JEALOUSY

JEALOUSY

EXPERIENCES AND SOLUTIONS

HILDEGARD BAUMGART

Translated by
Manfred and Evelyn Jacobson

The University of Chicago Press △ Chicago and London

HILDEGARD BAUMGART, who has a doctorate in Romance languages and literatures and is also a trained marriage counselor, has practiced at the Ecumenical Counseling Center in Munich-Neuperlach since 1973. She has published several articles on marriage and relationships and was the editor of a collection of letters from the German Democratic Republic, *Briefe aus einem anderen Land* (1971).

The University of Chicago Press, Chicago 60637
The University of Chicago Press, Ltd., London
© 1990 by The University of Chicago
All rights reserved. Published 1990
Printed in the United States of America

99 98 97 96 95 94 93 92 91 90   5 4 3 2 1

This book was first published as *Eifersucht:*
Erfahrungen und Lösungsversuche im Beziehungsdreieck,
© 1985 by Rowohlt Verlag GmbH, Reinbek bei Hamburg.

Library of Congress Cataloging-in-Publication Data

Baumgart, Hildegard.
    [Eifersucht. English]
    Jealousy : experiences and solutions / Hildegard Baumgart ;
translated by Manfred and Evelyn Jacobson.
        p.   cm.
    Translation of: Eifersucht.
    Includes bibliographical references.
    ISBN 0-226-03935-8 (alk. paper)
    1. Jealousy.   I. Title.
BF575.J4B38   1990
152.4—dc20   89-37321
                                                      CIP

⊗ The paper used in this publication meets the minimum requirements of the American National Standard for Information Sciences—Permanence of Paper for Printed Library Materials, ANSI Z39.48-1984.

This book is dedicated to two people
who were often in my thoughts.

As a jealous person, I suffer fourfold: because I am jealous, because I reproach myself for my jealousy, because I fear that my jealousy is hurting the other, because I allow myself to be enslaved by a banality: I suffer from being excluded, from being aggressive, from being crazy, and from being common.

—Roland Barthes
Fragments d'un discours amoureux

CONTENTS

Acknowledgments   ix
Introduction: My Cases and My Own Case   1

Part One: Jealousy as It Is Lived

1. The Jealous Individual   25
2. The Partner   32
3. The Rival   38
4. Normality and Justification   44
5. Destructive Solutions   50
6. Between Patriarchate and Sexual Revolution   61
7. Difficulties with the Concept of Possession   68
8. Compulsion to Freedom: A Paradox   71

Part Two: Tradition—Toward a History of the Emotion of Jealousy

9. On the Historicity of Emotions   79
10. The Jealous God   82
11. The Power of Emotions on Olympus   90
12. Jesus: Love and Freedom   100
13. The Difficulty of Expressing Jealousy   106
14. Bonding, Freedom, the Sense of Honor: Traditions of
    Love and Jealousy   114

Part Three: Psychological Theories

15. Freud's Essay of 1922   145
16. The Triangle: Husband, Wife, Child   168
17. From the Triangle back to the Biangular Relationship   199
18. Guilty Individual or Multilateral Entanglement   224

Part Four: Countermovements

19. Thirty Cases from Our Counseling Practice   257
20. Shock, Rage, Pain   266
21. A New Reality in the Relationship   271
22. Seeing Oneself Anew   276
23. The Reality of the Partner   283
24. Withdrawal from Symbiosis   289
25. Working through the Past in Marriage Counseling   292
26. The Meaning of the Rival: Fantasy and Reality   295
27. Severed Constituents   302
28. Homosexuality?   306
29. Letting Go and Returning   316
30. New Life, New Love   321
31. Laughing and Crying   324

Finale: The Solution of the Gods   335
Works Cited   341
Index   351

ACKNOWLEDGMENTS

From its first indistinct outline to its completion, this book took approximately six years of my life, and decisively shaped the last three. This work would not have been possible without the assistance and encouraging interest of friends, colleagues, and clients, and without the tolerance, helpful criticism, and loving sympathy of my family, especially my husband.

The first piece of encouragement came from Helm Stierlin, who also sent me several essays that deal with my topic and that otherwise would probably have escaped my attention. I owe special thanks to my colleagues from the working group on marriage at the Ecumenical Counseling Center in Munich-Neuperlach. They had to, and did, endure my frequent absences during the summers I was working on the book, from 1982 on. Gertrud Scheller, Maria Wagner, and Niels Königseder further supported me by allowing me to conduct follow-up sessions with some of their clients. I am grateful to Antoon Houben, for many years the head of Protestant Counseling Services in Munich, for eliciting from our financial supporters several months of unpaid leave for me, in three consecutive years.

The members of the Balint group for family therapists, of which I have been a member since 1979, also accepted my absence with forbearance. Our discussions of cases, under the leadership of Thea Bauriedl, were productive and important for this book.

I was especially fortunate in having the assistance of Hermann Gieselbusch, senior editor at Rowohlt. His expertise, the discreet consolation he provided in depressing times, and his involvement in this work and in my own method helped me tremendously.

And finally, the important last part of this book could not have been written without the willingness of about forty former clients to participate in follow-up sessions. Almost all of them unhesitatingly agreed to undergo the strain involved in confronting old pains. I have learned much from them and hope to be able to transmit to my readers some of what I have learned.

March 1985

INTRODUCTION:
MY CASES AND MY OWN CASE

Therapists who work with couples often have to deal with jealousy—this seems self-evident. But when my colleagues and I tried to locate past cases that would substantiate this statement, we had to think long and hard, leaf through old files, and search our memories to come up with something. It seems, therefore, that jealousy is not as prevalent a central theme in marriage counseling as is usually assumed, especially by those suffering from jealousy themselves. Counselors also seem to view it as an integral part of a larger context, rather than as an isolated phenomenon. My book, however, will deal primarily with this emotion, about which we cannot assert even that it is only an emotion. Yet this project could not have succeeded without such simplifications, even though I occasionally found them troublesome.

The experiences treated in this book, as the discussions with colleagues alluded to above suggest, could not simply have been culled from the everyday experiences of a counseling center. Rather they have, to a large extent, derived from my own preoccupation with the theme. Thus most of the catamneses (follow-up sessions with former clients) that I could use came about because of my own efforts; that is, a relatively large number of people have been in touch with me in the last few years, after I appeared on radio shows and wrote an article for a newspaper, the *Süddeutsche Zeitung*. Strangely enough, an exceptionally large number of conflicts involving jealousy have "coincidentally" wound up as part of my caseload in the four years since I started work on the book. This is in spite of the fact that appointments in our center are made by the secretaries in such a way that there is almost no possibility of assigning patients according to the nature of their problems, before the first direct contact between counselor and client. No one, except my closest friends and colleagues, knew anything about my project. Therefore, no new clients could have had recourse to special information (for example, that people in Neuperlach are especially preoccupied with jealousy).

1

When I think about what led me to work more intensely with this fascinating topic, a combination of personal and professional reasons comes to mind. I was working with a certain couple, in whom I rediscovered many of the things that had pained and pleased me in a past "triadic" relationship of my own. I also noticed that there were some elements of my own jealousy, dating back several decades, that I had still not understood and therefore not yet worked through. This kind of overlapping of one's own with another's experiences, which occurs frequently, poses for the therapist the danger of a lack of demarcation. It is very easy to abuse the power that is all too readily ceded to the facilitator in a crisis. One kind of abuse is for the counselor to have the clients try something that he could not or did not dare try. Acting in this way, the counselor, consciously or unconsciously, becomes the director of a production that holds an element of suspense primarily for the counselor. The clients do not experience their own catharsis in this production, but rather the one that the counselor wishes them to experience. The counselor's proper task, however (as I see it, in any case), is to promote the vivacity of the clients, while working with them to eliminate torpidity. This will allow them to learn to move again, but dancing to their own tune and not a counselor's. It is inconceivable that one's efforts will be successful if one does not recognize one's own torpidity and try to transform it into new mobility.

But instead, one often falls into a trap that is a variant of the repetition compulsion that characterizes all psychological disturbances. Even the counselor described above, in trying out the transference game, is hardly likely to escape from the prison of his own unactualized possibilities. At best, he will only see the vivid reflection of what could have happened in his own life, in all probability as an ephemeral play and not as a genuine solution to a problem that is not his own, in spite of all similarities.

I did not want to treat my jealousy, and that of my clients, in this way. Rather, I preferred to see and sense more clearly through reflection, remembrance, and thoughtful anticipation: I am here, and the people over there are the clients.

It would now seem appropriate for me to recount my own experiences, their pre- and post-history, and the course of the related treatment. In attempting this, however, I come up against an insurmountable obstacle that implicitly stands in the way of a book about jealousy: the question of discretion, which is more difficult to deal with in presenting cases of jealousy than in other cases. It has become relatively easy nowadays to write about depressions, phobias, compulsions, and even schizophrenia: some clients readily give their permission, some even think it interesting or useful, to have their story published somewhere. Even in our allegedly liberal age, writing about triangular relationships, betrayal, real or imagined infidelity, even reconciliation and self-control, is still problematic if the participants are recognizable. My own story is not only my own, but also that of several others. Therefore, I do not think I have the right to recount their experiences and emotions, since they would be seen primarily from my point of view. Without case histories, however, a book about jealousy is inconceivable. I was, therefore, compelled to modify my own experiences as well as my case histories, so that the individuals involved could not be identified. This will probably lead some clients to think they recognize themselves in these case histories, when they actually have nothing to do with them. As much as I would regret this, it would also be gratifying, because my purpose is to delineate that which recurs frequently, rather than to concentrate on isolated instances. Consequently, one of my goals would be achieved if as many people as possible were to see themselves in these examples. Moreover, I omitted some actual details that, had they been included, would have struck the reader as being badly conceived inventions. Jealous individuals often have notions that no dramatist or novelist could afford to use.

To circumvent the problem of maintaining anonymity, it occurred to me to use literary examples, as well as to modify the external circumstances as is common in psychological reports. In this regard, jealousy has a distinct advantage over other themes because no relational conflict has occupied writers, storytellers, and the amazed audience as consistently as the eternal triangle. Writers usually follow plot lines to their conclusion, while in real life these lines often become blurred. Stories, therefore, because they are only "fiction," are not worse but often better for our purposes than authentic, contemporary cases. *The Kreutzer Sonata* by Tolstoy (the Russian count whom Lenin characterized as the only peasant in Russian literature) illustrates this beautifully. In this novella, Tolstoy wove all that he suffered on account of the decadent bourgeois/aristocratic culture of the nineteenth century, and all his yearning for a true love, which even the people could no longer exemplify for him, into a powerful metaphor of jealous passion. The result was so obstinate, so one-sided, so incisive, and so true in its exaggeration, as reality, even Tolstoy's own, never could be.

Another source of "harmless" material to which I often had recourse is case histories previously published by physicians, counselors, analysts, and family therapists. However, it seems to me that the innumerable reports in the daily press of murders, injuries, arson, accidents, suicides—personal dramas associated with jealousy—are hardly useful. Except for their purely anecdotal content, they contain no information, and one can only speculate about the nature and significance of the backgrounds. The little that one does learn about the life histories, the social and family environment of the jealous individuals involved, actually tends conspicuously to support the hypotheses of those researching jealousy. Since I had, however, already suffered from not being able to give more detailed information about my own cases because of the aforementioned reasons, I did not, on top of that, want to document my theme with contexts that could not be tested to determine whether they existed only in my imagination.

In what follows, I will outline some of the questions I often confronted, using actual counseling sessions as a point of departure. It should be mentioned parenthetically that additional problems emerged as a consequence of deeper immersion in the topic. Many of these seemed to me difficult to solve or could only be solved in certain single instances. The connection to my self and my own history will be established here without indefensible indiscretions.

A couple, referred by a colleague, is waiting for me in the waiting room of the center. The colleague had time only for an intake interview and considered the convergence of the woman's jealousy and suicidal fantasies too dangerous to put the clients on his waiting list. He had seen only the woman, who was "sent by her husband." While arranging an appointment by telephone, I try to make clear the necessity of an interview with both of them. The wife does not think her husband would accompany her; he would not want to talk. I insist, but leave open the possibility that the wife could come to the appointment by herself. I would hold the hour open for the couple, even if he did not wish to accompany her.

I do not know what to expect, which is usual in such cases. The fear of painful confrontation often leads the partner making the appointment to project his or her own inclination to reject joint counseling onto the other person. But since I myself am convinced that it is very advantageous for them to come together and not individually, especially for the first session, I seem to be very persuasive. To my delight, they do arrive together.

I already know things about the couple that please me: I like the husband's occupation—he is a cabinetmaker and takes evening courses in art history. My colleague tells me that the wife seems to waver between feeling that her children are still completely dependent on her, and not wanting to lose contact with her profession as a physical therapist. Both spouses are in their early thirties. The three children are still small, and the spacing between them is similar to that of my own. I always have the feeling that it is more difficult to raise children today than it was during my time. On the other hand, I refuse to be convinced when someone says of the third, or fourth, or whatever, child, "It was just an accident" (in the age of the pill, IUDs, and the ready availability of abortion!). I assume at the outset that couples with several children, to put it in general terms, are fulfilling a need for more life. I have reserves of sympathy for such families because, for me, the time spent with my small children was a very beautiful experience, if not always easy, and I still somewhat regret its passing.

It is naturally a warning sign that the wife is thinking of killing herself, but this doesn't automatically alarm me. I have often found that such desires to stop living only mean that there is *something* that should finally stop. What is necessary is to discover what should "stop." I know from experience how far one can distance oneself from suicidal fantasies. I am also firmly convinced that basically no one, really no one, actually wants to destroy life. To be sure, it seems to me almost strange when people maintain they have never thought of suicide. I find that unbelievable, or perhaps a sign of a lack of imagination, simply because it is so easy to do (and because in West Germany there are annually about as many suicides as traffic fatalities).

Naturally, it does not seem at all surprising to me that the husband could have a love relationship outside marriage—my colleague wasn't certain whether the relationship existed only in the wife's imagination. But it was also not a cause for alarm. The reality of multiple partners, divorces, and the pressure to perform sexually is just as incalculable for a marriage counselor as the less spectacular, but still frequently experienced, reality of fidelity, which unfortunately is just not that common in happy marriages. Several times during our marriage, my husband and I have fallen deeply in love with others, but we get along well and enjoy living together, before as well as after these experiences. Therefore, the fear of being alone, of divorce and its irrevocable effects on the children, and so forth, is not automatically for me a necessary concomitant of such an experience. Obviously there is pain, however.

To return to my clients: as they walk ahead of me down the long corridor to my office, I have the feeling that they are well matched. I believe that it bodes well for the treatment of jealousy if the partners can agree to come together. This decision shows that they are still talking to each other, perhaps still want to live together, and that probably there are not too many secrets between them. These two even tell their story together, taking turns—entirely contrary to the expectations that the wife had communicated over the telephone. It has occurred to the wife that her husband's sexual behavior is now different. In what way "different?" Just different. She goes on: sometimes more distanced, sometimes more passionate than before; once he even cried during the night. At this, the wife became uneasy—he had never acted that way before. She tried to talk to him, but he became more and more withdrawn. In our three-way conversation, he also gives the impression of being more reserved than she, more formal, worried. She, on the other hand, is lively, articulate, and gestures gracefully while speaking.

And the story continued in this way: her questioning became a kind of obsession, she could no longer stop. Just tell me what's the matter—I can tell something is wrong—is it another woman? "But at first that wasn't even it," the client says, "I was such a fool! You can't imagine how long it took me just to suspect! My husband and I—we were such a team . . ." Did the husband also look at his marriage in this way? Actually yes, he says, until now; when they met, he also knew right away: "That's the one for me!" And even though she was sexually very attractive to him, he respected her sensitivity (one of the reasons for which was a near-rape by a friend of her divorced mother) and waited several months before attempting to kiss her. This made her think highly of him—she was finally desired as a person and "not only for her body"—and it was exactly his patience and reserve that won her heart, and that now "make her blood boil."

He, for his part, was fascinated by her warmth, liveliness, and vivacity. He had grown up in the shadow of the chronic illness of a cool and disciplined mother, whose husband had deserted her just because of this illness. She forced her son prematurely to play the role of an understanding, sympathetic, "head of household," responsible for organizing the externals of their life. His mother had died while he was still an apprentice. She had suffered greatly because she could only afford to have her son trained as an artisan, instead of being able to provide him with a university education.

The husband felt that the first ten years of the marriage had been very happy. Finally warmth, finally life—the three children!—finally a woman who, after getting something from him, gave him something in return. "We didn't need to talk much, we knew everything about each other." And now this change . . .

The wife, because of her strict moral upbringing, was accustomed to blame herself first when trying to determine who was responsible for unpleasant changes. Therefore, she wanted her husband to tell her what she should do differently. His response was, Nothing—no, really nothing— I don't know—for once just leave me be! When it occurred to her that another woman could be responsible, he denied it so vehemently, that once again she could not do anything but think, "I'm crazy." But then she once unexpectedly picked him up from an art history class that he attends because of his interest in antiques and their restoration. She came upon him in animated conversation with a young woman. "I knew right away— that's her!" She ran away without her husband's having seen her, got in the car, desperately drove out into the night, naturally driving too fast— and only broke out in tears after she stopped, with the brakes screeching, right in front of the bridge abutment into which she had wanted to crash. What had stopped her? "I don't know—I only thought of the children later . . ." Meanwhile, the husband had already called the police. When she finally arrived home exhausted, he bellowed at her, shook her; her upper arms are bruised because he grabs her so desperately—and then they make love and both say, with some embarrassment, that it was especially good.

Has this dangerously conflicted situation made them realize how much they belong together? Yes, naturally, says the husband. The wife hesitates. She says that, in some way, she felt loved by her husband, for the first time, "only for her body." When they made love on that occasion, he had talked to her just as he had talked to "the girl," but the most tenderness he demonstrated was occasionally to kiss her eyelid. But if I have understood you correctly, you still enjoyed sleeping with him on this horrifying night? Yes, says the wife, that's right; and this is what really confuses her now.

At this point, I myself feel anxious and uncertain. Successful sexuality in such an extreme situation is no measure of the dependability of the relationship at issue. Even the sexuality of so-called normal people too often involves elements of risk, danger, even enmity, not only of love, tenderness, and happy regression. Indeed, the experience demonstrates the ability of both partners to risk letting go. Jealousy does not always lead to denial on the part of the jealous individual, but rather sometimes leads directly to excesses of devotion. My main uncertainty does not consist primarily in not knowing how the two relate to each other, but rather very specifically in the question, Was the wife correct in her intuition? Or did she unconsciously use "the girl" to represent, in crystalline form as it were, all the elements of the disturbed relationship: if she were not there, would everything be fine again? Jealous individuals *always* sense something that is really there, but they often exaggerate its importance. I am also concerned that the wife could develop an obsession with this projection, which would then probably be difficult to dissipate.

But the husband says quietly, "The girl means a lot to me—my wife has again understood me correctly." The wife breaks into desperate tears. For fourteen days—since she has known about "it"—she has been pushing, literally day and night, to find out what "really" is going on between her husband and the young woman from the art history class. He says, It's nothing sexual. Then what? Just talk, About what—probably about him and the girl? . . . Yes, about that, says the husband, but not only that. Then about what? He can't exactly say. There must be something sexual between them? No . . . and so forth. Or another litany: she's done so much for him; at the altar he promised to remain true to her. He says, "I'm not unfaithful." How can he maintain this? Because he wants to stay with her . . . Or another approach: Is it her fault? In what way was he dissatisfied? Not at all, nowhere, he says, not even in bed. It just happened . . . And why did he always claim that there was no other woman involved? Because her persistent questioning was getting on his nerves. And because nothing sexual was involved. Is it now against the law to like other people?

What is my stance to be, vis-à-vis two such partners? After they have made so much progress in telling the story and attaining some insight, I deeply share their sense of being bogged down, their sense of the apparent hopelessness of the situation. At first, I was on the wife's side—I could understand her despair very well, also her going to pieces, her not wanting to believe, her deep anger at such a completely unexpected injury; it is, however, difficult for me to categorize the "guilt" of her husband in the same way as she does. Had the wife, as often happens in counseling, asked, "Would you have felt different in my place?" I would certainly have felt the need to be completely honest, completely "myself," and to reply in this manner: Probably today I would feel somewhat different but at times in the past I would have felt the same. Today I can tolerate seeing or only knowing that my husband is intensely preoccupied with other women. I can even tolerate his saying that they are important to him, without too much anxiety and often even with understanding and approval. There is a great danger, therefore, that I will pose as the model and standard for the couple. There is the consequent danger that I will find myself in a situation in which these questions will arise: whether this or that is right or wrong; or how I would have done some particular thing; or whether it is in any case desirable to do such a thing; or, perhaps, how I would feel if it were really true that sexuality . . . and whatever other personal questions of this sort may arise. Therefore, in order to avoid such a deviation from the therapeutic norm which, at least as far as "the world out there" is concerned, is supposed to be oriented towards the clients, the only possible answer for me would be, "I don't know how I would act in your situation—it is after all *yours,* and I would like to understand it; and I hope that I can do that."

I could also understand that, after something like this has happened, a wife at least wants to talk about it. At first I thought that the husband was too unwilling, if not even obdurate, vis-à-vis his wife. When it became obvious that he had submitted to his wife's persistent interrogation for two weeks, rarely losing his patience, I could hardly figure him out. At the same time, she was constantly "freaked out": she was screaming, breaking dishes, always on the telephone with girlfriends, and told the children that Daddy no longer loved Mommy. Does he have such a bad conscience that he believes he has to put up with this? Had he perhaps lied about not sleeping with his girlfriend? Suicide attempts are understandably very frightening—maybe the husband wants to spare his wife by not burdening her with the whole truth? Even I feel it would be wrong to continue digging for the facts. For one thing, I tend to believe the husband;

for another, the strain experienced by he clients simply in talking about the situation is already as much as they can bear. Were I to continue prodding, I would also inevitably wind up in a position parallel to the wife's, that is, I would be allying myself with her and attempting to force her husband into the role of sinner.

What role should I play in this stalemated situation? I feel as if each of them has grabbed me by a hand and is trying to pull me towards them. This can lead to nothing but immobility—not a good feeling, but one that is common in marriage counseling. I realize that there is something I would like to know, and this helps me let go of the symbolical hands and step back from the couple: Was the marriage that the two of them have been talking about really as happy as they have described it to me and to each other? I take a relatively daring leap. First I ask the wife if she can remember what it is like to be in love; then whether, perhaps, she had not found another man attractive or even important during her marriage. I don't think this is an unreasonable question, because I had already established the extent to which I am able to empathize with her suffering. I also want to see if she can cope with such a question. If either member of the couple is too sensitive and can't "share" the counselor with the spouse; if the jealousy, in this instance the wife's, is also directed at the "other woman" who is present (namely me); then the prospects for joint counseling are not very good. Perhaps then we would have to examine and work more closely on fear and mistrust in individual sessions.

As a consequence of my question, however, the scene changes completely. The wife's tears dry up with astonishing speed; the husband sits up; they look at each other for a while without speaking. Then the husband says, quietly but somewhat pointedly, "You'd better answer that yourself." The wife responds that it isn't as important as all that, and besides, there's a big difference between her flirting and his serious relationship. "And when you sit on other men's laps and even neck with them in front of me?" That was during the carnival season, she says—he says that, as far as he can remember, it was during the summer! She responds, well yes, but there was a carnival-like atmosphere. The husband retorts, that's no excuse for embarrassing him in front of the whole world. The wife's answer does not sound very logical, "My God, I always have to worry about other people! The kids all day long, and then you in the evening."

At this point, I would like to digress in order to fill in some background information. The husband had never flirted, and the couple's fun-loving friends sometimes teased him because of this. It is news to the wife that her participation in this teasing hurt him deeply. Why didn't he ever say anything? It wouldn't have done any good, he says, she would just have brushed it off, not taken it seriously; and basically she's right—it wasn't all that awful. But, the wife says, I wouldn't have flirted if I had known how you felt. Really? At this point, the wife strikes me as very spirited, almost as having a real zest for life, and I cannot completely accept her response. How has she been shortchanged by this marriage, which has been described as happy and which in many ways is a good marriage? In other words, what does her jealousy indicate? What is her husband unconsciously trying to suggest about the state of his marriage by entering into an extramarital relationship.

By the end of the hour, I am relieved that both their torpidity and mine has abated; that the dispute has settled down to a direct dialogue between the spouses; that the wife's despair has given way to reflection about her own real concerns; and that her references to what she has done for the good of the family are losing their accusatory character. The husband is emerging from his depressive withdrawal and stubborn entrenchment, and is expressing his own feelings of dissatisfaction and having been wronged. At the end of the first session, I am able to inform the couple that, in my opinion, the wife's insistent jealousy and the young woman are not the only things at issue. Rather, there is something between the two of them that will have to be worked out. At this point, I still cannot say what it is and therefore cannot yet give them any advice about what they could do about it. I would like to work with them mainly in discovering aspects of their relationship that they would like to change. I am also optimistic that they will come up with some of their own.

Each is disappointed with this, as well as with not being told he or she is in the right. Almost everyone who decides to get counseling hopes for such approval. Anyone who has ever been in a crisis situation will be able to empathize with this—one hopes for something like a magic trick; one wants to shed the pain and misery like a too-tight piece of clothing, so that one can breathe freely again. Since I am not an M.D., I cannot satisfy the occasional request for medication, which certainly has its origin in the desire for such a magical liberation. Sometimes patients also express a wish to be hypnotized, but marriage counselors can only frustrate such requests. They can, however, try to impart the hope that crises can usually be overcome. Generally, it is already a good sign if "something new happens" during the first session. The counselor can attempt to shift the focus of stress in the relationship, to interrupt the constant repetition of painful rituals (since this clearly cannot be eliminated all at once), and to substitute reflection for hot or cold desperation. Clients who leave the first session with such an experience of newness, and maybe even of reawakened curiosity about each other, will be less inclined to quit therapy immediately than those who were only understood on the therapist's terms and not their own, or who were given one-sided directives to change. If I had advised the husband in the case in point to give up his relationship with the young woman immediately, as otherwise his marriage would be finished; if I had pressured the wife to stop her persistent questioning and to "pull herself together"—nothing would have been gained. Both of them had already heard all of that from each other, as well as from friends, and it had not done any good.

I must say that, to me, sudden terminations of extramarital relationships, which sometimes occur soon after the start of counseling, are not all that welcome. This happens, however, in spite of my encouragement to change *nothing,* but first to have a closer and fresh look at what is actually happening in the marriage. When they do occur, however, it often strikes me that they are nothing more than the tricks of performing animals, and not a real farewell or renunciation. I can never ignore the fact that love outside marriage is a beautiful experience, and that parting will cause pain that must be worked through. One frequently hears talk of force, even rape, in marriage, and it is always the use of physical force against women that is meant. It is bad enough that such things exist, without making it worse by retreating into hysterical exaggeration or postures of feminist hostility. It is also important not to forget, because of the reality of physical force, the existence of psychological force, which women also exercise. It is my firm conviction, however, that the use of force will backfire if it is not confronted, understood, and transformed. Who knows how many men consciously or unconsciously will not forgive their wives for forcing them to kill off a love within themselves—too early, too inhumanely, too suddenly? Who can say how many women exercise the sublime power that every intimate relationship confers, to the detriment of their husbands and children, because they could not decide if they wanted to live through (which almost always means suffer through!) an extramarital relationship? Instead, they were forced to look, neither right nor left, but straight ahead and do what is called "their duty," without being presented with an alternative.

I have now come to those questions that originally moved me to write this book. Some of them have already emerged from the case outlined above. It did not take place exactly as described, but contains elements from several cases, without a single invention. Does jealousy represent only itself or is it a sign of something else? What is its relationship to the roles assigned husband and wife? The wife in my example set aside her career in favor of marriage and family. Is she perhaps not only jealous of the young woman, but also of the other possibility of self-actualization—her husband's greater freedom of movement? What rights does her upbringing tell her she has? What is the connection between jealousy and religion?

My work repeatedly and all too clearly demonstrates the extent to which adult attitudes have been shaped by the influence of the family during childhood. There is a series of psychoanalytic essays and case histories that deal mainly with the origin of jealousy in the early childhood experiences of the patients. Is this research still relevant for the general public? What about the undeniable fact that psychoanalysis is concerned exclusively with the individual? Jealousy, however, as a rule is a phenomenon that concerns at least three people. Are all manifestations of jealousy the same? In my outline, the husband has obviously been hurt by his wife's flirtations. But how does one explain the fact that he did not talk much about it, while the wife suffered the torment of an obsession with the need to talk, to question and pump him?

I would like to indicate the subsequent direction that the counseling took, by providing some additional information about the wife. After immigrating to West from East Germany as a little girl, she was plagued by a very understandable separation anxiety which she had not, as yet, worked through. It had been brought on by her overburdened father's threats to run away because the family had become too much for him, as well as by the intensely experienced death of a dearly loved grandmother. At that time, she literally had neither time nor permission to cry. After her grandmother's death, there was no one left who showed her that she was loved just for herself, and without her having to produce evidence of some achievement. She therefore came to believe that she could only earn love through sacrifice, but that she had a firm right to it in her role as wife and mother. Therefore, her whole world collapsed when she noticed her husband developing a serious interest in "the girl," who seemed to represent everything the wife was not, or was no longer. Another very important question: What is the relationship between the jealous individual and his or her rival?

The husband was oppressed by the experience with his mother. It soon became clear that he was trying to fulfill his deceased mother's wishes by upgrading the social status of his profession. The first thing he did to accomplish this was to take adult education classes in art history. During the course of counseling, he began to prepare for the exams that would allow him to attend the university. He has since passed these exams, and I have little doubt that he will study architecture, as he intends. He says that it will take him a long time, since he must support his family at the same time, but it is now clear to him that this is what he has always wanted. He also says that it would have made his mother very happy. And the mother of his children? She is going along with it; basically, he always knew he could depend on her. As a result of the new developments in his life, this man is at peace with himself. Perhaps this is what allows him to give up the romantic attachment to his fellow student after several months and without too much pain. The couple's friends no longer tease him, because the wife has all too clearly informed them that he was capable of developing an interest in extramarital relationships.

A new question: What happens to the third party after the dissolution of such a relationship? Is he or she jealous too? And another question: Is an extramarital relationship perhaps anything but a catastrophe? Maybe it is sometimes an opportunity, if not, to be somewhat blasphemous, a blessing.

Obviously, there has also been movement in the life of the wife, who has become the main subject of the therapy. She is trying to understand what significance flirting and ridiculing her husband had for her. Now she believes that it was to show him, just once, that she "could do something to him too, that he isn't always the person who is unreachable, superior, calm." Only with time did both of them come to understand that the husband became infatuated with the young woman because he felt his wife was naturally superior, because of her childbearing capability, as well as her willingness to make sacrifices. This was sometimes a burden that he could hardly endure. He projected onto his wife the guilt feelings he had experienced as a young man upon feeling relief at his mother's death. His needs dovetailed precisely with his wife's, because she could only imagine love as a reward for her self-sacrifice, and her self-esteem was entirely dependent upon her relationship to her husband and children. Her mania to know what had happened between her husband and his girlfriend would have been interpreted in classical psychoanalysis as curiosity about the primal scene, that is, as curiosity about sexual intercourse between one's parents. This does not strike me as absurd as it may sound to the reader because, as a matter of fact, it is not unusual— even now, in our "enlightened age"—for clients to talk about disturbing and uncomprehended early-childhood sexual experiences after only a few, often even in the first, counseling sessions. These experiences always involve a mixture of fear and desire, that is, negative and positive fascination, even when there has been terrible exploitation by overwhelming adults.

When working with couples, it is usually not possible to delve so deeply into the "well of the past" (Thomas Mann). There was no opportunity for me to test with my client whether this psychoanalytic model would be confirmed in her case. Something else, however, became obvious: her own repressed desire for genuine and complete infidelity, rather than flirtations that never turned into anything serious. Her husband had been her first and only sexual partner. Nowadays it would take considerable narrow-mindedness and lack of imagination for a woman in such a situation never to raise the question, to wish to know, or to think about how "it" would be with other men. My client was anything but narrow and unimaginative. She was, however, restrained by many things: her upbringing; the fear engendered by her father's threats to leave the family (should *she* impose such a burden on her children?); most of all, by her love for her husband, whom she did not wish to offend or hurt. The soul travels involuted paths. A least she could demonstrate her burning interest in a "different" sexuality and a "different" love, under the guise of a legitimate claim to witness her husband's intimacy.

As I was thinking all this over, it occurred to me how appropriate the German word for jealousy is—*Eifer-"sucht,"* zealous "addiction." This leads to another question: What expression do other languages use to designate this phenomenon? And further: How was jealousy seen and experienced in the past; how is jealousy reflected in religion and art, or how are religion and art reflected in the experience of jealousy at any given time? Was jealousy intensified or diminished with the progress of civilization or as the satisfaction of needs was refined?

I have not found exhaustive answers to all the questions above, nor to the many others that these subsequently engender. In a book that is primarily concerned with the intrapsychic and interpersonal consequences of jealousy, I could only treat the question of cultural background, for example, very cursorily.

To sum up, my research focuses on two questions: *How can one understand jealousy?* and its corollary, *How can one live with jealousy—one's own or another's?* It was at this point that I at first wrote down the words "you must come to terms with it." I have made some progress in understanding jealousy but hardly any in coming to terms with it. I am convinced that, because jealousy is so universal a problem, one can speak only of coming to terms with it. It is a delusion to think that it can be conquered or ever extirpated. As a consequence of my own reflections and a review of the pertinent clinical histories, I have become much more modest in my expectations. Fortunately, however, I did not lose faith in the possibility of helping clients deal more humanely with what is fundamentally a very archaic emotion. The reader, therefore, will find in the book a degree of confidence alongside great caution and skepticism.

As far as the literature of professional therapy is concerned, I can do no more than give a sort of interim report. I was astonished to discover that there is hardly any literature available by family therapists or systems theoreticians. The literature that is available, primarily case descriptions and theoretical reflections, has a psychoanalytical point of view. Thus I was unable to find a single case history dealing with the treatment of jealousy psychosis in an entire family. I did, however, locate several that described the successful treatment of pathological jealousy using individual psychoanalysis. They mention only incidentally how the elimination of jealousy affected the patients' families, but the entire system to which the patient belonged seems to have felt it as a relief.

Marriage counselors today are invariably caught up in the tension between traditional psychoanalysis with its plodding efforts at modernization, and the new methods of group therapy, which is developing erratically but with an extraordinary lack of predictability. Everything would appear simpler if one were to apply the criteria and methodology of depth psychology to the entire family structure, treating several persons at the same time, rather than just one. Only the smallest number of authoritative family therapists do this, however. On the contrary, they think of their work as something completely new, the result of a paradigmatic change in psychotherapy. I will discuss this fully at the appropriate time. For the purposes of this introduction, all that seems important to me is that the new direction never, or at least seldom, works to uncover what is hidden. That is to say it does not operate in accordance with Freud's fundamental intention of making conscious what is unconscious, but operates instead prescriptively, by which I mean that therapists give advice directly, even going as far as to give what are called "paradoxical directives." These are a particular form of directives on how to behave that at first bewilder and confuse the patient, because they recommend or praise precisely what the patient wants to be rid of. For example, in a family with a ten-year-old daughter who is exhibiting anxiety symptoms, the anxiety is reinterpreted as concern for her psychosomatically ailing parents. The family is instructed not to change anything, but consciously to hold on to the anxiety, because in doing so the daughter is helping the parents "a great deal" (Wirsching and Stierlin 1982, 240). This new method is not at all concerned with working through the relationship between therapist and patient, something central to psychoanalysis (transference, working alliance, auxiliary ego). The therapist expects and requires only that the patient faithfully execute the instructions. Of course, the therapist also wants to eliminate the anxiety but cannot say that, because then the prescription will not "take."

I actually think that both therapeutical methods share a common denominator: to prepare the way for those who seek help to change themselves. The exponents of each method, however, reproach the others precisely for not doing that. They accuse each other of manipulating patients by exploiting the power they have over them, in order to achieve their own preexistent goals. They are waging a hard-fought battle—the psychoanalysts, often very arrogant, claiming to possess the one true doctrine and theory; the systems theoreticians and therapists with all the visionary zeal attendant upon the awareness of breaking new ground. In my opinion, however, they often lack the culture and tradition of thought that characterizes at least the best of the psychoanalysts. What is desperately needed, and what we have so far had to do without, is a compilation of what they have in common, nonpolemical analyses of the opposing methods based on their own criteria. Until this happens, what are marriage counselors and their clients to do on this battlefield?

I can only speak for myself. I recognize that both sides have had their share of successes. It would be narrow-minded to deny this. I also believe in the reports of successes attributed to various forms of intervention, that is, communications-theoretical as well as systems therapies (even including paradoxical directives—see chap. 18, sec. 9) have been successful in treating jealousy of varying degrees of severity. My own experiences are limited to psychoanalysis, whether in individual, group, or marriage therapy. Perhaps this is related to my own experiences with my parents, but, whatever the reason, I can't imagine trusting a therapist so unconditionally that I would not be indignant or disappointed were he or she to describe as useful or essential to my life the very things I want to be rid of, while disallowing any discussion of these measures. What I am fully conversant and comfortable with is discussing what symptoms mean, and attempting to understand and internalize what their effect is on those closest to the patient. In my opinion, this is more easily accomplished in a traditional clinical setting or private practice (where one does not have a team of several people waiting behind a one-way mirror to come up with an effective prescription), than by using the new methods. Those who are knowledgeable about them also maintain that they will not work if the therapist is not convinced that the clients are getting the best he or she has to offer. Even here, then, there is an insidious intrusion of subconscious identification.

I remain most indebted to psychoanalysis, in spite of the fact that the elegance, the quick resolution, and the minimal effort sometimes necessary in directive systemic intervention are very attractive to me. This should be reflected in the book. However, I believe that I too am a systems therapist, in that my special field of expertise is the couple and, therefore, I must always consider several individuals.

I would like to make just a few observations about what my personal experience with psychoanalysis has taught me about jealousy. I am the oldest child in a family whose central figure is a powerful and extremely dynamic father. Perhaps because of this decidedly patriarchal family structure, the Freudian model, based as it is entirely on the world of the great father, made a strong impression on me and therefore has been therapeutically helpful. Some people may consider this old-fashioned; let us hope that someday it will be exactly that. Now, however, we still live in a male-dominated society and the most that can be said for it is that opportunities for women are increasing. In my daily work, I see again and again how all the models of the father-centered Freudian world cling like burrs to the subconscious, in spite of attempts at emancipation. This is reflected even in movements promoting change or separatism. Even as a child I must have thought it not very desirable to be a woman. One of the formative experiences of my life is jealousy of the male, which Freud treated under the rubric of penis envy. I often wished to be a man and, when I was depressed as an adult (fortunately always only for brief periods), regretted not having had only sons.

If it were not possible to be a man, one at least had to be loved by one or be able to love one. In our family, even that was not simple. My father was always able to make us feel protected by his power. For example, I can remember him taking us, dressed only in bathing suits, out into the backyard during thunderstorms and pouring rain, so that he could show us the beauty of lightning. Because of this, I naturally never had an irrational fear of thunderstorms and had hardly any fear of bombs during the war. His fiery temperament, however, sometimes expressed itself in fits of anger. These often had less to do with something occasioned by the family than with job-related stress that had built up and with his sensitivity, caused by a highly refined awareness, which itself had often stood in his way and was therefore repressed. This was difficult for a child to understand. It was unthinkable to protest or argue. Apologies, which I later found necessary vis-à-vis my own children, were unimaginable for him. My mother could do nothing but take his side and, at the same time, try to cushion us—an almost impossible task. My father also loved justice, and I grew up with the myth that all four children meant just as much and the same thing to our parents. Even as late as the beginning of my analysis I couldn't, in spite of my best efforts, explain what the differences might have been. They were, however, considerable, for my parents did love all four children and stood up for each of them, not with the same, but with different kinds of love. This resulted in very different experiences and very different treatment for each of the siblings, as is natural and appropriate.

Since I had once experienced the world as the "one and only" child of my parents, without any siblings, the claim to justice must have appeared to me as only the second-best solution. This is the situation of all first-born children who find it difficult to be dethroned. I assume that, because I was the first-born, I expected that the equal care and treatment that my father valued so highly must of necessity feel good to me too, since he loved me so very much. But a climate of sibling rivalry arose between me and my next-oldest sister, to which I with my internalized ideal of justice could not admit.

This sister is one of the most beloved and important people in my life. During analysis I first learned to look clearly at the negative feelings I had for her, even to call them envy and hatred, and at the same time to realize that my love and admiration were not invalidated by these feelings, not even devalued. In this connection, my analyst showed me how wise Goethe was to have Ottilie say, in *The Elective Affinities,* that the only remedy for the jealousy one feels for someone else's great advantages is love. Being close to this sister has enabled me not only to feel anger and annoyance, but also friendship, admiration, tolerance, and empathy for the otherness of later "sisters"—not only in my personal life, but also in my life as a counselor. It should have been clear that my sister also felt rivalry towards me, at least at the point when I called her to let her know I was pregnant, when she had already been married for five years but was still without the child she so desperately wanted. She was about to inform me of her own pregnancy. The calculated due dates fell on the same day. As it turned out, she delivered four weeks earlier than I did, and twins. Once again, she had outdone me.

In the relationship with my second, much younger sister, I could already benefit from my relationship with the first. My rivalry with her was less threatening, because of the great difference in age and because I already had the experience of acceptable coexistence.

Strangely enough, I have never been terribly envious or jealous of my only brother—even when looked at through the magnifying lens of psychoanalysis. My parents treated him completely differently from us girls. In some respects, they asked much more of him in terms of achievement and, in other respects, much less from him than from us. He was loved differently and punished differently—he was actually "incomparable." And for there to be jealousy, there must be some point of comparison. Besides, he is seven years younger and was therefore *my* "little brother." At the time of his birth, I had probably already succeeded in internalizing the maternal image. The older I became, the more clearly I understood that his fate, to be the son of so strong and powerful a father, is not exactly easy. In the meantime, he has become the "big brother" who puts his arms around his sisters' shoulders and whom we can ask for advice. But he has remained "other."

Extremely oppressive anxiety symptoms forced me into analysis, which placed an enormous strain on me and did not have only pleasant consequences. In modern terms, one changes the system when, after learning what is wrong with oneself, one looks for new ways of dealing with reality because the old ways made one unhappy. As I learned to admit to jealousy, envy, and rivalry, it seemed that *I* was the only one with such feelings in my family, which claimed to live according to ideals of justice and harmony. For a while, it even seemed as if these were the *only* feelings I had, and no friendly ones at all. Coming to terms with my father and his standards in me cost me an infinite amount of courage and strength. I probably would not have been able to muster these, in spite of my analysis, if I had not been convinced of his fundamental loyalty. He has often suffered a great deal on my account and probably, to this day, has not understood what motivates me. Was his suffering of use to him, as mine was to me? I don't know. He has mellowed and become calmer, and our relationship is very loving. The only thing he is able to love consciously (since he never learned or wanted to learn how to be in touch with his subconscious) has remained justice. And the fact that he understands that justice can only be approximated may be one of the deep disappointments of his life. But even this is only surmise.

As far as men are concerned, I consciously set out to marry someone "completely other" than my father, and these two most important men in my life are in fact very different from each other (although they are now on very good terms, perhaps precisely because of this). In spite of this, I find it extremely difficult, on a subconscious level, to keep my husband and father distinct and to refrain from ascribing to the former the qualities of the latter. My husband never wished to occupy the central position of patriarch that my father accepted as a matter of course because of his origins, his social bonding, and his personal history. As a refugee, my husband has been shaped much more decisively than my father by the collapse of Germany, even though he is a generation younger. For him, there are hardly any "certainties" about which he cannot have his doubts. This is particularly true of possessions, traditions, and social structures. It must also be noted that we all, of course, actualize the historical movements of our own lifetime. In the decades of our marriage, equal rights for women increased significantly and some hierarchical structures were dismantled. This did not pass over us without leaving a trace. The result for me is that I am less dependent, but also less protected, than my mother.

I have experienced jealousy in my marriage and would gladly never experience it again. My husband hardly ever feels jealous, at least of me. In this he is completely reality-oriented and "healthy," for he has never had serious reason to question my fundamental commitment to him. Someone less "reasonable" than he would actually have had occasion to be concerned, since I became very interested in other men on several occasions, thereby entering into new triangles. In classical fashion, I was unable to understand why this aroused the jealousy of other women, since I knew how much I was committed to my marriage. Moreover, I was occasionally jealous of those women who replaced me. Neither the insights into one's feelings, nor the ability to empathize with the feelings of others, gained through analysis, make life any simpler, only more lucid. The pain of overcoming one's own realities and conflicts, as well as those of others, is not thereby eliminated. When it is conscious, renunciation does not become easier—but maybe the new beginning, the return, is likelier to become so.

After working through my relationship with my parents and with my sister, I hope that irrational rivalries with other women will no longer be necessary for me. For decades there have been, at worst, only hints of these rivalries, and I have been spared the severe, obsessive, prying, and possessive form of jealousy. After several years of a very exclusive marriage, the first "grounds" for jealousy entered our lives. These years had provided me with a reliable and extended experience of solidarity. Two of my children had been born, and I had just started my own analysis. Therefore I was learning to think of myself more and more as an independent person, but also to recognize the ways in which I was dependent. Today it is hard for me to imagine that, in the first years of my marriage, I was delighted to "have" such a wonderful husband, with the promise of lifelong fidelity. But it is all too clear, from the reconstruction of my early years, that this was the case. At the same time, it never even occurred to me that my husband also had good reasons to be more than happy to have found me and to be living with me. The resolution of this unrealistic polarization—on one side, the most wonderful of men, on the other, the ugly duckling—was a difficult but indispensable process. We had entered into marriage with the conscious intention of having, perhaps not exactly an "open" marriage, but certainly one which allowed for important relationships with other people. Had this not been the case, my subconscious possessiveness, in conjunction with my desire for contacts outside of marriage which would then have had to be completely repressed, could have led to very severe jealousy. (Neither one of us ever considered losing touch with the most significant of our former loves. Rather, we hoped that they would later evolve into friendship. In both instances, it was they who broke off contact—because of jealousy.)

Anyone who consciously bases one's life on a relationship with just one person—and I had done that—quite rightly sees oneself in extreme danger when the light of one's life no longer seems to shine for one. It is my experience that the less I defined myself as my husband's wife and the mother of his (!) children, the more tolerant and realistic I could be. To be sure, I would be more determined now than previously to fight for him if there were real danger. I would also be less affected by the old feeling—derived from and identified with the "father": if he really wants something, I cannot do anything about it anyway.

My own uninhibited association with jealousy was made possible through a whole series of experiences: by acknowledging this feeling of which I had been ashamed earlier; by recognizing that ambivalence towards those one loves is unavoidable, and that this does not put the basic relationship into question; through the awareness that one will not necessarily be displaced, that one may coexist with and in addition to others; by relinquishing expectations of utopian justice, that is, no longer believing that the one who loves me is "just" only if he omnipotently and omnisciently satisfies my desires in the way I imagine they should be; by understanding that my parents' values are not everything, something intellectually simple, but emotionally extraordinarily difficult to do; and finally and fundamentally, by daring to have and try out my own point of view—an undertaking still, again and again, associated with anxiety, whereby my confidence in myself and in others grew, while I grew more independent.

Perhaps, in achieving this, I reached a stage that others arrived at long ago. They do not need to read my book. All around me, but especially in my work, I see many people with similar problems. It is these people I hope to be able to help with my own experiences. Approximately twenty years of difficult development, frequently accompanied by very happy experiences, provide the backdrop for this book.

Even when it isn't stressed, readers will find the book to be suffused with my own experiences, both as sufferer as well as facilitator. And if they read the *whole* book, they will be able to follow step by step the development of my thinking and research on the theme of jealousy. I do believe, however, that some parts can be read independently. I myself read handbooks that way, looking through the table of contents for those topics that interest me most.

Although I am a marriage counselor, I feel that I have neither the competence nor the right to give my professional colleagues guidance in the therapeutic treatment of jealousy. But perhaps this stocktaking, which is what I consider my book to be, can help them as they go their own ways.

Since my counseling work is the basis of, as well as the most important impetus for writing, this book, reading it should give jealous individuals and their partners a better idea of what happens during marriage counseling and what they may expect from it. To be sure, reading alone won't suffice.

PART ONE:
JEALOUSY AS IT IS LIVED

△ 1 △

THE JEALOUS INDIVIDUAL

What does jealousy feel like, both internally and externally? In what follows, I shall attempt to describe this condition and its vacillation between hate and love, reality and projection. Let us begin with the main character.

It cannot be emphasized enough that jealousy occurs in everyone's life. Encroachment on an intense love relationship between two partners by external demands, stimuli, and temptations leading to the formation of jealousy's basic configuration, the triangle, is inevitable. "The Other, simply by virtue of his existence in time and in the world, also necessarily relates to the rest of the world, and not only to the beloved." The jealous individual must come to terms with this "fundamental psychic reality of the rival" (Lehmann 1982) or, to clarify even further, with the world as rival, an individual appearing as its particular manifestation.

I shall begin as clearly as possible. Yet it will immediately become evident how multilayered and multidirectional jealousy is. In each case, jealousy is a relational conflict among three persons, usually among two persons of the same sex and one of the opposite sex. As a rule, the most jealous person is the one whose long-term relationship has been violated—in short, the husband or wife. That person feels him- or herself threatened, robbed, deceived, and cheated. But the new partner is also sometimes (not always) envious of the rights to which the long-term partner lays claim. He or she is both furious and sad to have to renounce, struggle, wait, or conceal. The long-term partner becomes, if not the enemy, at least an opponent, someone who is in the way. The person who stands between the competitors is spared jealousy, at least within the triadic relationship that has arisen in this way. But that person is also encumbered, at least in conflicts that are more than frivolous, by a severe burden of worry, disquiet, and often guilt feelings. Jealousy *outside* the triangle is not only possible, but frequently arises in the person being courted. This can occur when the wife, who seemed so much more unattractive than the new love, in turn makes herself more independent and possibly begins to notice other men. Or it can happen when the girlfriend, for the first time, puts out feelers from the new dyad into the rival world. Or there remains, as usual, jealousy of mother, children, work.

Jealousy per se is the same everywhere. Its intensity and significance in the life of the individual vary, but not the character of the feeling. The frequently raised question concerning the differences between male and female jealousy can be answered only in terms of its psycho- and sociogenesis, not in terms of what concerns the emotional state per se. Among the feelings that are to be expected in human life, there is nothing more agonizing, because grief is "greater" and morally blameless, anxiety situational and "more justified," envy more unequivocal, and hatred more clearly directed. The primary characteristic of jealousy becomes evident in this comparison with other strong and negative feelings: its murderous ambivalence, that is, being flung back and forth between love and hate, which is directed—and this too is decisive—only toward one's nearest and dearest. Among the aforementioned feelings, only grief can be compared with jealousy in terms of this last characteristic, and Freud saw them as parallel.

The close correlation between one's sense of self-esteem, on the one hand, and the beloved's esteem, on the other hand, is certainly one of the main reasons why even distrustful individuals so often remain long unaware of the situation that, in our culture, is a justification for jealousy—the love relationship of the wife or the husband with another person. They do not want to look at what is going on, because unconsciously they fear that they will have to look at it constantly, and—according to the frequently confirmed psychoanalytic thesis—they know how horrifying jealousy is, because they have already experienced it in their earliest history. In extreme cases, it can be seen that a woman, committed to a psychiatric hospital because of jealousy delusion, says, "I am not jealous . . ." (Lagache [1947] 1982, 6), and in a certain sense is correct. When jealousy is constantly suppressed out of subconscious fear, it can happen that it will burst forth as a psychosis, like fire from a seemingly extinct volcano.

Others whose fear is more conscious conduct a constant preventive war against the partner's possible external relationships. Sighing and with resignation, one says of them, "My husband [or my wife] is so terribly jealous . . ." These people sense that jealousy "actually substantiated" could overpower them and become their only concern in life. It is an integral part of the misfortunes and mysteries of a close relationship between two people that they directly conjure up a situation of infidelity. Modern systems theory has thrown new light on this (see chap. 15, sec. 2).

Let us call to mind what it is like once the defense mechanism has been breached—how agonizing, how galling, how unbearable even "completely normal" jealousy can be. Anxiety, disquiet, and an incessant compulsion to brood about the immediate situation endanger, even prevent, one's ability to conduct one's life as usual, in a certain sense one's "normal" life. One not only showers the rival with reproaches in one's imagination (often enough in face-to-face or telephone conversations as well) but also the beloved (really beloved?) partner. Hatred distorts the ability to see clearly and impinges upon other people close to one, either as nervousness and aggression or in an exaggerated, all-consuming devotion (for example, to the children, who thus become consolers or allies). One seems unattractive to oneself and deformed by depression, but, for all that, often exaggeratedly morally blameless. Efforts on behalf of the common cause, which earlier were managed cheerfully or were felt to be meaningful, become unreasonable demands—housework for women, for example; for men, being the breadwinner as per the classical division of roles. But other allotted tasks and assistance may also seem unreasonable ("intellectual interaction," constructive criticism of the other's work): "I am doing all of that for us, for the children—and you . . .?" Activities that used to be fun can no longer be fit into contexts in which they can produce pleasure. One can probably still do them mechanically, but the mood remains depressed, one's thoughts constantly stray—possibly to where the woman or girlfriend, radiating joy, is sitting across from this dreadful Other; to where the husband or boyfriend (that, at least, is what the jealous person thinks) does not waste a moment's thought on his unhappy long-term partner while doing with "the new" and perhaps much younger one what he is used to doing with his life's companion: going to the movies, attending art exhibits, or simply talking, laughing, being together.

It is self-evident that all these torments are intensified when it is also necessary to reckon with sexual contacts. Anyone who gets along well with the partner on a physical level, and felt happy until then, must wish that at the very least this most intimate, personal, and ecstatic form of association will be spared. The assertion, frequently heard in enlightened circles, that what is important is the relationship's intensity and not its actual sexual consummation—that infidelity can be even greater if it is "only" a matter of an intense emotional relationship—must be taken with a grain of salt. In the case of sexual difficulties *within* the marriage, the narcissistic sense of being wronged is perhaps even greater: "It isn't good with me, but with someone else, naturally, it's suddenly . . ."

In terms of the three people involved, the jealous person does not view any of them, including him- or herself, without ambivalence. Since those who are especially jealous are also especially righteous individuals, full of good intentions and also genuine friendliness, who would like to see the world as clear and ordered, this lack of clarity, this vacillation of their feelings, plunges them into profound discontent, even into unhappiness and despair. They do not understand the world anymore, because they want to prescribe how it should look and the world does not act accordingly. Nonetheless, they seem to seek out these discordant feelings. The dictum concerning "passion which zealously seeks what creates suffering" (see chap. 13) is only one of the definitions that point to this conspicuous feature of jealousy. Viewed dispassionately, it is a compulsion that is highly uneconomical but nonetheless powerful, one of the great proofs for the impotence of reason; and almost every jealous individual in despair, should he or she come to reflect upon it, will admit that Freud is correct in characterizing the ego as the "circus clown" between id and superego, torn between drives and moral imperatives, but in any case helpless, "impossible" (Freud 1914a). It is easy enough for all who warn against jealousy to say, "O, beware, my lord, of jealousy! / It is the green-ey'd monster which doth mock / The meat it feeds on" (*Othello*, 3.3.165–67).

In his baroque way, Shakespeare very nicely describes the paradoxical nature of compulsion (which mocks the meat it feeds on), which consists in the fact that what is necessary for the emotional state and its continued existence, namely the preoccupation with the beloved's infidelity, must be derided and mocked yet is needed and, indeed, never suffices. "I hate and love. You may well ask why I do that. I do not know, but I feel it happen, and I feel the torment." That is how Catullus expressed it two thousand years ago—perplexity, ambiguity, torment, and the inability to let it be.

Once the defenses have been breached, an exhibitionistic compulsion (see Bergler 1939) is added to the voyeuristic trait of staring, the need to stare. This exhibitionistic compulsion consists in the need to talk about it, the need to bring up again and again one's own sufferings and the torture that the Other is allegedly inflicting. Jealous individuals are often very talkative during counseling sessions. They repeat themselves and certainly do not always come to rid themselves of their suffering, but to receive confirmation that it is "justified" and to be listened to again and again in their torment. In this way, jealousy becomes the main preoccupation. It not only greedily ingests what it needs for its continued existence, but also devours everything else that once was worthwhile in the life of the afflicted individual—even and especially his or her own self-image.

"I never wanted to be that way," a man once said to me during counseling, and broke out in tears. But he "couldn't do anything else." During long business trips he could not, for example, think of anything but his wife's brief infidelity dating back two years. And every time he drove through the small town (remarkably often!) in which "it" had happened, he stopped at the local inn and imagined how his wife could have sat there with her friend.

The similarity to addictive behavior is conspicuous and is expressed linguistically in German. Addicts also need an external supply in order to feel "right" (or to be in touch with their feelings). Many addicts even talk affectionately about their drug (pills, alcohol, cocaine, etc.), just as they would about a person they cannot do without. Insight into the drug's harmfulness is denied for a long time (a doctor once said to me, "Seventy cigarettes a day will not harm me at all"). And once this insight has penetrated the consciousness, we find the same mixture of suffering and inability to stop that is found in jealousy. Murder and suicide are the final consequence of addiction, just as in extreme cases of jealousy. Drug addiction, as well as jealousy, fundamentally masks another addiction—an addiction to the relationship with a dependable early referent, ideally and typically the mother, which was never sufficiently experienced or never experienced as the proper mixture of withholding and giving. Underlying jealousy is the "addiction" to a person, the need for whose love one cannot forgo. In view of this, jealous individuals would be incapable of uttering Philine's words in Goethe's *Wilhelm Meister*: "And if I love you, what concern is it of yours?" Their primary concern is not, after all, loving but being loved and indeed in the manner that they themselves fancy. They are often amazingly subjective: should they for their part arouse jealousy, then they repeatedly ward off the concomitant guilt feeling that one would expect especially from them. They are often convinced that what they do is something completely different from what the partner does. And sometimes, by the way, that is also correct . . .

Seen from the outside—by friends, the partner, and the counselor—jealousy is never a "nice" feeling. At best, it is felt as positive only when someone finally reacts who, until then, seemed uninvolved, indifferent, cold, or all too superior. One could say it always retains something of the monster, even though some people may find green eyes beautiful. In comparison, tenderness, solicitude, and even amorousness that may be ridiculous are, without question, more highly esteemed. Reactions to jealousy vary from sympathy to a lack of understanding or aversion. Their own narcissistic sense of being wronged certainly plays a role, especially in the case of friends or family members: the jealous individual, after all, is so preoccupied with his or her own thing that little energy remains for other people, least of all for their worries or joys. Classically, they are used, indeed exploited, as sounding boards for complaints, successes, new facts. ("His car was in front of this person's house *again* . . .") This sentence is often heard in counseling sessions: "No one can stand listening to that anymore!"

The fuss made by someone in the throes of jealousy does not exactly elicit sympathy. The depreciation of one's feeling of self-worth reveals itself vis-à-vis the partner as dejection, apathy, and pessimism—manifestations that exert a depressive appeal and are difficult to bear for any length of time. Any role in the partner's alienation is often not acknowledged for a long time. Instead, one's own love is asserted all the more—to put it more clearly, the need, dependence, and exclusive relation to this most important person. The guilt feelings that this engenders in the partner are often so unpleasant that, precisely because of this, he or she escapes to where things are better—to the new partner. As an outsider, one can see most clearly (and heartlessly) that, were the jealous long-term partner at his or her best, as before when the two were in love with each other, there would be a good chance that the new love would be renounced. But this way?

If depression turns into active reproaches, the situation is not changed for the better. What woman enjoys staying with a man who beats her because he is jealous—what man with a woman who smashes a glass on his head? And even if friends or parents say, "You've just been too good!"—and in certain cases they may be correct—what unfaithful marital partner, when asking if the other has not perhaps also made mistakes, will be able to make something of this response: "My only mistake was in being too credulous, too friendly, too loyal." This is an assertion that, in its masochistic tearfulness, exhibits great inadequacy. Should the change in the relationship perhaps be, that in the future the other partner will become distrustful, unfriendly, and unfaithful?

An additional factor is that another basic behavior pattern of jealous individuals—spying, pursuing, surveillance—is viewed as fundamentally bad, even worse than the unfaithful partner's secretiveness. If one is well disposed to the unfaithful partner, one can at least ascribe to him or her the motive of wishing to spare the long-term partner. (Even in politics, secrecy has something meaningful, even noble, while espionage is an ugly business.) The pettiness, absurd scheming (which, however, always retains a residue of rational probability), cruelty towards the partner—all demonstrate how awful it is to have to insist on something that loses its value when it is not given freely. It is easy for outsiders to say, "Why don't you finally get your mind on something else?" It is precisely that which the jealous individual cannot do and—he or she, too, often understands this—does not even want.

The long-suffering of others causes impatience, especially when they appear to have chosen it themselves. An important factor here is certainly the observers' subconscious fear that something similar could happen to them. The cry for help—the appeal for closeness, for warmth, for being more important than all others—which in jealousy is like a shrill scream, as well as the horror in the face of abandonment and of the collapse of an order that was viewed as dependable until then, reminds one, if one follows all aspects of the situation to their logical conclusion, of the final parting—death. It is a great act of friendship to help bear the burden of such torments for a time. No one can perform this service for very long. Friends pull back. Neighbors feel themselves burdened and alienated should the fights become too loud and the surveillance obvious. The partner, partly out of helplessness, partly out of aggressiveness, takes refuge in the advice, "You have to go to a psychiatrist!" In general, no one has a clear idea of what this implies, except perhaps, the analyst will set it right and I will not have to concern myself with it anymore. In this way, forced into a childlike position, the partner no longer relies on his or her own decisions but instead desires help and salvation from someone who is fantasized as being omnipotent. This reaction is similar to that of the jealous person (if I may summarize), who, while acting irrational, imprudent, and insufferable, retains the absurd hope that the other will continue to love and accept him or her in the way that a normal person can expect only from one relationship in life, and even there for only a short time: as a small child is loved and accepted by his or her parents.

It may seem peculiar or perhaps disappointing that no distinction is made here between substantiated and unsubstantiated jealousy. I will treat this later in detail. Now I will point out only that not *every* person reacts to an extramarital relationship in the way I have just described, even though many characterize this reaction as "natural." What concerns me here is the jealous individual's internal state and its external consequences. I am concerned above all with the paradox of the need to torture oneself for the sake of successfully regaining the other in a way that is anything but successful.

△ 2 △

THE PARTNER

Whether or not the partner has actually been unfaithful is in no way of subordinate significance for the partner's interior landscape, although it may be for the jealous individual's. Let us begin with the "most normal" case: he has fallen in love, "it just happened to him"; he has a girlfriend, or she has a lover, and that is an event, a delight, a flattering intensification of the feeling of self-worth, an experience—in any case, a fact. Each person reading this has already fallen in love at least once. Recall how beautiful, how exciting and irresistible it is; how the whole world looks radiant; how a new, happy love makes one seem unusual and interesting. Recall also what strength it bestows and how creative it can make one with respect to goodness, friendliness, and consideration not only toward the beloved, but also toward all others. In a conversation Tolstoy said to Gorky, "He who loves, is also talented. Observe those who are in love—they all have talent." Above all, they have the talent to transform magically the completely ordinary person, with whom they are in love, into a fairy-tale creature deserving of all worship.

It is difficult to surrender this stirring and poetic condition of one's own free will. Further, the condition frequently includes (almost always at the beginning, yet often for a long time) the utopian delusion that it can be sustained and that one somehow will manage to integrate it into one's normal life. It seems, to be sure, that one still loves the long-term partner, in a different way perhaps yet also very much—this must be obvious. If not, the enamored enthusiast usually experiences his or her first dose of cold water.

A scientist who accepted a professorship in another city for the sake of his work, which is very important to him, regretfully had to leave his wife behind—the great love of his life—because of the children who were still in school. As planned, and after years of a commuter marriage, he returns to their permanent residence. In the other city he had, for a time, an affair with his secretary, who worked very closely with him professionally. The secretary had experienced an unhappy love relationship, and this triggered the affair. The professor, a friendly and idealistic man, comforted her and "finds it completely normal" that this resulted in a physical relationship. The young woman's admiration and gratitude were extraordinarily good for him, since he felt himself "incomplete" without his wife. He experienced himself in a new way. At the same time, he had the feeling of loving his wife all the more. He is extremely puzzled at her collapse when she learns of the affair. "But that is no reflection on *you!*" he says, and even that it is his love for his wife and everything he has gained in warmth and emotional richness because of her, which made him capable of comforting the secretary and building the hope in her that one day she would be able to have a marriage like his.

To a certain extent, this man was correct. (Moreover, when his wife learned of it, he had already given up the relationship with the secretary and was just as surprised at her reaction as at his wife's. To wit, the secretary looked for another job.) From his perspective, everything he felt was true. However, in terms of the relationships in which he had been involved, he had behaved extremely naively and thoughtlessly—in any case, not exactly empathetically.

This case of course belongs to the upside of jealousy counseling. The case is closed and the love between the marital partners had basically never been endangered. The wife, who would never have anticipated such a thing—in which she, for her part, was extremely naive—needed, to be sure, some time to regain her trust and to overcome her sense of having been wronged. However, she succeeded, with the help of her husband's patience, for he was able to cope with her depression and reproaches because she was in fact the most important person in his life.

It is different if the long-term relationship has cooled off and perhaps become boring, or if the partners have become disgruntled with each other. Then the all-embracing feeling of being in love is extended to the long-term partner, with at most a certain condescension. Furthermore, the pull of the place "where it is simply better," where more understanding, more open sexuality, a better mood, and perhaps even greater youth, beauty, and elegance are to be expected, appears much more strongly motivated to the ego. To be able finally to breathe freely, finally not to have to fight any more—after putting up with so much, it often seems that one may afford to splurge just once. Indeed, one has in a certain sense "earned" the right. Naturally, it is not supposed to last long; but "one only lives once," and anyway no one takes life-long fidelity as literally as in the past. "Women, in any case, get less out of life"—there are many clichés with which one may rationalize and justify an extramarital relationship. There are also those who claim that one will indeed spare the long-term partner by keeping everything from him or her and by continuing to carry on with one's usual, only tolerably satisfying, and somewhat bland life.

In spite of that, guilt feelings cannot be avoided (although they can be repressed!), and they are the partner's biggest problem. They become worse the longer the relationship to the extramarital partner lasts, and doubly so when the third person begins to change from the "intoxicant" ("In the seventeenth century, this expressive term was used for the beloved," Goethe, *Maxims and Reflections*) into a real person with demands, weaknesses, and perhaps jealousy. Male "intoxicants" obviously can also demand that the girlfriend should now finally leave her husband—he would be all right on his own. Depressions and suicide threats can come into play, possibly on both sides.

The enviable happy individual who is allowed to experience a new love thus clearly becomes the person who bears the burden of decision in the jealousy triangle. Above all, that person experiences what it means when a marriage or another long-term relationship based on love, a possible utopia, has become a battleground: he or I, you or I, she or I. The characteristic of the dissolution of triangular and jealous relationships, that one *must* hurt *someone,* affects the partner most painfully, because he or she is the one who has a positive relationship to the other two points of the triangle (or at least had one in the past).

What about the initial hope for the coexistence of two important enduring loves? It seems to me that the current view of marriage as the "grand" relationship, which tends to ignore its purely functional aspect, makes it difficult to maintain something similar to the relationships between wife and official mistress that were formerly common. Indeed, it makes it basically impossible. There are of course marriages that can tolerate outside loves, but I am not aware of any in which unambiguously preferential treatment in favor of one of the two relationships does not arise. The marriage is either only a formal bond, which may have its emotional, material, and societal advantages (for example, when a politician appears at official functions with his or her spouse, but feels that professional and sexual needs, as well as the need for understanding, are no longer gratified by the spouse, but rather by a close co-worker), or the extramarital relationship must take a backseat on every occasion, must be subordinated and even degraded. The latter is the rule in the many cases in which the long-term partner refuses to get a divorce. Women in this case are often more patient and optimistic. Men do not put up with this kind of thing for very long, or, so it seems to me, not as long as women. Nonetheless, such relationships sometimes drag on for years.

Although we assume schematically that the burden of decision lies with the person I here term the partner, that individual might not manage to come to a decision. Possibly one thinks that everything is fine for one the way it is, and the other two come to terms with that. In any case, a person with two loves, each having fully equal claims, is overburdened. A long-term triangle is in no way imaginable as equilateral, with equal angles. Often, then, a decision is reached because of the overburdening of the beleaguered party: he or she cannot go on any longer and gives up one of the two relationships.

Let us assume that one returns to the original partner. The aftertaste that remains with one is mostly grief, malaise, guilt feeling, which first conceals, sours, and invalidates what was beautiful in the extramarital relationship. Often the return is not made easy. One would perhaps like to be pitied, comforted, and praised for the renunciation, but it is exactly that which the jealous individual is unable to manage. If the partner decides for the extramarital relationship, similar problems arise in relation to the original partner. These problems can be perpetuated if there are children, who in a certain sense actually bind the parents together more indissolubly than the marriage itself.

Of course, it is a totally different matter when, in a relationship characterized by jealousy, the partner knows him- or herself to be innocent—when the accusations of infidelity were never justified or are very dated. One must then feel continually misunderstood and devalued and indeed, on a deeper level, plainly exploited for the jealous individual's emotional (or material) needs. It is constantly demonstrated to the partner to what extent he or she is spoiling the couple's life together, because the jealous individual is neither happy living, nor enjoys being, with the partner any longer. In addition, the psychological interpretation of sadomasochistic interplay, should this be at the partner's disposal, is not of much use to someone caught up in it. To a certain extent, unsubstantiated jealousy is still accepted as proof of love. Many men and women allow themselves to be circumscribed by this in a surprising way. One can do nothing but assume that they have such a need to be noticed, to be important, and to be in contact, that even someone's negative preoccupation with their existence provides them with something positive. When, however, things go so far that the television must be turned off when love making is portrayed; when only lonely beaches may be visited so that one will see as few scantily clad members of the opposite sex as possible; when every time the partner is five minutes late becomes an occasion for a cross-examination—then even former "good mutual understanding," even sexual compatibility no longer helps. Then the partner must finally say, That has nothing to do with me any more, that is *your* problem. That it nonetheless remains a shared problem occasionally leads such partners to counseling.

Thus we have arrived at the problem of how the jealous individual judges the partner. The commonsense reaction to the jealous individual's description is often, Why in the world is this horrible person so desirable that one cannot do without the person, even should it cost one's life? One constantly feels humiliated and frustrated by one's partner.

Anna needs support, but Dimitri is a weakling. Anna needs love, and she gets nothing from him but coldness and silence. During a hospital visit, she asks him, "Do you ever think of me?" His response is, "Oh yes, a little bit in the evening." She says, "He read my letter only once; he could not possibly have understood it." Anna needs to be able to trust, and Dimitri is a hypocrite: "I am nothing more than his maid." He is egotistic, spendthrift, perhaps a fortune hunter. A long time ago he impregnated a girl to whose sister he was engaged, and deserted them both. He also convinced Anna to have an abortion. He would rather have a dog than a child. Since then he almost always uses prophylactics. He is dirty and unhygienic . . . (summary of Anna's description of her partner in the pivotal "Case of Anna," Lagache [1947] 1982, 410ff.).

That the Other is not the way he or she should be is repeated argument by argument, almost word for word. The put-downs, which even "normal" jealous individuals engage in, can extend in a very unrealistic way to what the partner actually does well and, indeed, to what was perhaps a reason for choosing the partner in the first place: he needs a profession in which he is successful, only because he cannot live without work or because he has a weak sense of self (at such points in the session, psychological concepts gleaned from casual reading are often bandied about—"early childhood trauma," "hysterical," or simply "neurotic"); her charm, intelligence, and elegance only serve to increase the long chain of her admirers, whom she then sadistically drops one after another; she uses the children in that she "narcissistically concentrates her emotional energy in them." A main point of criticism is often that the partner is easily seduced: anybody who so desires can get her to do what he wants; he cannot walk by a miniskirt without turning around to look. Surveillance and the need to keep an eye on the partner are motivated by this. For the jealous individual knows the partner and "sees through" what everybody else, in his or her opinion, would misinterpret: if the wife cooks his favorite meal, it is only to divert attention from her infidelity; if she says she has never wanted to marry another because the other candidate had such and such flaws, then the jealous husband "knows" that is not true. If the husband does not see his girlfriend for months at a time, which the jealous wife has herself reliably witnessed, this is only camouflage— this witch will never give him up, and he is simply too weak to resist her.

Precisely formulated, those who are jealous wish for the partner to be the successor to an omnipotent parental figure, satisfying all desires and putting him- or herself completely at the child's disposal. Should these expectations not be fulfilled, then something happens that is the complete opposite—the jealous individual attempts to assume the posture of a mother who cannot transfer any responsibility to a child because it is too ignorant, too inept, too inexperienced. Where there should be a conjugal community between adults with respective separate needs, a community that is equal and continuously readjusts itself, there is–nothing. To express it concisely once more: to be separate, that is, autonomous, is not permitted.

It is not very productive for counselors to occupy themselves intensively with the external reality quotient of both partners' assertions. At most, it improves the counselors' position in the emotional storm but, because of that, perhaps allows them fewer possibilities for empathy with the jealous individual. They are concerned with internal realities and thus the difficult multidirectional bias (Boszormenyi-Nagy and Spark 1973; Stierlin 1978). In contrast, the categorization and evaluation of emotional and material facts, of right and wrong, is of central importance for friends and relatives and for judges, people who are primarily observers or advisors rather than therapeutically involved. They take sides and their attitudes range from understanding, malicious delight in the jealous individual's misery, and complicity in the "more suitable" new love to headshaking, knowing better, and condemnation. The observers' own fears and desires always play a role in determining these attitudes. Crisis situations that are drawn out for too long a time without a decision are, precisely because of the onlookers' projective concerns, so unbearable that either the observers exclude them from conversation and social intercourse (i.e., more or less repress them), or they "can no longer stand to look at" the whole thing anymore and withdraw. Many couples who are having difficulties, not only in jealousy crises, speak of their isolation.

THE RIVAL

What we know least about is the feelings of the individual who is disrupting a long-term relationship. Marriage counseling centers—perhaps because of the misleading word *marriage* in the official designation—are seldom sought out by couples or individuals who are suffering from a married partner's inability to reach a decision, or who must work through the loss of a partner with whom they hoped to remain but who has returned to the old relationship after much hesitation. It seems that problems of this sort, as distinguished from the jealousy of the person threatened by the partner's breaking away, do not yet unambiguously belong, in the clients' opinion, among those for which one can expect assistance from a counseling center. Just as there are changes in styles of illness, there are naturally changes in the way one assesses one's own psychic problems and in the way others assess them. Everyone's subconscious, even that of the abandoned "third party," probably protects the long-term relationship of couples. Therefore, in a certain way it holds true for the third party that the failure of such a rivalry is relegated to the "premarital" realm, that is, to the time before official entitlement. Under those conditions, one has to accept the collapse of one's hopes like a good sport, as "fair" and as easier to work through. Competition and rivalry that do not lead to the desired success are viewed as something normal. It is assumed that the renunciation of the desired person will not be mourned for a lifetime, because a lifelong relationship had not yet come into question. Therefore individuals afflicted by such a loss of hope are more likely to have faith in their ability to come to terms on their own with their frustration.

In contrast, having to give up a lifelong love because of the incursion of a third party into a long-term relationship is viewed as worse, arousing more sympathy, and as therefore more likely to require help. (See Davis [1936], who uses the concepts "rivalry" and "trespassing" and emphasizes the parallelism between jealousy and the reaction toward crimes against one's property.)

Occasionally people seek counseling because they repeatedly fall in love with married or otherwise unsuitable partners. Repeatedly they assume the role of the rival who is forced into renunciation. The shifting of positions in a relational triangle is demonstrated especially well by these lovers of impossible love: their internal reactions vary from those of the partner in love who feels guilty, to those of the jealous individual who feels bereft. The relation to the Oedipus complex, which according to Freud compels everyone to be at the same time the deceived partner (in the exclusive love for the mother) and rival, is obvious.

The rival will see him- or herself above all as parallel to that person whom I have categorized as the jealous individual. That both as a rule are of the same sex makes the rival all the more "related" to the other, and the rival often has a sense of kinship, which he or she naturally rejects, denigrates, or in rare instances sugarcoats and experiences positively.

The rival's most heartfelt problem is the long-term partner's unhappiness. Indeed, the reproach "If it were not for you, all this suffering would not have come about" affects the rival more than the partner. From the beginning, considerable strength (or in morally judgmental terms, ruthlessness, egoism) is necessary to stand by the intention to extricate the beloved from the former bond, simply because one would like to have the beloved oneself or because one "needs" him or her. A declaration such as the following, which a wife reported to me (her husband had passed it on to her from his girlfriend), is rare.

I understand, of course, that your wife is suffering and that you were not unhappy with her; but she has had you for twenty years and I am no longer as young as I used to be—now we have to exchange roles for the rest of our lives.

It is the rule that one looks away ("I just cannot concern myself with that anymore") or more frequently projects, based on one's own realities or desires, that the endangered relationship basically did not exist anymore, or at least was not good.

"Just imagine: every day she has to give her husband an accounting of her planned expenditures; he hits the baby; she experienced an orgasm with me for the first time in her life—what kind of marriage was that!"

One may not overlook the part played in such representations by the partner who is breaking away. The clearest cases, which practically never surface in counseling, are those in which everything was, in fact, already over. But frequently the partner mobilizes everything possible in the way of defenses, in order to protect against the possibility that the marriage might seem to him or her more than minimally bearable. It is only too understandable that the rival does not ask whether this is actually true, but rather believes the new love. That also holds true when the marriage is represented as good, but the couple's agreement on the freedom to have relationships outside the marriage is stressed.

In spite of that, the rival cannot avoid a confrontation with the jealous individual's suffering. According to the model "one cannot not communicate" (Watzlawick, Beavin, and Jackson 1967), it holds true for the rival that he or she cannot not react. No reaction is also a reaction. I do not know how similar situations are mastered in Islamic or Buddhist cultures. In my culture Christianity, with its respect for suffering, has definitively stamped everyone's attitude to it, regardless of how distant the individual may be from organized religion. The compulsion to self-determination (see chap. 8) here becomes, in a special sense, a torment. In a love triangle, of course, justice does not confront justice, but at most, (subjective) justification confronts justification. If the (objective) legitimacy of the former lifelong partner were as inviolably established for partners and rivals as the prohibition against killing, then neither would have been likely to begin their relationship—or, in any case, there would not be fifty thousand divorces annually in the Federal Republic.

It is apparent that, in many cases, the third party must at the end consider him- or herself to be exploited and abandoned. Hopes have not been fulfilled, promises have not been kept, enthusiasm has retreated before reason, and reason counsels resignation. Here again, the task of mourning that the discarded rival must accomplish comes into contact with the difficult working out of the jealous individual's narcissistic sense of being wronged.

The jealous individual in the triangle is preoccupied above all and most intensely with the third party's external aspects. The rival's sense of kinship, and sometimes of having a doppelgänger or being reincarnated, of course does not prevent the jealous individuals from (but rather pushes them to) far-reaching supposition, speculation, insight—seldom of anything good, mostly of extreme negatives. It happens more frequently than one might think that the two individuals of the same sex know each other in the real world. The French psychoanalyst Lagache, whose extensive examination of jealousy, dating from 1947, is very important for my study, provides statistics from his cases which show that the "rival is chosen" from the common social environment (neighbors, family) or from the partner's professional sphere. In only thirty of his eighty-one cases is jealousy directed toward individuals met by chance. If family members are involved, then the kindred relationship in its various modalities clearly predominates (brother, sister, half-sister, sister-in-law; Lagache [1947] 1982, 441ff.).

In a more recent study from the Netherlands (Buunk 1982) that examines fifty couples involved in extramarital relationships, about two-thirds of them have personally spoken at least once with the rival about the triangular affair, and 44 percent viewed the third party as somebody belonging to their circle of friends, or later became friends with the third party. Since the group that was interviewed exhibited elite characteristics—with at least four years of college and large incomes, which was also true for 42 percent of the working wives—such a behavior pattern may not be representative for the average population. The lower middle class especially is probably more conservative and avoids, in "an old-fashioned" way, open communication—that would, in any case, correspond to my (statistically unsubstantiated) experience. Nonetheless, one may consider Buunk's sample—ranging in age between twenty-seven and forty-six and therefore clearly stamped by the 1960s—as indicative of a trend, certainly in its modernity. What seems important to me in this is that the rival's sense of kinship, which has already been frequently noted, is confirmed by the possibility of direct communication.

In the acutely painful stage of the triadic relationship, this sense of kinship is demonstrated not in a friendly manner, but primarily by the jealous individuals' ascribing to the rival things that one can actually only know about oneself. What psychoanalysis terms "projection" manifests itself here in all of its forms: "He has what I do not have; she has precisely what I also have—of course, she wants to take my place; *naturally* he thinks like this or like that—all men and women are like that (except for me; or, more insightfully, perhaps I would also be like that); she is like my mother, sister, or like the girlfriend who always challenged my position in school; he has the bad traits that I resist in myself and, therefore, luckily do *not* have"—and so forth and so on. As a rule, jealousy has a hard time with objectivity and "being rational," whether or not the third party is known to the jealous individual. The floodgates are opened to a chaotic confusion of projective fantasies, so that one often has the impression that the jealous individual is much more preoccupied with the third party than with the partner per se (to whom a projection is, under certain circumstances, also ascribed—namely that of being totally fulfilled by the rival).

"I had the feeling that she was looking for me," a client said about her rival, who had many traits that were lacking in the client—she was younger, more elegant, and more open with men. Without jealousy, there would have been no possibility for the client to occupy herself so intensely with the other woman, to observe her, and to mimic her in conversation with the husband and the counselor (that, after all, means putting herself in the rival's place, at least in terms of game playing). Fundamentally, the client was looking for the rival, at least internally, and not the other way around.

That the rival as well as the husband participated in this game again shows how obsessive jealousy is part of a triadic relationship. She flirted with the husband although he did not like her at all, and inflated the wife's jealousy into a major event. The husband reacted to surveillance by submitting and by curtailing his activities, and thereby increased his wife's mistrust, because she assumed that his reaction was just a tactic.

In such cases analytic psychoanalysis presupposes a deeply repressed homosexual component (Freud 1922, Pao 1969, M. Balint et al. 1972, Seidenberg 1953, Barag 1949). In the case of male jealousy, it calls it by its proper name in a way that is certainly shocking for laymen: as it is frequently expressed, the repressed utopian goal is the "union of penises" in the woman loved by both men. This crude image may well be a construct, may tax one's credulity and be an irritant—it is, in any case, therapeutically efficacious. Case histories demonstrate this. The paradox of psychoanalysis once again proves itself here. It neutralizes and, at best, dissolves fantasies in that it does not exactly prescribe them, as systems therapy does (see chap. 18, sec. 9), but nonetheless intensifies, admits, and precisely examines them and, in any case, does not forbid them.

When people other than the jealous individual judge the third party, their own situation naturally plays an important role. "The closer to it, the less objective they are" is certainly the rule here. To be sure, even positions taken calmly do not necessarily have to be objective, but can also serve to protect oneself.

A man asserted in despair and rage, "And my children don't think that things are that bad. They've even had the nerve to tell me, 'Let Mom have her fun. She's so attached to you, she'll be sure to come back.' '' The children were at the age of puberty and pushed aside all pressures to take sides, in a way that was insulting for the father but, in the final analysis, understandable. They wanted to keep both parents so that they could devote themselves in peace to their own pressing problems. To accomplish that, they chose—unconsciously at first and then rationalizing it—this "casual" attitude.

Another man said, "My mother is always on my wife's side! Couldn't she see just *once* how my wife's eternal nagging and her know-it-all manner have tortured me, how constantly being put down almost drove me to suicide—until I finally found my girlfriend, who always has time for me, understands me, and who treats me like a king! A man needs something like this just once!" This man had also never been "the king" for his mother. She had carped and nagged at him, and in keeping with "the self-fulfilling prophecy," her son, "really very dear and gifted, but undisciplined," had now on top of everything else deceived his wife. How could the mother think that was good? She clung too tenaciously to her own dogmatism for that. And to countenance the idea that even a marriage can become untenable could have endangered her own not exactly glorious relationship to the son's father.

The stance taken towards the rival also depends on the ideological orientation of the person making the judgment, as well as on the social environment in which the participants live. Therefore, in a book originating from the orthodox Catholic milieu (Portmann 1952), the rival is viewed as a priori bad (or at least stupid, or not Catholic). In other circles where people are inclined to live more freely, the rival is more likely to be the embodiment of the emancipative principle and his or her claims and desires are often taken more seriously than those of the long-term partner, whose bond poses an unconscious threat to the observers and their needs for freedom. And thus the reactions of the "sympathizers" (in the truest sense of the word), even to the breakup of an extramarital relationship, vary from malicious delight to compassion.

△ 4 △

NORMALITY AND JUSTIFICATION

The question of whether jealousy is based in reality must be important to anyone reflecting upon this topic. To start, what this implies is the question, Does the partner have a relationship with the rival or not? This question must be unconditionally settled, whatever the therapeutic method. Otherwise grotesque misunderstandings may arise, such as those reported by Melitta Schmideberg (1953).

> Some analysts are so much preoccupied with "intrapsychic" factors that they overlook the more obvious ones. A colleague claimed that by analysing specific aspects of analytic material a certain patient developed "almost delusional jealousy." This patient happened to be the lover of a patient of mine, and I knew very well that his jealousy was only too justified. Yet a scientific paper was published largely based on his analysis (5).

In this way, an interplay between therapist and client can arise, which reinforces the symptom instead of overcoming it; the client feels misunderstood because of the false assumption and must prove to the therapist again and again, in reality as well as in therapy, how right the client is in distrusting the partner. On the other hand, an "almost delusional jealousy" is certainly not always the reaction to the partner's real infidelity; other people would handle the same infidelity differently, and pathological jealousy remains obsessive even when jealousy is "justified." It remains, if you will, not "normal." Why are my fingers so terribly reluctant to write down this word "normal," which Freud, after all, used so uninhibitedly?

Freud had it good: people came to him, the "Professor," whether they had been referred or not, because they felt "ill" and needed medical help. Given this point of departure, he could then prove to them the internal logic, the "normality" of their illness and, in many cases, cure them by this means. In a counseling center, as a rule, things are different. Here the word "normal" is often used as a weapon to prevent change in a system due for change. What is normal does not have to be called into question. It can remain as it is. For example, "I am normal—you are ill, and thus you must become healthy, or (more likely) the counselor should make you healthy." This presupposes that the counselor is also "healthy." There arises a new triadic relationship, in which two healthy individuals confront someone who is ill. And there is also a great danger that, for the sake of his or her own normality, the abnormal individual must simply remain abnormal and therefore ill—in this instance, jealous— even jealous of the counselor, who then "talks the client out of it" for the sake of a happy ending. To overlook transference processes in this way, and to overlook one's own inclusion in the therapeutic system, will in all probability fail to enable one to contemplate the jealousy with any degree of clarity. The counselor is too afraid of it.

However, without dispensing with the most exhaustive reality testing possible, it seems better to me not to question jealousy's normality, but to question its *import* from two perspectives: the inner- or intrapsychic and the relation-oriented or interpsychic. On the one hand, therefore, the question is, What is the significance of jealousy for the jealous individuals themselves? On the other hand, What impact does it have on marriage, family, the rival, and the milieu? It is very striking how early psychiatric studies (Jaspers [1910] 1963, Friedmann 1911, Lagache [(1947]1982) do indeed deal briefly with the patient's surrounding field—with heredity, ancestry, profession, the partner's attitude—but then view the jealousy exclusively as the "patient's" concern— as *his* or *her* illness, craziness, delusion, or whatever one may wish to call it. There is often no mention of therapy. There is, at the most, a single mention of a sleeping pill or medication for a concurrent physical ailment. The jealous individuals are discharged when they behave calmly or when the partners, whose posture is basically that of a pitiable sacrifice, desire the discharge.

Psychoanalytic reports of psychiatric cases, in a more limited sense (Mack-Brunswick 1928, M. Balint et al. 1972), also deal only with the jealous individual, even though the effect of the partner's reactions is taken into consideration and, especially in Balint, included in a limited way. (He allows his patient's wife to come along to the sessions a few times. However, as a rule she leaves again after a short time.)

These two examples of psychoanalytic work with psychotics prove that, contrary to Freud's view, even serious disturbances of this type can be eliminated when the conditions of the case are favorable and there is corresponding competence on the therapist's part. The catamneses in these two instances, and also in some less difficult cases of the psychoanalytic literature (Seidenberg 1953, Barag 1949, Pao 1969), contain indications that, because of the cure, the total surrounding field has changed for the better. This is not surprising since, of course, all members of a system are connected to one another and constantly affect one another.

In the treatment of individuals, however, the oft-described danger of symptom transference to another person in the system remains (see Richter 1969, Stierlin 1975, Boszormenyi-Nagy and Spark 1973, Bauriedl 1980). To my knowledge, there is still no detailed study of therapy directed at family dynamics that has jealousy as its specific focus. Only Vaukhonen's very precise and meticulous study (1968) deals at all with the patients' relational field, with their marriage, their ancestries, and the meshing of both partners' psychic structures. The author says nothing of the therapy—perhaps joint therapy—that results from this. The study is purely diagnostic and descriptive.

Let us return to the question of normality. I believe that, in cases of jealousy conflicts, it is helpful to keep in mind the whole structure, especially the various triangles to which the client belongs. At least two must be kept in mind: the earlier oedipal triangle, which is still in effect, and the actual rivalry relationship. Then neither the client nor even "the jealousy" has to be treated the way one treats "the appendix," but rather the client's disturbance is understood as an expression of the disturbance of a relationship. From this standpoint, the criterion of normality loses its disqualifying significance. *Every* possible reaction then becomes understandable, "normal," in the context of a relationship. Whether it is justified does not play any great role in this, because "unmotivated jealousy can also be a response to a (real) situation; conversely, when a delusional structure corresponds to a real fact, it remains a pathological error in spite of that" (Lagache [1947] 1982, 25). Further, "only the least circumspect judges view its objective substantiation as a characteristic of normal jealousy, or its objective nonsubstantiation as a characteristic of abnormal jealousy" (Marcuse 1950, 762).

However, one should not be left with the impression that one jealousy is like another or that there are no differences between reactions to accusations based on facts and those based on false interpretations. The experience that "nothing human" can be alien to a human being who perceives things as they are—let us say perversions, murderous desires, or "only" conscious low-down dirty tricks—should not lead to the inability to call a spade a spade, or to equating thoughts of murder with the commission of a murder. The way in which these phenomena are dealt with therapeutically, however, is different from the way in which they are dealt with privately. In the therapeutic realm, it is obviously not the acting out of aggressive and libidinous drives that constitutes humanity and "health," but their recognition, which makes possible their integration.

In the final analysis, there are only two criteria on the basis of which the jealousy tableau can be evaluated: the burden of the participants' suffering and the question of delving for a solution. There is a great difference in how and when jealousy and its less-manifest predecessors—surveillance and displays of possessiveness—are felt as unbearable. What is deemed normal in one marriage and family, seems in another to be an unreasonable demand.

All counselors will soon—and should!—wean themselves from missionary notions directed toward their own conceptions of loyalty and freedom. At the same time, they must be clearly conscious of their personal values, precisely in order to affirm clearly their position in counseling. Jealousy is not "bad," as far as I am concerned, as long as what can also be called—with care— neurosis is meshed in the desires and needs of both partners; as long as they both "feel well"; as long as no difficulties arise from confrontations with the environment ("attention-getting behavior"). It is not "bad" because it is not upsetting and therefore does not need to be treated.

However, when one or both of the partners suffer from restriction or aggressions, the situation is different. When one looks closely, it is common pressure that usually leads the couple to seek help, even when it seems as if the jealous individual is being sent because the situation is becoming too much for the partner. At the beginning, indeed, jealous individuals usually want their jealousy to be confirmed and not questioned. In the end, however, they want to be rid of it, if only, as they may desire initially, insofar as the other person becomes different or at least behaves differently. The task of the therapist is to work out the communality of the whole.

The criterion of the burden of suffering is, moreover, just as valid for jealousy that is felt to be a character trait ("he was always jealous, even with his first wife") as it is for the kind of jealousy that is triggered by a specific incident. Whether or not this incident is legitimized, in our culture, as the generator of understandable jealousy plays no role in this. (Karl Jaspers's differentiation between an independent psychotic process and the development of a personality [(1910) 1963], especially on account of the other conception of causality in psychoanalysis, seems to me to have lost its significance. This is also confirmed by the psychiatrist Shepherd [1961], who on the basis of a wealth of case material was led to conclude that Jaspers's differentiation was imprecise.)

It seems to me that the question of whether or not the triadic condition is felt to be a crisis that must be resolved is important for the evaluation of the seriousness of the disturbance and consequently for the therapeutic prognosis. In relation to jealous individuals, the question is whether they have been preoccupied with their feeling for a long time to the exclusion of other concerns and do not want to "surrender" it, or whether they desire a decision that will either end the jealousy or, possibly, the relationship to the partner. Here I can lean on Lagache ([1947] 1982, 361ff.).

We feel that we can empathize with *psychological* jealousy. The suffering it causes likewise appears to be appropriate, although a conflict, and consequently disquiet and maladjustment, has arisen. "What characterizes such a jealousy is its 'becoming,' i.e., its orientation toward finding a solution to the conflict." Possibilities are the reintegration of the partner and new "crystallization" (according to Stendhal [1822] 1926), partial renunciation, or breaking off. "In this sense, jealousy appears to be 'work' and the ambivalence has a positive functional value." The jealous individual's posture tends less toward self-control than to self-defense. He or she suffers, but grits his or her teeth. "The person transcends the conflict psychologically, morally, and spiritually," before he or she has put it behind him or her "in time." He or she has not become "another person" because of and after it.

One can, to be sure, still empathize with and understand what Lagache terms *pathological* jealousy. The jealous individual, however, persists in conflicted ambivalence. The jealousy becomes a negative functional value. "Everything proceeds as if the jealous individual is seeking nothing but his or her suffering." The concentration on the conflict and the time-space constriction shrink the contact with the world. The jealousy is no longer normal, "precisely because it has become the norm for the jealous individual, his or her accustomed stance." To be sure, we can still understand the person but can no longer identify with him or her. Aversion, unease, and defense reactions take the place of sympathy. In order to muster some understanding (and, as I would interpret it, for our own protection), we reach for the hypothesis of a "pathological predisposition."

Lagache speaks of *delusion,* in the narrower sense of the term, when "the connection between the situation and the reaction is no longer rational and objective." The interpretation of material facts and the statements of other people is no longer tested on reality, but is washed away by the omnipotence of thoughts. The result is a "perversion of the evidence." The jealous individual rejects the persuasiveness. The delusion is inaccessible to reason and experience but remains fixated on one, the "beloved" person.

This is also true in most cases of jealousy *paranoia.* Here the observer only senses a shift in emphasis: the jealous individual no longer wants, above all, to express his or her inexpressibly bad condition. Rather, "he or she again finds him- or herself" in jealousy, that is, a deeply changed ("crazy"), anxiety-ridden person "clings to what is emotionally closest to him or her, the more he or she loses himself and the world."

In this way we obtain an ascending scale of jealousy. Is it of any use to us? Yes and no. Lagache also acknowledges the defense function of concepts such as "pathological predisposition." Naturally, however, not every intellectual effort to understand and classify can be understood as a defense mechanism. In marriage counseling, one deals almost exclusively with instances of the first and second types of jealousy. The diagnosis and treatment of the third and fourth types are actually a matter for psychiatrists. Nonetheless, people with those kinds of serious psychiatric disturbance occasionally appear in counseling centers, and dealing with them then poses a difficult problem. They resist the diagnosis that they must go "to a psychiatrist," because the effect of such a characterization can be devastating for them and for the family system, not to mention that, again and again, there are reports of cases in which the clients have "not arrived" at the psychiatrist's office, probably because, for the most part, they just did not want to be crazy and therefore never made an appointment. Because of this, on top of everything else, they lose contact with the counselor who wanted to refer them. One possibility, if not the only one, seems to me to lie in marital or family therapy, even for serious cases. However, it is not only difficult to convince the family of the "crazy person" of this, but most psychiatrists have neither the time nor the training for it. In recent years, the combative situation, if not open hostility, that exists between physicians on one side and counselors and psychoanalysts on the other seems to have relaxed somewhat—fortunately. Because the best solution would naturally be a collaboration between psychotherapy and medicinal intervention, which cannot be rejected in the case of dangerous delusional states.

The above classification based on Lagache and its application are useful for keeping one's distance. On the other hand, it is therapeutically less helpful— because in therapy things only start moving when one is, to a certain degree, involved again and when empathy and (multiple) identification are used as instruments. In that way, the concepts of normality and justification take on another meaning. To quote Lagache yet again, no conceptual and emotional content is (in delusional jealousy) "so unique, so 'against nature,' that it could not also appear in the healthy individual's dreams, fantasies, or free associations. . . . Conversely, the healthy individual, that person who . . . resolves the conflict, makes us aware of the possibilities that jealousy suffocates. . . . Pathological jealousies elucidate the possibilities of normal jealousy, but their pathology is only clearly delineated if we compare it with an ideal, typical normality" ([1947] 1982, 364). Early psychiatrists, too, repeatedly discussed the manifold transitions between what is normal and what is pathological. Bleuler found the distinction between health and illness as meaningless as, for example, the attempt to classify photographic tones as black or white: "Most of them are just gray" (cited in Marcuse 1950, 762).

△ 5 △

DESTRUCTIVE SOLUTIONS

There is a gruesome novella by Lope de Vega (1562–1635) titled *Jealousy unto Death.*

It deals with a hunchbacked, ugly, stupid, but rich married man and his beautiful, well-bred young wife. In a subtly engineered farce, in which a prince's entire court participates, the husband is forced to sign a declaration that he will never again be jealous. Otherwise, the Moorish king, whose prisoner he believes himself to be, will have him picked up and made a galley slave. He is mistreated, duped, and made the object of general ridicule. The observers amuse themselves royally at his expense. He, of whom it is said that he "completely lost awareness of his own self" in jealousy, keeps his promise accordingly, but he cannot change his jealous disposition "and, since he did not dare express it, languished to such an extent that he was afflicted by a serious illness which ended his life." The last sentence of the novella describes how, after a year, his wife marries a man whom she likes and "with whom she led a satisfying and cheerful life" (Vega Carpio 1979).

The great dramatist Lope de Vega was, without a doubt, primarily concerned with the idea that an entire court, for what is, in its opinion, a good cause and for its own amusement, stages a complete drama, the illusion of which is never suspended for the main character, acting willy-nilly to the end of his life—a dis-placement of reality, an induced delusion. In terms of the content, however, Lope does not give a damn—in Spain, this most Christian of countries—for this poor fool's suffering, but rather takes the side of the young, healthy, charming wife and thereby the side of esteemed normal life. And this, in a country that has made nothing short of a ritual out of jealousy, which for its part was viewed as "normal" and as one of the primary motives in literature and life—the cause of many murders, court actions, and instances of being forced into a cloister (see chap. 14, sec. 5). There is no salvation for the jealous individual in Lope's novella. He finds no understanding, and his young wife's entire lack of sympathy for him is apparently considered to be a matter of course.

What characterizes the genre of the novella is that it narrates "an unheard-of occurrence." This occurrence, however, is not at all so unheard-of. Lope's novella treats the exclusion of a person who, to be sure, is caricatured but who experiences and endures a feeling that all know—"odd man out": the projective elimination, present in all eras, of one's own distorted feelings onto "those over there" who seemingly are different from us. In terms of its tone, Lope de Vega ascribed this novella to the comedic muse; seen in human terms, it is a tragedy.

According to Goethe's famous maxim, there is "in every major separation . . . a seed of madness" (*Maxims and Reflections*). Analogously, one could say that in each jealousy there is a seed of murder. That applies to the killing not only of people but also of feelings: warmth, understanding, and, naturally, love but also mobility, openness, the courage to quarrel—many other signs of vivacity can be killed off. Goethe's sentence is rarely quoted to the end: ". . . one must guard against its [the seed of madness] germination and cultivation." Goethe knew whereof he spoke. He survived many separations and much renunciation and transformed them into new life. My book was written in the hope that this is possible also with jealousy, that it can be possible. For now, this chapter deals only with "murderous" solutions.

Jealousy cannot be resolved without demarcation, without a line of separation, and therefore without change. It does not simply cease to exist. Something has to happen, not only in the partner and in the rival, but above all in the jealous individual. One often expects that putting an end to the relationship with the extramarital partner would automatically eliminate the injured party's jealousy. That is, however, not at all always the case.

A man had a relationship with a female colleague, with whom he did not work closely. "She cannot hold a candle to my wife," he said. "I would never marry her; but sexually it always works with her, and without problems, whereas with my wife. . .! Besides, she is lovable and does everything for me." This friend not only never wanted the man to marry her, but also went to another city for a serious operation she had to have. She told her friend that she was taking a vacation. Only later did she inform him that she had wanted to spare him the worry and frequent secret hospital visits.

The wife never learned anything of these details (although she knew perfectly well about the relationship) and even now considers the girlfriend, whom she has never seen, to be a depraved and ruthless person. Her own attempts at a solution consisted of the following: at first, when her suspicions about the existence of the love affair were confirmed, in a state of shock she made a fairly serious attempt at suicide. This set into motion a whole tangle of allied reactions: the wife's parents were against her ("How could she do that to us!"), as was her adolescent daughter; her husband was partly against, partly for her, but also against the "insolent" daughter; the husband's mother was for the wife (she "would have done the exact same thing").

The husband put an end to his relationship, but for a long time his wife did not believe this. He was attentive to her, but she rejected him while exhibiting depression and her sense of having been injured. Sexual relations were finally normalized to a certain extent, but the wife did everything to avoid orgasm, which the husband very much desired. In spite of gradually improving harmony, the wife remained distrustful and was suspicious of telephone conversations, business meals, and the husband's evenings playing table tennis with friends. Again and again she wanted to know precise facts about the girlfriend and to see her at least once, even if from a distance. In counseling, too, she always spoke of "that one": what a tramp she must be to just go up and make overtures to a married man with a wife and children, what tricks she must have at her disposal, and so forth. She did not believe her husband's claims that the affair was not very important to him, that there was not much internal involvement (which the counselor could have confirmed but was not allowed to because of the duty to maintain confidentiality). The husband denied the wife the information she so desperately desired. Perhaps he was somewhat embarrassed that his girlfriend was not terribly attractive. Mainly, however, he wanted to preserve for himself a protected area of "his own concerns" against his wife's incursions.

In counseling, the wife came up with many fantasies about stepping out on her husband and about a greater independence from housewifely duties. Because of this, there was a further easing of tensions. However, when the wife learned that her husband had again met his beloved and slept with her a few times, the whole game started over again. During a quarrel, the husband himself threw this confession in her face: "You essentially drive me to it with your eternal distrust and your frigidity!"

This time, thoughts of suicide were not at issue, but rather, as it seemed to the counselor, the wife's *internal* deadening. Sullenly and reproachfully, she buried herself more and more in housework and contempt for her husband. She resented his occasional evening appointments. She saw all women as his potential lovers. She herself, however, never found her way to the local gym or even to driving school. In counseling she speculated vivaciously and imaginatively about what a driving license could mean for her in terms of freedom and opportunities. However, when the counselor, who sensed and knew from allusions to what extent her need to torture herself (as well as to torture the counselor and the husband by clinging to the torturous situation) was related to her earliest experiences, insisted on working more intensely with her and on increasing the frequency of the sessions from one to two hours per week, she terminated counseling. "I can't get away from home that often, and in any case I don't need all that anymore. My husband doesn't deserve to be liked by me anymore, and therefore I'm also no longer jealous." Every syllable of this was untrue. She could get away from home more often; she still liked her husband; and she was still jealous. But it was more desirable for her, "better" for the economy of repression, to persist in this ominous state than to confront the unpleasant facts of her childhood and puberty.

Many jealousy conflicts are resolved in this way. The basic problem—in the above case, the couple's sexual difficulties and the failure of engagement of one with the other—is not actually dealt with, but rather suffered and survived without the mourning that should occur. Consequently, one receives the impression that all this enduring, as well as the refusal to let oneself go, stiffens the limbs of the psyche and restricts internal (often enough, also external!) mobility. In the case described above, there are no victors and not even someone who has grown because of a new experience. The wife is moody, depressed, and sexually unsatisfied. The girlfriend feels herself abandoned and alone. The husband feels that he is treated without compassion, hemmed in, and misunderstood. The climate of the marriage is cool and lifeless. The despair that underlies the marriage is, so to speak, frozen in. The husband sometimes escapes into senseless car trips without a destination. Once he also escaped into a lonely (!) night spent drinking, but he always returns.

The tendency of jealousy toward torpidity, expulsion, revenge, and the inability ever to forget is often unrelenting and irreversible. In this it can function as the negative image of fidelity, as the dark side of love that has endured (indeed, it relies on this love). The greater the internal sacrifices of the jealous individual, the more intrusive the hidden (self-inflicted) wounds that arise from it, the more aggressive will its resolution appear to be, even in spite of occasional attempts to be generous and tolerant.

Two young people became acquainted at the university. After a carefree semester of being in love, the man's financial situation, which had been very favorable until then, changed completely because of his father's bankruptcy and consequent suicide. For his girlfriend the man's depression, as well as his sudden poverty, was a challenge that she accepted, so to speak, by rolling up her sleeves. She "let her literature studies fly out the window," became a foreign-language secretary, and was soon earning enough money to make it possible for the man to continue his studies.

Their success during the following years must have given the couple a kind of high. The woman made herself indispensable as the boss's right hand in a large international enterprise. The man got his degree in physics with such high honors that he immediately thereafter found a high-salaried position. They thought of themselves as "a combat unit," "a working team," but above all, as inseparable.

They married, a daughter was born, and the wife stopped working. The financial loss that this entailed was made good by the husband's further advancement, which, however, required him to put in many more hours, take many trips, and be away from home to attend business conferences in the city where they live. The wife had to spend a lot of time waiting for him. "I gradually came to see myself as being like the queens in certain Egyptian group sculptures—are you familiar with them?" she asked me in counseling. "The king is represented as immensely large, the queen as being so small that she only comes up to his knee. She supports—naturally in hierarchical immobility, just like the king—his calf from behind with her tiny hand, thereby insuring his ability to stand. The Egyptians apparently thought of it in this way, and I also came close to thinking in the same way." A queen, shrunken down to a doll's dimensions—how could that work out? "And when my husband came home, he always rushed to his [!] daughter. I was dismissed. Sometimes I just couldn't look at their billing and cooing anymore."

While waiting for him in the evening, she began to mix herself cocktails, which gradually became stronger, so that, more and more frequently, she needed a whiskey for her hangover in the morning. Within a short time, she was deeply dependent on alcohol and became unattractive, slovenly, and inactive.

A catastrophe, as she phrased it, led to her awakening. She discovered that her husband did not have to go to conferences as often as he claimed, but instead had a girlfriend. The scenes between the two of them must have been exceedingly stormy. All this woman's energy, which formerly had been exerted so tirelessly "for us," exploded in jealousy. Suddenly alcohol was no longer a danger. Instead, she occupied herself relentlessly with the girlfriend, her husband's business colleague, and became incredibly inventive in scheming to make her look bad at work. She followed her as she went about her daily activities, in order to see whether perhaps she was still meeting her husband, who had no choice but to put an immediate end to the relationship. She also tortured the girlfriend by making nighttime telephone calls. Finally it became too much for the ex-girlfriend. She sued the wife for slander and harassment and won the case. At the same time, it had become intolerable for the husband to continue in the firm. He had to change his place of employment, which entailed moving to another city. The wife moved with him.

Her defeat and the loss of all familiar circumstances—friends, house, leisure time—again elicited one of the reversals characteristic for this client. She began to think about herself and arrived at the conclusion that life at home, alone with the child and spending her time waiting, had done her no good. She offered her husband, who had a very bad conscience, a reconciliation: they could try to make a go of it again, if he would now do for her what she had previously done for him—namely, finance her education. She had given up her real major interest, the study of German literature, for him when she was already in her sixth semester. She had accommodated him to such an extent that, in the end, she did not even read anymore. The husband was agreeable to the suggestion and was basically happy that his wife again "had taken the lead."

She burrowed into her studies with characteristic energy and, in the shortest time possible, wrote such an excellent final exam that she had no difficulty in finding a position as a teacher.

The marital climate was changeable. The wife still occasionally reverted to surveillance and remained suspicious. The relationship between her and her daughter was very difficult, for the daughter naturally sensed the emotional estrangement that was an inevitable concomitant of this intense woman's commitment to her studies. Because of this, the daughter clung to her father all the more. The wife's relationship with the "child who was a product of the reconciliation," a son, was better.

When I became acquainted with her, she was working forty hours a week as a teacher. The daughter was eight and the son three years old. The husband had met his girlfriend again, which he did not in any way deny. He said that the affair happened years ago, the whole thing had been very important for him at that time, and he simply wanted to see how things were going for this woman. Yes, he still liked her, he replied to his wife's insistent questioning. He had not slept with her because in the meantime she had become a happily married woman. Moreover, he says he has finally had enough of his wife's interrogations.

In the few counseling sessions I had with this couple, the husband was silent much of the time. Both had come only at the recommendation of the family court judge. The man had moved out on his wife after the recent outbreak of jealousy, whereupon she filed for divorce. He said, "She's just too hardworking for me. And then she's so nasty to our daughter. And sexually she still rejects me." Whereas the wife said, "He's deceived me—at that time with his girlfriend, now by meeting her, and always with his work. I didn't work my fingers to the bone just so that we can't ever see each other anymore, and so that I have to take care of the children by myself, in addition to holding down a job."

The wife refused to take custody of the daughter, and the family court judge also felt she would be better off with the father because of the rivalry between mother and daughter. In response to the question as to how he should manage that financially and in terms of time, she said, ''You're certified too. Or extricate your old girlfriend from her marriage. She's sure to come. Then you'll finally have the wife you've always wanted.''

In this case, there was little motivation for counseling. The wife thawed somewhat only in individual conversation. It seemed to me that the basis for what one may, in a very unpsychological manner, term a desire for revenge, lies in the fact that the wife had given too much of herself, that she had lived, so to speak, too much against the grain for the sake of her relationships. I cannot say why her revenge lay in a kind of rejection of her daughter and in the attempt to force her husband to give up the profession he really loved. Without more precise knowledge of the backgrounds, I am just as perplexed and horrified as the person now reading this probably is.

The examples cited to this point contain something murderous, but in them it is not a matter of life and death in a physical sense. Anyone, however, who is concerned with the resolution of jealousy conflicts encounters murder and suicide over and over again. Every few days, newspaper reports appear that illustrate, incidentally more strongly than other arguments, the sense-lessness of demanding more police as a prevention against murder, or even demanding the death penalty as a deterrent and an atonement. How would the police gain entrance to the conjugal bedroom in which a jealous husband first rapes and then strangles his wife? Would the prospect of punishment deter a woman from ramming a bread knife into her husband's back because now he wants to move in with his girlfriend, who is twenty years younger? And no traffic regulation will be able to stop a desperate young man from driving over the edge of a cliff or crashing his car into a tree because he cannot bear that his girlfriend has taken up with someone else.

For the outsider, such actions are abnormal, pointless in terms of what they hope to achieve, and ''sick'' from a psychological perspective. None-theless, one can empathize with them to a certain extent, and they—murder as well as suicide—come to be viewed with more understanding, and even sometimes sympathy, than crimes motivated by greed or compulsive acts. Historical examples include the many enthusiastic judgments of Goethe's Werther, which were expressed by his contemporaries. They identified not only intellectually but often actively with Werther's suicide, which was mo-tivated by the fact that his beloved was unattainable since she belonged to another man. Another example is an anecdote from Stendhal's book *De l'amour* ([1822] 1926): he tells of a Leipzig tailor who, in a fit of jealousy, lay in wait for his rival in a public park and stabbed him to death. The death penalty was felt by the population to be too harsh, but could not be reduced. "On the day of the execution, the young girls of Leipzig came together, dressed in white, and accompanied the tailor to the scaffold, while scattering flowers in his path."

Before one may precisely understand the internal aspect of such a case, a long association with the perpetrator is required. This kind of thing is not part and parcel of the everyday experience of a marriage counseling center. Suicide fantasies and death wishes, however, certainly are. Just once, I myself had a client who, one year after a long period of counseling, made a serious murder attempt on his wife and committed suicide a few hours later. At the funeral, the man's friends from his local pub, all of them upright Bavarian artisans, did not even offer to shake the wife's hand.

I learned much about jealousy in counseling this case. During the course of counseling, the wife underwent an indispensable development toward greater independence (not, by the way, with other men!). The husband, who prior to this had often been violent, could not overcome his fear of her withdrawal from the thought patterns and life-style that he had inherited from his family. This case made the limits of counseling all too painfully clear to me. Before counseling, their family life was intolerable and especially harmful for the son, whom the father viewed as a rival. Treatment of the conflict, which was desired by all, also had to include the growth of the wife. Because of this, however, the husband felt himself threatened to the core. For a time, the external aspects of their life together improved somewhat. Internally, however, it became ever more impossible, and when the wife insisted on a trial separation, the catastrophe happened. The case is relatively easy to identify, and therefore I would rather not take advantage of my precise knowledge of what took place within the husband. Nonetheless, I think that a closer look at such an entanglement should not be omitted from a book about jealousy.

Therefore, as an example of the hopeless internal logic of a murderous resolution, I will turn to a great author's short story—Uwe Johnson's "Sketch of an Ill-Fated Individual." With the candor that a psychologist first would painstakingly have to work up and reconstruct for a case report, it conveys— adhering to the highest literary standards—the internal landscape of a man who kills his wife.

The content may be easily summarized. A German, Joe Hinterhand, who emigrated first to England and then to the United States for political reasons, discovers in 1947, after twenty years of being with his wife, that for fourteen of those years she had carried on a relationship with a Fascist. Then he murders her. His own suicide attempts are thwarted, since he is in prison. After completing his sentence, he continues to live in torpidity and loneliness for around twenty years. He has "invented his own death sentence, doing his time by experiencing a living death."

As far as the facts are concerned, what strikes one first is a twenty-year union, fourteen years of which were spent in marriage; "carnal knowledge" between the wife and her Fascist boyfriend until 1937 (the story's hero, perpetrator, and sufferer translates the German phrase "fleishliche Bekanntschaft" into English with conscious embarrassment and awkwardness); thereafter, apparently only an exchange of letters (anything else would, of course, not have been possible between America and Europe during the war) until, in 1947, there is a two-day meeting, a side trip during the couple's European vacation. Although it is not completely clear, the son does not seem to be the husband's. Nonetheless, there is a "kind of symbiotic relationship between the two," that causes others to smile condescendingly at the Hinterhands' behavior toward each other. There is a joy in being together, perceived as completely dependable, at least by the husband from whose perspective everything is seen. A few economical pages convince one of the central significance that the love for his wife has for this man. He "immediately" liked her when she was a girl, "her face and voice, her skin and hair, at first and last sight." One may read how tenderly and fervently the young love is described (22ff.), with what unbelievable happiness Joe Hinterhand experiences the marital union which is finally achieved in England (35ff.), and with what tenderness he dreams about growing old with her (29ff.). It is said that he has surrendered to her "the single, irreplaceable, and irreparable place within him, which used to be referred to with the word 'soul'. . . . And this offering appeared to him neither as a sacrifice nor as a loss; quite the opposite, as a safe haven" (25). Thus an exchange of souls, devotion, a merging of the two.

And on her part? Is there any question of exchange, of reciprocity? We only see her through him. We hear the hesitant pledges, and his interpretations of what she says—brittle, enticing details. No great avowal, but consent; not a word about vital necessity, that is, the inability to live without him; but loyalty, being there, solicitude, togetherness.

We do not learn what precipitated the wife's confession. Neither do we find out what importance the unknown rival had in Mrs. Hinterhand's own internal relational system. Her husband is apparently indifferent to that. Some important information that would interest a reader or a friend lies outside the bounds of what touches him: Why did she stay with him? How does the son relate to him? Doesn't all that count anymore—the twenty years of his own experience?

The answer is no, this invisible stretch of his wife's individual existence changes *everything*. And after he is released from prison, Joe Hinterhand will attempt to reinterpret the past by repeatedly looking at photographs from the long years of marriage which he now wants to or must understand differently. He can no longer ask his wife whether this interpretation is accurate. For him, in any case, everything is *"Untrue. False. Poisoned. Devalued. Invalid."* His wife has been revealed as someone "who is out to do him in." The horrified reader asks, Why? Was it not she who was murdered? According to Joe Hinterhand, she suddenly seemed to him to be transformed "into a principle, an embodiment of all powers that are opposed to his existence, like the threat of doing away with the *validity of words*" (italics mine). She was therefore a principle, not a person anymore. This threat is so strong for him that he "could only wish that it would disappear from the world." The inevitability of what consequently leads to the "act of self-defense" is obvious and deeply moving—and yet, with what breakneck speed normality is inverted; what a violent act for a person who has committed his life to the battle against Fascist violence; what a monstrous presumption for one who consciously wants nothing more than to submit himself in service to a cause recognized as right. A person who has committed himself to truth can only respond to an alien truth in the following way: since you are different, you must die.

What is depicted here with the precision of a psychological x ray, although at first glance is appears to be a whisper and unclear, contains the fundamental principle of the fatal solution to jealousy, which is perceived by the perpetrators as an act of justice, as a response to the (individual, not juridically comprehensible) experience of suffering injustice (cf. Lagache [1947] 1982, 605ff.). In order to live in peace, these people who, in objective clinical terms, are "oversensitive to setbacks" need a delicate atmosphere of sympathy and confirmation, which is "consciously calm, peaceful, less aggressive, less disturbing for others." If this life environment changes, the change is ascribed to the hostile intention of others (those closest to one) and, in a state of crisis, can only be reacted to with violence. (Joe Hinterhand is certified to be not legally responsible for his actions.)

The conspicuous intermingling of subject and object, of internal and external reality, and of perception and interpretation points to very early childhood, to the time in which the small child cannot yet experience him- or herself as separated from the mother (see chap. 17, sec. 6). In exaggerated terms, it can be said that murder and suicide are the same. They both affect the combined, inseparable oneness of codependability. It is therefore significant that the following quotation is to be found on the dust jacket of Johnson's short book:

> Is it One living being,
> That divided itself into itself,
> Is it two, who choose each other,
> So that one knows them as One?

In the face of this merging, a judgment like Lagache's, according to which murder motivated by jealousy is "self-affirmation [*affirmation de soi*] to which the reality of the other is decisively sacrificed," strikes one as moralizing and one-sided. In these most severe cases, of course, it is not actually a matter of *you or I*, but rather of *you and I* and otherwise nothing at all. Thus, when the you is killed, the I is not therefore saved, but rather the entire internal world and at the same time the external life *of both* are destroyed. This is demonstrated not only by the biographies of common murderers, but also by the great literary examples such as Othello, Herodes, Pozdnishev, and Joe Hinterhand.

The fact that, in spite of all the horror, we are intellectually able to understand all the solutions that were presented in this chapter because they exemplified some basic characteristics of destructive jealousy, shows how fundamentally questionable are all classifications such as "healthy and pathological," "normal and abnormal." What makes it so painful to contemplate these histories of relationships, however, is our helplessness and powerlessness when we are called upon to provide helpful fantasies as an alternative. Again and again we remain trapped in the dead ends of the labyrinth of feelings. Why must this be so? Jealousy is, like all symptoms, a sign of constricted vitality. What is the source of this constriction? It is the purpose of this book to circumscribe more closely some of the possible responses to this question.

BETWEEN PATRIARCHATE AND
SEXUAL REVOLUTION

After all the changes that sexual and other relationships between men and women have undergone in the course of centuries, there remains in our time, in modern industrial societies, fundamentally one primary characteristic of these relationships: love, the characteristic that is the last to be stressed, although not exactly new on the scene. Everything that formerly was of decisive importance for the relationship can now be dropped: civil or religious recognition of the marriage; joint property, even joint maintenance of the household (there are many marriages in which it is clear that each partner is financially responsible for specific areas); childbearing as a reason for marriage; work in which a spouse is indispensable; similar background (class, race, religion); related interests—all of these ingredients may be lacking and often are. But there must be love. This is taken for granted to such an extent that in counseling, in answer to the question of what made the other person so lovable at the time the choice was made, there is a helpless repetition of what had just been said, with only slight changes in the wording: "I just liked him, we were just in love." Or extremely impersonal characterizations are given in response: "She was so pretty. It was so romantic. He was just nice." They often add with some amazement, "But that's always the way it is." There is, in fact, almost no young couple (with older couples the situation is occasionally different) who begin what they have agreed will be a long-term relationship, with or without a marriage certificate, which is not predicated on a great love. It is rare for someone to say—and therefore it gives one cause to pay close attention—"It was more a marriage of convenience." (I have not come upon this statement without the limiting "more" or something similar.) It is also true that even today an unexpected pregnancy still leads to marriage, more often than one would expect. But even then, it is almost always stressed that, while the marriage did take place earlier than planned, they would have gotten married in any case. Other explanations often prove to be retrospective projections of the current situation.

Thus, as one reads in Goethe's *Stella,* "everything for love"—everything for the sake of bonding one person to another, which is felt to be of central importance. In the face of this enormous emotional burden, the high divorce rate is not surprising. Indeed, one must rather wonder that so many marriages still function at all. A wise proverb has it that "loving and praying cannot be compelled"—and all of us base our most important adult decision to enter into a relationship on such uncertain ground!

Very often no thought at all is given to further expectations. To be sure, however, such expectations exist subconsciously, even if some clients at first do not know (or want to know) anything about them. It is to Jürg Willi's great merit that he clearly designated and considered therapeutically important the couple's "common unconscious" in his "collusion concept" (Willi 1975; see chap. 18, sec. 7 below). The different varieties of interlocking expectations, that is, demands to receive something and readiness to give something, will continue to occupy us with respect to jealousy. At this point, only one aspect will be considered: the possible relationship to other individuals.

Freud speaks of the "dis-sociable character, which is, without a doubt, peculiar to all sexual relationships. Lovers find enough to satisfy them in each other, and even the family resists incorporation into more inclusive associations" (Freud 1933, 144). Love, therefore, tends to exclusivity. Nonetheless, or precisely because of that, no couple in today's environment will be able to avoid developing their own stance toward the problem of fidelity, whether consciously or subconsciously. The person who comes to marriage counseling because of a triangular situation often assumes that all counseling deals only with real or imagined "infidelity," by which is understood relationships to the rival in love. That assumption is in no way correct, especially not when one understands by it only the most direct rivalry, that of a sexual partner endangering the marriage. (Other frequent causes are, for example, unresolved relationships with parents, difficulties with the children, disagreements in general, sexual incompatibilities, not having anything more to say to each other.) Nonetheless, in most counseling, jealousy plays a role at some time— besides jealousy of a direct competitor, also jealousy of past loves, of the (vital) importance of parents, children, and siblings, of pets, of the wife's girlfriends, and of the husband's professional colleagues; and further, of areas that take up so much room in a person's thinking, feeling, and time (!), that the partner, with some justification, feels toward them almost as if they were people. The "unfaithful" individual really does invest so much internal energy and is internally so engaged (in the Freudian sense, sublimated libido). Often this is expressed accordingly: he is a "passionate" glider pilot or deep-sea diver; she "simply can't do without" getting together at least once a week with friends from church or with a woman's group to exchange views; he could not live without his "beloved politics" (but, at the same time, is knocking himself out for it)—or a middle-aged woman, who constantly listens to classical music through headphones, has no idea "how she could grow old without it."

But whatever the competition may be, I repeat, nowadays everyone who is in a dyadic relationship that is meant to last must take a position in relation to the surrender of the exclusivity that love intends. The utopia of merging into each other, of constant codependability, in which one often believes against all reason but in spite of that with all the fibers of one's heart, can of course never be sustained, but can at best be achieved for fleeting moments (certainly, however, not only in moments of orgasm). What then is one to do about separation, and about jealousy?

Let us consider some simple examples from the counseling practice.

A man, happily married for years, flies into a rage every time the name of the person whom his wife loved before their marriage is mentioned. He forbids even harmless contact which would be natural for a previously important, but now faded, relationship: rare visits, birth announcements, notifications of a change of address.

A woman, who knows of an affair her husband had with a girl many years ago, cannot refrain from examining his coat pockets for movie ticket stubs, his wallet for love notes, and even his socks for traces of carpet fiber from another house.

Another man's world falls apart and he hints at suicide fantasies, when he hears that his wife went to the movie with a common friend during a three-week trip (which the husband took!) and after the movie spent another hour with him in a bar.

These examples have two aspects in common: the jealous partners cling to marital fidelity and to their agonizing worry about it. They themselves do not appear to question their own certitude in this matter—at least, that is the way it seems. The front lines are clearly drawn, even if they are defended with inappropriate means, which probably will be the reaction of some readers. Or . . . Is the husband perhaps correct in forbidding his wife any contact with her old boyfriend? Considering the movie theater's darkness and anonymous intimacy, is it not better to prevent something from possibly developing between the wife and the family friend? And the wife who played the detective ("once a liar, always a liar!"): Doesn't someone who was deceived once have cause for constant distrust?

It is natural to expect this seemingly conservative attitude, especially on the part of older people who think of the husband as living in a hostile world (and occasionally being with women who are not at all hostile), and the wife as protectress of the home, hearth, and children. In many cases, that is certainly correct. In this connection, it will be worthwhile to recall a tolerant and frank book from 1957 (Wydler), in order to make clear how different was the world in which today's fifty- and sixty-year-olds began their marriages: the Kinsey report had just appeared in English, but the jacket photo of a woman in a bikini, which from today's perspective was completely harmless, excited storms of indignation. Back then the author, who was progressive for his time, explains the woman's greater emotional stability as a consequence of the fact that her sensuality was continually claimed and gratified by the children, while the man found only short moments of sensual gratification in the sexual act and "has to seek this moment again and again" (144–45). A serious marriage was inconceivable without fidelity, which meant that whatever loves one might have had before marriage were to be definitively renounced. The psychoanalyst Wilhelm Stekel, who for a time belonged to Freud's inner circle, recommended something similar in his 1931 book *Marriage at the Crossroads,* that is, a general confession before marriage, the purpose of which was to make the decision for exclusivity appear all the more serious and believable.

Given the conditions prevailing today, embittered jealous individuals of this type expect an attitude toward sexuality and fidelity from those around them completely different from that with which they grew up (the pernicious and negative, as well as positive, aspects of which they have often personally experienced). Marriage counselors cannot confirm this expectation. Obviously what is called "the sexual revolution" has left its mark on the conduct of relationships, and birth control devices have eliminated one of the major obstacles to a more open sexuality by abolishing the fear of pregnancy. The subconscious, however, is stronger than what is permitted at any given time, and family as well as class traditions can stand in complete contradiction to what is "technically" possible. "The" permissive younger generation does not exist for marriage counselors. Statistics probably do not support this view. Counselors, of course, see only a conflicted sample of problems that seem to the afflicted individuals to be so bad but, on the other hand, still just treatable, that they seek out a counseling center. In any case, many young people show up there, and their jealousy is based on "conservative" notions of marriage as lifelong fidelity. An example:

A twenty-four-year-old man has known his twenty-three-year-old wife since they were in a dance class together. Sixteen and seventeen years old at the time, they knew after fourteen days that they belonged together. Now they have been married for three years and have a two-year-old daughter. The wife went to a sanitorium for convalescent care after a skiing accident. She had to discontinue treatment after a few days, because her husband stopped eating and could not work, for the idea of his wife being "so far" (about 150 kilometers) away from him and living with other people, especially men, in the same house ("One knows what goes on during this kind of treatment!") is unbearable to him. The couple had practically not been apart for even an hour since they were married, except when they were at work (both had jobs until the birth of the child; after that, only the husband), and when the woman was in the hospital during childbirth and after the accident. The wife tells the counselor, who is shaking his head, that she did feel "somewhat restricted"; she missed getting together with her girlfriend and going to her sports club; and both she and her husband used to enjoy going dancing together so much. But the husband insists that, after all, he did not get married in order to sit around by himself again once a week in the evening. It seems to the counselor that a compound leg fracture was the only means available for the wife to escape her marriage for a short time—a marriage that she too considered to be completely happy. At the same time, however, the gruesome Spanish proverb occurs to him: "La casada, la pierna quebrada y en casa" (roughly, the wife's leg should be broken, and she should be confined to the house).

To be sure, more and more young people are entering into marriage with completely different conceptions. The petrified bourgeois family structure is being attacked from many sides and has been represented as a place of lovelessness, of exploitation, and for the education of subservient citizens. Therapists who deal with couples know better than others to what extent these accusations are justified. If they do not, however, also know that in marriage and its extended form, the family, security is still possible through the experience of quarreling, making up, and allowing for differences, as well as of intimacy, poetry, and humor; if they above all do not believe and have not experienced that the family, in our society at least, can only under very rare circumstances be satisfactorily replaced by other forms of living together—then they could hardly practice their profession. The marriage counselor who subversively undermines marriage may appear in the fantasies of paranoid conservatives, but in reality such a counselor is difficult to imagine. That means, however, that the counselor, like the clients, is also caught in the tension between the validity and dubiousness of the norms of the right as well as the left. He or she will, therefore, have to make more room for ambivalence, for mutual acceptance of differences, and for experimentation with life-styles based on the "other" orientation, than is agreeable to the exponents of all extreme positions.

But what about the situation of young people in "modern" marriages? Many of them—and also a group of older forerunners and fellow-travelers—at first believed, especially since the protest movement at the end of the sixties, that they could do without what slogans call the patriarchate, the nuclear family, alienation, and sexual repression. Jealousy also was part of what one wished to eliminate. "We want to live more honestly. If there is—at least in the imagination—nothing like fidelity, why then act as if it did exist. My husband had a simile for that: the love for different people is like the relationship to different landscapes . . . at home one may perhaps be in only one landscape, but one also feels oneself drawn to others" (Gambaroff 1984, 44). The young woman who said this, like her husband, is fully cognizant of, and ready to accept as part of the bargain, the painful side of extramarital relationships, which both are allowed. She did not complain to her therapist about jealousy but rather that she is not able to be "seized" by a truly sexual "emotion" with anyone other than her husband. She was, so to speak, surprised by her own fidelity (and this is in no way to be understood as sexual exclusivity). When it became clear to her that something like this is possible, "she became very reflective and was silent for a long time."

A rather large group of younger people, especially from the middle class, could, I believe, commit themselves to a similar program, just as the young woman did in Marina Gambaroff's example. These couples are trying out a new way of dealing with jealousy, and hope to make progress with advice such as, "There is actually no reason for an adult to be jealous, unless he has so many 'flaws' that he is not worthy of love. Or he is so incapable of love, that he cannot experience joy anymore. But these flaws and disabilities can be eliminated" (Körner 1979, 69). In spite of such high hopes, men and women are showing up at counseling centers and psychotherapeutic practices ever more frequently. They are disillusioned about precisely what others believe to be their perfect right: that they are jealous, that they have a bad conscience because of an external relationship, or that they can bear neither their own infidelity nor the partner's. They believed in a beautiful, bright, difficult freedom and often fought stubbornly to defend this belief against their own desire for security and permanence—and they fail. Even they are afraid. Some examples from this new type of marriage:

A woman, with her husband's sullen tolerance, kept up a passionate relationship with a married friend for two years. When her husband also falls in love, she totally loses her composure. That, she says, is "something entirely different." She herself, on the other hand, even during her "infatuation with the other," always loved only her husband.

A man has had a girlfriend for years. His wife suffers a great deal on account of this, but realizes that she must allow him his new life. She insists on a separation. Two hours after the divorce became final, the former marriage partners sleep with each other again. Nonetheless, there is no question of giving up the solution at which they have arrived. When the wife, who has struggled to achieve inner freedom, begins a friendship of her own with another man, her husband gives up his own love from one day to the next and, since then, has been pressuring his wife to remarry him.

A man in his mid-thirties says that it is, after all, obvious that marriage nowadays does not signify any claim to sexual exclusivy—and has lived his life accordingly for many years. He is a bachelor who has many love affairs with married women, is used to pleasurable but fleeting relationships, and finds jealousy simply ridiculous. He marries a much younger woman, naturally retaining the same premises that defined his bachelorhood. An unexpectedly close and satisfying relationship develops in this marriage. When the wife falls in love after a few years, all the husband's old arguments collapse. He is helpless in the face of his friends' malicious delight at his situation and their lack of understanding.

In this series of examples from cases, people have attempted to live in aware-ness of and with external relationships—on the one hand to tolerate them, on the other to assert the right to them. The hope of avoiding jealousy in this way, or at least of being able to deal with it in a more humane fashion, results in failure. The reaction of conservatives to these life-styles and ways of suffering is clear: they say, for example, "That's just the way it is! People who live like that bring it on themselves. They take risks and then cannot take it when it really gets dangerous. Some constancy and renunciation have never done any harm. The claim to exclusivity in the most important union of one's life, which has been entered into freely (!), is natural. Therefore, there is only one measure to be taken against jealousy—not 'sleep around!' but rather 'guard against its inception!' "

△ 7 △

DIFFICULTIES WITH THE
CONCEPT OF POSSESSION

The fervor with which one or the other of the positions on fidelity is defended speaks for itself. Because neither of the two is any longer supported by unambiguous societal approval, supporters of each feel threatened by the other. The conservatives can, of course, still count on the protection of laws and institutions, but these are often felt to be questionable, even hollow, in any case attacked from many sides. In the public arena, a flood of images in the media, art, and literature reflects common life situations, and it is not always possible to discount them as being irresponsible, determined by commercial interests, or shameless. For if there is one thing that jealous individuals don't have, no matter how much they resist it, it is immunity to temptations. The intensity with which they insist on their rights is frequently a sign that they are terribly unsure of these rights.

A marriage, and in many cases that which is described as "living together like a married couple," is a situation regulated by contract and involving personal obligations, that is, rights to a person, like no other contract. More succinctly expressed, to a certain degree it involves one's "property." Fichte and Hegel have, to be sure, already disposed of Kant's much-quoted definition of marriage as the right to the "reciprocal use of sexual attributes" (see Duden 1977), but this right, and purely in its crude genital sense, remains just what distinguishes marriage from all other long-term, legally regulated human alliances.

> I love you,
> I hold you dear,
> I have you.
>
> We belong together,
> you belong with me,
> you belong to me.
>
> You are mine,
> you are my wife,
> you are my possession.

This compilation (Körner 1979, 81) reproduces very well the attitude of one segment of the younger generation. It is significant that a man is speaking here, because awareness of the problem, as well as the guilt feelings of men, was intensified by the rebellion of women in the feminist movement. Political terms such as exploitation, marketing, alienation, repression, and conditioning are used more and more to explain psychic phenomena. The concept "possession" is especially discredited in this context. Jealous individuals, who are already rubbed raw, react with corresponding sensitivity when it comes up—men as well as women. For of course it is primarily women who, willingly or not, are used to think of themselves as a man's "beautiful possession" (Duden 1977). But one does not have to be so entangled in such a perplexing, as well as comical, identification with the aggressor as Esther Vilar (1971) in her theses about the man who is trained to perform tricks like a circus animal, in order to realize that the man also—his capacity for work, his esteem, his money, his sexuality—can be considered, claimed, and defended as property by a woman.

Becoming aware of this claim to property, the desire to own the other, is often very painful, and it sometimes requires a lengthy effort before the person suffering from jealousy is at all able, if only under the protection of the therapeutic situation, to try out what it sounds like and how it feels: Yes, I wanted to do that, I wanted to possess the other *completely*. The jealous individual often feels the need to mitigate this sentence with something like a justification: Yes, I did want that, but only because that's the way it's supposed to be—isn't it? Or, because we agreed it was supposed to be that way. And then what often follows is, But I also gave myself completely! Giving up this defensive congruency signifies another step forward: Did I really want that? Is it actually desirable to be completely another's possession? The dual meaning of the word "possessed" gives one food for thought.

Conversely, it is unimaginable for love to have nothing to do with possession. Research on small children by psychoanalysts and family therapists demonstrates unequivocally how vitally important it is for "human young" to evoke and discover in other people—parents, but above all the mother—appreciation, concern and solicitude, separation anxiety, and pleasure in possession, which are bestowed on a valuable and, in the best of circumstances, on one's most valuable property. "The need to belong to someone" (Stierlin 1978, chap. 2) is a fundamental human fact and is associated, in a dialectical spiral, with the possibility of taking possession of oneself, as well as with the courage to lay claim to someone else as belonging to and being part of one and thus, to a certain degree, as being one's possession. Being able to make demands, wanting to have, and holding fast are all part of psychic health. A person who never makes demands, but only gives, lays a burden of guilt on the other person, which can hardly be borne and which, in a twisted sense, often does not serve the other (or only in a superficial way), but instead caters all the more to his or her wishes and fears.

The psychoanalyst Max Marcuse states concisely and clearly, "We want to 'possess' the person we 'love.' That person is to be 'ours.' And no one may share in our possession'' (1950). Marcuse considers this kind of love to be normal and also to be inevitably associated with jealousy if this "internal claim to possession" is violated or disregarded by a third party. Today, over thirty years later, no one who reflects on erotic relationships will be able to accept such a statement without question. Rather, one will notice its origin in the patriarchal order and will more likely consider such a claim to exclusivity as neurotic. (Marcuse also recognizes the many exceptions to his axiom and depicts them in rich variety and with sensitivity—but he classifies *these* as deviations.)

Nonetheless, the possessive pronoun—"a pronoun indicating possession," in the words of language teachers—cannot be eliminated, least of all in subconscious usage. "My" husband, "my" wife—how is one to express this differently? In Bavarian dialect, one says, "the husband, the wife," with emphasis on the noun—as if there could only be one single person for this function, or even, because the person is apparently defined by the function. In this instance, written German is more precise and personal, but it is true for all languages in Western culture that, except for "father" and "mother," there is no other designation for a human relationship, other than that for marriage partners, which by definition is thought of as unique, at least for as long as they both live. The difference is that everyone a priori assumes that parental love is divisible, and even that it can be divided justly. Love between spouses should, in the strictest sense, be indivisible, untransferable, untouchable. We experience the opposite, however, on a daily basis. What are we left with between the two extremes?

△ 8 △

COMPULSION TO FREEDOM:
A PARADOX

What should be engraved on wedding rings? The old German saying upon getting engaged, "Yours willingly?" Something beautiful about love? The popular wedding vow that, in context, has absolutely nothing to do with marriage or sexuality: "The one should carry the other's burden?" Or a laconic name and date, by which is to be understood, with you, from then on? The phrase used in Japan during courtship, "I would like to grow old with you," appears to be gaining in popularity here as a definition of marriage, surely because of its discretion and sobriety and because it contains no moral or emotional implications. But one can also grow old with neighbors, friends, and siblings—although one does not make a formal decision to do this.

All these nice phrases, each of which elicits a whole flood of tradition-bound associations because each designates an important aspect of long-term dyadic relationships, illustrate very clearly that these helpful paradigmatic ideas still do exist, but one must choose them for oneself, and one's confidence in being able to live by them is becoming more and more a psychological problem. When everything is permitted, each person must find his or her orientation, and that is often more troublesome than the retreat into what is time honored and customary. Our freedom compels us to self-determination and therefore to self-limitations. Marriage of course always contained the utopia of the freely made decision (the church, regardless of social pressures, could never do anything but recognize a marriage that the partners entered into of their own free will, discounting all social conventions), but people have never before in the history of this institution been as free as they are today. Never before have so many possible kinds of partners or so many different forms of marriage been available. One result of this is the heavy use being made of marriage counseling centers, because the entire burden of decision has shifted from external to internal considerations. It has been shifted onto the entirely personal creation of what is usually called a "relationship" rather than love, whereby it is stressed over and over again how singular and incomparable each individual union is.

Parallel to the enormous revalorization of the person-to-person encounter, there is often a concurrent demand to develop a strong emotional attachment to the extramarital partner. A married woman said to me, "When I sleep with a man, it is because it simply *has* to be, because I have gotten so close to him that it would be a lie if I did not do it." She spoke contemptuously of "business-trip affairs." She could not reconcile them with her sense of self-esteem. "If I'm going to be unfaithful, then it has to be something important—I'm not a whore!" I have heard similar statements from men, although traditionally it is easier to think of men as being capable of one-night stands. Such an attitude may not be the rule, but neither is it rare.

Thus one expects a "grand" relationship even outside marriage, and in addition demands that the everyday experience of marriage should also "somehow" always be exciting, uncommon, and alive with love. With such expectations, it is no surprise that today a marriage is considered to be radically and irreparably broken much more quickly than in the past. One could pointedly say that the divorce rate is climbing because it is always the whole person who is involved, by which we understand the person primarily in psychic aspects. If this "whole person" does not get his or her due in terms of what he or she has dreamed of and expected, then many of those who are disillusioned prefer to accept the great material, social, and emotional sacrifices that divorce brings, rather than making compromises.

The following case should serve to clarify the jumble of paradigmatic concepts, family traditions, and "personal predisposition" that can arise in jealousy conflicts, as well as the compulsions to make a decision associated with them.

A couple moved in together on a trial basis. After five years, the woman presented the man with an ultimatum: either marriage and a child, or it's over. The man could not decide for marriage, and therefore they separated. Both had some brief flings and then both landed in longer and more serious relationships with much older partners, with whom, however, neither marriage nor having a child together was possible. After two years, the man and woman got together again and decided to marry. Their plan was to have at least one child and to allow brief "insignificant" relationships: they have enjoyed their freedom for too long to give it up completely.

With the help of the man's parents, the couple got a large apartment and had a beautiful wedding. From then on, the husband very rarely sleeps with his wife. His parents, who live in another city, visited often. Once, when the wife stayed out late at night (as arranged), she found the door locked at five in the morning. The neighbors heard her furious ringing, but not the husband ("I am always a very sound sleeper") or his parents ("at our age one simply doesn't hear that well"). A fight broke out; the wife banished the parents from the apartment. The husband "doesn't get involved in that."

He is terribly busy anyway, because he went into business for himself as a television repairman and often has to work late, even at night. His wife gave up her job as a saleswoman and works as his girl-Friday: she is the cleaning lady, chauffeur, and secretary, who, however, is a rather slow typist. The husband thinks it is too complicated to explain the ins and outs of the business to her. He needs to go bar hopping and have other women "for relaxation."

In the meantime, the marriage has lasted three years. There is no child in sight, and gradually both become too old for that. There are a lot of quarrels, and the husband is drained by the wife's constant jealousy. This is the occasion for marriage counseling. A short time before, the wife went on vacation, exhausted and defiant—alone!—and had a passionate affair. The husband has no objection. In fact, he thinks it is good that his wife "has her fun too." He says that he cannot really remember the agreement to try and have children. As far as sex goes, he asks his wife during counseling if she could not understand that one would rather eat chocolate if it is given right away and with a smile, than if one must be a good boy before and after and give something in return (namely children). The wife is not visibly hurt by being equated with a simple sweet that can be bought in a store. She only says that the agreement concerning extramarital relationships has, in her opinion, not been kept, because she predicated this on a *good* relationship between her and her husband, and he is not fulfilling this condition. Therefore, her jealousy is justified.

She says that what she expects from the marriage is to be a good wife to her husband, to communicate well with him, "to have a few children," and to help him relax in the evening after work. She would certainly be less jealous *with* children, because then she would have someone who needs her, with whom she could have fun, and who likes her. Her mother had been happy in her role as a wife in a farming family in spite of her many children, even if her father had often gone to the bar and worked hard the rest of the time.

It is obvious how poorly coordinated are the various segments of what these married singles imagine they want in life. The man gets married but does not really want to become a father. Rather, he wants to assume a position similar to that of a son, that is, he wants to be viewed benevolently and perhaps even with pride, when he—one is tempted to say *like,* but not *as,* a real man—works hard, frequently spends the night drinking, and "goes through" a lot of women. The woman is satisfied with a subordinate, virtually servile function and has an extremely conservative concept of marriage, but in spite of this experiments with casual extramarital relationships. Moreover, it turns out that she has very vague notions of parenting: she could still continue to work; the child would go along in a car seat, or she could put the portable crib next to her typewriter.

Her external appearance reflects a corresponding contradiction: a well-defined gentle face, with a provocative hairdo and always tight jeans and "sharp" low boots. The "disco look" during the work day. Her husband is the center of her life, but this sun revolves around itself and, in any case could use something moonlike that reflects him gently and whose orbit never comes into contact with his own—but not a living being with demands on his body and soul. It is also difficult for the counselor to sense in what respect this small disco-moon is really alive.

The oedipal problem, that is, the helplessness and indecisiveness in the face of assuming the parental role, is quite obvious: both avoid "adult" engagement and choose "impossible" partners even in their important extramarital relationships (during a marital interval, a love affair while on vacation). Is the wife's jealousy "justified"? Is her failure to please her husband his defense mechanism, which protects him from becoming too involved with her (and thus becoming unfaithful to his mother)? How can the couple proceed, individually or together, with such different desires and anxieties? The anguish of the compulsion to make a decision is all too clear; therefore, what the couple expects from marriage counseling is *help* in making a decision. At first they are disappointed that this is not extended in the form of advice, but they do not react by staying away or with vehement reproaches and instead continue to come punctually to the sessions. They therefore behave in a well-mannered and appropriate fashion toward the institution of counseling, just as they do toward their internal (and even to some extent) their external parents.

It is possible to imagine both partners as being different under different circumstances. In a different age, the husband would perhaps have followed a pastor's advice, would have fathered children as was appropriate, and would have sinned by violating his marriage vows, as was also quasi-appropriate. The wife would then possibly have been as happy or unhappy as her mother. Today they have nothing at their disposal but their freedom, but they cannot do much with it that is convincing, because, in a deeper sense, they are not free individuals. They are obsessed by unclear notions of "self- actualization."

It should be remembered that both the Protestant and Catholic churches handle this word gingerly. A Protestant theologian writes—and intends it as criticism—"One likes to explain 'emancipation' to the amazed congregation as 'wrenching oneself from God's hand,' and 'self- actualization' is treated like a dirty word" (Moltmann 1979, 761). On the Catholic side, we hear without any critical qualification, "If the family is seen today primarily under the aspect of self-actualization, then every other person, the child as well as the partner, must appear as a competitor who diminishes one's own freedom" (Cardinal Ratzinger, a specialist on marital questions, in his Lenten letter, 1980; cited in *Süddeutsche Zeitung*, 25 February 1980).

This one-sided and negative evaluation of freedom seems to apply to the case described above. It seems as if one could do nothing better than forcefully remind the husband of his duty toward family and state (and church), and support the wife in her tendencies toward a more or less servile existence. Such desires cannot be alien to any marriage counselor. Nonetheless, I hope that there is no marriage counselor who is able to affirm the cardinal's words and who does not feel that they exhibit a profound misunderstanding of the purposes of marriage counseling.

Self-actualization does *not* mean that one necessarily views the Other as a competitor. A glance at extraordinary lives, such as those of many saints, shows how flat and thoughtless such a notion is: Was their devotion to God and humanity not also *self*-actualization? And was there not conflict and competition within the families of those exemplary Christians because in the face of their vocation it was irrelevant to them if they caused suffering to members of their family? It is true, of course, that many people today use the term as carte blanche to act ruthlessly. No one, however, who works with couples and families can want this form of self-actualization, precisely because it is not the result of a strenuous investigation of one's own orientation. Rather, it consists only in the imitation of frequently changing models and attitudes and contains something that is almost asocial—to express it pointedly, something autistic and therefore pathological. Nonetheless, a preoccupation with one's own self and its needs is indispensable for the person who wants to find his or her way through the current maze of guidelines. It is unavoidable that one will occasionally offend others in doing so, will hurt them and leave them, and that one will have to expose oneself to being hurt. No one, however, passes judgment in a space devoid of context, on the negative or positive effects of the development of individual norms and possibilities, even when one imagines one is doing so. Of course one must come to some decision on one's own, but this is not conceivable without the influence of others. The technical term that Helm Stierlin coined for this is "related individuation."

The way out of jealousy, which is in any case a lacerating emotion, is not exactly made easier by the compulsion to internally directed self-determination that has been externally imposed. The paradox is "You are free, but you must come to a decision." The logical impossibility of this sentence (whoever is free *must* not do anything, and whoever must come to a decision is not free) contains something confusing and very unsettling when one looks at it closely and tries to understand it. This paradox, however, also contains the possibility of creativity and of a leap into another order and state of mind, as is true for every far-reaching disturbance in a living organism (for jealousy, above all in the systems of individual, marriage, and family). I believe that this possibility will be felt, if not as freedom, then as liberation.

PART TWO:
TRADITION—TOWARD A HISTORY
OF THE EMOTION OF JEALOUSY

ON THE HISTORICITY
OF EMOTIONS

Emotions have their own history. This is true in more than one sense. Everyone who thinks about oneself can follow the course of many of one's emotions (although not all of them)—from their inception, intensification, and possibly their development into something overwhelming; then their decline to something no longer so important and finally to insignificance, until they are forgotten. This can apply to the "major" emotions—love, hate, envy, enthusiasm, rage, grief—as well as to the "minor" emotions—annoyance, feelings of competition or friendship, enthusiasm for sports, and negative or positive affective reactions toward certain political or cultural attitudes. The list of examples could be much longer. One can always imagine the person (the "subject") who is living or has lived with the aforementioned experiences, saying, It was very important to me then, but today it doesn't affect me anymore. Neither the specific time when emotions are "major" or "minor," nor the stretch of time spanned by the emotional curve, plays an immediate role. Jealousy can also be "major" or "minor," can last for a short or a long time. What is important is that there is a beginning and an end.

We feel other emotions as constants in our lives. Elderly people can say, for example, "I always hated my father-in-law"; or, "The love for my wife has been a constant factor in my life"; or even, "The oldest of my three sons was always the closest to me." For one's entire life, one can "passionately enjoy" traveling, listening to music, walking in the mountains, bowling, sleeping, or eating. One's relationship to the last-mentioned basic needs of life is something else again. In spite of that, one can imagine them being juxtaposed with the words "passionately enjoy" and "my entire life." Many people can thus say of themselves as well, "I have always been jealous"—or others say it of them.

Upon closer examination, even such lifelong feelings are naturally subject to change. They can be directed toward different people or things. They have high and low points, crises and times of indifference, even when their beginning and end coincide with the lifespan of the feeling individual in terms of a subjective evaluation or in the view of a later observer. Emotional rigidity, that is, a compulsive need to hold fast (behind which there is generally an inability to let go, or a prohibition against it), is, at least for me, more likely to be a suspicious phenomenon. This is true not only of negative but also of positive emotions, or a demonstrative display of them. People who constantly speak of their marital happiness usually find this essential, even if they have not noticed the danger that they are warding off by doing this.

Therefore, the historicity of emotions, "my" emotions, is accessible even at first glance, or at least the first somewhat more thoughtful glance. We can call up emotions into consciousness without any difficulty. Since the beginning of this century, however, we have also become familiar with another history of emotion: that of the unconscious. Freud completed his *Interpretation of Dreams* in 1899 but dated its completion as 1900 because he rightly felt that he had written a masterpiece for that century. The proud epigraph that he took from Virgil's *Aeneid*—"Flectere si nequeo superos Acheronta movebo," "If I am unable to bend the gods, then I shall move the underworld [Acheron]"—describes in prophetic and at the same time precise form its incalculable effect. The gods—for example, reason, recognized order, the upper world, perceived reality, everything that is powerful but also debilitating—the "gods," therefore, I cannot change. Thus I will go where no one has yet been, except in dreams, and from there get the strength to change and, in the best of cases, to become healthy.

The labelling, revalorization, and therapeutic use of what Freud termed the unconscious have added a dimension of depth to our knowledge of the individual history of emotions that was unimaginable before. Many often very ragged sprigs and branches of Freud's work have penetrated the public consciousness. It is still true, however, for the great majority of people who find themselves in a state of personal euphoria or need, that they know almost nothing of Freud's discoveries and to an even lesser extent have experienced them per se. What is remarkable (and often questionable) about psychoanalysis is precisely its division into a highly complicated and abstract theory and a practice that follows the course of experienced facts with inexhaustible patience, precision, and concreteness. A layperson reading a case history often will not understand at all what is meant and therefore cannot begin to imagine that, in fact, not one theoretical term is used in a well-conducted psychoanalysis. But let us not digress. The unconscious roots and history of individual emotions will be treated extensively later in this book.

For now, the factuality of feeling, its character, its actual presence—this is, to be sure, a human constant. Love and fidelity have always existed; envy and jealousy play a role in the earliest biblical stories. When I am in love today, I experience exactly the same thing as an infinitely long series of people experienced before me. Many clients in marriage counseling see things in this way—and naturally not only they. That is also the way they want it to be, because then the justification of their present emotion would be buttressed by human history. Every counselor would also have it easier if there were eternal laws governing emotions. But unfortunately, there are none. Love— what we understand by this term today, and what some authors rather imprecisely term "romantic love"—was, to overstate it, invented in the eleventh century in Provence. For a long time to come, it was in no way the basis for marriage as we like to conceive of it now, and least of all for every marriage. Hate and mercy still had a completely different character in the (Christian!) Middle Ages than they do now. Punishment and personal cruelty were unimaginably harsh (see "On Changes in Belligerence," in Elias 1936), without the perpetrators being ostracized by society. Death was viewed and experienced differently than today; children were loved and raised in a completely different way; and even such a fundamental "instinctive" emotion as maternal love (Badinter 1980) was subject to far-reaching sociological changes and the emotional changes deriving therefrom. Some few basic instincts, such as the drive to procreation and to self-preservation, are certainly the common basis of all emotions. Clients, however, are not referring to that when they speak of the universally valid and ever-present form of their actual reactions; they are not referring to any scientific abstractions, but rather to a complicated construct of emotions—their own current ones.

What does the history of emotions have to offer us? More precision, in any case, perhaps greater peace, as well as the relativization of our all too absolutely fixed emotions, injuries and losses. A current psychotherapeutic slogan is "Here and Now." As far as I know, it originated with Frederick Perls and his Gestalt therapy, and it is directed against "classical" analysis which, in his opinion, is too backward looking, that is, oriented toward individual histories. It seems to me that every efficacious psychotherapy, even one that is oriented toward behavioral psychology, must begin with the Here and Now, with the therapeutic situation, but can only change the There and Then, or what is "outside," if it takes into account and works through the There and Back Then.

Since this is my opinion and since it also gives me more pleasure to understand larger connections than only individual ones, that is, to place myself within traditions or to disassociate myself from them, I would now like to consider the roots that link our present feeling of jealousy to the past.

△ 10 △

THE JEALOUS GOD

My culture is described as Christian and Western. It cannot be my task to determine what is Christian about it, but in any case the Christian (and Jewish) Bible is one of the fundamental and founding texts of this culture. I am only able to read the Bible as a layman does—but everyone in love, everyone who wants to get married, and everyone who is jealous reads it from the same perspective (if they read the Bible at all).

The way I see it is that a powerful jealous being stands at the beginning of the religion that today determines this cultural sphere: God. From the beginning, the Old Testament depicts him as being vulnerable, with a tendency to fits of anger, and as it is written before the Flood, he can take terrible revenge when he decides that "My spirit shall not strive with man forever" (Gen. 6:3, *New King James*). God's jealousy (*qineah* in the language of the Bible, *kinah* in modern Hebrew and still semantically undifferentiated from "envy") may be explained in terms of religious history by the tribal origin of Old Testament religion, constantly threatened by other ways or possibilities of relating to the transcendental, by the powerful Egyptian mythology as well as by many less significant "idolatries." It is both fascinating and moving to see how in the Bible the concept of the *one* God is formed out of the mist of early phenomena, dreams, and thoughts; the God not only of a small desert people, but of the whole world. Differentiation, however, was and remained important for this religion up to and including the time of Jesus, as well as the current schisms and efforts at unification. The Ten Commandments were the first clear legal code, and they remain one of the foundations of Western religion and morality. For the descendants of Jacob-Israel, the code was related to the difficult separation from the high culture and religion of Egypt—to the exodus from Egypt, the refusal to serve the Egyptians, and thus the first slave rebellion in the Judeo-Christian cultural sphere. The Law begins with the definition of God as a lord who tolerates no other gods beside him and who describes himself as so jealous that he will visit the "sins" of the fathers upon the children unto the third or fourth generation. (That Luther uses the word *zealous* is because in his time there was still no distinction made between *zealous* and *jealous*.) To be sure, God will also be merciful a thousandfold if one loves him and keeps his commandments.

Even in the case of God, jealousy is what it always is—a triadic relationship: God, his people, and the other gods are the participants. For them too it is a matter of love, possessiveness, and being hurt. Is justice also a concern? That children should be punished for what their parents have done totally contradicts our modern sense of justice. But—it still happens, again and again, in many societies even juridically. Though no one is sent to prison for one's parents' transgressions, one may still inherit their debts. Above all, however, society often judges people on the basis of whether they come from a "good" or "bad" family. Many family therapists agree that what parents do with their children has an impact, sometimes a devastating one, that lasts precisely unto the third or fourth generation—not longer than that, but usually for as long (for examples, see Preuss 1971, Boszormenyi-Nagy and Spark 1973, Bowen 1960).

Is the jealous, vengeful, and in the philosophical and juridical sense unjust God therefore old-fashioned? Yes—because he is the embodiment of a patriarch, that is, of a father in the classical sense of a male-, phallus-, and possession-oriented culture, whose texture is starting to unravel. Furthermore, belief in the Old Testament attributes of God has become extremely fragile. No—because the laws of this culture are still in effect everywhere, externally and most especially internally, in what psychoanalysis, for example, designates with terms such as superego, introject, and ego-ideal. Later we shall see what Jesus had to say about this; unfortunately it had little impact on the history of the emotion of jealousy. For the purposes of this book, there is little point in considering what God *should* be like. In any case, God the Father, in whose image humanity was created (as man *and* woman), who was viewed throughout almost two thousand years of Western history as the revealed and therefore true God (and still is), and who is mentioned in constitutions, names of political parties, and school regulations—this God is jealous.

Let us look at how a Catholic theologian evaluates this religious fact. Renaud states that the concept of God's jealousy has the advantage of allowing one to avoid two dangers: "too great a familiarity with what is sacred, and a too negative concept of a terrible God of vengeance." When we consider God's jealousy, we arrive at "the innermost part of the personal and living God, and are led to admiring contemplation of the *mirabilia Dei*" (1963, Preface). Jealousy as a "mirabilium Dei," something that is to be admired in God—not, therefore, how awful that God is jealous, but how wonderful. Furthermore, it is less a matter of the concept of jealousy (and possibly its exemplariness) than of showing what God is like, with the help of the concept of jealousy. Because, as we may conclude, jealousy is something so well known everyone is familiar with it (even if the pious author claims, "We are at a great remove from marital jealousy"); on the other hand, it is something so strange, alien, and fearful that it qualifies as an attribute of God, who is termed "the hidden one" by theologians in many different centuries. "He is jealous, because he loves": this assumes that it is obvious that someone who loves is also someone who is jealous.

Very early on, jealousy in the Bible is associated with anger, even with the threat of total annihilation. As Renaud says, the concern is not with justice but "with a psychological climate of intimacy between lover and beloved" (56). It is, however, difficult for us today to understand how a lover may punish the beloved the way God does (my contention, not Renaud's). "And the people began to commit harlotry with the women of Moab. They invited the people to sacrifices of their gods, and the people ate and bowed down to their gods. So Israel was joined to Baal of Peor . . . Then the Lord said to Moses, Take all the leaders of the people and hang the offenders before the Lord, out in the sun, that the fierce anger of the Lord may turn away from Israel." Thereupon Moses asked the judges, those charged with responsibility for religion and the people, to kill any of their people who were joined to Baal of Peor. God's plague upon his people, which is a concomitant of their infidelity and to which twenty-four thousand are sacrificed, only ceases when a great-grandchild of Aaron, Moses' brother, secretly stabs to death an Israelite and his wife who is not of the people. The Israelite had brought her along with him against God's commandments, and Aaron's great-grandchild stabbed them both through the body and in her tent. Aaron's descendant is praised because his deed "has turned back My wrath from the children of Israel, because he was zealous with My zeal among them, so that I did not consume the children of Israel in My zeal" (Num. 25:1–11).

The ambiguity of the word *qineah* is obvious here. Luther always translates it with the word *zeal*. In current linguistic usage, it can mean jealousy, envy, and zeal (i.e., fervent striving for something), but also passion, as for example in the Song of Solomon 8:6, where it is written, "For love is as strong as death, jealousy as cruel as the grave." But this word, when it is a matter of God's *qineah,* is always associated in the Old Testament with the concept of anger and power, as well as with fire, the sign of his divinity. "For the Lord your God is a consuming fire, a jealous God" (Deut. 4:24). *Qineah* is such a basic characteristic that Renaud terms it the actual "energy of God's divinity" (89). It is "the violent reaction of the sanctity of divine love as it is revealed in the scope of the covenant, against everything that would encroach upon the relationship between Yahweh and his people" (148).

The direction of this conflagration is of interest for us: it is first directed exclusively against the people of God, as illustrated in the above example, and *never* against the alien gods (in human terms, only against the partner, never against the rival). In the postexile era, *qineah* is transformed into the

avenging power of the God of redemption, who no longer tolerates the suffering of his people. In our terms, it becomes only zeal: God wants to lead
Israel home out of the Diaspora. And even if the people no longer remember
their covenant with him, he will do it anyway because he is "jealous for My
holy name" (Ezek. 39:25). What he expects is "that you may remember and
be ashamed, and never open your mouth anymore because of your shame,
when I provide you an atonement for all you have done" (Ezek. 16:63). The
catholic author does not go into God's compliance, which one could in psychological terms call an exercise of power by showing kindness, but rather
warns against anthropomorphisms, "for I am God, and not man" (Hos. 11:9).

In order to make God more understandable, the authors of these sacred
texts use human characteristics. Freud sees in this process no revelation, no
growth and self-development of human knowledge of a real God, but rather
an unconscious projection device, through which the individual has accounted
for the "impersonal forces and fates," to which he or she is subject and which
remain "eternally alien." The forces derive from a person, an extremely
powerful will, easier to deal with than what Freud, the enlightener and atheist,
thought of as the only principle of universal occurrences: completely merciless
natural laws. Therefore, where Freud saw in death nothing but material attrition which must necessarily lead to the extinguishing of organic life, projection provides for a divine will that determines when the end shall come,
and the individual feels him- or herself "at home in what is sinister" (Freud
1927, 338). One still believes that one will find the familiar where before
there was only the sense of helplessness and of having been delivered up to
natural forces.

For me, there is more religiosity in Freud's atheism than in the many
thoughtless utterances of so-called believers (cf. Preuss 1971). In one of his
main works on this theme, *The Future of an Illusion,* Freud's fictive opponent
expresses such a precise and distinct faith that it is difficult to accept that
someone who is able to write something like this does not know what religious
feeling is. To be sure, respect demands that one not simply co-opt Freud as
a supporter of religion. Freud, however, never deals disrespectfully with
religion, even if he is pitiless in relation to the psychodynamic processes that
can be observed in religions. I have never understood why Christians could
feel themselves threatened by this. Their faith must not be well developed if
it cannot endure being tested in terms of how it functions psychologically.
No one concerned with honesty in this field will be able to deny Freud's
observation "that one's personal relationship to God is dependent on one's
relationship to one's biological father, that its fluctuation and transformations
are a function of the relationship to the biological father" (Freud 1913, 177).
Thus *all* forms of psychic intercourse are made possible, not only equating
the father to God but also, for example, inversion to its opposite, idealization,
masochistic submission, and the dream of participating in omnipotence. Who

can conclude from this that objectively God is totally Other? Moreover, he can only be believed and experienced internally since, in the final analysis, neither his existence nor its opposite can be scientifically proven. In this sense, Freud's atheism was also a "belief," and the eternally alien, impersonal natural law can be a father projection just as Yahweh is.

God's attributes, therefore, tell us something about the feelings, yearnings, and customs of the people during whose lifetime they are ascribed to him. The texts, which in the Old and the New Testament were culled from a doubtless much greater number of extant texts, belong to societies that disappeared long ago—Moses died in approximately 1200 B.C. They are nonetheless important, even if we live completely differently today, because they still have the aura of a claim to divine authority, because a whole scientific field is devoted to their study, and because every believer who is not merely following conventions is called upon to come to terms with them.

Without any doubt, the culture represented in these texts is thoroughly patriarchal, to such an extent that not a single female deity appears. In the tenth commandment, the wife is called one of the man's important possessions, whom another man should "not covet": in the enumeration of possessions, the home comes first, then the wife, then slaves and animals. Marriage is always understood as the husband's marriage, which, to be sure, he may not violate. The penalty for adultery is death for both participants (Lev. 20:10, Deut. 22:22). Divorce, also only the husband's prerogative (Deut. 24:1–4), was possible if the wife found "no favor in his eyes" because her husband discovered "some uncleanness" about her (the standard German translation cannot explain this word precisely; in a footnote it is said that there is perhaps no restriction to one specific reason for divorce). Clearly phrased laws protected women against unjust accusations of feigned virginity and against rapes (Deut. 22:13–29). However, the criteria determining the severity of the sexual offense are to a large extent based on how seriously the property rights of another man, of course a Jewish man, were violated. The women (and children and old people) of alien conquered peoples, whose men were all killed, obviously were, like objects, part of the spoils of war (Deut. 20:14). A legal marriage with a female prisoner of war was possible after certain conversion and mourning rituals had been observed (Deut. 21:10–14). This, however, only pertained to more distant cities. In the land that Yahweh had promised to his people as their inheritance, the great jealous God desires that "you shall let nothing that breathes remain alive," with the justification, "lest they teach you to do according to all their abominations, which they have done for their gods, and you sin against the Lord your God" (Deut. 20:16, 18).

Among the laws that Moses receives from the Lord on Mount Sinai is one that is directly concerned with jealousy (Num. 5:11–31): the "jealousy sacrifice," as Luther translates it; in the standard German translation, the "jealousy ordeal'' (''ordeal'' means God's judgment); in the New King James version, ''the grain offering of jealousy.'' It deals explicitly with substantiated as well as unsubstantiated jealousy, and serves as the means to ascertain guilt and thus to confirm for the husband whether his wife is faithful or unfaithful. The wife who—with or without cause—has allowed her husband to harbor the unconfirmed suspicion that she has slept with another man is subjected to a solemn and intricate ritual: she is led before the altar, her head is uncovered, and a small offering is put in her hands, one-tenth of an ephah of barley meal (an ephah measures a little over a bushel, or 36.4 liters). The priest holds an earthen vessel containing holy water, into which he puts some dust from the floor of the tabernacle. In the imprecation that he now speaks over her, she is promised that this ''bitter water that brings a curse'' will prove her innocence if she has remained faithful. If, however, she has slept with another man, it will cause her bitter pains, make her belly swell and her thigh rot, evidently as a sign of illness and sexual inadequacy. The woman is to say, ''Amen, so be it.'' After the offering is burnt, the woman must drink the water. Verses 27 and 28 stress explicitly that the predicted effect will occur: if the woman has remained pure, she ''may conceive children.'' If it is demonstrated that she was guilty, ''then the man shall be free from iniquity, but that woman shall bear her guilt.''

This kind of magic ritual can only be explained within the context of the history of religion. In the time in which Moses lived, approximately thirteen centuries before Christ, people in the ancient Orient believed in the efficacy of such formulaic imprecations and blessings—in Israel, too. The Chosen People were distinguished from their neighbors by their fundamental concern for purity before the holy and fear-inspiring God, whose *qineah* is always to be feared. This concern is also the theological basis for a man's fear of becoming impure because—perhaps—his wife has sinned. Nonetheless, the floodgates are opened for speculation. How many guiltless women may have developed anxiety-induced physical symptoms after partaking of this water? How many cynics were liberated enough not to allow themselves to be influenced by it? But also, How many men were perhaps ridiculed because of suspicion carried to absurd extremes? And in decadent times, such as those lamented in the prophetic books of the Bible, How many corrupt priests may have put genuine poison in the harmless magic water when a husband wanted to take revenge on his wife?

This kind of ritual for the elimination of suspicion is unique in Mosaic law. One could imagine, for example, similar prescriptions being used to solve a murder in the medieval ordeal or even to establish paternity. However, nothing like that has been transmitted. Apparently jealousy was viewed as an especially pressing and troublesome problem. It cannot have been conceived of as contemptible, since it was one of God's main attributes. One could empathize with this and, reciprocally, with human jealousy. Indeed, perhaps a believing Jew had to reflect on this and could see himself confirmed in his own jealousy. The analogy to jealousy of the beloved or to marital jealousy is obvious when, for example, it is still written in the New Testament, "The Spirit who dwells in us yearns jealously" (James 4:5). Here it is also a matter of an emotion that the Jealous One has at one time evoked, which he very much desires, and upon which the love object, here God's people, casts doubt. Just as in a human relationship, the Bible shows the "beloved's" uneasiness at the jealousy of the jealous individual, which leads to the unavoidable compulsion to reorder the relationship in its totality.

One cannot deal with the Old Testament God's jealousy without looking at the words of the prophet Hosea, the first who "designates God's devotion to humanity with the word 'love' " (*Die Bibel* 1980, 1021n). Hosea lived in the eighth century B.C. in a time of political and religious instability. The text transmitted under his name alternates, as in all the prophetic writings, between lamentations and threats in view of the people's infidelity, and reminders of God's promises. Hosea must bear, however, a special and remarkable fate: his life, and explicitly his marital life, becomes a sign of God's treatment of His people. God commands him to marry a girl who has participated in the sexual rites of the cult of Baal (literally, "a wife of harlotry"; Luther translates it as "whore," the German standard translation as "cult whore"). It was indescribably presumptuous to make such a demand of a believing Jew, fundamentally shaped by the Mosaic law of purity. Hosea does what God demands of him, fathers three children with this woman, and gives them defamatory names in accordance with God's instructions: he calls one girl Lo-Ruhamah (no mercy), a son Lo-Ammi (not my people). What follows is the symbolic description of Israel's falling away in the form of the metaphor of a woman who has many lovers, allows herself to be paid by them, celebrates feasts, and bears them children. This woman—Israel—is promised that she will be punished: "I will hedge up your way with thorns, and wall her in. . . . She will chase her lovers, but not overtake them. . . . Then she will say, 'I will go and return to my first husband, for then it was better for me than now' " (Hos. 2:6–8). The promised reward for repentance and conversion, which is also present in other prophetic books, here takes the following form: "Therefore, behold, I will allure her, will bring her into the wilderness, and speak comfort to her" (Hos. 2:14). There follows, in the form of the metaphor of marriage, the vision of the new covenant: "In that day . . . you will call Me 'My Husband,' " and God promises, "I will betroth you to Me forever; yes, I will betroth you to Me in righteousness and justice, in lovingkindness and mercy" (Hos. 2:16, 19). Hosea himself is ordered to draw the parallel between human and divine behavior: "Then the Lord said to me, 'Go again, love a woman who is loved by a lover and is committing adultery, just like the love of the Lord for the children of Israel" (Hos. 3:1). It is not clear if the reference is to the woman previously mentioned; more likely the reference is to another woman, because Hosea reports the bride-price he paid. It is all the more startling when a prophet of the holy and pure Lord takes an impure wife for the second time and says to her, "You shall stay with me many days; you shall not play the harlot, nor shall you have a man; thus I will also be toward you" (Hos. 3:3). Luther, the passing of whose clear and direct language one must regret yet again, translates, "Consider yourself mine for a long time and do not whore around, and do not give yourself to any other man; because I also want to consider myself yours."

It is now extremely easy to ask, What is this authoritarian father—God—doing here with his allegedly beloved children? How might the sexuality between Hosea and the impure women have been viewed? How did the children feel, whose names weigh on them like stigma? But these questions are too easy, too psychologizing. In the face of the enormous effort to understand God, which the Bible documents, his reduction to a father projection and the related critique of the people whose remarkable fates are reported—as, for example, Alice Miller attempted in her books—seem to me banal and ahistorical. Here I prefer to side with Freud, who considered the father's impact on the concept of God as "very important" (and admittedly was concerned exclusively with this) but who spoke as a matter of course about the "other meanings and origins of God, which psychoanalysis cannot illuminate" (Freud 1913, 179). What seems important to me here, at least for the person who reads the Bible today, is overcoming through love the hurt that the jealous individual has experienced. Even for God, this means through changes in the person who has been hurt.

△ 11 △

THE POWER OF EMOTIONS
ON OLYMPUS

The other, nonreligious strand of the Western tradition, which does not derive from the pensive Chosen People on the northern rim of Africa but from the bright world on the other side of the Mediterranean, nevertheless contains just as much religion. The Greek gods were, in contrast to the Germanic gods, never suppressed, but were loved and preserved as a cultural inheritance throughout the centuries of Christianity. Only, one did not believe in them any more. Therefore children will obviously be affected differently when they read that the God to whom they pray at night is jealous, than when they listen to stories about Zeus and Hera, who quarrel about their conjugal rights and duties in an extraordinarily human way. And the children, when they become older and if they have not unlearned how to trust their own reason and eyes, will perhaps find the classical assertion that the essence of the Greeks is "noble simplicity and quiet greatness" quite incomprehensible. Greed and jealousy, as well as murder, revenge, rape, kidnapping, and abduction of women as well as boys play an overwhelming role in Greek mythology.

Why is it that many people at first do not think of this substantive aspect, that the purifying, "cathartic" effect of the tragedies sticks in our memory and emotion longer than the preceeding excesses, gruesomeness, and deliverance into the hands of a fate that dooms greatness, at least as far as people are concerned? We associate concepts such as light, serenity, and moderation with Greece and its gods; perhaps Antigone's aphorism occurs to us: "I am not there to hate with you, but to love with you." In doing so, however, we forget that she was not only someone who loved, but also a proud, privileged child of her haughty father Oedipus, in whose family one atrocity after another occurred, even *after* the cathartic realization of his own unconscious crime.

In comparing Jewish with Greek tradition, an orientation toward oneness (the One) stands in contrast to an orientation toward multiplicity. The strict demand to be faithful to the law contrasts with the possibility of negotiating with the gods, the exclusive relationship to Yahweh with a constantly changing and developing polytheism, which was open to other religions and one of whose characteristics was allowing itself to be influenced by other religions. Instead of the commandment not to make a graven image of God, instead of the single Temple, there are manifold images of the gods and many places of worship. The glorification of God is not the primary concern in this tradition. Since the border between humans and gods can be crossed—gods and goddesses love human beings, people can be accepted among the gods—a divine glow descends even upon human emotions. And Greek beauty does exist—the dreams of a nobler, freer, more perfect humanity realized in stone and verse. Everyone who is not limited by constraints of reverence, which is evoked by association with a religion still believed in today, can recognize the projections with which Olympus is populated: figures of rulers who live a more carefree existence, who are invested with a great measure of power, but with whom one can empathize, who are not distant and "totally other" like the God of the Israelites.

Jealousy does not play a dominant role as it does in the Old Testament *history* of God's people and therefore the world. Rather, it is the motivating center of an abundance of *histories;* because of its multiplicity, it is less threatening to us, and because of its transformation into and preservation in art (exaggeration, representation, and neutralization in form), we are able to grasp it in a symbolic construct, upon which we can reflect without it coming too close to us. In amazement at the gods' violent solutions to jealousy, and in trembling witness to punished human hubris, the ancient Greeks could experience—just as we can—the power and impotence, justice and injustice, meaning and meaninglessness of this primal emotion. In view of the antiquity, profundity, and beauty of all these stories, enlightened attempts to do away with jealousy seem stupid as well as far removed from life and art.

The triangles and alliances, as well as their disruptions, are innumerable, and jealousy not only expresses itself but also stands for rights and duties, for anxieties and desires, and often for their incompatibility. Above all, jealousy brings with it mobility that can be fatal as well as life giving, most frequently both. If one proceeds from the Freudian model of jealousy in which children are the jealous parties in a triangle with their parents (which, as one knows, is named for a Greek myth), then one cannot help but notice that the reverse form of envy, namely that which parents feel toward their children, occurs with surprising frequency in many stories. Especially among the pre-Olympic Titans, who are not yet subject to any laws, terrible things go on.

Uranus, the supreme god, of course fathers children with his spouse the earth—Gaea—but he hates her from the beginning and pushes her back into the earth's innermost core. There much pushing and shoving arises among the offspring because of the crowded conditions, causing Gaea to groan under the burden. She enters into a conspiracy with these children, especially the sons, who apparently can be both outside and inside at the same time. They are to punish the father, who is expressly designated as the one who was first hostile toward his wife and children. One of the sons, the great Kronos, whose name is related to the word for time (*chronos*), decides to act: when his father again comes to his mother and spreads himself completely over the earth, the son grabs a huge sickle that his mother has made and cuts off his father's penis (Kerényi 1951, 1:23ff.). Still, Gaea is impregnated by the drops of blood and gives birth to many creatures—giants, dryads, and the furies, the terrible goddesses of blood vengeance. Kronos throws the severed member into the sea, which begins to foam, and Aphrodite rises from the foam. Spontaneous generation comes to an end, and Kronos becomes the new ruler among his brothers.

He now marries his sister Rhea, but he too hates his children, who also disappear into a cavern, an interior, where he considers himself safe from them: into his own body, because he devours them immediately after their birth. The alliance against him is formed not only between the mother and her strongest son, Zeus, but also between Rhea and her parents, who are also the parents of Kronos: Gaea and Uranus assist her at the secret birth of the divine child Zeus (on Crete), and deceive Kronos with a stone swathed in diapers, like in the fairy tale of the bad wolf. Zeus, now an adult, defeats his father Kronos and frees his siblings who were devoured by their father. Kronos is—a proclamation of Olympian benevolence— bound and removed to the Isles of the Blest. This is the most perfect illustration of the ethnologist Frazer's formula for dealing with chiefs and kings among primitive peoples, cited by Freud in *Totem and Taboo:* "One must watch out for them, and one must watch over them" (Freud 1913, 53).

In these stories of jealousy and sex, everyone is closely related to everyone else, brothers marry their sisters, fathers envy their sons, but also—and especially threatening—the Great Mother consorts in various forms and under several names, above all as Rhea, but also as Cybele and as Nana in Asia Minor, with handsome young men who are her children and her lovers at the same time.

In the story that illustrates parental jealousy most clearly, the mother is called Agdistis, generated by a rock, Agdos, on which Zeus's seed fell. She is a wild hermaphroditic being, gruesome and not subject to the laws of Olympus. Dionysus, who brought wine to humanity, intoxicates this unnatural being and, while it sleeps, ties a rope made of hair around its penis and then fastens it to a tree. Jumping up, Agdistis castrates himself. A beautiful tree sprouts from the drops of blood, and its fruit impregnates a "Nana." Her son Attis is so beautiful, that Agdistis, at this point feminine only, falls in love with him, spoils him, and gives him gifts—a symbiosis that is obviously seen as sinister by gods as well as people. King Midas wants to separate Attis from his father-mother and gives him Midas's daughter as a wife. At the wedding, however, Agdistis appears and drives the guests mad with Siren sounds. While castrating himself, Attis shouts, "For you, Agdistis!" and then dies because of the bond to his mother.

One can understand that Bachofen, in his research on matriarchy, could extrapolate from such stories a slow development in universal history. He sees movement from a state in which mothers are allowed to have children not only by their husbands but also by fathers, grandfathers, and sons, to a condition of marital legitimacy of Apollonian clarity, in which men and women are benevolently assigned to appointed, permanent places and in which un-ambiguous paternal descent becomes the rule. Bachofen therefore understands Oedipus, the husband and son of his mother, as someone suffering greatly because of the old laws (see chap. 17, sec. 7). The fact that all these stories of incest exercised a great attraction (and still do), which supplements and most likely explains the danger, is illustrated in the story of the proverbially beautiful Adonis, who came into being as a result of incest initiated by a daughter with her father. The daughter, therefore, is the active party here. She usurps the role that is rightfully her mother's—therefore, Freud's theory of the desires of children, which are responsible for emerging disaster, may finally be confirmed in this story.

Myrrha's love for her father is, to be sure, viewed as so reprehensible that it is explained as being caused by a deception perpetrated by angry gods, perhaps by Aphrodite, who is jealous because Myrrha is supposed to have considered her hair more beautiful than that of the goddess. Myrrha sleeps for twelve nights with her father, whom she intoxicates. He thinks she is a "girl he does not know." When he realizes for what purpose he has been seduced, he pursues her with a drawn sword (at this point, adherents of Freudian symbolism would not omit drawing the comparison penis-sword and could say, Well of course he too!). The gods transform her into a tree, the myrtle, out of whose bark Adonis is born. If gods and people, however, abhor a sexual relationship between father and daughter, why does no monster arise from this union, but rather a being of irresistible beauty? To be sure, Adonis is also a metaphor for the transitoriness and unattainability of beauty—because he becomes Aphrodite's youthful lover, but she must share him with Persephone, the goddess of the underworld, in keeping with the will of Zeus. Therefore, each year he must die and then be resurrected, and Aphrodite is allowed to love him but must also mourn him (Kerényi 1951, 1:62).

In this story, it is striking that the king, father of a daughter and therefore most likely married, very clearly has the right to sleep with a "girl he does not know." The patriarchate already seems to be in full force here.

In Greece, it is primarily Zeus who stands for this world order. Zeus, as Homer puts it, is the "father of gods and men" but also the father of countless other beings, the spouse of many goddesses and human women, and additionally the lover of beautiful boys. It seems that Zeus is hardly jealous. Among his epithets are some that identify him as the protector of marriage, such as Gamelios (god of marriage), Teleios (he who dispenses wholeness), and also Heraios (belonging to his wife, Hera) (Kerényi 1951, 1:93). He does not have to be afraid for his marriage. In one way or another, he always gets the other women whom he wants to have: as a bull with Europa, as a swan with Leda, as golden rain with Danaë, in the form of a human husband with Alcmene—and he leaves them without anguish on his part, in order to return to Olympus and, therefore, to Hera. Anguish—flight, revenge, pursuit, disbelief—is for the women and their Zeus children. He is, of course, often angry— lightning and thunder are some of his most familiar attributes—but he does not get angry because of jealousy, in any case not because of jealousy typified by the usual triangle. He is concerned about and rages for his rights, majesty, honor, and other values that are sacred to him. Moreover he is not only someone who protects laws, he is also subject to them.

Hera, on the other hand, is jealous. She is not *a* wife of Zeus, but *the* wife per se. One is reminded of the ancient maternal goddesses because she, his sister by the mother Rhea, was there before him and chose him for her husband at his birth. That they both had the same mother, which would be an obstacle to human marriage, here becomes an advantage: it is written that Hera is the only female being who got a husband who is her absolute equal. This equality of birth makes it possible for her to defend her rights with enormous power, but also with the cunning of love and charm. Much less is said about the children of Hera and Zeus than about the children of his many other unions. Therefore, paternal descent, even in mythology, is much more significant, important historically, and important for individual histories than maternal descent. Without a doubt, it is also more important in historical reality at the time of the golden age of the Olympic cult of the gods.

Kerényi, the Hungarian classical philologist and student of mythology, whose books about the Greek gods I recommend that one read and reread, writes that Hera, of all the goddesses, was the one "who did not seek motherhood from her husband, but fulfillment" (Kerényi 1951, 1:79). Once again like the ancient maternal goddesses, she could give birth to children by herself—Hephaestus, for example, who was not exactly a success and whom she thereupon angrily hurled into the sea, and the dragon Typhon, "the fearful scourge of mortals." He came about because of a rivalry with Zeus, which again illustrates Hera's claim to equality of birth: she was angry because Zeus had given birth to Pallas Athena by himself, though not as autonomously as

Hera but by making use of the clever Metis, who may well have been his first wife and whom he first seduces and then submerges in his belly, where she carries the pregnancy to term.

Hera is the protector of marriage, her own as well as that of all people. Her epithets are Pais (the girl), Teleia (the fulfilled), and Chera (the lonesome). These epithets are very expressive of the destiny of the married woman— every woman, but also Hera, who is loved, fulfilled, and deserted by Zeus over and over again. But she also has the power to leave him and thus to send him into a rage—and how different this makes her from human wives in the era of the Olympic gods. Zeus, the epitome of the defiant husband, says to her during one of the many quarrels depicted in the *Iliad,* that she should feel free to go, even if to the end of the earth: "You may go on and on till you get there, and I shall not care one whit for your displeasure; you are the greatest vixen living" (Homer *Iliad* 8.483–84). He knows that she will always return, just as he returns to her. Homer's description of a second wedding as a sign of their reconciliation is magnificent (*Iliad* 14). Before sleeping with her, Zeus says he has never before felt such desire. He then enumerates many women whom he has loved, including Hera herself—he has never wanted her as much as he does now. She lets him speak, enjoys her victory and making love on a bed strewn with flowers—but the whole thing is nothing but a trick of hers, because she wants him to fall asleep so that her will shall be done on earth.

Transposed into timelessness and agelessness, Hera actualizes in divine invulnerability what jealous individuals dream in vain: she can cast a spell on her opponents, such as the boy Aetus, whom she suspects of being Zeus's lover. She turns him into an eagle. She transforms Io, whom Zeus desires, into a cow so that he must make love to her in the form of a bull. Hera has the power to cause her rivals the deepest affliction, like Alcmene, the mother of Heracles, whose labor she interrupts; or like Io, on whom she sets a gadfly to drive her all the way to Egypt. When marital laws are transgressed, she can set a monster like the Sphinx against Thebes (it made her angry that the boy Chrysippus was to replace the wife of Laius, later the father of Oedipus); she can obstinately defend her secrets: thus Tiresias, the seer, is to decide the quarrel between her and Zeus as to whether men or women get more out of love. When he—truthfully—answers that women get ten times as much pleasure, "experiencing joy to the depths of the soul" (men only physically?), Hera punishes him by blinding him because of what he has said. She can cause storms to blow, which send the ship of Heracles, Zeus's son whom she hates, to the edge of the underworld. To be sure, Zeus avenges himself in this instance with a terrible punishment: in order to make her finally give up her jealousy, he suspends her from golden chains between heaven and earth, with two anvils on her feet, and none of the other gods can set her free.

Zeus and Hera always reconcile and Heracles, whom she pursued so re-lentlessly, is finally accepted on Olympus and married to her daughter, Hebe.

Heracles—his name alone indicates his closeness to her—is not only Hera's enemy but also her servant and protector. Yes and no, anger and reconciliation stand in close proximity among the gods. Nothing really endangers their immortality; this is apparent in the most detailed divine jealousy story, that of Hephaestus and his wife Aphrodite, in which all the experiences and hopes of human jealousy are summarized in such an exemplary fashion that I would like to save it for the end of this book.

The differentiation between gods and people was, however, of central importance for the Greeks. All Niobe's children were killed by the gods, and she herself was turned into a stone that still weeps today (Homer *Iliad* 24.602–12), because she boasted to the goddess Leto, Zeus's beloved, of having twelve children, whereas Leto had borne only Artemis and Apollo. A human couple, Ceyx and Halcyone, who out of arrogance addressed each other as Zeus and Hera, were turned into birds as punishment (Kerényi 1951, 2:129). Human beings were permitted to observe, wonder at, and honor the powerful emotions on Olympus and the way in which they were resolved—but they were not accessible to humans in this great and transfigured form. This is probably most true for Hera's equality of birth, if one compares it with the complete lack of rights for Greek women. They were not even permitted to view the great figures depicted in the theater—only men were permitted there, and women's roles were played by men. Hera, moreover, with all her divinity, can still only be victorious in a specific circumscribed situation—her victory is never a final one. Casually formulated, There's sure to be a next time! For Zeus represents the paternal as the higher principle. He dispenses progeny as a divine gift and therefore cannot stand in an exclusive loving, or even devoted, relationship to one single woman. Hera, on the other hand, represents the monogamous marriage of both spouses and therefore stands in permanent opposition to Zeus (Kerényi 1951, 1:126). Human wives can pray to her, but she cannot protect even her own marriage. Perhaps it was comforting to unhappy Greek women that she could at least demonstrate rage and desires and make demands.

To this point, I have written exclusively of stories about the gods that could not actually come to a tragic end, since the gods are immortal and in the final analysis immune to injury. The situation of the heroes, the demigods, hybrids of gods and humans, is different. Their divine origin is apparent above all in the immortality of their suffering as well as in their pride. All important tragic figures have gods among their ancestors, which is proven in reverently reported family trees. They are not only the children of the gods, figures of light and wisdom, but in a certain sense bastards and monsters. The tension between mortality and immortality leads to a "characteristic intensification of the human aspect—not least in the gravity of their fate and suffering," which leads to tragedy, "the place of ever-new emotional shocks caused by ancient material'' (Kerényi 1951, 2:19ff.). This tension is presented, represented, and identified with; it is not happily resolved but is concluded in a tragic, fatal, and gruesome way.

The heroes transmit the explanation and foundation of human history. Let us consider the best-known event in Greek mythological history—the Trojan War, based, without a doubt, on actual events—the destruction of a powerful city. Even though these events were not reported according to current principles of historiography, it is known that they deal with the war of the allied Greek kings against Troy and, indeed, with the revenge a husband takes for the injury suffered on account of his wife's abduction—revenge against the abductor and his people. A war due to jealousy, because the Trojan prince Paris has taken from the gentle King Menelaus his beautiful wife, Helen: that is going too far. However, upon more careful reading, we find that several levels of jealousy and rivalry are concurrently intertwined in this glorious and gruesome cluster of stories.

The gods' concern that human beings have become too numerous is uppermost (Homer cannot get enough of describing their huge multitudes— see especially *Iliad* 2). Zeus had already wanted to wipe them out with lightning and flood. Greek mythology is, in any case, saturated with the jealousy and envy of the gods, who reward moderation and restraint but severely punish rebellion and attempts to usurp divine prerogatives. The destinies of Prometheus and Tantalus, as well as that of Niobe, are among the best-known examples of this. A further concern of the gods is their fear of a new ruler of the world. Zeus, who himself defeated his father, calls a halt to a fight with his brother Poseidon for the sea goddess Thetis, when he learns that a son of one of the divine brothers would have the power to bring about a change in who governs the world. Instead of fighting for Thetis, he condemns her to marriage with a mortal, Peleus. The issue of this union is Achilles, the greatest Greek hero in the Trojan War. Zeus himself, in the form of a swan, fathers Helen with Leda— according to one of the many (different) versions, with the conscious intention of bringing about the result that arose from these two events: the Trojan War, in which the human race almost exterminated itself, and in any case was greatly weakened.

The prologue still seems peaceful: the consummated marriage (if only reluctantly tolerated by Thetis) to Peleus is celebrated, and it is written that this event was the last time that immortals and mortals sat and ate together. The goddess Eris, "dissension," uninvited like the evil Fee in the German fairy tale, throws among the guests a golden apple that has on it the inscription, "for the most beautiful." The three most powerful goddesses grab for it: Hera, Athena, and Aphrodite. Zeus himself appoints the Trojan prince Paris to decide the victor, and he, blinded by Aphrodite's promise to give him Helen, the most beautiful woman in the world, grants the prize to the great love goddess.

Thus we arrive at the occasion for war, and the sides taken by the goddesses are predictable: Aphrodite helps the Trojans, Hera and Athena support the Greeks. Nonetheless, Zeus has determined that Troy will fall, as the *Iliad* often attests. Achilles' anger, whose origin, consequences, and overcoming is the theme of Homer's epic, intervenes as a powerful retarding moment. Neither Achilles' death nor the fall of Troy are depicted in the *Iliad* but are expected as something inevitable.

The poem begins, "Sing, O goddess, the anger of Achilles son of Peleus." This anger arises as a result of a quarrel between men over a woman: Agamemnon, the commanding general of the Greek army, must hand back his war prize, Chryseis, the daughter of a priest of Apollo, because the god has been offended and punishes the Greek army with a plague. Agamemnon demands Achilles' "prize of honor," Briseis, as a substitute, and Achilles, the most powerful of the warriors, must acquiesce. All that is said about Briseis is that she leaves Achilles "against her will" (in the German translation of Schadewaldt), "reluctantly" (in the German translation of Voss). She is obviously not asked what she wants.

Achilles, however, "went all alone by the side of the grey sea, weeping and looking out upon the boundless waste of waters," and refuses to fight (1:349–50). Is it, for him, a question of love? More likely it is one of honor. Like a child who has been ignored, he complains to his mother Thetis that, since he has already granted him such a short life, Zeus should at least give him some respect. (But common jealousy, which has no heroic resolution at its disposal, always has something to do with honor and respect.)

The Trojans almost force their way to the Greek ships—their means of retreat—and many fall. Achilles continues to harbor resentment; concerned about Briseis, "he wastes with sorrow for her sake" (18.447). However, when he fights again, it is not because of the woman "with the beautiful cheeks" but to avenge the death of his friend, Patroclus. The same immoderation that caused his anger, expressed in his egocentric refusal to fight, to become a disaster for both gods and men, is transformed into its active opposite, heedless fighting. Achilles behaves like a demon, as Homer repeatedly describes. The force of the injury done to him corresponds to the force of his aggression, and both are evidently a function of Achilles' determination—including his self-determination. Briseis remains nothing but a cause, and only once is she permitted to speak, after she is returned to Achilles by Agamemnon, to mourn Patroclus, but more "her own sorrows." She says, "Thus do fresh sorrows multiply upon me one after the other": Achilles has killed her husband and three brothers. Zeus did not allow her even to weep for this but promised her that Achilles would marry her, and now that he is also preparing himself for death, nothing is left for her but to grieve (19.282–303).

Reading between the lines, a psychologizing and imaginative interpretation of this kind of relationship between men and women again suggests itself—getting married cannot have been understood as a personal union between two real people in this context, in which a woman is pushed from one master to another like an animal. I would prefer to go along with Schadewaldt, who writes, "After the *Iliad* has put people through the confusion of anger and passion, and as a result of that has driven them to misery and death, it finally culminates in human awareness of their common vulnerability." We are dealing here with figures who are larger than life and not with portraits, no matter how much psychological wisdom may be apparent in them. This is what makes the Greek myths such an inexhaustible source for intellectual contemplation and observation. Kerényi speaks of the "archaic massiveness and freedom" and of the "documentation of what is human that is not easy to surpass in terms of spontaneity," which Greek mythology is in its totality (Kerényi 1951, 1:8).

A reflection of what is narrated by the Greeks as reality is present in mankind today in the dreams and fantasies specifically associated with jealousy. Three citations should serve to prove this.

An anonymous American says of his affair, "It was as if I were playing God. In one hand I had my wife, in the other I had my girlfriend, and I had the power of decision over death and life" (McGinnis 1981). A jealous fiancé writes, "If I would have the power to destroy the whole world, including us, in order to let it start from scratch, risking that the world would not again generate me and Martha [his fiancée], I would do it without a moment's hesitation." This was written on 6 August 1882, and the man was Sigmund Freud (cited in Jones 1953–57, 1:143). And in conclusion, let us listen to a young wife. On 16 December 1882, a quarter of a year after her marriage, she writes about her husband, "I would like to burn everything, everything. There should be nothing left to remind me of his past. And because jealousy has made me terribly egoistic, I would not regret the loss of his writings. If I could kill him and later recreate him as the person he used to be, I would joyfully do even that." The writings to which she refers are those of Leo Tolstoy (S. Tolstoy, 1982).

△ 12 △

JESUS: LOVE AND FREEDOM

What does the central figure of Christianity, Jesus of Nazareth, have to say about the topic of jealousy? Jesus was addressed by his disciples as Rabbi—"teacher"—and they believed that he was the promised redeemer of world history, the Messiah. The answer is that he has nothing to say about jealousy, and little at all about the topic of male-female love and sexuality. Coming from the Old Testament to the New Testament, generally we find ourselves in an atmosphere of freedom, relief, and friendliness. In terms of marriage, however, Jesus is stricter and not more liberal than Mosaic law: Jesus refers to divorce, which was a given for the Israelites, as adultery (Matt. 5:31–32, Luke 16:18; Mark 10:11). The law against divorce is, to be sure, qualified in two places by the case of the wife's "lasciviousness"; here Jesus stands within the old male-oriented tradition. With unusual severity, however, he condemns adultery even in thought—and explicitly the adultery of men: "But I say to you that whoever looks at a woman to lust for her has already committed adultery with her in his heart" (Matt. 5:28). Are we not confronted here by a new type of law, one that is even more agonizing, since the law is shifted from without to within? Whoever wants to hear the words of the New Testament is forced, and not only here, to come to terms with the dialectic peculiar to Jesus: the law of forgiveness and freedom is juxtaposed with the absolute, pointed demand for purity. (I mean here the text per se, and not what tradition and the church later made of it; see chap. 14). The same Jesus who coined the notion of adultery in one's heart prevents, with a single sentence, the legally prescribed death penalty of stoning in an actual transgression: in the story of the adulteress reported in the Gospel according to John. The complete text of the New King James version follows to refresh the reader's memory:

> Then the scribes and Pharisees brought to Him a woman caught in adultery. And when they had set her in the midst,
> they said to Him, "Teacher, this woman was caught in adultery, in the very act.

"Now Moses, in the law, commanded us that such should be stoned. But what do You say?"

This they said, testing Him, that they might have something of which to accuse Him. But Jesus stooped down and wrote on the ground with His finger, as though He did not hear.

So when they continued asking Him, He raised Himself up and said to them, "He who is without sin among you, let him throw a stone at her first."

And again He stooped down and wrote on the ground.

Then those who heard it, being convicted by their conscience, went out one by one, beginning with the oldest even to the last. And Jesus was left alone, and the woman standing in the midst.

When Jesus had raised Himself up and saw no one but the woman, He said to her, "Woman, where are those accusers of yours? Has no one condemned you?"

She said, "No one, Lord." And Jesus said to her, "Neither do I condemn you; go and sin no more." (John 8:3–11)

As happens so frequently in the Gospels, Jesus' interrogators are less concerned with the actual case in hand than with the hope of being able to set a trap for Jesus and gaining a reason to condemn him, thereby rendering harmless his radical questioning of the existing order. The way Jesus is reported to act seems to show clearly that he does not ascribe the same importance to the problem as his apparently excited interrogators: he writes with his finger on the ground. After his pronouncement, which shifts the question to a totally different level than that of the (unquestioned!) legality of the punishment, he bends down again and continues this activity, which is so inappropriate to the drama of the situation. Just as in the problem of looking at a woman with lust, it is again a matter of one's own conscience pronouncing the guilty verdict. It is written that they leave, "one by one, beginning with the oldest." Jesus remains alone with the woman in what is certainly the most important hour of her life. The scene could not be more impressive. The sentence, although it has already been morally passed, is voided. "Neither do I condemn you." And there follows the summons to change one's ways, known to us from the entire Old Testament, but invested with an entirely different meaning by Jesus: "Go and sin no more."

Today it is important to point out, as Romano Guardini does, that Jesus was not a "revolutionary of the heart," that he does not stand for "the right of passion against petrified order and hypocritical morality" (1949, 6), and also that he did not see himself as a social reformer. According to the Gospels, he was executed for blaspheming the established religion (as so many others were later, in the era of the new religion that bears his name). His blasphemy consisted in following his own law, which was "not of this world," cutting through all established order. He evidently considered marriage, sexuality, and marital decrees as things of this world. This is demonstrated in the following example: members of the Sadducees, who denied the resurrection of the dead, ask him whose wife a Jewish woman would be in the hereafter, if after her husband's death she had married his six brothers one after another. She therefore had seven husbands during her lifetime, obedient in this to the Mosaic law of marriage to one's brother-in-law. This is a question whose theoretical-schematic character is obvious. Jesus characteristically takes it seriously: "The sons of this age marry and are given in marriage" (Luke 20:34). He also answers the challenge to the resurrection—to be sure, quite like a biblical scholar: Moses already calls God the God of Abraham, Isaac, and Jacob. From this the conclusion may be drawn, "For He is not the God of the dead but of the living, for all live to Him" (Luke 20:38).

I cannot judge whether Jesus actually spoke these words. What is important to me is that the people who first documented his teaching were concerned with showing continuity with the Jewish tradition. What becomes of the concept of jealousy in the New Testament? It is only mentioned in a single place, and not by Jesus. In the second letter to the Corinthians (11:2), Paul says that he loves the young congregation with godly jealousy, because he wants to lead them "as a chaste virgin to Christ." Hosea's image of marriage, therefore, continues to have an influence; it develops into the union between Christ and the Church and leads to an interpretation of the Song of Solomon as an allegory of this relationship. This magnificent love poem, which glows with color and sensuality, is indeed accessible to my Protestant way of thinking and feeling, but the leap into mystical and symbolical exegesis is not. In any case, jealousy does not appear in the poem, and if one really views Christ as the bridegroom, and the Church as his bride, then this bridegroom is not jealous. The Song of Solomon celebrates in song a condition of extreme harmony, of extreme joy in one another, the culmination (in German the word for wedding is *Hochzeit*, literally "sublime time") of a love in which suspicion is unimaginable. Neither in the Song of Solomon nor, as far as I know, anywhere else in the symbolism of the Church as Christ's bride does jealousy play a role.

Even though God's jealousy is not mentioned verbatim, Paul still understands humanity's forlornness—the forlornness of all people, and not only of the Children of Israel, because the Gospel is explicitly meant to be for "everyone" (Rom. 1:16)—which is a result of God's anger at the refusal to honor him, to thank him, and to be aware of him, therefore to live in relation to him. The basic sin is no longer worship of alien gods, but that one "worshipped and served the creature rather than the Creator" (Rom. 1:25). The "vile passions," to which God gives up humanity, are first and foremost sexual deviations (Rom. 1:26–27) but also injustice, greed, envy, murder, dissension, pride. From this, Paul derives the human race's incompetence to judge others (Rom. 2:1). That does not mean that moral principles are invalidated, but that they are evaluated in a completely different way. I do not wish to stray here into a discussion of the doctrine of justification, but would like to point to one remarkable way Freud stands within the tradition of "being nonjudgmental."

I do not, however, want to skirt the question of how one who would like to orient oneself toward Jesus can deal with jealousy. Everyone must find for oneself the truly pertinent and meaningful answer. Unfortunately, although I work at an institution that is supported financially by both the Protestant and Catholic church, I can refer to hardly any convincing experiences with believing clients. Furthermore, our clientele does not expect Christian counseling, but simply counseling per se. On the contrary, it sometimes seems to me as if more stones are cast in the marriages of churchgoers than in those of others. Insight into one's role in the shared unhappiness of the relationship, into one's guilt, as guilt is understood in Christian terms, is often resisted in an especially stubborn manner: generally, it is asserted that obviously no one is without sin, but in the relevant arena of sexuality and fidelity one is most certainly without sin, and only the other partner has broken and betrayed the promise made at the altar. I have not yet encountered anyone who has drawn the conclusion from the words of the Sermon on the Mount relating to adultery based on lustful thought that, in that case, everyone has already committed adultery at least once (except in Freud; see his essay on jealousy, 1922).

However, perhaps I have here fallen prey to an ethical misunderstanding of the Christian message, whose core, after all, remains the offer of conversion and forgiveness and whose rules are directed less at behavior than at the internal relationship between God and humanity, at least if one sticks to the words of the New Testament and not certain church prescriptions. In the Epistle to the Romans, Paul writes, "Therefore we conclude that a man is justified by faith apart from the deeds of the law" (Rom. 3:28)—for Luther, the central tenet of redemption. And Jesus, asked about the most important commandment, responds with two quotations from the Old Testament, "You shall love the Lord, your God with all your heart, with all your soul, and with all your mind" and "You shall love your neighbor as yourself" (Matt. 22:37, 39; similar in Mark and Luke). Whoever takes this seriously is free of the constraining prescriptions of Israel. In any case, three "objects" are to be loved: God, one's neighbor, and oneself. How this is to happen simultaneously must seem to an observant unbeliever as being akin to an attempt at squaring a circle. It is probably possible in a constantly changing and therefore vital relationship to God, to others, and above all to oneself. Perhaps a comparison with the best and most blissful form of maternal love would help: upon the birth of a new child, this love is not divided or displaced, but is doubled and expands.

Expressed in psychological terms, in the New Testament an adult attitude of being solely responsible for oneself is expected from the subject, in contrast to the Old Testament where a dependent attitude is expected, dependency on directives. Jesus' statement that the Sabbath is there for the person and not the person for the Sabbath shows in clear focus that he in no way considered the law of Israel the final word of God, which should be followed unconditionally. He opened up the law to human beings so that they could contemplate it and make an independent judgment, thus allowing even for possible violation of the law. However unimaginable it is that Jesus could have thought of marriage in a modern psychologizing sense, it is just as unimaginable that he saw marriage as good, or at least as less evil, but sexuality otherwise as bad. While Paul represents this attitude, it is not to be found anywhere in the Gospels. It is evident that, for Jesus, good and evil, friendliness and enmity, forgiveness and condemnation, acceptance of one's neighbor as a child of God and arrogant inflexibility in adherence to the law, are present in *all* areas of social life. In this, marriage is one common human situation among many and not one that is governed by special rules. When Jesus says that one should forgive one's brother not seven times, as Peter suggests, but seventy times seven (Matt. 18:22), this applies to spouses as well—and is probably just as utopian. However, it shows the primacy of love and forgiveness versus dogmatism and vengefulness, as well as the large chasm between divine dictates and human possibilities. In Matthew, at another point where the theme of justice is addressed, it is written, "But Jesus looked at them and said to them, 'With men this is impossible, but with God all things are possible' " (Matt. 19:26).

Thus Paul also counts love as one of the gifts of the Holy Spirit—and I will not relieve the reader of the effort of taking the Bible (by far the most widely circulated book in the world!) down from the shelf in order to look up the magnificent and comforting thirteenth chapter in the first Epistle to the Corinthians. In this chapter, the love that should govern the congregation of Christ is described and celebrated in song. On the theme of jealousy (1 Cor. 13:4), Luther chose the word "to be zealous"; the Zurich Bible used "is not jealous"; the standard German translation, "is not agitated"; in the New English Bible, "envies no one." In any case, this belongs to the characteristics that love does *not* have. "Love does not envy; love does not parade itself, is not puffed up." And further, love "is not provoked, thinks no evil"; and expressed in positive terms, love "bears all things, believes all things, hopes all things, endures all things" (1 Cor. 13:4–7). Paul, however, explicitly points out that what is possible for people is temporary: "For we know in part" and "for now we see in a mirror, dimly, but then face to face" (13:9, 12).

Paul thought that the end of the world was imminent and had fewer objective grounds for thinking this than we do today. In spite of this, an adjustment geared toward the imminence of the Kingdom of God is denied to us. I cannot conceive of a believing Christian ordering his or her moral life according to a belief that the atom bomb soon be dropped, no matter how convinced he or she may be of this. The saying attributed to Luther, but which cannot be found among his writings, is more widespread: "Even if I knew that the world would end tomorrow, I would still plant an apple tree today." In any case, it would be unimaginable to attribute to Luther the saying, "Even if I knew that the world would end tomorrow, and if I were jealous of my Käthe, I would still remain jealous."

I wanted to conclude this chapter on Jesus and jealousy with the reference to a biblical saying that stresses individual responsibility: "You see to it!" I had forgotten the context, but here it is: when Judas saw that, because of his betrayal, Jesus was condemned to death, he took the thirty pieces of silver he had received back to the chief priests and elders "saying, 'I have sinned by betraying innocent blood.' And they said, 'What is that to us? You see to it!' " (in the standard German translation, "That is your affair!"). It is known how the story proceeds. Judas hanged himself (Matt. 27:3–5).

I will allow this connection to stand, because jealousy certainly played a role even between Jesus and Judas. The whole history of how the church deals with jealousy is a continuation of what Paul writes to the Corinthians: "for you are still carnal. For where there are envy, strife, and divisions among you, are you not carnal and behaving like mere men?" (1 Cor. 3:3). Thus, of course, "You see to it! That is your affair." I too would be grateful for more accommodating assistance, but I do not find it in the Bible.

THE DIFFICULTY OF EXPRESSING JEALOUSY

> I could boldly maintain that ignorance of our own psychic life
> is so extensive that we do not even know what we are saying,
> even when what we say is uttered in the spirit of total clarity
> and deliberation.
>
> Richard Sterba, "Eifersüchtig auf. . .?"

"Jealousy is worse than a toothache." In order to comprehend completely the meaning of this Old French saying, one must know that toothaches were uncommonly feared in medieval France. When one wished something especially bad on someone, it was a toothache. People considered jealousy to be not only *just as* embittering and uncontrollable but to be even worse, even more incomprehensible and agonizing. One could always pull teeth, and a toothache was at least unambiguously negative. Jealousy, on the other hand— did one really want only to be rid of it? Was it not also the sign of a noble and passionate emotional life, the sign of a noble and delicately cultivated love, which had been invented in eleventh and twelfth century France, that is, at the same time in which the saying was first recorded (see chap. 14)? In any case, the lack of clarity in how the emotion of jealousy is valuated and the ambivalence that makes dealing with jealousy in therapy so difficult would explain the peculiar fact that jealousy, although it plays an important role in many of humanity's archetypal stories, was difficult to express in all languages and therefore was first expressed late in history.

From the beginning, there were difficulties in distinguishing jealousy from other concepts, especially from envy and from zeal. I have already written about the ancient Hebraic terms. In modern Hebrew, all three meanings are conveyed by a single word, *kinath,* and therefore the particular meaning intended can be derived only from the context. In Greek, too, the designation for what we today call jealousy is first found, according to the dictionary, "in Late Greek, poetic," that is, in Plutarch, who lived during the time of Christ (ca.A.D. 48–122). The word is *zelotypia* and is not clearly distinguished from *zelos,* "zeal." Classical Latin has no unambiguous word for jealousy at all. The word *zelotypia* was a late borrowing from the Greek, but since the first syllable was considered long in Greek, the word did not fit into latin verse and therefore could not be used in love poetry, epics, or verse dramas. Instead of *zelotypia*, it was customary to use other words, as in Ovid's *The Art of Love*, in which jealousy often comes up: *aemulatio*, literally "the effort to do the same as another," thus competition, emulation; *invidia*, "envy," etymologically related to "evil eye" (*in video*); *rivalitas*, "rivalry," originally "two with access to the same water" (*riva*, "shore"). Ovid also uses the phrase *amoris stimulis agitatus*, "driven by the sting of love," where we would simply write "jealous." Love and jealousy, therefore, were very much considered to be inextricably intertwined. Or jealousy was precisely and painstakingly paraphrased: *sollicitus propter alienum amorem*, "troubled because of alien love"; *uxor pellicatus dolore cruciata*, "a wife tormented by pain because of [her husband's] association with a concubine."

Zelotypia, however, was adopted in medieval Latin and played an important role in the love doctrine of the French cleric Andreas Capellanus, which I will deal with later. Its use originated in the second half of the twelfth century, and it was widely circulated in the following centuries.

Linguistic development logically followed the fate of Western culture: after the Germanic tribes inundated the Roman Empire, Latin virtually went underground. On the one hand, it was handed down in the major texts, and the language of literature no longer changed at all. On the other hand, it became the language of expanding Christianity and its theological scholarship, and as a result it also became the language of secular education. At the spoken level the various Romance languages developed out of Vulgar Latin.

In the German-speaking area, as it is defined today, various Germanic dialects or languages were spoken, of which almost nothing is preserved until the eighth century, and until after the year 1000 only spiritual texts are preserved. The monasteries, which had exclusive control over the transmission of the written word, viewed the world of Germanic gods and heroes as manifestly so inferior to the world of antiquity that they did not make the now unimaginable effort involved in copying and preserving documents that doubtless existed. The consequences for the German word for jealousy are that we do not know how this emotion was designated, although it nonetheless played an important role in the Nordic sagas, as may be concluded from the texts that were later written down. Neither is the German word for zeal recorded. The Middle High German poets used *nide, nit,* that is, the early form of the German word for envy.

The brothers Grimm, whose fairy-tale collection represents only a small part of their lifelong efforts on behalf of the linguistic monuments of ancient German culture, in 1838 began their inventory of the German language, the *German Dictionary,* whose first volume appeared in 1854, and the last only in 1971. The entries for *zeal* and *jealousy* appeared while the learned brothers were still alive. For the sake of a more precise definition of the concepts, they always made available the Latin words, since they could assume a thorough knowledge of Latin on the part of scholars and educated people. Thus we learn from their dictionary, the German word for zeal, *Eifer,* appears "suddenly in the fifteenth century," as *fervor, studium* (fervor, passion, zealous effort). "It earned its right to a firm place in New High German because of Luther," that is, because of his translation of the Bible, which was so important for the development and definition of modern German. Luther, however, does not distinguish zeal from what we today call jealousy, not even in unambiguous contexts such as Num. 5:11–31 (see chap. 10). The earliest citation of jealousy in the Grimms' dictionary comes from Sebastian Brant (1457–1521), the German humanist and legal scholar who has become famous through his popular moral satires, especially the *Ship of Fools,* which appeared in 1494 illustrated with Dürer's woodcuts. Moreover, it was the greatest German publishing success before Goethe's *Werther:* "The time of jealousy is not the best, it fears strange cuckoo eggs in its nest." The German word for jealousy in the quote is *Eifer.* The first recorded use of the modern German *Eifersucht,* "jealousy," is found in Hans Sachs (1494–1576), the Nuremberg shoemaker, dramatist, and poet at the time of Luther. But the use of *Eifer,* modern German "zeal," as a synonym for *Eifersucht* continues for a long time. The verb *eifern,* "to be zealous," synonymous with "to be jealous," has been preserved to this day in the southern German and Austrian area. Only in the eighteenth century do the concepts of zealousness and jealousy become distinct. That the need for such a distinction ever arose can be attributed to the influence of French literature, which was far ahead of German literature in psychological refinement and in which there had been a separate word for jealousy, *jalousie,* for a long time.

When one considers the origin of this word, one again must go back a few centuries. Whoever wants to pursue the winding paths of philological research should read the 1937 scholarly study of how jealousy is designated in the Romance languages, written by Margot Grzywacz, a German Romance philologist who taught at the University of Shantung. What is of primary importance for our purposes is that the people, in the centuries after the decline of the living culture of the Roman Empire, gave up almost all abstract concepts and greatly simplified the language. Students of Latin, who turn to the study of living languages with a sigh of relief, can speak from experience. A concept like jealousy, which is so difficult to express and on whose designation ancient Greek and Latin labored almost without success, could therefore only be injected into the language from above, by the educated class.

Zelosus is, without a doubt, the root of words for jealousy: *jaloux, jalouse* (French), *geloso* (Italian), *celose* (Spanish). Grzywacz, however, proves that this word did not yet exist in Vulgar Latin. The etymologically related word for jealousy, *gelōs* or *gilōs,* is definitely in use in the vernacular of the former Roman area, first in Provence in the art songs of two troubadours (educated love poets and singers) with the beautiful names of Cercamon and Marcabru, who lived in the first half of the twelfth century. Even in Provençal, *gilōs* was thus not a vernacular word, but a word used by the educated (in folk songs, derivatives of *invidiosus,* "envious," were used).

Where then does this word *zelosus* come from? It did not occur in the spoken Latin of the Roman Empire, and if it had existed, it would not have meant "jealous," but "zealous," because *zelus* only means "zeal." Language here makes an unusual and revealing detour: in the Latin translation of the Bible, the Vulgate, which dates from the fourth century and remained the only available text of the Holy Scriptures in the French-speaking area until well into the twelfth century, the adjective *zelotes,* "jealous," is often used for God's jealousy. (At the beginning of the twelfth century, a French translation was produced, but naturally there was no printed text until the fifteenth century.) When it was adopted into the vernacular, the foreign ending was romanized to *zelosus.* Grzywacz writes, "The suspicion arises that some clever person [or several at different places] identified the husband, who does not want to tolerate other men besides him receiving veneration, with the 'jealous Jehovah' " (33). That would also explain why *jaloux,* still used to mean "zealous" in Old French, is expressed today with *zélé, empressé,* or *fervent.*

Here, therefore, we again find the connection between religion and jealousy, between a secular, generally familiar emotion and the highest divine claims, or in a broader sense, the general connection between religion and sexuality. Transposed into the psychological, one may say that even linguistic development reacts with great sensitivity to the strong narcissistic role of jealousy.

A glance at the contortions language had to undergo to create a word for the deceived husband shows that assertions about the difficulty of linguistic development are not pulled out of the air, but rather that unpleasant circumstances are hard to express. A *cuckold* is actually a cock with antlers. Capons, castrated roosters, were called this, because in earlier times there was a strange custom of inserting the severed spurs into the comb of capons like horns. In many languages, "to wear horns" or "to put horns on somebody" is the expression that characterizes the deceived husband, and it doubtless has a denigrating, pejorative, phallic meaning. The development, therefore, is from the castrated rooster to the impotent man—he who allowed himself to be deceived, he who is deceived without his knowledge. It is without question the expression of a male-oriented culture that a word with a similar involved and circuitous development did not have to be found for the deceived woman. In that instance, one could simply call the thing by its proper name.

The expression for jealousy that finally became rooted in modern languages contains yet another deep psychological insight: in all languages, it is used in conjunction with a preposition, *jealous of, eifersüchtig auf, jaloux de, celose de, gelose di*. And in all languages, two answers are possible in response to the question, "Of whom are you jealous?"—of the rival or of the beloved, let us say of John or Margaret. Therefore, when the context is unknown, it remains unclear whom the speaking subject, whether male or female, actually loves and whom the subject hates—John or Margaret. At a time in which everyone believed (and had believed for a long time) that one knew what was meant in speaking of jealousy, it remained for psychoanalysis to point to the underlying uncertainty and to make it therapeutically productive. In 1930 Richard Sterba, a member of Freud's psychoanalytic group in Vienna who later emigrated to America, referred to Freud's findings on the homosexual elements of jealousy (Freud 1922; see below, chap. 15): he writes that the bisexual experience of jealousy may be viewed as just as universally valid as bisexuality itself, "which after all stands at the beginning of everyone's libidinal development. Overcoming the homosexual components of this bisexuality signifies for our cultural epoch the normal conclusion of psychosexual development" (Sterba 1930). Conversely, it plays an overpowering role in pathological forms of jealousy. But a residue of universal bisexuality is preserved in the "very obvious ambiguity of such a commonly used expression."

While German has this extremely instructive ambiguity in common with other languages, the German expression for the condition, the emotion, the passion of jealousy is clearer than in those languages: it is not a suffix that characterizes the German word (a precise correspondence to the Romance words and the English words dependent on them would be, in German "Eiferei"), but the compounding of *Eifer* (zeal) with another noun, *Sucht* (addiction). The magnificent capacity of the German language to form compounds allows one to draw inferences from the word alone about how the emotion is classified. *Sucht* does not, as many think, come from *suchen* (to seek) but is related to *siech* (sick). It is a very ancient Germanic word, which earlier spanned a far greater range of meaning than it does today. *Sucht* was the generally used expression for our current word *Krankheit* ("sickness," which came into general circulation much later and is related to the word *Krampf*, "cramp"). The word *Sucht,* according to the Grimms' dictionary, has a "demonic undertone," since physical illnesses originally "were conceived of as something that infiltrated from the outside, as an invasion, that is, as the manifestation of demonic power." The word "appears in the early stages of its occurrence as the sign for a living spirit"; it is used in exorcisms, imprecations, and verbal formulas that ascribe activities to the illness itself, as if it were a living being: the illness "strikes one to death, kills, causes trembling, persists, continues, reigns." In Luther's *Table Talk* one still finds the curse, "May the illness strike him." The meaning of *Sucht* as dependency and addiction to narcotics does not come into existence, according to the

Grimms' dictionary, until modern times, the nineteenth century. There was, however, from the beginning a weaker secondary meaning for this term: "moral, psychic, mental illness." As a general designation of illness, *Sucht* was archaic in the written language by the second half of the eighteenth century, and by the nineteenth century was extinct. Its meaning as "a (pathologically exaggerated) compulsion" is, according to the dictionary, "today almost the only accepted meaning."

The introduction of *Eifersucht* in the second half of the sixteenth century shows that the condition indicated by the word was in the first place perceived as an illness. If we consider its "demonic aspect," we are further able to conclude that this illness was viewed as "ego alien" (the psychological technical term is "not ego-syntonic"), at least in the classification imposed from the outside, since at that time many jealous individuals would have considered their condition to be completely normal, just as they do today. In this instance, too, it was psychoanalysis that was first able to postulate a therapeutically efficacious theory about the forces that possibly move the human soul to construct a delusion in regard to jealousy, or allow it to collapse again. That we are today able to understand jealousy as "dependency" because of its linguistic history, although it is a false etymology, has invested the concept with a depth of meaning that cannot be rendered as directly in other languages.

As far as I can tell, there is in German only one figurative usage of jealousy, "to guard something jealously" and related expressions that transpose the personal triadic relationship to impersonal objects and activities. The same phrase exists in both English and German. The Romance languages, on the other hand, bubble over with a wealth of idiomatic metaphorical expressions from the military, botanical, armament, and naval spheres, all of which I do not want to enumerate here. Is the fact that a comparison with jealousy so readily occurs to them related to the greater passion of southern peoples?

I would like to deal briefly with one of the figurative meanings: with *jalousie,* a foreign word that is used in German and English as the designation for a blind or shutter with adjustable horizontal slats. This is an instance of a metaphor that is no longer felt as such and which, in using an abstract concept for a concrete object, documents a rather uncommon linguistic change (the opposite is more common). The abstract concept—jealousy—must have been so familiar to the speakers of the language that it seemed appropriate as a designation of an unfamiliar object. (These blinds were probably invented in the Orient.) There is evidence of the word *gelosia* already being used in this sense in Italy before the beginning of the sixteenth century—for the first time in 1493, when it was applied to the latticed door that screens the sanctuary, so that the people can observe the sacred rites but do not interfere with the priest (Grzywacz 1937, 121). The explicit meaning of *jalousie* in somewhat later occurrences is "to see without being seen"—therefore not the being exposed to the intense heat of the sun or to an undesirable view. The projective power of language here stresses the voyeuristic aspect of jealousy, which likewise was first understood and classified by psychoanalysis (see chap. 17, sec. 3). A time comparison again shows the Romance languages in the lead: about seventy years before an unambiguous word for jealousy can even be found in German, it was already possible to use the word metaphorically in southern Europe.

To conclude this excursion into philology, I would like to take a look at the quotation that confronts one most frequently if one is involved in the study of jealousy: "Jealousy is a passion, which zealousy seeks what creates suffering." Many consider this to be an adage, but it is too ingenious for that. Many educated people attribute it to the Protestant theologian and Prussian patriot Schleiermacher. However, it cannot be found either in his works or in his letters. In Büchmann's *Familiar Quotations* (33d ed., 1981), I find the following explanation: the quotation comes from a translation of Cervantes, the great author of *Don Quixote*. In one of his small pieces (*entremeses*), a soldier cries out, "!O zelos zelos!

¡Quán mejor os llamaron duelos, duelos!" To translate it rather literally: "Oh, jealousy, jealousy! How much better if you would be called grief and pain!" This verse, which in Spanish sounds both comical and clever at the same time, in keeping with the character of the comic figure of Gracioso, was rendered by the translator, Hermann Kurz, as "Oh, jealousy, jealousy, passion which zealously seeks what creates suffering!" Although the stated date of publication for Kurz's book is 1917, and Schleiermacher had died in 1834, it is nonetheless possible that this notion occurred to Schleiermacher and then began to circulate as an adage, making it possible for Kurz to take over a ready-made figure of speech. However, it seems much more plausible to assign it to the Spanish cultural sphere, both on the basis of its understanding of jealousy, as well as the witty and shrewd use of language.

While looking for the reason this adage was attributed to Schleiermacher, it became ever more improbable to me that he was its author because of the wording—Schleiermacher's language was not witty, but extravagant, effusive, and emotional. That one thought him capable of this bon mot is probably indicative of how his contemporaries and posterity judged Schleiermacher, and perhaps also indicative of his life: he was a great ladies' man but never fell in love with a girl, always with married women—as he writes in an exchange of letters with his fiancée, a friend's very young widow (Schleiermacher 1919). The contemplation of jealousy, therefore, would have been a necessity for him. We are indebted to him not only for the *Intimate Letters* (1800) about the love manual of romanticism, Friedrich Schlegel's *Lucinde*, but also for the beautiful *Catechism of Reason for Noble Women* (ca. 1797; see below, chap. 14, secs. 8, 10, for a more extensive discussion of this), which is a comprehensive compendium of the new conception of love that was arising around 1800. He himself attempted a very strange resolution of jealousy: soon after his marriage, when his young wife fell in love with his friend and pupil, Alexander von der Marwitz, there was "no thought of disapproval; he valued Marwitz over everything, and Marwitz worshipped him" (as reported by August Varnhagen von Ense). Schleiermacher therefore tried, by secretly decreasing his food intake, "to let himself die in order to escape his own misery, and in order not to be an obstacle to his beloved wife's happiness." He did not succeed. Marwitz died in the Wars of Liberation, and the marriage between Schleiermacher and his wife, who was twenty years younger than he, once again reached an even keel (Varnhagen 1967, 433).

I wrote this book in order to discover precisely what I myself understand by jealousy. For when I look closely, I see that we indeed have a word for it today in all modern languages—but is the word clearly apposite? Is the emotion of rage and the sense of injury in the case of actual infidelity really jealousy? Or is jealousy only the exaggerated preoccupation with the wrong that has been done? Or only the "addictive" looking around and surveillance, which is not at all dependent on fact? When does an actual jealousy delusion (yet another new word!) begin—when suspicion that "something is going on" is borne for years, or only upon the acting out of an entrenched delusional "knowledge," which leads to aggression and perhaps to murder and suicide?

△ 14 △

BONDING, FREEDOM, THE SENSE
OF HONOR: TRADITIONS
OF LOVE AND JEALOUSY

1. Love in Marriage?

Some banal assertions that can be made: without sexuality the human race would die out; love has always existed, jealousy as well; marriage as a protected institution has been around for a long time. But how did what was called love look? What was taken seriously as a reason for jealousy? What was derided? The most important question is, What was the connection between love and marriage, which we are today accustomed to seeing joined? In older novels and biographies descriptions of marriages entered into for rational or financial reasons strike us as being strange and alien. Today we of course expect love *outside* of marriage too, but under no circumstances can it not be present *in* marriage. Today it is no longer really possible to comprehend emotionally that the reverse was once true—love could be evident *in* marriage too, but it was not held to be a necessary prerequisite.

What is extremely remarkable in all of this is that, upon closer examination, we see that our notions of love are rooted in centuries-old reflection upon extramarital relationships. Because of this, one must draw the psychological conclusion that jealousy has been introduced into our nest from the beginning as another bird's alien egg. For how could the person who is passionately active or fixated outside marriage not have a deep inclination toward mistrust of fidelity in his or her own marriage?

The first great golden age of independent Western culture, the Christian Middle Ages, which was marked by knightly ideals, developed, indeed even invented, just that which we now call love. For the first time since the age of antiquity, a construct arose of rules, a "code," linguistic prescriptions, by which the leading figures of the time strove to live—and educated people, the upper class, the nobility emulated them. These rules of life and love can still be gathered from the cultural monuments: from art and even architecture, from poetry, and most clearly from the theory that originated at that time.

For a theory of love did exist. The treatise *De amore* was composed by a royal chaplain, Andreas, an influential court cleric, in the second half of the twelfth century, probably under the influence of Countess Marie de Champagne. It is the pivotal example for such a theory. (The Latin text is preserved in twelve manuscripts; there were two French versions in the thirteenth century, two Italian in the fourteenth, and two German in the fifteenth—an unusually wide distribution.) In keeping with the scholastic model, the treatise consists of three books: the first deals with how one wins love, the second with how one keeps it, the third—which comes as a great surprise to us— with what is to be rejected and what is shameful in love and women.

In this complicated web of maxims, definitions, and model dialogues, love is understood exclusively as extramarital love (and the Christian chaplain speaks with the greatest matter-of-factness about the "service of Venus"). In one of the disputations (Andreas Capellanus 1972, 141ff.), a man of the upper nobility explains to a married lady that he is very surprised when the word *love* is used to refer to the marital relationship, "since it is unequivocally true that love can have no claim to a place in the relationship between husband and wife." For what is love, he asks, other than the "immoderate striving [*ambitio*] for a greedily desired secret and hidden embrace?" There can be no question of something like this between marriage partners. In place of this, between them there is friendship, *amicitia*. But there is yet another reason why love cannot play a role in marriage: an essential quality (*substantia*), without which "true love cannot exist, namely jealousy [*zelotypia*], is condemned by married people in every instance, and must be avoided by them like a harmful illness; however, it is always appropriate for lovers to honor jealousy as the mother and nursemaid of love." The lady resists: love is, after all, nothing other than the desire for unlimited carnal pleasure, and no one forbids this between married people—therefore . . . ? The nobleman responds that it would be good, beautiful, and admirable *if* jealousy were not actually the prerequisite of true love. Two opinions are contrasted: the man thinks that jealousy is indispensable for love; to the lady, it is "nothing other than an ugly and repulsive suspicion of the woman."

Thereupon, the man gives the following definition of jealousy: it is "a genuine passion [*passio*] of the soul, in which we fear that the strength of love in our beloved could wane; it is trepidation about the inequality of love [*inaequalitatis amoris trepidatio*]; and it is suspicion of the beloved which arises without ugly thoughts." Three aspects characterize jealousy: "The person who is genuinely jealous always fears that all his devotion [*obsequia*] will not be sufficient to preserve his love; that he is not loved as he himself loves; and he always broods [*recogitat*] on the pains that would torment him, if his beloved should happen to enter into a union with another lover, even though he also believes that this could not happen under any circumstances." The psychological precision of this earliest Western definition is astonishing, and the structure of the language itself takes us even deeper than the words:

as in the case of "jealous of," it is unclear in this entire paragraph whether "the beloved," *amans*, is a man or a woman, although the jealous individual, *zelotypus*, is clearly masculine. Furthermore, "his love," which he would like to preserve ("*suum conservandum amorem*"), based only on the wording could be his own active love as well as the love tendered him—which is without a doubt the conscious meaning and therefore the correct translation.

When the nobleman further maintains that such jealousy cannot exist in marriage, since the husband, of course, need not have such fears because of the protection afforded by all sacred rights, his argument appears to be less convincing for us today. Approximately eight hundred years after Andreas, we view the marital relationship much more from the perspective of emotions than of rights. The disputatious nobleman further explains to the lady that passionate love between spouses is a violation of the code, which one must condemn all the more since it is a matter of the abuse of something sacred. "The worst instance is a wife who is caught with another man. But, as apostolic law teaches, a passionate lover (of his own wife) is viewed as an adulterer with his own wife."

The disputation ends indecisively; a judge who is responsible for matters of love is summoned. This is the "comitissa Campaniae," the countess of Champagne, probably Marie. She writes a letter to the two on 1 May 1164, confirming the man's opinion, substantiating it primarily with reference to the second of Andreas Capellanus's thirty-one rules for life: "He who is not jealous cannot love." Therefore, since the countess is of the same opinion as the nobleman, that jealousy is not possible between married people, what binds them together cannot be called love. (This small example shows that reality in the medieval-scholastic way of thinking was not tested experimentally or scientifically, but was measured against the standard of an a priori thesis.) The countess views Andreas's thesis as correct, as a kind of minor dogma. She scrutinizes the concepts of marriage held by the disputatious nobleman and the lady by testing them against Andreas's thesis and, using the thesis as a point of departure, subordinates reality to this system of thought. Such an interpretation, for which the thesis is more important than actual experience, seems questionable to us today; from the perspective of modern systems theoreticians, "reality" seems "invented." However, who can guarantee that our current view of love, marriage and jealousy is the "true" and "correct" one (see chap. 19, sec. 4)?

Accordingly, what is termed "ugly suspicion of the woman" seems to remain the husband's concern. It is not true and noble jealousy. In this way, the medieval theory of love solved the problem of the ambivalence of jealousy: in many literary works it is viewed as something to be rejected completely, and in many folk songs the jealous husband is derided, yet everyone who is jealous wants to think of his or her suffering and passion as something justified and noble. One could further conclude that jealousy is all the more ugly, the more it is related to physical rights of long-term possession. For the distinguishing characteristic of the love that earns this name in the medieval sense is its mobility (rule 4: It is a fact that love continuously waxes or wanes), its changeability (rule 17: A new love drives the old love to flight), its transitoriness and secrecy (rule 13: A love that has become familiar rarely endures). The medieval codification is, on the whole, extremely elitist, so that from the sociological standpoint one of the main concerns of courtly love seems to be that it "not be vulgar"—an interpretation that is much more pivotal and important than the much-discussed question of whether the troubadours and love poets had, in fact, slept with their lady or not (Luhmann 1982, 50).

The evaluation of the lady is closely related to this: she is elevated into a stylized and ideal figure who alone decides whether to grant favor or not and to whom the man subjects himself unconditionally. She has the power to help him to perfect himself morally: expressed in simpler terms, to help him become a better person. Love for her is nothing less than rational, even if it occasionally leads to excesses. For what could be more understandable than loving someone who is invested with excellent characteristics that are completely obvious. Other women are not loved in classical medieval literature, unless this love is caused by magic potions and witchcraft.

Psychoanalysts have convincingly emphasized the oedipal aspect of courtly love as described by Andreas Capellanus: the condition of jealousy that is directed not against the husband, but (transferring) against other people courting the favor of the venerated object; the exaggerated idealization of the beloved; the experience of her (sadistically colored) superiority in view of which nothing but (masochistic) submission is possible—all this is nothing short of a classical reflection of an infantile oedipal conflict, such as Freud, for example, describes in the essay "On a Specific Type of the Object Choice by the Man" (Freud 1910, Koenigsberg 1967). This context also allows us to understand Andreas Capellanus's ambivalence toward women. His third book is a model of medieval-Christian contempt of women, which cannot be explained only as the tactical addendum of a cleric daring to enter forbidden areas. Rather, it is all too understandable in psychological terms and is an integral element of the tripartite structure of the work. The adult knight, who is guided by Andreas's rules, does not behave like a child who desires his mother and hates his father, according to the strict Freudian conception; the child can, however, not *only* love the mother because in the end she remains with the father and rejects the son. In reaction formation toward his latent hatred, he must invest her with immoderately magnificent characteristics in order not to devalue her—more precisely, in order to be able to deny that she, as Freud notes, does "the exact thing" with the father that whores on the bottom rung of society do. Resisted hatred and the denigration of the "mistakenly" beloved person is revealed in Andreas—as well as in his contemporaries—in misogyny, to which the third book of *De amore* bears persuasive witness.

Is courtly love then a collective neurosis? If one wishes to see it this way, yes. But neuroses always have a rebellious aspect as well. To express it in positive terms, they have a revolutionary and creative aspect, and revolution consists here in the revalorization of the woman (even if not of sexuality). Medieval idealization signifies a liberation, if one contrasts it with the patriarchal order of antiquity, in which nothing was as dishonorable for a man as passivity in love. Passivity was viewed as the basic attitude of women and not-yet-full-grown adolescents, whom men could therefore love without shame in the same way as they loved women (Veyne 1982). It is also a liberation if one contrasts it with early Christian reserve, and even wariness, toward worldly love. Koenigsberg correctly writes that, "for the next ten centuries, men could fall in love according to the rules of courtly decorum without falling into disgrace" (48).

In spite of the veneration of the woman, however, the world remained male-oriented, and the splendor that surrounds the "lady" has as its purpose only "the purification and ennobling of the knight, the nobleman, and his refinement by raising him to her level" (Kremers 1973, 107). Nonetheless, since love is what is at issue, the highest ideals and eroticism draw closer together. The clean separation into "courtly" and "noncourtly" love cannot be maintained forever. To be sure, sexual activity within marriage—which was not a matter of free choice, but was entered into for economic, dynastic, and other reasons far removed from emotions—was primarily for the purpose of having children and therefore to continue and maintain the family. It will continue to be viewed for a long time to come as something totally different from passionate affairs outside one's own four walls. Both coexist, and both are common and normal.

2. Love as a Frenzy That Explodes the Established Order

Because of the emphasis that the Renaissance placed on the individual's uniqueness and freedom, women, in real life as well as in literature, are brought from the heavenly splendor of the medieval courts of love (which probably never existed in reality) down to the level of a tangible living being. Unreality and the universality of the ideal make way for individual characteristics, which no longer exclude sensual, demanding, even negative aspects. These women are nonetheless loved, even if they no longer fulfill the condition of love that was most important for Andreas Capellanus—overall perfection. Love, from now on as *passio* in the sense of suffering as well as of passion, correspondingly becomes more immoderate, restless, crazy; it is no longer something only of concern to the noble person, who is overwhelmed by what is noble, but a force that enslaves everyone, that can strike everyone in an arbitrary onslaught, and that no longer respects societal order—a symbol for the dissolution of medieval hierarchical structures. (In Andreas one still reads, in spite of all the extramarital affairs, "It is not seemly to love someone whom one would be ashamed to marry.")

A good example of these changes is Ludovico Ariosto's *Orlando furioso*, which was written between 1505 and 1515 and first published in its completed form in 1532. It is a work of enormous influence on European literature. The hero is described as "raving," but in Boiardo's verse epic, which Ariosto wanted to continue and far outstripped, the hero is described as "in love" (*Orland innamorato*). The hero is none other than Roland, the central figure in the Old French *Chanson de Roland* (ca. 1100). This solemn and powerful figure from the cycle of legends that revolve around Charlemagne belongs to the world of religious wars waged by the knights. In accordance with convention, the Roland of the *Chanson de Roland* is engaged, and at the news of his heroic death his bride follows him to the grave. It was an unheard-of novelty for Boiardo's time that Roland—known in Italian as Orlando—should have nothing in his head but love. Boiardo not only invented this change, but also introduced jealousy into Italian love poetry (Friedrich 1964, 283). "Either 'Orlando' or 'in love' " (Kremers 1973, 30)—and in Ariosto's work he even becomes insane because of the infidelity of the venerated Princess Angelica, who is neither married nor especially good and noble, but simply attractive. She turns men's heads when she wants and is in the mood, and is no longer the elevating medium of refinement associated with the core meaning of the world, but simply a girl one wants to possess. Orlando's insanity—as far as I know, the first insanity caused by jealousy in European literature—erupts when he can no longer close his eyes to the fact that Angelica prefers the simple foot soldier Medoro to him and surrenders herself to Medoro. She is also a victim of Amor, who blindly shoots his arrows, no longer respecting class boundaries. In this way, the bravest knight no longer gets the most beautiful woman—the world is out of joint. Orlando is incapable of bearing this. His reason flees to the moon; he storms through the countryside like a wild, almost bestial, naked figure and hacks down everything he meets, barely excepting Angelica and Medoro, whom he no longer recognizes. Unlike the knights driven crazy by love in earlier verse epics, Orlando cannot be healed simply through magic or an ointment. Much stronger means are necessary to rectify this radical collapse of the world order. A friend goes to the moon in Elias's fiery chariot and retrieves Orlando's reason with the help of John the Evangelist. Only Heaven itself can help. Only then can the recovered Paladin assist the Christian cause in gaining final victory over the heathens, and allow himself to be acclaimed in Paris for this accomplishment.

One cannot speak here of a jealousy delusion in a more narrow clinical sense (i.e., the delusional-paranoid preoccupation with rivals, who either do not exist or are seen in a distorted, completely obsessive way). There is not a single reference to the imagined or actual reality of the preferred rival. Jealousy, if it is still jealousy, no longer has anything noble about it. It neither nurtures nor sustains love, but throws people's normal and correct contacts into such radical disorder that murderous bestiality appears the only fitting symbol for it. What is hurtful and contemptuous about jealousy, the desperate "I have to be the way I do not want to be," has shifted out of all proportion to the foreground. A refined, enjoyable passion is no longer experienced, but rather "the brave knight, the bloom of every tournament, / Weeps in bed like a simple stable boy" (Boiardo 1.2.22). That such a decline of the emotion should be unbearable and cause insanity may perhaps appear to be irrational, arrogant, and misanthropic if it is not placed in its historical context. However, whoever wants to deal with jealousy must avoid such psychodemocratic ways of formulaic thought. Precipitous decline—what Freud termed the narcissistic sense of injury—is a basic element in each jealousy. It needs to be understood, and not to be condemned.

3. Jealousy in the Popular Imagination

Naturally, there was also a popular literature—verses, dances, pamphlets, and adages—concurrent with the aforementioned examples of a high-aristocratic literature, in which the entire world is reflected in its dubiety as well as its splendor. In the popular literature, jealousy has nothing to do with collapsing social structures and cosmic connections; it is not interpreted and is not seen as something awkward, but is simply there and is either derided or held up as a warning in street ballads. For instance, in medieval France there were the May dances, which possibly go back to old Venus cults and provided a kind of Mardi Gras freedom. A "queen" grants complete freedom to those in love, and the jealous husband is derided. (The May songs contain some of the earliest recorded examples for the occurrence of the word *jealousy* in Old French.) What is striking is that one hears talk only of jealous men. We may conclude from this that women represented vitality, which was valued but could never be fully domesticated, while men represented boring duty and order. One never confronts tragedy in such popular satires.

In the German- and English-speaking area at the time of the waning Middle Ages, there was already a long thematic tradition of adultery in the popular ballad, in which sympathy is reserved exclusively for the adulterer (Roth 1977). The norm of marriage is not questioned, but getting around it is evidently a good thing. Until well into the nineteenth century, adultery is always the violation only of the man's marriage, above all juridically. The man cannot violate his own marriage in any way. Although the church officially judged the violation of the holy institution of marriage with equal severity whether committed by the man or the woman, views and judgments that favored men lasted subliminally almost to the present time. Women were almost always punished more severely by the courts, and in any case social ostracism was disproportionately harsher for women until the present century (one need only think of Fontane's Effi Briest). One may well imagine that there was an undercurrent of malicious delight among the people at the circumvention of such attitudes and prescriptions. The lesson to be drawn from popular theatrical farces is not, therefore, that one should behave more morally, but that one should be more cunning the next time.

4. Were Women Permitted to Be Jealous?

It is conspicuous how seldom jealous women appear not only in popular literature but also in the literature of the high culture. The evil, the power-hungry, and even the lascivious woman exists, but apparently one did not have to trouble oneself about the jealousy of women in an unquestionably patriarchal society. During times in which emotions and passions were under the control and at the service of internal as well as external principles of order, to a much greater extent than we expect today, the damage that a woman sustained if the suspicion of her husband's infidelity should be confirmed was "only" psychic. The man, however, had to stand before all the world as a cuckold, if the children born in his marriage were not biologically his. Esteem was the motor that drove suspicion and anxiety, as well as the prophylactic and vengeful cruelty of men, and esteem plays a greater role in jealousy today than one would reasonably expect (if one does not look at it from a psychological perspective) in our society, which is more permissive in every respect. Medea is the powerful figure who causes a horrible bloodbath because of her rejection by Jason, her husband, and because of his intention to marry Creusa. She even kills her own children by Jason, and it may be significant that even antiquity viewed her as the Stranger, the sorceress from far away, "not one of us." And it is probably just as significant that she only surfaces again in seventeenth- century France, in Corneille, at a time in which more freedom and control over their own destinies had accrued to women, at least in the upper classes which set the standard.

And what about Kriemhild and Brunhild? The *Song of the Nibelungen*, which originated around 1200 and was elevated by the romantics to the national epic of the German people, who did not exist at the time it was written, contains two larger-than-life female figures whose passion drives an entire people to death and destruction. But is this passion jealousy? I will briefly recapitulate the story.

The splendid Siegfried, who cannot be wounded because he has bathed in dragon's blood, loves Kriemhild. However he may marry her only if her brother, Gunther, the king of the Burgundians, attains the beautiful and strong Brunhild, who intends to marry only the person who defeats her in battle. Siegfried, made invisible by a magic cloak, guides Gunther's actions, and a double wedding takes place. On their wedding night, however, Brunhild ties up Gunther and hangs him on a nail. Siegfried, invisible, has to help again. Brunhild believes that she has been defeated. Siegfried takes her ring and girdle and shows these trophies to Kriemhild, who therefore knows of the secret. Only ten years later, upon the famous quarrel between the queens at the entrance of the Worms Cathedral, does she reveal her knowledge to Brunhild. Brunhild's pride is mortally wounded. She has Siegfried murdered by her vassal Hagen, who kills him by striking him on his only vulnerable spot—when he was bathing in dragon's blood, a leaf fell onto a spot between his shoulders.

Kriemhild's rage and vengefulness know no bounds. Remarkably, however, Brunhild is totally exempt from this. Kriemhild is interested only in Hagen's death. Later she becomes the wife of Attila, the king of the Huns. In his country, thirteen years after Siegfried's death, not only Hagen but the entire Burgundian army find their death—as well as Kriemhild herself, who has become a "she devil."

What was going on between these two women? Was it a matter of jealousy for Brunhild? Certainly it was a matter of injured honor, as well as the feeling that, as the strongest woman, the strongest and most splendid man was actually her due. But does Brunhild love Siegfried; does she really want to "have" him, as we would say today in a way that is totally inappropriate for this context. And is it jealousy that drives Kriemhild to reveal the secret that then precipitates the catastrophe—jealousy of Brunhild's higher rank; jealousy of the intimacy of the battle between her husband and another woman.

The thematic history of the *Song of the Nibelungen,* in any case, tells us a lot about the development of love and jealousy. These two powerful queens are surely imaginable only as the late descendants of a culture, the Germanic culture, in which women occupied a more powerful and thus more dangerous position than in Christian times, in which the preserved manuscript versions originate. The first reappearance of this literary material in a prominent place is in Hans Sachs's "Tragedy of the Horned Siegfried," from the year 1557. A great change has taken place: the rivalry between the women is missing completely. What is at issue is only the men's interaction and the unruliness of a bold prince who is finally murdered because of envy. The moral of the story is that one should raise one's son more strictly—a reduction and restriction of a story about kings to the level of the Nuremberg bourgeoisie. The offended woman as the central figure only surfaces again in Wagner. There she is superdivine and superhuman at the same time, a symbolic figure for a new view of woman, still not clearly focused and at the same time of extraordinary dimensions: here Brunhild is Siegfried's wife (and almost the one who creates him). The deception of Brunhild is the action that symbolizes dependency on a decadent world, which is destroyed in the *Twilight of the Gods* (first performance in 1876), without there yet being any hint of a better world to come. Right, as well as all of Wagner's sympathy, is on Brunhild's side. (His last written words, during which he suffered a fatal heart attack, are, "The emancipation of women . . . contradictions . . .")

5. Jealousy in the Quest for Honor

Another step in the history of this topic in European literature takes us to Spain, the classical land of pride and jealousy, which always—until the present time!—had to struggle with its conception of itself, with the question of whether it belongs to Europe or not. Its history is stamped by the *reconquista,* the reconquest of the country from the Islamic Arabs who in the beginning of the eighth century had penetrated as far as the Pyrénées. The power of the Arabs was not finally broken until 1492, more than seven hundred years later, with the conquest of the kingdom of Granada by the "Catholic royal couple," Ferdinand and Isabella—in the year that has been impressed upon our memories as the date of the discovery of America, which is actually closely associated with the other event. The *reyes católicos* were determined to support the Italian Christopher Columbus's plans of exploration, but only *after* they had attained their sacred main goal. In April 1492, when the city of Granada had fallen, they signed the agreement with Columbus; in October he landed on the first island in the Caribbean, still believing that he had discovered the sea route to India. This was the foundation of Spanish world rule. A vital feeling of greatness, happiness, and pride became widespread in the mother country, which led to great cultural achievements but finally was lost in hubris, narrow-mindedness, and melancholy about two to three centuries later.

What does this have to do with jealousy? A lot! Germans use the phrase "proud as a Spaniard," and justifiably—because the problem of honor became the central theme in the literature of the so-called Golden Age (from about the middle of the sixteenth to the end of the seventeenth century). The centuries-long struggle against "the others," meaningful and justified in its historical context, apparently could not be maintained without the development of a special sense of honor, possibly just because of what the Spaniards felt to be the cultural and human superiority of their opponents. "Pride of nobility, pride of conquest, pride of race, and pride of religion" (Pfandl 1924, 76) were not directed in the first instance against the rabble in one's own camp, but above all against the Moors, who were, in the view of many, very ancient, very noble, and very refined, whereas the Spaniards were descended from the "barbarians," the Visigoths being one of the main sources of their bloodline. With the final victory and the gold showered upon them from across the sea, Spanish pride was robbed of its meaningful grounding and led to a cult of honor that was completely reoriented toward the external, toward a desire for the esteem of others. Lope de Vega writes (*Los comendadores de Córdoba*), "To be virtuous and to have merit—this does *not* mean, to be honorable; but to give occasion for one's fellow man to treat us with honor." The Spanish world empire was destroyed because of this externalization, which led also to contempt of physical and manual labor and to the internal incapability of the large number of noble Spaniards to engage in manual labor or to become merchants. Great Spanish literature, however, found in honor, which was almost always associated with love, one of its great motivating forces.

Love and honor harnessed together lead to jealousy. Brothers, fathers, and especially husbands saw their honor physically incarnated before them, so to speak, in the form of their sisters, daughters, and wives. If he does not want to be considered dishonorable, the only thing that a *christiano viejo*, an "old Christian" (i.e., a racially pure and not newly baptized Spaniard), must demand of himself if he is at all suspicious is to duel with sword or dagger. The law and church regulations were opposed to this, but one's own honor, as it is reflected in the esteem of others, is clearly ranked higher in the system of values. There is still time for regret at the moment of death, should the duel end negatively for the participant. A serenade in front of the gate of the person who is desired and guarded is enough to precipitate the jealousy reaction. It is like pushing a button, unbelievably mechanical. Apart from religious works, there is certainly no Spanish drama of the Golden Age in which jealousy is not the motivating force at least of a subplot. It is unimaginable for a transgression to be forgiven—in Spain, the most Christian of countries! The only resort is bloody revenge on the adulteress and her beloved.

Such events were apparently also frequent in real life, which allows us to conclude that women had considerable freedom in sexual mores. In view of this, jealousy was a noble emotion that was to be summoned up, as well as a monster that one looked at in awed astonishment. Not even its association with love seems certain any more; Calderón (*El escondido y la tapade,* "The man in hiding and the veiled lady") says that someone was of the opinion that jealousy could only arise where there was also love; but it is much more likely to be some sort of insult, to which one is subjected: "and it does not necessarily have to be the child of love; sometimes it is generated by a sense of honor." The comedic resolution leads to the marriage of the couple who are in love; the more serious resolution—not necessarily felt as tragic—leads to revenge and often to the replacement of the murdered wife by another. From our point of view, she is thereby characterized as a possession, as an "object," in an inhuman way. However, it must not be forgotten that the background of all baroque art is the conviction that the world is only an illusion. Thus where everything is a dream, a game, and transitoriness, the misaligned elements are mutually interchangeable. This explains the improbability of many plots, as well as the interchangeability of people. Lope de Vega's highly acclaimed and very successful drama, *Los comendadores de*

Córdoba ("The commanders of Cordoba," 1596), provides an example of this. It is based on an actual event.

A noble councilor of Cordoba returns from a trip and finds his wife in an adulterous relationship with his nephew, a young commander (*comendador*). Thereupon, he kills not only the couple but also his wife's niece, who has yielded to the nephew's friend, and kills as well all the servants and animals in the house—dogs, cats, a monkey, and a parrot. At the end, the king of Spain appears, explicitly praises this action, and points out to the citizens of Cordoba, that they can count themselves lucky to have such a man on their city council. That is a greater honor than the fact that the Roman poets Seneca and Lucan were born within their walls (about which all of Spain was not a little proud). The king betroths the highly honored man to one of the noblest girls of the land. Don Fernando, the hero, thereupon can confirm, with the consent of the satisfied public, that he has regained everything he lost.

One has to rub one's eyes and put this evaluation of actions and events into historical perspective. Our current moral viewpoint is totally unsuited to the task. "Soy quien soy"—"I am who I am"—this is the standpoint that the Spaniard considers in a crisis, obeying the internal laws of his time. He thus reflects on his social aim "to be this and nothing else," which consequently imposes very specific duties. The person who does not fulfill them falls into nonbeing, into social death. Because of his wife's infidelity, which is absolutely intolerable for a person of his social status, Don Fernando falls from a condition of a person enjoying the most highly esteemed existence to the condition of a person who has been deprived of the highest value, honor. He can do nothing but try to fight to get it back as quickly as possible, especially since he knows that restored honor confers even more standing, even more presence in the world than unimpugned honor (cf. Larson 1977). The suspicion arises that this kind of "being" was invested with such high value because the historical situation, especially the undermining of Spain's hegemony by England, which was becoming ever more obvious, contained to a high degree the real danger of "nonbeing."

One must keep in mind that, from a psychological perspective, this kind of jealousy is much more a matter of self-love than of love for others. In view of this, narcissistic confirmation is not derived from one's internal being, but exclusively from the external. One expects of love that it will set in completely or not at all, and it is always associated with jealousy or at least with the possibility that jealousy could be summoned at short notice. Seen from today's perspective, all these figures are at least neurotically jealous: but what we today consider neurotic was viewed at that time not only as normal, but as something that one owned to one's self- image.

This held true not only for men. The energetic intervention of women, who took their own destiny in hand out of love, injured honor, and jealousy, is an innovation in literature which, originating in Spain, set an example for all Europe. Marriage is always the goal. Correspondingly, in Spain there was no system of rules for extramarital love, but at most one for premarital love. Especially in comedy, there frequently appear young women who, ensnared by glowing promises, surrender themselves to an admirer and then are deserted because of another (after all, the figure of Don Juan originates in Spain). Driven by *los celos* (jealousy), they reconquer the unfaithful one with passion, wit, and unbelievable inventiveness—it is also a *reconquista* during which they dupe their rivals, who generally know nothing of them, with mischief and a delight in the game. It is no coincidence that these young women disguise themselves as men who then are wittier, braver, and more attractive to other girls than their genuine admirers. Fantasy opens up to women an aspect of human experience, at least on the stage or between the covers of a book, which is otherwise not accessible to them. The novelty and freshness of the experience turns them, so to speak, into the better, even if beardless, men.

The success and frequency of the theme show how attractive such a dream was. Like all dreams, this one also has to do with reality, although it does not directly reflect it. It could only anticipate, transform, and rework what historical reality, in spite of all evidence that the woman was an object, already contained, even if it was only implied, suppressed, or existed in exceptional situations. The active, and actively jealous, woman with rights and real claims to love and fidelity (or even to her own infidelity, which does not demand bloody revenge but can be understood and forgiven) did not exist in reality either as a postulate or even as a norm; she was, however, born in fantasy.

6. Jealousy as a Sign for the Paradoxicality of Love

Next the spotlight falls on the development of concepts of love, marriage, and infidelity at the time of Louis XIV. In the second half of the seventeenth century France was the glorious center of Europe, while neighboring countries were shaken by radical changes, rebellions, wars, and revolutions. In France sexuality is included in the problematic of love much more forcefully than in even the Renaissance or baroque Spain. What is totally new is that in France, in life as well as in literature, it is *extramarital* sexuality, the sexuality of the married woman, who was much more liberated than in Spain and Italy and also in the Protestant countries, which were more strongly committed to morality and inwardness. If the medieval lady, at least as reflected in the ideal, was committed to sexual denial; if a young Spanish girl contemplating marriage could possibly allow herself to be seduced to surrender to passion;

then the French woman of the standard-setting upper class, who was carefully guarded until marriage, actually became free to love in marriage. She no longer had her hand to bestow, but she did have what was euphemistically called her "heart," *coeur,* to give, and the danger was very great that in doing so she would psychically lose everything.

For the whole rule-governed game of the art of love, which surfaced again and which was primarily an art of seduction, was played to the detriment of the woman. If she decided for love, then she had to become unhappy, because love ceases (and marriage remains). If she renounced love, like the princess of Cleves in the novel by the refined and courtly ritualistic Marie de La Fayette, her renunciation brought her at most spiritual happiness, which was, however, tied to a retreat from the vital wellspring of the courtly environment, on which all values were based. Not without reason did Louis XIV have himself called *roi soleil,* the Sun King. Today we can barely imagine the solitude and quiet of the existence of a woman who lived alone on her estates.

However, when love was at issue, that is, the granting and denying of favors, the woman was an active partner in the game. "In this game the man values the woman's resistance as a condition for the intensification of his own efforts; likewise, the woman values the persistence and endurance of the man's efforts. And both know, that both know this" (Luhmann 1982, 77 n. 19). Extravagant, excessive, and immoderate love was the prerequisite that made possible the woman's surrender, that justified the man's claim, and that was considered socially acceptable (unlike the seduction of unmarried girls). The prerequisite was *amour passion,* "passionate love," which led to a joyful and sorrowful loss of identity, to partial insanity. In this, the new concept of love is connected to two medieval traditions: on the one hand, the tradition of mystical union; on the other, the tradition of *amor pestis,* love as an illness. (The latter can be seen most clearly in *Orlando furioso,* but it appears again and again as a topos in Spanish drama.) The rules and experience of love in the seventeenth century agree with modern system-oriented theories of schizophrenia, that what causes insanity consists in the paradoxification of love in a culture that placed a very high value on rationality and the apparent logic even of emotion, as well as on moderation and control. Since the congruence of love and eternity, ideally found in marriage, could no longer be attained, the short time of passion became an elaborate playing field for strategies that no longer had a clear goal ("healthy," "normal") but were antithetical, that is, paradoxical. (The German word for marriage is *Ehe,* which clearly expresses the connection to eternity, since *ê* and *ewe* are the early forms of the modern German word, and both also mean "eternity, eternal law.") The ideality—beauty, noble birth, wealth—that formerly made love so clear and self-evident played only a secondary and unimportant role, even if it had not yet totally disappeared. (In a difficult but thoroughly stimulating study, itself a literary work in the sense of a personal interpretation of reality, Niklas Luhmann [1982] has limned the dedifferentiation of the "code, love as passion".)

What seems important to me for the purposes of my theme is that excessive passion, something that is per se rare and improbable, an extreme condition, was demanded for love, as if one could actually demand something like that. This is the fundamental paradox. At the same time it could not last, because the woman could no longer bestow her hand in marriage. Nonetheless, this desire also wants, as Nietzsche formulated it much later, "deep, deep eternity." One could almost say that its fulfillment, however, already contains the danger of the beginning of the end. The proximity to an insanity-producing relational paradox of the kind "come close to me in order to remain distant from me" is obvious—as well as the proximity to constantly lurking jealousy, first because a third party in the form of the husband had always been present, and second because a new extramarital partner could appear on the scene at any time. For there were no commitments other than those generated out of and preserved by emotion.

Since extramarital love was no longer forbidden but was almost a courtly duty in spite of the church's sustained opposition—kings had mistresses; queens had lovers; extramarital progeny, the "bastards," were recognized within the upper class and were often very successful—another paradox arose: keeping things secret and making them public. In this, love as such was never subjected to social ostracism, although its inelegant conduct was, as one can observe in Molière's comedies. Thus love, as well as imperilled love, the loss of love, and jealousy, took on primary significance for self-esteem in a courtly culture, in which the highest priority was to represent something—it was, if you will, more important to seem to be rather than to be.

This state of affairs among a small upper class, this refinement of seeing through things and nonetheless playing along, this intermingling of the most complicated activity and the melancholic foreknowledge of its inevitable failure—all of this is unimaginable without taking into account the interaction of social reality with the psychological perspicacity of a literature that observes, exposes—and unmasks. We are indebted to French ethics (the German word is *Moralistik,* and shares with the word *moral* and *mores* a common Latin root, *mores*), which sets no norms but shows the world and people as they are and not as they should be (cf. Friedrich 1949, especially chap. 4), for a long series of clear-sighted definitions of jealousy. The most famous come from La Rochefoucauld (1613–80), a great nobleman involved at the highest level in affairs of state and the heart, who avers in a self-portrait from the year 1658 that being melancholy is his first and foremost characteristic. Although he describes this special melancholy as "rather bearable and rather gentle," it does not stop him from describing, with the most extreme incisiveness and precision until his death, what he saw around him—and for him this means that he looked through things. His contemporaries were horrified—but between 1664 and 1678 the count saw six editions of his *Maxims* appear.

It is impossible that jealousy could be a noble emotion, as it was at the time of Andreas Capellanus. To be sure, it appears in noble-minded individuals, the *honnêtes gens,* among whom La Rochefoucauld included himself and was included by others. Possibly therein again lies a paradox that makes one melancholy. La Rochefoucauld's central thesis is "jealousy contains more self-love than love" (1967, p. 447, maxim 324). For the author, this amour propre is behind all genuine and apparent virtues, and he considers it to be an outright evil, even if an unavoidable one. A similar situation obtains for jealousy: it is born with love. Many saw this before La Rochefoucauld, but not this: "it does not always die with love" (451, maxim 361). Nor did they see that, "like other passions, pride has its bizarre aspects: one is embarrassed to confess that one is jealous, and yet one counts it as a point of honor to have been jealous and to be capable of jealousy." In the last edition of the *Maxims* to appear during the author's lifetime, one still reads the cutting remark (and this time even with a moralistic undertone), "jealousy is the greatest of all evils and the one that has the least pity on those who bring it about" (469, maxim 503). And is there any salvation? None! except a very difficult one, as the maxims repeat in several variations: "the remedy for jealousy is the certainty of what one fears, because it will bring about the end of one's life [in a duel] or the end of love; that is a terrible remedy, but it is sweeter than doubt and suspicion" (379, maxim 240). However, let us remember that jealousy does not always die at the same time as love. . . .

It is obvious that his contemporaries resisted this overly caustic description of the unavoidability of sorrow that must come from love. People today naturally ask if loyalty and constancy were really in such a hopeless state, and whether marriage as a way of life was actually so unattractive. La Rochefoucauld answers, "There are convenient marriages, but no delightful ones" (418, maxim 113), and what he calls delightful, that is, the glow of extramarital transitory love, must have been irresistible for him in spite of all sorrows. "In love with love" is a phrase that frequently appears in his work. It was most likely his experience and conviction that such an experience, on the part of men as well as women, can only end in renunciation, resignation, and melancholy.

Nothing is as appropriate as an illustration of what love was and could be in his time and his class as the novel of his young friend, Marie de La Fayette, *The Princess of Cleves* (completed in 1672, published in 1678). La Rochefoucauld advised her on the writing of this work. The basic plot can be quickly summarized.

The recently married princess is admired by the duke of Nemours. He hopes to make her his mistress. She resists him out of a sense of decency and morality, although she also loves him passionately—and he knows this—whereas only tenderness, duty, and friendship bind her to her husband. Her husband dies of an incurable infectious illness. Perhaps, however, his life-force had been weakened by the importunings of the duke of Nemours. The princess retreats into genuine and heartfelt grief; in spite of that, the duke believes that he can count on her marrying him. She refuses and sticks to her refusal, with the justification that she cannot believe in the constancy of his love should they marry, and that she wants to spare herself the torments of jealousy and being deserted. She retreats to a convent, to a pious and lonely life. The duke still fights for her for a while and believes that he "will die of pain" when he receives her final refusal. "Finally, however, time eased his pain, and constant separation extinguished passion."

This apparently simple story is interwoven in a net of love intrigues and court machinations. What sticks in one's memory is, above all, the figure of the princess, drawn with great psychological sensitivity, so strong in her delicacy and so resigned in her strength. The situation is not "tragic," but only sad—as well as very noble, courtly, and measured in spite of great passion. La Rochefoucauld writes, "There is a certain kind of love, whose excess prevents jealousy." This presupposes that it is unavoidable that, one day, jealousy will make its appearance, because such a love does not last. And it is this transitoriness to which the princess does not want to surrender herself.

7. Nonetheless: Love in Marriage

Since the excessive passion required was so difficult to put into practice and so dangerous, and since it is also imaginable only in the interaction with a society that was still rigid even in its frivolity, French classicism superficially and cynically built into its conception of love decline, descent into libertinism, and sexual immoderation. A good century after the Golden Age, the French revolution would inspire, horrify, and convulse Europe—and fundamentally change it, because much had already changed.

The revolution's points of departure were not only economic but primarily moral stances that are also of interest for the theme of this book. Upper class norms no longer prevail. New impulses came from the bourgeoisie, with whom the princess of Cleves, the Countess La Fayette, and the duke of La Rochefoucauld had no contact, about whom they knew nothing, but whom they nonetheless despised. The middle class could not afford love that was not goal oriented, and it could and did not want to conceive of marriage as fundamentally unhappy. Their own experiences spoke against this, but also in part the experiences of the nobility, especially the provincial nobility. At the end of the sixteenth century, the great Montaigne already writes in his

Essais (book 3, essay 5) that "no woman" who has once tasted marriage "would want to take the place of her husband's mistress or girlfriend." Because, should one ask him "whom he would rather have humiliated, his wife or his mistress, whose unhappiness would touch him more, whose greatness he desires more," then there is no doubt as to what the answer would be "in a healthy marriage" (1962, 829). There is no talk of jealousy. Indeed, one reads in the same passage, "A good marriage . . . rejects the etiquette of love. It seeks the etiquette of friendship." One sees ever more clearly that the concern is not with lack of love within marriage, but with what to designate as love. For in a letter on the death of his thirty-two-year-old friend, La Boetie (1357ff.), Montaigne reports, for example, that his friend calls his wife "ma semblance" (my counterpart) and says to her in farewell that he has "loved, cherished, and valued" her as much as he could (*aymee, cherie, estimee*)— thus there is love within marriage, even to the choice of words.

The main difference for us, who designate both forms as love, consists in the passionateness that is always felt as transitory (Luhmann 1982, especially chap. 6), and especially in the highly esteemed *measured* sexuality within marriage. In addition, there were things about which one did not speak, and conjugal love was one of them (Ariès, Béjin, and Foucault 1982, 71). There was a long tradition of the modesty of the decent woman, which, for example, made possible the frequently reported substitutions during the wedding night. (The first and most famous is contained in the biblical story of Jacob, who cannot distinguish Rachel, whom he desperately desired and had won through seven years of service, from the substituted Leah. Jacob's love for Rachel is, however, so great that he serves for another seven years to win his promised bride.) One could never mistake the beloved for another. Her sexuality was more individual.

The question apparently was not whether there was love, tenderness, friendship, and fidelity in marriage, but how one could combine this with passionate sexuality and being in love, that is, the lovers' being emotionally in tune with each other from the outset rather than only reaching this state in the course of time. Predecessors of our concept of "a marriage of love"—which for many centuries was an almost unimaginable conceptual monstrosity—were developed especially in England and America, where love as marital duty shifts to love out of sympathy with the marital "life's companion." Furthermore, in the eighteenth century the woman is revealed as a human being; emotion and nature become leading concepts; happiness for all becomes something that is no longer left to God and that he denies to the majority, but something one begins to *demand*.

8. What Is Romantic Love?

I will save myself from the danger of generalizations with a leap forward, to Friedrich Schlegel's small work *Lucinde,* which appeared in 1799 (almost exactly a century before Freud's *Interpretation of Dreams*), at a time in which the "bourgeois" had already advanced from being the vanguard to the established norm, from which a new avant garde was disengaging itself. (Friedrich Schlegel and his wife split their sides laughing at Schiller's poem "The Song of the Bell," which had become a textbook model for the bourgeois family of the nineteenth and twentieth centuries. They almost "fell from their chairs" laughing—according to a letter from Caroline Schlegel to her daughter on 21 October 1799.) *Lucinde* is cited again and again as the primer for the modern form of marriage; I have my doubts whether it is read. It is a strange, unfinished, brief work, consisting of conversations, reflections, allegories, letters—all in all about ninety pages long, fanciful, ironic, garrulous, melancholy, and sensual (but not at all obscene). It is in no way a novel, which it is called in the modern edition. It tells no story nor does it show development, although it contains a series of stories. But its appearance caused an uproar that today we can no longer comprehend. Schlegel, who was twenty-seven years old at the time, was not allowed to remain in Göttingen, whereupon his friend, the theologian Schleiermacher, who was four years older than he, published his *Intimate Letters* about Schlegel's *Lucinde* a year later in 1800. In these letters he defended the offensive little work. He too was disciplined by his superiors. In a letter to Goethe, the indignant Schiller called *Lucinde* the "height of modern deformity and abnormality" (cited in Klessmann 1975, 184).

In Henriette Beese's afterword, one can find the reasons that were responsible for the scandal. Regardless of what they were, that a scandal arose at all shows how much conceptions of decency and indiscretion have changed in the last two centuries. The most offensive aspect of the book was apparently its description of the "most beautiful situation," by which is meant the sexual reversal of the male and female role. This is hinted at very subtly, but probably referred to whether the man or the woman was on top during sexual intercourse, and therefore, in a figurative sense, to courting, demanding, and desiring on the one hand and on the other yielding, granting, and letting things happen. The representation of a child, "little Wilhelmine," was also viewed as indecent. Uninhibited, lying on her back, she sticks her legs into the air so that her little skirt slides back.

Lucinde was read as a roman à clef, and the disclosure of what was private, which one justifiably saw in it, only made everything even worse. People pitied Schlegel's beloved, Dorothea Veit (and most likely also greedily admired her), because her intimate feelings were put on public display. This did not seem quite right to her either, even though she loyally stood by Schlegel. For what was important to her, as well as to him, was the depiction of a new conception of life and marriage which is more closely related to our current one than any other in history. What we consider "normal" was at that time the project of a small group of courageous individuals, who consciously and with conviction set themselves against convention and law. The fact that they later became more conservative, conforming, and resigned anticipates the general trend in the second half of the nineteenth century.

Schlegel's own life evidences many of the important leading characteristics of his time—like the significance of friendship which, according to Luhmann (1982, 105), almost outdid love in terms of intimacy in the eighteenth century. Schlegel lived with Schleiermacher in the same apartment for two years, in a relationship that Schleiermacher called a "marriage," referring, however, only to the intensity of the exchange and not, for example, to sexuality. Also typical of the time was the admiration of women, who are not simply conquered or seduced, but only with whom the man really becomes himself and "whole," just as she does through him. It is also a characteristic of the late eighteenth and early nineteenth centuries that emotion comes to set the standard for real life. Caroline Böhmer, the great letter writer and one of the most fascinating women in romanticism, was especially highly esteemed by Friedrich Schlegel. When she was expecting an illegitimate child, Friedrich and his brother, August Wilhelm, protected her; Wilhelm simply went ahead and married her. (Caroline could not, to be sure, raise her child as a "bastard" but had to place it into care, where it died. They were after all still that bourgeois . . .) Friedrich fell in love with the Berlin Jew Dorothea Veit, who was ten years older than he. As already mentioned, she was the model for Lucinde. She got a divorce for his sake. Both brothers lived for a time with the two women and several other friends under one roof in Jena in a "family of like-minded spirits" (Hoffmann-Axthelm 1973), thereby making room in their real life for companionship—also a favorite notion of romanticism. To be sure, human reality was stronger than lofty theory: this early predecessor of our communes soon fell apart, above all because of the jealousy and rivalry between Caroline and Dorothea, but also because Caroline fell in love with Schelling, who later became her husband and was fourteen years younger than she. The divorce from her friend and husband Wilhelm was painful and probably also a disgrace for him, in spite of all the "modern" tolerance.

With what does the famous *Lucinde* deal? It only deals with the love between Julius and Lucinde, who can be called romantic without qualification and without any references to linguistic prescriptions. And what is "romantic love?" In the letter in which Julius reacts to Lucinde's announcement that she is going to be a mother, he quotes from a "French book" where it says, "Each was the other's universe." Julius has to smile at this—and at the same time reveals to the reader that there were already precursors of this new conception of love. But there, "in such a French passion," it is "hyperbole"; however, it has become "literally true" for him and Lucinde. In the French book, each finds "the universe in the other, because they lose an appreciation for everything else. This is not the case with us. Everything that we used to love, we still love, only even more dearly. An appreciation for the world has only now been properly opened up to us. You have through me . . . and I have through you . . . '' and so forth. Thus, the other is viewed as a world unto him- or herself, as unique and totally inexhaustible, which also implies that he or she is infinitely changeable and capable of development. This diversity in unity, which can be expressed psychoanalytically by the concept "self," is probably the most fundamental basis for marriage and thereby for the ability of love to last, because through this, boredom, weariness, and the termination of love can be circumvented.

What later became of the expectation held of love shows that it is not really that easy to live with these noble thoughts: the demand made by this ideal plainly *necessitates* divorce, if the partner is not able to fulfill it. Thus the model figure, Caroline Böhmer-Schlegel, only attained peace, happiness, and fulfillment in her third marriage, with Schelling. One finds in *Lucinde* a division of women into two large classes: "the ones who value and honor the senses, nature, themselves, and masculinity," and the others who "have lost this true internal innocence and pay for every pleasure with remorse, leading to bitter insensitivity toward internal disapproval (24)." (One could, by the way, also describe the state after and before successful psychoanalysis in the same way, although the description would be more poetical than is usual.) Men must learn true love from these women of the "good" class— from the liberated, natural, never prudish, but also not shameless women, each of whom "already contains love completely within herself," but each "in a totally different and totally personal way, as personal and as different as their uniquely characteristic way of being (23)." True love is not the usual relationship of "crudeness and vulgarity" between man and woman—men are already familiar with this—but the relationship that contains everything: "friendship, a beautiful association, sensuality, and also passion." Nonetheless, not every man can learn everything from every woman. Julius says to Lucinde, "Many would understand me better than I understand myself, but only one would understand me completely, and you are that one. (25).''

9. Jealousy as Romantic

In this environment of German idealism, which allowed Germany to emerge from its backwardness in relation to the rest of Europe for the first time since the Reformation, the woman is enthusiastically idealized for the first time in centuries. Indeed, she is totally idealized, from head to toe, body and soul— and not only to her advantage, as is later revealed. Julius says, "Let me confess that I do not love only you, I love womanhood itself (24)." And in this there now lurks ancient, eternal, never enthusiastic jealousy, although it is more charming than it was earlier and can be quickly placated. In the chapter "Loyalty and Jest," Lucinde complains that, the day before, Julius spent too much time speaking with Amalie at a social gathering and "forgot her for the entire evening, which was unkind." A calm didactic conversation about jealousy ensues, in which the danger of triangles is treated in a totally different way than it was formerly. Lucinde would like to be reassured that the relationship with Amalie is nothing but "clear, pure friendship." Julius vigorously defends himself: Oh no, how could she even think of attributing such foolishness to him. "It would of course be vulgar to speak with such an attractive girl as if she was a sexless amphibian." On the contrary, he says outright that he "loves" Amalie, but not seriously. He loves her playfully, in jest. "One must actually love all women in jest." Lucinde says, "Julius, I do believe that you are becoming completely foolish," and continues by sarcastically saying that now we again have "nothing more than what the French call gallant and coquettish." In this she, the great teacher of pure sensuality, behaves very thoughtlessly in terms of romantic love, because Julius has arrived at a central point of the theory of art and life subscribed to by his circle of friends and can counter on the spot, "Nothing more, other than that I think it beautiful and witty."

"Wit" here does not mean our more narrow concept of pointed humor. A few pages before the above, Schlegel has his wit appear in the allegorical figure of a beautiful, young, courageous man. (The word has more to do with the modern term for intellect, with *shrewd,* or words such as *curiosity, conceit,* and probably even *lunacy,* which in German are all expressed by compounds with the word *wit.*) Society is "chaos" without this wit; it can only be brought into harmony through wit, "and if one does not joke and flirt with the elements of passion, then it congeals in thick masses and obscures everything." Romanticism, the enthusiastic champion of emotion, of merging and blending together, of desire and dreaming is, on the other hand, the continuation of the Enlightenment as well—and Julius, as far as jealousy is concerned, is essentially a predecessor of Freud, who in an essay in 1922 praises the playful possibilities of socially sanctioned infidelity, that is, flirting, as a healthy and wise arrangement. Freud also would have been in agreement with Julius's stipulation and description: in this matter too, "people must know what they are doing and what they want, and this is rarely the case. In their hands, a refined jest is again immediately transformed into crude seriousness." And Freud—as well as later psychoanalysts—could well agree with the statement in which Julius says that jealousy redounds on the jealous person. Julius says that love—and love is always understood as unity in duality or vice versa—can no more insult than it can dispense charity; everything is natural and self-evident. "Therefore it has to be uncertainty, a lack of love, and infidelity toward oneself. For me happiness is certain, and love is one with fidelity (36)." Julius states this boldly, in a somewhat know-it-all fashion, and very much as a male. For the male-female role reversal had not gone so far that he did not lecture, and she listen.

However, both together go still further; in spite of, or precisely because of, the uniqueness and greatness of the all-encompassing love of one's life, it is possible not only that one can toy with a love outside the relationship, but also that one can be true many times over. Julius and Lucinde speak of their former loves in the section "Desire and Tranquillity." Lucinde: "You still love her and, eternally mine, will also love her eternally. . ." Julius: "I see you leaning on my chest, running your fingers through your Guido's hair . . ." Jealousy and love triangles have never yet been spoken of so calmly, so generously, and so kindly. At the end of the short didactic conversation, the lovers come to an agreement to allow Lucinde a *little* jealousy, since in love "there should be everything, and one thing should strengthen and mitigate, animate and enhance the other." Julius as well is allowed "a small dose of cultivated, refined anger." This is the climate in which the inscrutable Goethe, when he was almost seventy years old, could say to chancellor von Müller, "Jealousy is resentment of an alien elective affinity" (1 March 1819).

The history of the nineteenth century shows that these windows of opportunity were closed again; these ideals were eroded by reality; moreover, they were the business of the elite ("To love with 'romantic irony' is not meant for workers and servant girls" [Luhmann 1982, 175]); and the utopia of the merging together of the man and the woman was at the expense of the latter ("The man loves love, the woman loves the man" [172]). It also shows the avalanche of effects that Freud precipitated, whereas he and his research would have been superfluous in a world in which love were really such a free and generous thing.

Nonetheless, the expectation of "love for love's sake," which is open to an infinity of nuances and associated emotions, creates "a possibility for all talents and situations; it does not unconditionally demand the labor of passion" (Luhmann, 1982, 175). Love becomes marriageable because of this, that is, because love does not restrict the self like an illness, but expands it. It even leads the self completely to itself in the interaction with the other. Love becomes marriageable because a shared separate world is created that changes again and again of its own accord and therefore does not lead to boredom.

That is what remains of this design, even if it is the period after the peak of romanticism until the end of the First World War that appears to us today as especially patriarchal and bourgeois; even if marriages were still entered into for rational and economical reasons; even if there were still prudishness and a double standard; and even if Julius's characterization remained (and remains) apt: "There what the man loves in the woman is only the category; what the woman loves in the man is only the degree of his natural qualities and his bourgeois existence; and both love their children only as their product and their property. There fidelity is a reward and a virtue; and there jealousy also has its proper place. For they feel uncommonly justified in silently believing that there are many others like them, and one is worth about as much as the other as a person, and all together they are not worth terribly much (36)."

10. Does the Church Offer Help Against Jealousy?

To conclude this cultural-historical survey, I would like to deal briefly with the attitude of the church. The citation from Schlegel speaks of equality. Better yet, it speaks of the equal inferiority of all people. On the one hand, the church could subscribe to this, for in its view, "all have sinned and fall short of the glory of God." On the other hand, for the church each individual soul has an infinite value, because God sacrificed his son for their salvation. The result is that in the moral realm a huge spectrum ranges from contempt of mankind and sin on the one hand, to tolerance, love and forgiveness on the other. Within this spectrum, the church as a whole, and its individual representatives in particular, have assumed the most varied positions in the course of centuries.

Where depravity and justice were at issue (in the sense of being embraced by God), sexuality evolved into a central theme—in contrast to what has been transmitted to us about Jesus. It goes without saying that the theme that the church could use as a point of departure by appealing to the Bible was the indissolubility of marriage. However, this came to prevail as the normative conception of the church remarkably late, that is, in the twelfth century, at about the same time as the celibacy of the secular clergy. The involvement of the church in the marriage ceremony is, in general, relatively new. Marriage was seen for a long time as something akin to a contractual arrangement between private parties. Ariès shows (Ariès, Béjin, and Foucault 1982, 192ff.) how the priest's jurisdiction expanded from a mere blessing of the marriage bed in the ninth and tenth centuries, to the marriage ceremony in front of the church doors in the fifteenth and sixteenth centuries, to the shifting of the entire ceremony to the interior of the church in the seventeenth century. The course that this development took in Germany is similar (Weber-Kellermann 1976). Written registration of the marriage became a rigid requirement parallel to the growing importance, even absolute necessity, of the priest. Only in 1563, at the Council of Trent, did it become canon law that a marriage was valid only when it was contracted before a priest in the presence of two witnesses. Also in the Tridentine era, marriage was finally declared a sacrament, for which there is no basis in the Bible. The seeds of this were present in church tradition since the time of Augustine. As is well known, Luther rejected this interpretation. In any case, the church increasingly came to stand for order and public control and was no longer simply one authority that attended upon a private proceeding with its blessing.

The general development of its relationship to marriage and sexuality shows that the church's need to impose as much control as possible on this most dangerous of all instinctual behaviors is becoming ever stronger. The dependence of humanity on nature is reflected most clearly in the sex drive; from a theological perspective, it reflects that humanity has fallen to the world.

The remembrance that God himself created humans in *his* image pales in view of the competition between love of God and human love. The entire burden of ambivalence subsequently descends upon the image of the woman: on the one hand, in each individual life she can be "virgin, mother, queen," even a "goddess," like Mary; on the other hand, she can be a witch with incalculable possibilities of forbidden sexuality (cf. Dross 1978), like Eve, who has been fixed in the role of man's seducer. Although men have at all times committed adultery much more often than women, the guilt for it has been ascribed to women, when one draws the bottom line. This is the paradigmatic example of a projection: one's part in one's own sexuality, which is condemned by one's conscience, is shifted to another—I accuse, therefore I am not guilty.

Hedges of mistrust were planted closer and closer together for the purpose of keeping sexuality out, even in marriage. Finally, in the nineteenth century, Catholic moral theologians designated sexual intercourse as "evil in itself" (*in se malum*), just like, for example, the taking of human life. These actions can become good only under very specific circumstances: sexual intercourse within marriage, but only when it is directed toward creating new life; the taking of human life in the case of a just war or as punishment of a criminal. Voluntary masturbation, birth control, and all extramarital sexual intercourse, as well as (that too, at least!) the outright taking of innocent life, remained "once and for all time, that is, intrinsically evil" (*intrinsece malum*) (Gründel 1977, 94–95).

Of course such a negative, harsh, and pessimistic judgment of sexuality by the beloved and feared authority of the church caused severe conflicts for many people, especially since in the preceding century the expectation of personal happiness was conversely ever more firmly tied to marriage. An anemic Protestant church, which was closely tied to the bourgeois-patriarchal society that was establishing itself, pointed in the same direction as the Catholic church, although not as sharply and clearly, that is, toward the suppression of sexuality or allowing it as a necessary evil under specific conditions. These tendencies continue to exert an impact up to the present time in spite of all the efforts of courageous and progressive theologians of both confessions. In this context jealousy must appear to be an extremely understandable emotion, protected by the most important legal claims.

To be sure, in a Catholic moral-theological dictionary of the nineteenth century (*Wetzer und Weltes Kirchenlexikon* 1886), I find the rejection of unfounded jealousy, because it is unworthy of a trusting marriage and insulting to the partner. However, if on the basis of tradition sexuality is to be feared to such an extent, how is one then to distinguish between good sexuality within marriage and evil sexuality outside marriage? According to the dictionary, one may no longer really speak of jealousy in the case of proven infidelity. This is a naive observation in terms of the psychology of those who are within the bosom of the church. And naturally God's jealousy is something completely different.

In any case, the church has provided little assistance for what after all would seem to be provided for in its teaching: for forgiveness, turning one's life around, beginning anew, but above all for the transformation of *both* participants. The rejection of the physical was so strong in both churches until well into the present century that divorce in the case of infidelity, as well as spontaneous murder because of jealousy and wounded honor, was tolerated, if not plainly permitted—again, of course, only for men. To be sure, duels had to be secretly arranged, like the one in Fontane's *Effi Briest* (1894–95), where the lover is killed by Effi's husband, although the affair took place years in the past and, in the meantime, he himself has come to view his marriage as cheerful and worth living, even as having actually just *become* good. However, a second from a good family could always be found to go along; the victor (and murderer) came out of it more or less unscathed and could peacefully continue to pursue his career, even in state service—in Fontane's novel, as a jurist. The child of the marriage stayed with him. One must imagine all of this as taking place in a milieu in which a solemn Protestant marriage ceremony was a matter of course. Effi, who is on a trip at the time the affair is discovered, never sees her husband again and sees her child only once after several years have passed; her pastor, perhaps not without compassion, may well have viewed this as the unavoidable consequence of her deed, which she had to take upon herself as repentance. Possible changes in the direction of a less rigid sexual morality can at most be surmised from the author's apparent emotional partisanship for his main character.

On the Catholic side, there is one example (as far as I know, unique) of a forgiving resolution of the ancient jealousy conflict that preoccupied the Spaniards so greatly: *Divine Words* (1920) by Ramón del Valle-Inclán (1866–1936), an author who is not very well known in Germany. He belonged to the "generation of 1898," named for the year in which Spain finally lost the last of its overseas possessions—Cuba. He was, even in his external appearance and in his nobility, goodness, and craziness, a knight of the same melancholy demeanor as Don Quixote. His play could not succeed as anything other than a tragicomedy. It is set in a village among simple people. A *hidalgo* (a member of the minor nobility) could not have afforded to do, even in the nineteenth century, and in spite of all the criticism that Valle-Inclán and his friends levelled against the backwardness, the false pride, and the inner laziness of their compatriots, what a simple sexton does.

His wife deceived him with a traveling mountebank, and when he leaves her, the people, yelling with enthusiasm, bring her naked on a hay wagon to the front of the church in which her husband is serving. The peasants hope to be allowed to attend a spectacular punishment. Instead of that, the sexton, previously stylized as a grotesque, cowardly, narrow-minded, but also pious man, takes his wife by the hand and leads her into the church in which he married her years ago. He bewilders the people, who already are holding stones, with the biblical saying—spoken in Latin—about the first stone being thrown by him who is without sin. Although the peasants do not understand the sentence, they are moved by the "mysterious liturgical magic" of the words; everything that Christianity has preached about forgiveness and meekness throughout the centuries—and how often was it only preached, and not practiced!—suddenly becomes effective. They disperse and drop the stones as in the Bible.

There is nothing comparable to point to in the Protestant camp. However, one can surmise how many rooms there once were in the house of the evangelical church and how free and human its representatives were permitted to be without falling victim to official ostracism, if one reads Schleiermacher's manual for "noble ladies"—which will be the optimistic conclusion of this chapter. It was written between 1796 and 1798 and imaginatively recast the Ten Commandments. To be sure, it was not really well known. It first appeared in the "Fragments" of the journal *Athenäum*, and was reprinted only in 1870 in Dilthey's great biography of Schleiermacher. Schleiermacher was highly esteemed as a university theologian and was valued and beloved as the pastor of the Church of the Holy Trinity in Berlin. His influence on nineteenth- and twentieth-century theology was very great, and in spite of this—would a contemporary urban clergyman be able to write in this way about women and love? In any case, the theses that are postulated below show how right we are in viewing "romantic love" as the basis of our contemporary marital and feminine ideal.

"The Ten Commandments"

1. You shall have no other beloved beside him; but you shall be able to be a friend, without toying with the suggestion of love, without flirting, without worshipping.

2. You shall not make for yourself any ideal—neither the ideal of a heavenly angel, nor that of a hero from a poem or novel, nor that of one who is created out of one's own dreams or fantasies; rather you shall love a man as he is. For she, Nature, your mistress, is a strict goddess, who avenges the fanatical ecstasy of girls and of women unto the third and fourth generation of the emotions.

3. You shall not misuse even the least of love's sacred relics; for the one who desecrates her affection and surrenders herself for the sake of gifts and offerings, or only to be a mother in peace and quiet, will lose her tender feeling.

4. Remember the sabbath of your heart, that you celebrate it, and when they embrace you, make yourself available or be damned.

5. Honor the individuality and the idiosyncracy of your children, so that they may be well and live vigorously upon the earth.

6. You shall not intentionally arouse.

7. You shall not enter into a marriage that must be broken.

8. You shall not want to be loved where you do not love.

9. You shall not bear false witness for men; you shall not gloss over their barbarity with words and deeds.

10. Covet men's education, art, wisdom, and honor.

If one tones down certain pomposities in this text; if one eliminates the parallels to the Decalogue which impose several linguistic mannerisms, so that the text approaches contemporary speech; and if one concentrates on what is said about women, men, and the granting of rights—have we, almost two hundred years later, really made any progress?

PART THREE:
PSYCHOLOGICAL THEORIES

15

FREUD'S ESSAY OF 1922

1. Authors before Freud: Gesell and Friedmann

Emotions have their own history, even in terms of the scientific attitude toward them. The expansion of medical knowledge and theories in the nineteenth century naturally affected psychiatry as well. It is obvious that the interest of physicians was primarily directed toward pathological jealousy, that is, the jealousy delusion, which was initially included as part of the research into paranoia. Very early on, special attention was given to the relationship between alcoholism and jealousy (see the relevant chapters in Lagache [1947] 1982, Vaukhonen 1968, Germano 1960, and Jaspers's essay of 1910 for historical perceptions). These studies give one the impression of great practical experience, but at the same time of theoretical uncertainty and therapeutic helplessness. It remains unclear what actually happened with pathological jealous individuals when they were hospitalized, primarily for their family members' and their own protection, in a psychiatric institution.

The first questionnaire-based study of the general phenomenon of jealousy that I know of was written by the American Arnold L. Gesell (1906). The questionnaire was answered by approximately one thousand people (without a medical objective being set) and was distributed in the years 1905–6.

Questions were asked relating to the following themes: (1) the role that envy and jealousy played in your life; (2) envy and jealousy, as you see them in others; (3) a description of the condition of jealousy as you now know it, based on self-observation (an introspective description); (4) a description of the "jealous" temperament. The author classified and worked up the answers, which were often long and detailed. His most important conclusions follow: Since in the animal kingdom jealousy is closely connected to the basic instincts of feeding, mating, and breeding and raising progeny, it appears very early in human history. Jealousy is a "self-feeling," whose content is determined not only by instinctive reality but also by the influences of the social environment. It evolves into complex and refined forms parallel to the differentiation of the consciousness of the self. The jealousy of children is mostly open, aggressive, and instinct-driven, whereas from puberty on, melancholy and depression frequently accompany it. Jealousy is perhaps the most painful of all human emotions. Gesell has nothing to say about the therapy for jealousy in adults. The best upbringing is "probably indirect and prophylactic" and consists in fostering a healthy sense of personality.

The description of the emotion in this long, precise, and vividly written study shows how little people have changed in terms of their psychic and social reactions, in spite of the enormous technical, scientific, and political changes of the last hundred years. Gesell is not interested in showing a way out of jealousy. He only wants to describe it. He does not cite Freud, and one could hardly expect him to do so in 1906.

The first German work about the psychology of jealousy was written by the psychiatrist M. Friedmann (1911)—to our modern eyes, it is a long-winded, involuted, even if sympathetic work, in which deliberations on passion, affects, politics, research results from the field of zoology, interpretations of cultural history, and medical and personal experience are laboriously interwoven without any clear result. Friedmann considers jealousy in the true sense to be possible only between rivals of equal rank. If "a black man in North America" has a relationship with a white woman; if "a genteel woman engages in sexual activity with her coachman"; then the husband can feel no jealousy, but at best "a thirst for revenge" or "contempt" or "bitterly angry" enmity. The author observes that one "can even continue to like" the person toward whom jealousy is directed, but also "can become the person's deadly enemy." In connection with the equality of the competitor, Friedmann comes upon something that he calls the "duplication of the subject"—all of which are tentative efforts in an area that later becomes clear through psychoanalysis. His definition of jealousy is, "jealousy is the emotion or the affect that arises with competition, or even only with another's participation on a field of action in which emotion is strongly emphasized, and it is expressed as a feeling of painful agitation, which is connected with the impulse to suppress the competitor" (17). Aside from the fact that the meaning of such a sentence is revealed at the earliest upon a second reading, nothing in it is incorrect. But there is something missing: for example, the relation to the partner, to one's own life history, or the reason for the "painfulness."

In the concluding summary of his work, the author names two remedies for this "affect that is so extraordinarily widespread, and that is so generally dangerous": first, the diminution of real oppositions of interests (legislation, social assistance, care provided by professional cooperatives), and second, self-knowledge that is fostered by appropriate pedagogy. It is gratifying and touching to see how, three years before the outbreak of the First World War, a German professor of psychiatry reminds one that, "in cultivating ambition and a feeling for national greatness, the impulses of jealousy will also become active." The extent to which Freudian terminology has, in the meantime, penetrated our linguistic consciousness, is shown when Friedmann calls one of the two main characteristics of the affect "the prevalence of strong suppression impulses" (the other characteristic is the "continued lack of peace, as well as the impossibility of bringing the entire battle to a conclusion"): it is not one's forbidden impulses that should be suppressed, but the opponent!

2. "Some Neurotic Mechanisms in Jealousy, Paranoia, and Homosexuality"

I have presented Friedmann's book, which is hard to get hold of, in some detail in order to make clear to what extent Freud's brilliant discoveries helped to shed light on and liberate even this field. At the same time, Friedmann's study sheds light on the distance that existed at that time between official psychiatry and psychoanalysis (this has not changed very much up to the present time): in 1911 Friedmann could have long known of Freud, but he makes not a single mention of him. Not even Jaspers mentions him, a year earlier.

As we see it now, however, with a single stroke in a ten-page essay Freud pushes aside the fog in which his predecessors and colleagues had lost their way. Actually only two and one-half pages are *exclusively* devoted to jealousy. The title of this brief essay, which was written in 1921 and first appeared in 1922 in the *Internationale Zeitschrift für Psychoanalyse,* points to the context in which Freud sees jealousy: paranoia and homosexuality. The latter, in connection with jealousy, that is, the classical expression of passionate love for the other sex, is certainly the more confusing component. Let us, however, allow Freud to speak for himself.

Jealousy is one of the emotional states that, much like grief, one may designate as normal. If it appears to be missing in a person's character and behavior, the conclusion is justified that it has succumbed to a strong repression and therefore plays a much greater role in the person's unconscious psychic life. The cases of abnormally intensified jealousy, with which analysis deals, prove to be divided into three levels. The three levels or degrees of jealousy may appropriately be named 1. *competitive* or normal, 2. *projected,* 3. *delusional.*

There is little to say analytically about *normal* jealousy. It is easy to see that it is essentially composed of grief, of pain at the imagined loss of the love object, and of the wound to narcissism to the extent that this may be separated from the other; furthermore, it is composed of hostile feelings toward the preferred rival and of a more or less significant ingredient of self-criticism which wants to make one's own ego responsible for the loss of love. This jealousy is, even though we designate it as normal, in no way completely rational, that is, originating in real associations, in proportion to things as they really are, and entirely governed by the unconscious ego, because it is deeply rooted in the unconscious, continues the earliest impulses of infantile affectivity, and originates in the Oedipus or sibling complex of the first sexual stage. It is nonetheless remarkable that it is experienced bisexually by many people; that is, besides pain for his beloved wife and hatred toward the male rival, what also becomes operative in the husband as reinforcement is sorrow for the unconsciously loved man and hatred toward his wife. I even know of a man who suffered acutely from his attacks of jealousy and, according to what he said, underwent the most severe torments by consciously putting himself in the place of his unfaithful wife. He himself associated the sense of helplessness that he then felt and the images that he found to describe his condition, as if he, like Prometheus, had been sacrificed to the vulture or had been thrown bound into a nest of snakes, with the impact of several homosexual attacks that he had experienced as a boy.

The second level of jealousy, *projected* jealousy, derives in the man as well as the woman from personal infidelity, actually committed in life, or from impulses to commit infidelity that have been repressed. It is an everyday experience that fidelity, particularly the fidelity demanded in marriage, can only be maintained in the face of constant temptations. The person who denies these in himself still feels their pressure so strongly that he gladly enlists an unconscious mechanism for his relief. He attains this kind of relief, which is indeed an exoneration by his own conscience, when he projects his own impulses to infidelity onto the other party to whom he owes fidelity. This strong motive can then make use of perceptual reality, which betrays the same unconscious impulses on the part of the other, and could then justify itself by the consideration that the male or female partner is also probably not much better than oneself.*

Social mores sensibly have taken this general state of affairs into consideration, in that they allow a certain latitude for the married woman's coquetry and the husband's lust for conquest, in the expectation that this will drain the unavoidable inclination to infidelity and render it harmless. Convention stipulates that both parties are not to hold these small steps in the direction of infidelity against each other, and usually obtains the result that the enflamed desire for the alien object is satisfied in a certain return to fidelity toward one's own object. The jealous individual, however, does not want to recognize this convention of tolerance. He does not believe that one can stand still or turn around on the path once taken, or that social "flirting" can also be insurance against actual infidelity. In the treatment of this kind of jealous individual, one must avoid impugning the material reality on which he relies. One can only want to move the jealous individual to evaluate it differently.

Jealousy that has arisen through this kind of projection has, indeed, an almost delusional character. However, it does not withstand analytical work, which reveals the unconscious fantasies of one's own infidelity. The situ-

---

*"Cf. the stanza in Desdemona's song, *Othello,* act 4, scene 3: 'I call'd my love false love; But what said he then? . . . If I court moe women, you'll couch with more men' " (Freud's note; see also below, sec. 10).

ation is worse with the third level of jealousy, that is, jealousy that is actually *delusional*. This also derives from repressed attempts to be unfaithful, but the objects of these fantasies are of the same sex. Delusional jealousy corresponds to dormant homosexuality and rightfully claims its place among the classical forms of paranoia. As an attempt at defense against an excessively strong homosexual impulse, it would be paraphrased by the formula: *I* certainly do not love him, *she* loves him. In a case of jealousy paranoia, one should be prepared to find all three levels of jealousy, and never only the third (195–98)

To begin with, Freud counts jealousy among the emotional states—and in doing so he makes it parallel to grief—"that one may designate as normal." Therefore, in a way characteristic of him, the pressure of "you may not," "you shall not" or "you must" is not applicable. The jealousy of each person is simply a fact. (It should also be mentioned that Freud was sixty five years old at the time this essay was written, that twenty six years had passed since the publication of his *Studies on Hysteria,* which is generally thought of as the beginning of analytic research, and that twenty five years had passed since the discovery of what was later called the Oedipus complex.) Correspondingly, if jealousy is not present, one may draw the conclusion that it is repressed and "therefore plays a much greater role in the person's unconscious psychic life." In this, Freud obviously proceeded from psychic and social states that he had before him, as well as from his own history and psychic disposition. During the time he was engaged, he himself was extremely jealous. Even though it is known that Freud was a very great authority figure to his disciples and successors, it is still remarkable that not until almost thirty years later did a psychoanalyst give more careful consideration to the absence of jealousy (Marcuse 1950) than Freud.

One of Freud's basic assumptions is that there is an unconscious, which is kept from consciousness by repression. A further discovery is that psychic phenomena (and also disturbances) are rooted in childhood. In 1921 Freud saw no further cause to defend this or elaborate it. Therefore, one simply reads that jealousy "is deeply rooted in the unconscious," that it "continues the earliest impulses of infantile affectivity," and that it originates "in the Oedipus or sibling complex of the first sexual stage." With this the triangular nature of jealousy is specified: just as on the one hand the child "competes" with one parent for the love of the other, on the other hand the siblings compete for love, attention, preferential treatment from the parents, even perhaps for an exclusive relationship to the parents. In revitalized form, this is also the shape it takes with the adult engaged in love conflicts. One thereby makes the assumption that, the better the experiences of the child were, the more affectionately the parents have helped the child overcome the conflicts of the early years, the better the child will then be able to deal with jealousy as well. Nonetheless, the child will not get away without experiencing jealousy.

However this refers only to "normal" jealousy, which is composed of (1) pain at the imagined loss of the beloved person (the "love object" in Freud's language); (2) the wound to narcissism, "to the extent that this may be separated from the other," that is, the sense of injury felt by the rejected person who has suffered a blow to the very core of his or her ego; (3) hostile feelings toward the rival; and (4) self-criticism, which is related to the role played by one's own ego in the loss.

What is missing here is aggressiveness toward the "object," as Freud with impersonal coolness termed the loved individual. There are probably various reasons for this: in the first place, aggression toward the beloved, whether male or female, does not in fact regularly occur in "normal" jealousy, but on the other hand the other four characteristics always do. Perhaps a question mark would be appropriate even for self-criticism; but the presence of this regulative factor is just that which may be a sign of normality, consequently making possible the overcoming, working through, and integration of the agonizing state without outside assistance. In the second place, "love" for Freud is always ambivalent. Hate is always also contained in what we are accustomed to call love. Indeed, one of the functions of love is to render hatred harmless. At the same time, love alone is an unrealistic abstraction. And in the third place, it is characteristic for Freud that he primarily works on the intrapsychic conflict. Indeed, "conflict" for him is always only the opposition of internal demands—an important starting point for later criticism of psychoanalysis. In connection with "normal" jealousy, the mention of hatred toward the beloved person would perhaps deal too much with an external conflict and with the participation of the other in one's own suffering, which already appears to have been mentioned sufficiently in the "pain at the loss."

An additional point that Freud advances somewhat hesitantly, and as being applicable only for "some individuals," is the bisexual component; only here, not as a regular manifestation, does "hatred toward the wife" appear (in the husband). Very early on, Freud introduced the concept of bisexuality into psychoanalysis under the influence of his friend, Wilhelm Fliess, whom he truly loved passionately, although not sexually, for a time during middle age. In part, this conception has biological foundations (convincingly, the man's nipples). For jealousy, this signifies that just "some individuals" experience, in addition to the usual feelings, their opposites as well, therefore sorrow for the unconsciously loved man and hatred for the partner who deprives them of the possible love object. Understanding such feelings is, to be sure, only possible through analytic interpretation.

Freud distinguishes a second type of jealousy from "normal or competitive jealousy"—that of "projected jealousy." Projection is an extraordinarily important concept for psychoanalysis (and upon close examination is correspondingly complicated and can be used in many different ways). For the purposes of this book, it is sufficient to keep in mind what is understood here by projection: several rejected emotions, characteristics, and desires are transposed to the outside, "projected" as onto a screen. The individual drive to infidelity is projected, by both men and women. Projection can feed on other relationships experienced in reality, but also on repressed desires or fantasies. The formula, so clear for Freud that he does not even mention it, is, It is not I who am unfaithful, it is she or he. Individuals on this level of jealousy do not completely deny their desires, but are more likely to be inclined to make use of the formula, It may be that I too would like to be unfaithful, but in my case it is something different.

According to Freud, it is easier to lay the blame for infidelity at the other person's door and to feel injured by him or her, than to admit it in oneself and to work through it. In order to be able to do that, one would have to be aware of the fact that it is difficult for *every* person to keep the promise to be faithful (we ascertain, perhaps in some amazement, the proximity between the atheist Freud and Jesus, who considered adultery in one's heart a real guilt, just as he protected the adulterer from punishment because *no one* is without guilt).

Freud then briefly deals with the sensible social rule of allowing both married men and women a certain latitude for "flirtations," in which the "small steps in the direction of infidelity" usually lead back to the partner and in which the desires that others have awakened are satisfied "in a certain return to fidelity toward one's own object (197)." Precisely for jealous, projecting individuals, it is difficult to come to terms with this conventional tolerance. Since they basically are afraid of their own impulses, they cannot accept that this license, this "game," can also be insurance against actual infidelity. They therefore see, in unrealistic exaggeration, something that is actually there—the desires that *all* people have for multilateral relationships. Freud calls this second level "almost delusional," but it is not impervious to analytical treatment.

In contrast, the situation of the third and most severe variety of jealousy, really delusional jealousy, is essentially worse. For here the projection of infidelity has derived not from hetero- but from homosexual desires. Because of the great psychic and social danger that the admission of homosexuality would entail, Freud considers jealousy paranoia to be analytically untreatable, even if it can be understood and interpreted. The defense mechanism is expressed as "*I* certainly do not love him, *she* loves him." (To clarify, I of course love *her*.) It is significant that Freud here uses only the masculine version as an example. The feminine version is naturally just as conceivable. Freud additionally points to the fact that all levels of the emotion are always to be found in jealousy paranoia, and never solely the homosexually projecting level.

Jealousy delusion is a severe psychiatric illness, which in its acute stages can totally disable afflicted individuals and make them a real danger to others as well as to themselves. It rarely surfaces in marriage counseling. Nonetheless, the boundaries are unclear, and I would almost prefer to turn Freud's concluding statement around: in each and every case of jealousy that comes up in counseling—and many of these cases nonetheless must be counted as "normal" jealousy, even if they are acutely painful—all three levels can be observed.

3. A Brief Glance at the Freudian Method as It Applies to Jealousy

Who, according to Freud, would be especially disposed to jealousy? People who themselves were unfaithful or would like to be unfaithful, as well as people with strong but repressed homosexual impulses. With the aid of jealousy, therefore, both types resist their own escape from a relationship that, once entered into, they established as the norm. It is characteristic of Freud that he ignores all other aspects. His question is primarily, What am I do with myself? Other questions are not totally excluded, but play a subordinate role, questions like, What am I doing with the others? What are the others doing with me? What are we doing with each other? Freud has often been reproached because of this limitation—unjustifiably, it seems to me. Even a person with Freud's enormous energy and imagination is not omnipotent. Without the power of this one-sidedness, the foundations of psychoanalysis would certainly have not been laid with the clarity that made possible the disengagement from other positions and, consequently, further work on building a new structure. In spite of that, and especially as a marriage counselor, it is important to keep in mind the deficiency of the Freudian conception.

I have previously mentioned the therapeutic importence of earlier authors. In their works, it seems as if only reason actually helps—and every jealous individual knows how powerless reason is. Or one must wait until the disturbance, the aggression, and the insanity stop "of their own accord." In Freud the situation is different. At the time of the essay on jealousy (1922), psychoanalytical treatment was already a tested and widely deployed method of treatment, which was crowned by success in numerous cases. The basis of this complicated theory is a very simple insight: understanding cures. And this means not only understanding oneself, but also being understood (by the analyst), as well as understanding others. What is not understandable, the confusion, is to be transposed into what is clear and simple—an "enlightening" process in the literal sense. It is of course unimaginable without a lasting fascination with the irrational. Freud's writings are imbued with an unceasing delight in the unconscious, with a constant amazement at, indeed one could even say with a kind of veneration of, the world deep within. Perhaps this is connected to the fact that moral condemnation plays no role in his work. (His letters, however, show that he was completely capable of moral condemnation in his personal life.)

What Freud occasionally called his "cure" refers to the relation between two people, the patient and the doctor, between whom nothing more occurs "than that they speak with each other" (Freud 1926, 213). During Freud's time, this conversation still took place for an hour each day, therefore a considerable time commitment (however, his analyses were as a rule much shorter than those today). "One can posit the goal of treatment as bringing about the most extensive ego integration and reinforcement by the elimination of resistance mechanisms and the examination of repression mechanisms on the part of the patient, to spare him the psychic effort for internal conflicts, and to make him as far as possible capable of accomplishment and enjoyment" (Freud 1923a, 226). With reference to jealousy, this would mean that one does not concern oneself directly with jealousy, but rather with the person's total structure. One thereby reveals what is repressed, for example projections, by means of uncontrolled random thoughts (the basic rule of "free association") and dreams. The analyst absorbs and interprets these with "evenly suspended attention," which is as much as possible unimpeded by his or her own unconscious.

"The psychoanalytic procedure is distinguished from all suggestive, persuasive, and similar procedures in that it does not want to suppress by authority any psychic phenomenon within the patient (1923a, 226)," that is, one does not persuade, advise, or educate, but instead one permits everything. Naturally, the influence of the analyst cannot be completely avoided. This influence, however, is primarily used to support patients in the work of healing which they themselves must accomplish, in that they overcome resistance to therapy that reveals, that is, they actually overcome their resistance to self-knowledge. In this working process, the relationship to the physician plays an eminently important role. The suffering experienced at the hands of people from early childhood, which is the basis of the disturbance, of jealously in our case, is revived in the person of the physician and reintroduced in a gentle process of a more realistic working through, in accordance with the principle of "remembering, repeating, and working through" (Freud 1914a). Consequently, "the elimination of the painful symptoms is not the goal to which one aspires, but follows . . . virtually as a kind of icing on the cake (1923a, 226–27)."

As we have learned, Freud does not view normal jealousy as a symptom in the clinical sense. In terms of the abnormal forms of jealousy, which to be sure often appear without a rational external cause, the afflicted individual would perhaps no longer be at all jealous upon completion of analysis, therefore "after the phenomenon has been fathomed and after the enduring transformation of the conditions for its emergence (ibid.)." Or jealousy would be reduced to normal proportions. The patient's ego is strengthened by the "cure" and has again become capable of accomplishment and enjoyment because of it: to express it more precisely perhaps, has become capable of work and love. The person who is cured will thereby be in the position of coping with normal jealousy him- or herself, if it should persist or reappear. Freud says nothing about this coping. However, each of us is familiar with realistic possibilities of coming to terms with jealousy, which no one will categorize as neurotic or abnormal. Such solutions are, for example, to endure the frustration for a time, to forgive, to win the partner anew, but naturally also to distance oneself, even to separate forever.

Othello is considered the classical drama of jealousy in world literature. I shall try to apply Freud's categories from 1922 to this drama, at the same time taking into account where they may not (yet) be adequate.

4. *Othello* as an Example

William Shakespeare's *Tragedy of Othello, the Moor of Venice* premiered in 1604, two years after *Hamlet,* one year before *King Lear.* The drama was an immediate great public success. The first printing appeared in 1622. The basic story can be told in few words.

Sergeant Iago suggests to Othello, a noble and highly esteemed black general of the Republic of Venice, that his young wife Desdemona is deceiving him with Lieutenant Cassio. Iago's motive for the accusation is revenge: Cassio has been promoted ahead of him. By cunning intrigues, Iago arranges an unbroken chain of clues that make Othello's jealousy appear to be justified. Desdemona's lost handkerchief, her husband's first gift, plays an important role in this. Othello smothers his wife. When he learns that she is innocent, he stabs himself to death.

5. Shakespeare's Source and Its Transformation

The story as just outlined is obviously the roughest possible sketch. Shakespeare took the story from an Italian novella (by Giovanni Battista Giraldo Cinthio, 1566), and even the transformation of the source is instructive for our purposes. The hero is a Moor in the Venetian version, therefore an Other, but Iago's motive for spurring him on to jealousy is spurned love: Iago himself is rejected by Desdemona and therefore assumes that a captain who, however, has not been shown preference by Othello is her lover. It is therefore Iago who, in the first place, is jealous in the most direct and classically oedipal sense: jealous of a married couple, whose fidelity he denies in inventing a brother rival. Iago is also a scoundrel in the source: he not only wants to kill the captain, but since he cannot have Desdemona, he does not want the Moor to have her either—she too must die.

Everything is more direct and less complicated than it is in Shakespeare: the Moor and Iago kill the woman together, with a sand-filled stocking—phallic aggression can hardly be symbolized more clearly. The actual perpetrator is Iago, but the Moor is present and in agreement. To cover up the murder, the house is destroyed. Subsequently, the Moor is so troubled that he has a falling out with Iago. Court proceedings, which have been set in motion by intrigues, lead to the banishment of the Moor, who is killed by Desdemona's family. Finally, Iago is also arrested and dies under torture. The Cassio figure survives an attack on his life, just as he does in Shakespeare.

6. Iago: Othello's Alter Ego, the Motivator, and Judge of Human Souls

Shakespeare's tragedy is infinitely richer than Cinthio's novella, so rich that I must limit myself to a discussion of a few psychic and relational stimuli.

The increased number of characters and their clear characterization make possible a more complicated plot. The lover of the Moor's wife, in Cinthio Iago, is split up into three characters. Iago himself no longer loves her, but hates her. The motif of preferential treatment for promotion is the invention that is uniquely Shakespeare's own. The second character that has been split off from Iago is the somewhat stupid Roderigo, who is fervently in love with Desdemona. The third character in this alliance, the favored Cassio, is a friend of Desdemona's family. Othello "loves him," but Cassio has no designs on his wife. All his thoughts and wishes in the drama are concentrated on regaining Othello's favor, which he squandered in a drunken quarrel. Brabantio, Desdemona's father, plays a further important secondary role. Othello was his friend but abducted his daughter. Desdemona also is given a character that functions as an alter ego, her lady's maid and intimate Emilia, who is Iago's wife.

Two phenomena stick all too clearly in every reader's memory: first of all, Othello's jealousy, which is generated only by false proofs and irresistibly leads to the murder of his innocent young wife whom he loves above all things and who loves him above all things—an induced jealousy delirium, a delusion. Just as in a genuine psychosis, Othello incorrectly evaluates real phenomena and orders them within a system that makes murder appear to be the only and, above all, the just solution. But this development is not generated from within him; rather he is forced into it by another person whose goal it is to generate the delusion in him—something that in this form is hardly imaginable in reality, even though what is often at issue in psychoses is "driving the other crazy" (cf. Searles 1959).

The tragedy's second unforgettable characteristic is the figure of Iago, the motivator of the plot, a true devil (*diabolos* means the one who "throws things into confusion") in whom one seeks in vain for sympathetic traits. He defines himself in his first self-characterization as a persiflage of God who says, "I am who I am" (Exod. 3:14). Iago, driven by rage and hurt, acknowledges his intention of causing the Moor's ruin by means of all possible deceptions and pretenses, because he has been denied promotion, and concludes with the words, "I am not what I am."

Iago stands within the baroque tradition of theatrical scoundrels. This type appears fairly often in Shakespeare, and it is usually easy to defend oneself internally against his power. A monstrosity such as Edmund in *King Lear* barely moves us. Iago, on the contrary, fascinates in spite of all the "improbability" of such an unambiguously evil character. However, what fascinates is his relationship to Othello. After thinking about the centuries-long impact of the drama, I must agree with the psychoanalyst Martin Wangh (1950): "The drama's magic consists in its hidden content, which speaks directly to each spectator's unconscious." Wangh designates this hidden content as "Iago's tragedy," with which I will deal extensively below. Here I would like to note only that I consider it an exaggeration to represent *Othello* as the tragedy of Iago, of all people. In order to feel that a character is tragic, I must be able to empathize with his or her irresoluble conflict, suffering with the character. I can do this with Othello. With Iago, on the contrary, I cannot suffer; he is simply too base.

One can, however, say that Othello decides Iago's tragedy. What is dramatic about the play derives from the fact that Iago represents a darker side of Othello, a side that is split off from him—using Jung's terminology, he is his shadow. And he is certainly also "every spectator's" shadow, as Wangh suggests. Iago is at the same time the alter ego of all other characters, because he moves them out of themselves. For he is, as Othello says, a good judge of human nature, a person who "knows all qualities, with a learned spirit, of human dealings" (3.3). In this one may understand him as a kind of negative image of a psychoanalyst: he manipulates empathy and knowledge of other people's souls in order to get others to accept his values. Instead of "ego integration and reinforcement," as we read in Freud, he pursues the ego's destruction. He claims to be fostering the "capacity for accomplishment and enjoyment" in Othello, who trusts him and again and again calls him "honest." But instead Iago's goal is to destroy this capacity for accomplishment and enjoyment. Othello's resistance is overrun. Nonetheless, Iago can justifiably state at the conclusion, "I told him what I thought; and told no more / Than what he found himself was apt and true"—a very apt definition for the interpretative work of a psychoanalyst. Othello's "desire" that Desdemona actually be unfaithful and his own internal compulsion to kill her cannot be overlooked, especially in the murder scene (5.2).

7. Othello's Jealousy: "Competitive or Normal"

For the time being I will stay with Otheollo's jealousy. It very obviously contains the first level of jealousy identified by Freud, who calls it "competitive or normal.'' Nowhere in world literature has the ''grief [and] pain at the imagined loss of the love object'' been so movingly expressed as in Othello's words. He, a rough commander, falls as in a fit when he finds himself convinced by Iago of Desdemona's infidelity (4.1). His moving desperation is expressed poetically: ''O thou weed, / Who art so lovely fair, and smell'st so sweet / That the sense aches at thee,—would thou hadst ne'er been born!'' (4.2). There is certainly no more tender, loving, and desperate murder in world literature than that of Desdemona (without any suggestion of perverse motives!). He kisses the sleeping woman three times while weeping, before he awakens her to death. When he has realized his injustice, run through with his own sword, he falls over her body with the words, ''I kiss'd thee ere I kill'd thee: no way but this, / Killing myself, to die upon a kiss.''

To be sure, the unification of lovers in death is something that goes far beyond Freud's oedipal rationality and can only be explained psychoanalytically by later studies on biangular relationships, merging, and symbiosis.

The Wound to Narcissism

The wound to narcissism, which Freud designates as one part of jealousy, is also all too clearly present in Othello. Shakespeare's ingenious stroke of choosing a Moor as the model of jealousy, someone ''who is not like us,'' who is a stranger, although highly esteemed, in a powerful and firmly established social order, lays the groundwork for an insecure self-image. Othello, although a commander and a friend of Desdemona's father, Brabantio, did not dare to court the noble girl in the usual way, and Brabantio's horror when he discovers the secret wedding confirms what Othello already knew: he and Desdemona are a couple too dissimilar to find normal recognition. The black-white dialectic imbues the entire drama, and undisguised racist rejection is expressed in several scenes. Othello, moreover, has unambiguously negroid features and not only Moorish or North African ones. Right at the beginning he is called ''thick-lips'' by Roderigo. In act 1, scene 2, Brabantio complains that it is unbelievable that his delicate daughter, who rejected the land's wealthy young men, should of all things have fled ''to the sooty bosom of such a thing.''

Othello himself is also amazed at this: in his calm and impressive self-characterization, which forms such a contrast to the tirades of hate previously hurled by Iago, he tells how his love for the beautiful white girl (''fair'' was the time's ideal of beauty) developed. She wanted to hear over and over again the stories of his wild and difficult life. Her sympathy seems to him to be ''. . . in faith, 'twas strange, 'twas passing strange; 'Twas pitiful, 'twas wondrous pitiful!'' (1.3). In this great scene, when the entire senate of Venice has been summoned to act as judge, Desdemona shows herself to be a determined young woman who stands by her choice of a man before the Doge himself, without fear and with all the decorum of her upbringing, in opposition to her widowed father to whom she was everything. Brabantio's jealous competitive behavior toward Othello—almost like that of a lover, who is cut out by another—shows us an aspect of the relationship between parents and children that seldom occupied Freud. Desdemona, on the other hand, introduces the example of a mature oedipal solution: she emphasizes that she will continue to recognize her duties toward her father,

> . . .but here's my husband,
> And so much duty as my mother show'd
> To you, preferring you before her father,
> So much I challenge that I may profess
> Due to the Moor my lord.

She is, therefore, not at all only a delicate "chuck" or "wretch," as Othello calls her, or the "white ewe" that, in Iago's lewd language, "an old black ram is tupping." Rather, Othello would have every reason to trust that she, as Freud says, is "blamelessly faithful."

However, danger and improbability, with which Desdemona's possession by Othello seems to be surrounded, are so great that doubt and self-doubt are lurking in the background at every moment. Iago therefore has an easy time convincing Othello. The person who himself confronts his good fortune as something unbelievable—that person's faith can be easily shaken. Othello does not have the feeling that he may claim a right; a miracle has happened to him. The literally "improbable" beauty that has come to him has revalorized his blackness and his condition of being an outsider. It has in his eyes certainly offset it. Loss signifies a wound to the core. When Othello loses Desdemona, he simultaneously loses an indispensable part of himself.

Hostile Feelings, Self-Criticism

The "hostile feelings toward the preferred rival," who Othello thinks is Cassio, are too obvious to require documentation with quotations. The "more or less significant ingredient of self-criticism which wants to make one's own ego responsible for the loss of love" results from Othello's personal insecurity, shown above. He calls himself too old, not adroit or gregarious enough, and says "youthful drives" have died out in him—he should not have married. It is also probable that he, who is described even by Iago as a "constant, noble, loving nature," has a bad conscience because he took his friend's daughter. It is also probable that his readiness to be jealous, which has a strong masochistic aspect, corresponds to a need for punishment.

Bisexuality

The bisexual components noted by Freud, which "some people" exhibit, are not missing in Othello. Cassio, who is depicted as very attractive, educated, and handsome, was so dear to him that he preferred him to his sergeant Iago, who would have been entitled to promotion because of long service. Therefore, he will lose both wife and friend should Iago's projections of infidelity be borne out.

Projections of Infidelity

So much for Freud's first level of jealousy. We can only surmise the presence of the second level in Othello, that is, projected jealousy, which derives from one's own impulses to infidelity. It is, of course, the task of the patient and the analyst to uncover and interpret these impulses in actual cases of jealousy as well. Usually they are at first consciously denied.

A man, experienced in the art of war and no longer young, may well have had experiences with women, and *one* motive for Iago's revenge is said to be that Othello (as well as Cassio) is supposed to have had a sexual relationship with Iago's wife. Iago himself says, however, that he only knows this as rumor. This motive seems remarkably weak, something that occurred to Shakespeare incidentally as just another obvious justification for Iago's hatred, which is there anyway. Not the slightest hint of such a relationship is anywhere confirmed by Othello.

Tender fantasies of infidelity are, on the other hand, entertained by Desdemona. She speaks dreamily about the attractiveness of a Venetian relative, in the famous scene when she is being undressed before going to bed, a scene that is surrounded by premonitions of death (4.3). Desdemona is alone with Emilia. She has been beaten by Othello in public, has fallen from her serene and "fair" love, and is helplessly conscious of a crisis. It is here that Shakespeare has Desdemona sing the willow song, which a lady's maid, when she was dying of unhappy love, sang to Desdemona's mother. It is sung here in the context of the intimacy between two women, in a kind of maternal warmth, where social controls fall away with one's clothing, and the ego world loses its power in the face of approaching sleep. This girl's lover "prov'd mad and did forsake her"—thus, as the spectators know, it is an exact parallel to Othello. The song says not only "Let nobody blame him; his scorn I approve," but also "I call'd my love false love; but what said he then? . . . If I court moe women, you'll couch with moe men."

This is the only passage in *Othello* that Freud quotes, and with precise reference to the theme of projected jealousy—projected because of one's own repressed thoughts of infidelity. In terms of the "noble Moor," this would mean Othello either remembers experiences with other women or has felt drives within himself that are not exclusively directed toward Desdemona. Freud writes, "It is an everyday experience that fidelity, particularly the fidelity demanded in marriage, can only be maintained in the face of constant temptations" (1922, 197). Even in the case of Othello, who is so movingly in love, and just married? In the case of the man who would like to die of joy after his sea journey when he again holds his "fair warrior" in his arms? (Desdemona does not wish to be separated from him and remain at home like a "moth of peace"; she follows him to the battlefield, where the drama takes place.) Yes—even in the case of Othello.

Psychoanalysis presumes—always given that the "case" is as serious and dangerous as Othello's—that jealous individuals have two characteristics: first, an especially delicate conscience (a punitive superego) and consequently an unusually great need for justice; and second, "an extraordinary attentiveness to the promptings of the unconscious" (Freud 1922, 198) of the beloved person as well as one's own. The latter are repressed because of this same love of justice, because it would be entirely too painful to be the first to abuse the idealized bond of love. The jealous individual "attains . . . exoneration by his own conscience, when he projects his own impulses to infidelity onto the other party to whom he owes fidelity." With this, equilibrium is created; it alleviates unconscious guilt feelings if it can be assumed—likewise unconsciously—"that the male or female partner is also probably not much better than oneself." And at this place Freud points to Desdemona's song.

Perhaps it is necessary to point out again that *anxiety* makes one aggressive. Neither Desdemona nor Othello is unfaithful. They love each other, as it is expressed in "normal" language, without reservation and wholeheartedly. Admitting and permitting sensuality on both sides, which—how could it be otherwise?—is also not blind to the charms of another, as well as a concurrent trust in the decision for marital fidelity, would be the "rational," the "healthy" solution. Desdemona's life convincingly exemplifies this solution for the spectator. One can certainly say of her that she, who previously rejected individuals who were accessible and suitable for her and who had never fallen in love, is awakened to the serene sensuality that we are able to observe in her, precisely by her love for Othello. She even asks for praise from Iago himself—of all people!—in the euphoria of her arrival after the long sea journey: "What wouldst thou write of me if thou shouldst praise me?" (2.1). Iago thereupon produces some clever verses that clearly demonstrate his distorted sensuality and his incapacity to respect and love women.

Othello himself, already on the brink of a pathological condition, makes yet another attempt to remain with the reality principle: he says that there is no cause to be jealous, when everybody sees that "my wife is fair, feeds well, loves company, Is free of speech, sings, plays, and dances well; Where virtue is, these are more virtuous" (3.3). Even his own deficiencies, as he attempts to convince himself, do not have to cause his anxiety: "For she had eyes, and chose me." All this reflectiveness, however, is of no use. The internal compulsion to destructive jealousy is stronger.

8. Why Jealousy as a Means of Revenge?

All this still does not provide an explanation for the basic question of the drama: Why is it jealousy with which Iago destroys Othello? A typical theatrical villain could produce a sufficiently interesting plot by poisoning the commander who he feels has treated him unjustly, or by luring him into traps. Indeed, he could even stab him from behind in battle. Why does Iago draw Desdemona into his need for revenge if, according to the text, Cassio is his rival?

Freud's third level of jealousy—that of projected jealousy because of repressed homosexual impulses—provides a conclusive explanation for this. It is important to remember that Freud warned the reader that, "in a case of jealousy paranoia, one should be prepared to find all three levels of jealousy, and never only the third." Thus an entire chorus of jealous voices makes *Othello* such a breathtaking and spellbinding drama. If only it is viewed correctly, it is like a fugato whose main theme is Iago's repressed homosexual fascination with Othello.

This thesis certainly poses a great challenge for the reader or spectator. Nevertheless, I was not the first to whom this possible interpretation occurred. In a 1935 production, Othello and Iago (played at that time by Laurence Olivier, who in 1964 gave an unforgettable performance as Othello) appeared as a homosexual couple (the afterword to the German prose translation of 1971 refers to this performance). This direct representation appears to me to be questionable. It is more than unlikely that Shakespeare was thinking of a *real* love relationship between the two. Every performance, however, should contain suggestions of homosexuality; for the delusional outbreak of aggression derives its internal probability, even necessity, from the subliminal attraction of the men for each other that at the same time is surrounded by extreme anxiety.

Shakespeare's own homosexuality has been a constantly recurring topic of research, without having yielded a clear biographical result. He married Anne Hathaway when he was eighteen years old, but his magnificent love sonnets from the year 1598, when he was thirty four years old, are dedicated to a Mr. W. H. (Mr. was at that time the abbreviation for master, a *young* man.) Even if one takes into consideration all the conventions of the art of the sonnet at that time and, therefore, relativizes their genuine emotional content, the sonnets unambiguously contain erotic, passionate undertones that are directed by an older man to a beautiful youth. The youth is unfaithful to him with the poet's own beloved, a "dark lady" who leads a questionable life but exercises great sexual fascination (even though she did not fit the time's ideal of "fair" beauty). Here again we see love *and* rivalry in both men. Consequently it does not seem to be completely unreasonable, even as far as the author is concerned, to examine from this perspective the tragedy that was written six years after the sonnets.

When one pays heed to Othello's and Iago's unconsciously homosexual utterances, it is as if one's eyes had been opened. Before I cite some of them, a glance at the significance of women for both men seems necessary to me.

9. Women in the World of Men: Symbiosis as Danger

As previously mentioned, Shakespeare's genius consists for me in having Iago act out a part of Othello's jealousy. Parallel to this, Desdemona and Emilia manifest two sides of the "feminine," which actually belong together in a person who is mature in the psychoanalytical sense. Emilia stands for the sense of reality, for maternal force, strength, and warmth, and therefore can easily be cast as the "strong wife" of a man with homoerotic tendencies. Self-aware, almost in the sense of a modern feminist, she stresses that she feels herself free to dispose of her sexuality according to her own lights—to her own advantage and even to her husband's (4.3). Desdemona, on the other hand, represents delicate, devoted love, love that is unconditionally submissive, until death, to the husband as lord. Who knows if perhaps Freud wished for something similar from his Martha during the time of his engagement, which was fraught with jealousy. Desdemona's last words, when she speaks once again after the strangulation, almost as if pronouncing a divine judgment, are, "Commend me to my kind lord." She is referring here not to God, but to Othello. In this same passage (5.2), she says that she is dying an innocent death, and to Emilia's question as to who has killed her, she responds, "Nobody; I myself." That is correct in a very deep sense. For it is mentioned more than once that Othello would never have dared to court her had she not taken the initiative. In this way, it was she who lured him away from the world of men in which he had lived until then.

During highpoints of his self-characterization (1.3, 3.3, 5.2), Othello invokes his earlier clear and glorious identity, with the same degree of yearning. Now, however, Iago can say, "Our general's wife is now the general" (2.3). It is obvious to every reader or spectator that, in the most exact and at the same time most general sense, Desdemona's intrusion into Othello's previous life has brought about her death. As Othello reports, at the very beginning of their love relationship, when he has won her by stories of his rough, brave life, she already wishes, with the exquisite empathy of lovers,

> That heaven had made her such a man [like Othello]: she thank'd me,
> And bade me, if I had a friend that lov'd her,
> I should but teach him how to tell my story,
> And that would woo her. (1.3)

Expressed in psychoanalytical terms, she senses that only the experience of becoming narcissistically understood by, and feeling herself one with,

Othello can bind him to her, an aspect that also plays a large role in homosexuality. Not her being different, but rather her wanting to be the same is what convinces him: "Upon this hint, I spake." Brabantio, who is indignant when he sees that his daughter was "half the wooer," must yield. The couple is inseparable and not just because of the secretly consummated church service.

Strikingly, Iago is hereafter the representative of the world that Othello leaves. The military rank in which Iago was left, if not "left *behind*," which is thus the manifest basis of his desires for revenge, is that of "ancient" in Shakespeare's language, that is, the elder, the earlier. Cassio, who is close to Desdemona not only in age and sympathy but also in education, aristocratic origin, and "fairness," receives the rank of lieutenant, which is taken from the French *lieu-tenant*: someone who defends a position for the highest commander, stands in his place, is a deputy. Iago's concern is to eliminate *all* deputies of his previous relationship to Othello, and Desdemona is one of them.

Wangh (1950) shows the subliminal homosexuality in Iago's interruption of intercourse between Othello and Desdemona (the "primal scene"), during the wedding night in Venice (1.1) and again during the night after the arrival on Cyprus (2.3). Finally, the bedchamber, upon whose bed Desdemona explicitly has spread the wedding sheet, becomes the place of execution: Desdemona dies on her marriage bed. And she dies, as we come to understand ever more clearly, precisely *because* she has shared this bed with Othello.

10. Iago's Jealousy

Oedipal envy (which begrudges the father the mother's love) is only *one* possible interpretation here. Iago is doubtless also envious of Othello's love for Desdemona. In this, he conforms to the schema observed by Freud: "*I* certainly do not love him, *she* loves him." He continues in this vein again and again, often repetitiously and unmistakably: "*I* of course hate him" (therefore, I do not love him).

As in the case Freud describes of someone suffering from jealousy paranoia, Iago has "formed no friendship and no social interests" (Freud 1922, 200). Shakespeare has him emphasize that, for him, there is only egoism, pretense, and money. Consequently, the penetrating words right at the beginning of the drama that are directed at Roderigo, Iago's clownish alter ego, "Put money in thy purse," clearly suggest an oral-sexual interpretation. One may say in a totally unpsychoanalytic manner that Iago loves no one, neither man nor woman. He is afraid of love and concurrently has an uncontrollable desire for it. Probably the only possibility for the actor playing Iago to gain empathy from the audience is to show the dirty, fawning, suppressed, but nonetheless present desire for love in the evil and scheming person, whose lust for power only proves how excruciatingly lonesome he is.

It is only hate that makes possible Iago's preoccupation with men, "as if," as Freud writes about his patients, "it is only delusion that has taken over the further development of his relationships to the man" (ibid.). This does not apply only to men: hatred and contempt are the leitmotifs in, and at the same time the only possibilities of breaking down the barriers to, speaking and thinking about sexuality.

For Iago hardly speaks of anything except sexuality in its most vulgar manifestation, and in this his misogyny and contempt of women is all too clear. It is certainly no coincidence that the only people in the drama who die at the hands of another (naturally a man) are the two women. Emilia is stabbed by her husband, after she has discovered his "villainy" and, in a tremendous outbreak of indignation, sounds the alarm about it like a fire bell. As we already know, Desdemona also dies at her husband's hands, which are basically guided by Iago. The third person who dies is Othello. The two others whom Iago would have liked to see dead, Cassio and Roderigo, come away with wounds. The rival whose death Iago intended is not Cassio—or Cassio only secondarily—but Desdemona, and as Wangh very correctly observes, only by scheming to blacken Desdemona's name again and again does Iago have the opportunity to emphasize his love for Othello in an "unsuspicious" manner.

11. Why Does Othello Become Jealous unto Death?

That Othello for his part can be made jealous at all—while Desdemona believes that one could not conceive of such a thing because of his generous and trustful soul—is connected to the significance of women in Othello's life. He understands men, but not women. "O curse of marriage, / That we can call these delicate creatures ours, / And not their appetites!" (3.3). In other words, how can we feel at all secure in our "possession" of them, since they are so different from us?

And here we get into areas that Freud in 1922 had not yet explored. Latent homosexuality is not the issue, but the unity experienced as unbelievable, the being one and all with a person of the opposite sex, which is just as wonderful as it is unconsciously frightening. Othello as well as Desdemona frequently makes use of metaphors of the love that signifies and replaces the whole world and therefore guarantees order (which Iago wants to destroy). Thus Othello says, when Iago begins his seductive efforts, "But I do love thee! and when I love thee not, Chaos is come again"; or "If she be false, O, then heaven mocks itself! I'll not believ't." Therefore, the world is out of joint if what Othello assumed upon his unconditional involvement with the delicate creature is not correct: that she loves him and only him. Only then may he to a certain extent become unfaithful to his past. Otherwise he is bound in duty to fidelity toward masculine solidarity; otherwise Iago's "love" is again more attractive, and expressed in Freud's language, this might mean, "*I* certainly love neither Iago nor Cassio—*she* loves Cassio and not me. Therefore I must hate her, and out of loyalty to everything that was dear to me, but above all for the sake of justice, I must kill her.''

The motif of justice belongs to the sphere of mature humanity. The person who sees *Othello* does not, of course, despise in the main character a frivolous or egoistic person, and much less a ruffian, but is moved precisely by his trusting humanity, his naturalness and warmth, and his poetry even at the point of destruction. Cassio's eulogy summarizes these feelings: "he was great of heart.'' Othello sees himself, even as far as the esteem of others is concerned, as someone for whom justice is more important than anything else; therefore, for example, he immediately dismisses Cassio, to whom he has shown preference, from the desired lieutenancy, because of a brawl that one could view as a kind of peccadillo. In the murder scene, the compulsion to justice is addressed and defended several times. The famous beginning of act 5, scene 2, is only one instance of this: "It is the cause, it is the cause, my soul.'' Even more important is Othello's response to Desdemona's clear and true defense, that she has not given the handkerchief to Cassio. If that were true, he says, what he understands as a "sacrifice" would become a "murder" (5.2). At this time, he is already so possessed by the notion of sacrifice and justice, thus also by his *duty* to kill, that he can no longer listen. He has "lost his mind.''

For this man is a murderer, not a just avenger, and he *wants* to be this precisely because of the greatness, indeed the boundlessness, of his heart. "I had rather be a toad, / and live upon the vapour of a dungeon, / Than keep a corner in the thing I love / For others' uses" (3.3). But here it is not a matter of just anything that he does not want to share in his all-or-nothing pride, but he feels himself wounded "there, where I have garner'd up my heart, / Where either I must live, or bear no life; / The fountain from the which my current runs, / Or else dries up" (4.2).

These poetic images from his conversation with Desdemona, who barely understands Othello because he is imprisoned in the world of his own delusions, show only too clearly the relationship to the first and actual source of love, the mother. In his delusion, Othello regresses to the early dyadic state (see chap. 17, sec. 6), in which the power of control over the life of the person with whom one lives and to whom one is symbiotically bound is not yet regulated by the laws of the paternal world. Rather, omnipotence and impotence are merged into one. He is like a child who out of rage and desperation wishes the beloved person, who does not do what he wants, "away"; and in typical fashion, after the fact he also has the fantasy that is characteristic of jealous individuals, that it is possible to recreate the destroyed world: "had she been true, / If heaven would make me such another world / Of one entire and perfect chrysolite, I'd not have sold her for it" (5.2).

Iago's intrigues cause Othello to be so much "beside himself" that this force of death and life, which is experienced genetically at a very early stage and which is normally held in check by everything that belongs to the ego-world, is again released. However, all later levels of jealousy also appear in this "being beside oneself." What is most especially striking is the self-fueled, agonizing preoccupation of Iago, Othello's black fraternal soul, with the imagined intercourse between Cassio and Desdemona; according to Freud, therefore, with the primal scene. Iago lewdly asks, "Would you, the supervisor, grossly gape on? Behold her topp'd?" (3.3). Othello's notion that entire hoards have had his wife is soon added. This is also similar to what is described by alcoholics experiencing jealousy delirium (Llopis 1962). In addition to this, the "concern" with Desdemona's fidelity makes possible the preoccupation of both with the sexuality of other men. This peaks in Iago's telling of Cassio's dream, which Iago has invented and in which he describes a homosexual love scene: he, Iago, not so long ago shared a camp bed with Cassio. In the dream, Cassio took him for Desdemona and lay on top of him as if he wanted to make love to him, all of which is elaborated with unambiguous details.

The compulsion to remove Iago's female "rival," in that she is made guilty and may therefore be killed, is so great that even Othello unconsciously participates in the loss of the handkerchief that later appears to Othello as the final and irrefutable proof. After the scene between Othello and Iago at the beginning of the third act, which one is fully justified in viewing as a seduction scene, Desdemona sees that things are not well with her husband. He complains of a headache. She wants to caress him and pat his forehead with the handkerchief. He indignantly pushes it aside with the words, "Your napkin is too little," and it falls to the floor. And now it is Othello himself who says, "Let it alone. Come, I'll go in with you."

Some other passages document the thesis of unconscious homosexuality. Above all, Iago's ominous "I am not what I am" contains a new meaning, namely, "I am not the *man* I appear to be." But also in the murder scene, an exchange of words between Desdemona and Othello is transformed from delusional nonsense into a truth, which only delusion brings to the light of day:

> *Othello.* Think on thy sins.
> *Desdemona.* They are loves I bear to you.
> *Othello.* Ay, and for that thou diest.

Another statement by Iago, about which translators note that it is characteristic for him in its ambiguity and that it escapes definitive interpretation, is understandable from the point of view of the homosexuality thesis. After Othello has changed, a concerned Venetian nobleman asks, "Are his wits safe? is he not light of brain?" whereupon Iago answers, "He's that he is: I may not breathe my censure / What he might be: if what he might he is not, / I would to heaven he were" (4.1). Not only the contrast to Iago's self-definition is obvious here, but also his impotence in the face of what Othello is: a man who loves his wife—and not a man who loves Iago. If one were to interpret this sentence based only on the superficial level of the relationship between general and sergeant, that is, "he is not the general who will make me a lieutenant, which he could do and which I want for myself," then it would be most unlikely that an outsider would doubt Othello's clear-wittedness.

12. Catharsis

The delusion takes its course, and the fatal solution, as if it were unconsciously desired, becomes unavoidable—Othello, however, returns from murderous narcissistic regression into omnipotence, to the social world of regulated and just relationships. In this he is different from many mentally ill criminals who also believe they are carrying out an act of justice, but after the murder they maintain this conviction and are not capable of regret and reconciliation (see Lagache [1947] 1982). The elevating and stirring impact of the drama also lies in this: we need not hate Othello, but may continue to love and admire him.

At the moment of his demise, he once again proves his greatness: "Here is my journey's end . . . where should Othello go?" He asks Cassio for forgiveness and in a few sentences takes stock of his life.

> Speak of me as I am; nothing extenuate,
> Nor set down aught in malice: then must you speak
> Of one that lov'd not wisely but too well;
> Of one not easily jealous, but being wrought,
> Perplex'd in the extreme . . .

Yet again he returns to the pride and significance of his life, to military glory: just as he once stabbed to death an enemy of the Republic of Venice, he now stabs himself to death—and thereby equates himself with this enemy. At the same time, however, he again becomes completely himself, for this act too takes place for the sake of justice. His continued existence would be an insult to Venice, which here stands as a symbol for the moral and defensible society of human beings humanely living together.

Iago, moreover, in his own way also returns to truth: his last words on the matter are the only ones, except for those he has with himself in monologues, in which he does not lie. To Emilia's question of whether he told Othello that Desdemona was unfaithful to him, he responds, "I did," and then strengthens the statement with the words "with Cassio." However, his last words are "Demand me nothing; what you know, you know: From this time forth I never will speak word."

And even under torture, he will not reveal his secret. He is destroyed in a more radical way than Othello because in the end he, the little man, the fearful man, the man who is incapable of love, could not harm a person who was great, not only in hatred but also in love.

16

THE TRIANGLE:
HUSBAND, WIFE, CHILD

You two! But that is the beginning of jealousy, that I think:
you two, the couple, you two!

Max Frisch, *A Wilderness of Mirrors*

No one who experiences jealousy as an adult is doing so for the first time—
this is the thesis of psychoanalysis. The Oedipus complex, much admired and
often castigated, remains one of the basic components of psychoanalysis and
one of the most important theoretical bases of therapy. Happily it is not the
task of this study to come to terms with the criticism it has drawn. Like Freud
himself, I can only counter with the following objections: "These are certainly
nothing other than constructs, but if you practice psychoanalysis [or marriage
counseling], you will find that they are necessary and profitable constructs"
(Freud 1917, 338).

The construct of the Oedipus complex is based on facts that everyone who
dares look can see exhibited in little children between the ages of about three
and six. In this age range, they develop a lively interest in their own and
other people's genitalia and find themselves in a conflict that often expresses
itself dramatically: they want the parent of the opposite sex for themselves
alone and therefore wish the other parent gone, whereby "being completely
gone" can also be conceived of as "being dead." The painful experience
that the parents belong together and that neither of them can be possessed by
the child completely and alone forever, leads to renunciation of these unrealistic demands and to identification with the parent of the same sex, that
is, to an assumption of the "correct" role of one's own sexual identity ("the
annulment of the Oedipus complex"). In this, the child is ideally supported
by the unshaken, sustained love of *both* parents, who are not offended by the
child's exploratory efforts, its love, or by what Freud liked to call its "badness."
They are also not offended by the child's failure, but neither do they trivialize
it. Rather they help the child endure what is, in many respects, a difficult
and passionate age as, in the final analysis, a good and necessary experience
and help the child integrate it into the unconscious.

For it is in the unconscious that the results of this life stage are preserved. "What is unconsciously present as a psychic outcome of incestuous impulses to love, is no longer assimilated into the consciousness of the new phase; what was conscious in it is again expelled" (Freud 1919, 208). Therefore memories like the following are very rare without the aid of analysis; these memories come from Stendhal's autobiography ([1835] 1981, 37ff.).

> My mother, Henriette Gagnon, was a charming woman, and I was in love with my mother . . . . When I loved her, perhaps at six years of age (1789), I had the exact same character as in 1828, when I was madly in love with Alberte de Rubempré [a demimondaine]. The way I pursued the chase had not basically changed, except for a single point. In terms of the physical aspect of love, I was in the same position as Caesar would be if confronted by the use of cannons, if he were to return to the world. I would have learned to use them very quickly, and that would not have changed my tactics in any way. I wanted to cover my mother with kisses, and I wanted her to be naked. She ardently loved me and often kissed me. I returned her caresses with such fervor that she often found it necessary to leave. I detested by father when his arrival interrupted our kisses. I always wanted to kiss her on the breast. I was as criminal as possible, I was madly in love with her charms . . . . [Stendhal lost his mother when he was barely seven years old.] Thus forty-five years ago I lost what I loved the most in the world. . . All the happiness of my childhood was carried to the grave with my mother. . . At this time my inner life begins.

Stendhal's report clearly shows how complex the oedipal relational structure is, and that the child's "criminal" desires are not a matter, for example, of being too familiar with an asexual madonnalike mother: "She ardently loved me and often kissed me." Perhaps her flight was also a flight from her own desires? If we concede that Stendhal's descriptions of his father have some basis in reality, and do not see them only as colored by oedipal jealousy, then this father was certainly not exactly an affectionate partner for the "plump, perfectly fresh, very pretty woman" who "often neglected to give orders to her three lady's maids" but instead read Dante in the original. In one small scene, Stendhal reports of her that, "one evening, when by happenstance I had been put to sleep on a mattress in her room, in order to get to her bed more quickly she jumped over my mattress with the spriteliness and ease of a doe." As far as Stendhal's father is concerned, Edmund Bergler, whose literary psychobiography (1935) I have to thank for the reference to Stendhal's relation to his mother, speculates that the son not only felt manifest hatred for him, but also unconscious love. According to Bergler, it is only because of this that he can remember the positive Oedipus complex with such uncommon precision, because the homosexual bond to his father is thereby all the more deeply repressed. The following quotation indicates what Freud meant by the concepts "positive" and "negative" in reference to the Oedipus complex: upon close examination, one gets "the impression that the simple Oedipus complex is in no way the most common, but corresponds to a simplification and schematization which, to be sure, often enough remains justified in practical terms. A more thorough examination usually uncovers the entire Oedipus complex, which has two aspects, a positive and a negative, dependent on the original bisexuality of the child, that is, the boy not only has an ambivalent attitude toward the father and lovingly selects his mother as his mate, but at the same time he also behaves like a girl, in that he displays a loving feminine attitude toward the father and the corresponding jealous-hostile attitude toward the mother" (Freud 1923b 261).

Here, under the central rubric of sexuality, Freud expresses the fundamental relational problem of early childhood, whether one calls it oedipal or not: the child experiences in its family for the first time a relational triangle, such as will later be experienced again and again by some people. In this primal triangle, which occurs during the age when the greatest imprinting occurs in humans, not just a beloved and a hated person confront the child, but *two* beloved persons whom the child needs and dares not lose. How is it possible for the child in this situation *not* to become conflicted? To express it in metaphysical terms, this loyalty conflict—to introduce a term used in family therapy—leads to the first experience of the unavoidability of guilt. How strong the guilt *feelings* are is a psychological problem that will continue to occupy us often enough in connection with jealousy.

In reference to the Stendhal quotation, Bergler's observation does not therefore mean, for example, that the adult author simply imagined the passion for his mother; he also experienced it. He can describe it in such vivid terms for two reasons: first, because this passion is still more permissible than something that would place his father in proximity to the temptation of pederasty and would place Stendhal, writing his autobiography, in proximity to homosexuality; second, because at the time he is writing, Stendhal already possesses the cannons that Caesar did not have at his disposal, that is, fully developed genital sexuality. Therefore, like every historian whose later experiences influence his or her description—in this way Freud explains the connection between childhood experiences and those of the adult neurotic—he changes what he describes: "Hatred for the father and desires to see him dead are no longer shyly intimated; tenderness toward the mother acknowledges the goal of possessing her as a woman" (Freud 1917, 348).

The Oedipus tragedy demonstrates how incest experienced during the age of maturity terribly offends the sensibility of gods and men. It shows how dangerous it is, as well as the close connection between incest and schizophrenia. Therefore, what Freud called the destruction or annulment of this "cursed desire" (Caroline Neubaur, afterword to Chasseguet-Smirgel 1974) must also appear to be very desirable, even necessary. Each of us is urgently set the task, but "it is worthy of note how seldom its annulment succeeds in an ideal way, that is, in a way that is both psychologically and socially correct" (Freud 1917, 349).

The preceding descriptions of jealous individuals may evoke this question, "What in the world do their problems have to do with their parents?" Uwe Johnson's Joe Hinterhand also concerns himself with this question (see above, chap. 5) and says he has "indeed been able to acknowledge as a model, [that] a male child envies the father his mother and substitutes another woman for the lost person; treated by several foster parents as a burdensome orphan, such envy, loss, and substitution are unreal to him" (1982). The oedipal conflict is unreal if one understands by this that it is not conscious and not remembered. According to psychoanalytical theory, to begin with it is natural to (almost) everyone who gives it some thought; in the very first instance to Oedipus himself, but also to every neurotic who goes into psychoanalysis, or to every marriage counseling client who would like to overcome a crisis. Unreal does not, however, mean inoperative, and that "burdensome orphan," Joe Hinterhand, certainly had no possibility of "psychologically and socially" surviving the childhood oedipal crisis "correctly." How many frustrated hopes, how many temptations, how much hate without the possibility of discussing it and working it out, must the child, who had been pushed around, have experienced when it was time to accept the challenge presented by the first triangle! The incapacity to speak, to correct oneself through one's experiences of others, characterizes even the adults in Johnson's story. That a child has no, or no proper, parents obviously does not mean that it would not know that parents are due to a child. Nor does it mean that the child does not see any other husbands and wives or fantasize about what goes on between them. Joe Hinterhand therefore behaves in a more narrow-minded and unknowing way than is necessary, and the reader gets an idea of what "resistance" in analysis and counseling can be.

Let us attempt a brief interpretation of Joe Hinterhand's denial: behind it lies the fear of having to give up the unjustified claim to total possession of a beloved person, of having to "share" her; to concede that she (to remain within the context of the oedipal relationship) can love both father and son in different ways. After such a working out, which would have required resignation and grief deriving from a sense of reality, a different ending to Hinterhand's drama would be possible. He would no longer be at the mercy of apparitions resulting from his orphan's fantasies, but would have been able to perceive his wife's reality and not only an idealized image of her. He would not have forced her, who after all lived with him because she *wanted* to live with him, to silence and lies with his unconditional demands. The pain at her infidelity would still have been immense, but since it had already been overcome once before in his life, the wound would not seem so great that it could only be compensated for by murder. This murder is, of course, not only punishment of the unfaithful wife, but also in a destructive way of the deceived husband. Seen psychoanalytically, not only rage at the mother's successor is the issue here, but also atonement for the reappearance of oedipal hatred for the father.

Why is it so difficult to leave the Oedipus complex behind? First of all, it is important to remember that Freud's starting point was individuals with nervous disorders (among whom he himself, who was for a long time his own most important research subject, also belonged). Once his eyes had been opened to the point at which he could exert the leverage to overturn neuroses, he and his disciples searched for what was viewed by society as a monstrosity. They sought further and possibly more convincing documentation— and found it, happily in of all places the most treasured cultural documents: in myths and religions, in literature, as well as in the biographies of important men. All of it was certainly an expression not of everyday life, but of great feelings, great dangers, and extraordinary, even if symptomatic, symbolic events.

That we can follow the lines of our own minor fates in the magnification of tragedies such as those of Oedipus, Medea, or Antigone; that we can feel ourselves cathartically uplifted, understood, and liberated in our pity and fear at them—this does not mean that the unresolved triangular bond is constantly operative in all our lives as a powerful barrier to feeling and development. We are not usually so exceptional, so passionate, or so absolute, and naturally the resolution exists in "normal" heterosexuality, which is experienced by the millions. Especially as a marriage counselor, one must here guard against an occupationally determined blurring of vision.

Remnants of the conflagration of the childhood world smolder in everybody's unconscious, and they can occasionally be fanned into large fires by the storms of adulthood. Based on my own experience I can say that, in all cases of jealousy with which I have dealt, or which I could observe in team conferences or in the reports of colleagues or interns, reaching back to the relationship with one's parents was extraordinarily enlightening and helpful.

All difficult primal triangles do not result in overtly jealous individuals, but all jealous adults had to deal in their childhood and youth with problematical parents (or substitutes). This is true even if, as is often the case, they perceive their childhood as happy, view their parents as the dearest people, and can only slowly approach their early wounds and fantasies.

The question from which the reality of the Oedipus complex may now be deduced can only be answered in individual instances and always through laborious effort, that is, the "struggle to remember" (Mitscherlich 1969). This is a painful and sobering experience for people who would prefer to be quickly rid of their torments. A further disappointment, and one through which Freud also had to work (Freud 1914a), is that not only remembering, that is, making conscious, but also repetitions and working through are part of the cure and are necessary before new solutions are possible.

It seems to me that the most convincing indication of jealousy's genesis in the child's early years is, and remains, in the first place the fact that it is concerned only with the most important persons, and in the second place the obvious fascination with *both* of the other persons in the triangle. This fascination is obvious to the observer, even though it is often first resisted by the jealous individual.

1. The Damaged Third Party

Many of the projections that play a role in every jealousy indicate how difficult it is to accept victory over successors to paternal and maternal figures, because victory was originally forbidden. It is difficult because one then concedes to the old rivalry a different ending than in childhood, even if or precisely because one is oneself a man or woman in the biological sense and thus—potentially or actually—a father or mother (see Gambaroff 1984). The adult role is still so blocked by old guilt feelings that it must at least be compensated for by the torments of jealousy; if no jealousy appears, the role may not be assumed on a permanent basis and joyously.

The "Type of Object Choice by the Man," already described by Freud in 1910, belongs in this context. It is characterized by the fact that, for this kind of man, the prerequisite of a "damaged third party" for his loves must be met. He only falls in love with women who already have husbands, fiancés, or steady boyfriends, who are firmly committed, just as his mother was indissolubly committed when he was a child.

Goethe was a genius of this impossible love. He had a very difficult, bad-tempered father, who did not make love and life exactly easy for his son, and a cheerful, exquisite mother. She loved her pampered child beyond all measure, and she spoiled him—a fact that was sometimes critically noted by her friends. When he left, however, she was also able to let him go. In view of the profusion, liveliness, constancy, and warmth of her letters, one can well imagine that, in terms of psychoanalytic theory, it must have been difficult for her son to find a woman who could assume the place in his life that "Lady Aja" once had. None of Goethe's relationships to women took any shape other than that of a more or less uncomfortable triangle, which, however, also allowed him the possibility of withdrawing.

With his only girlfriend, Lili Schönemann, who was a socially appropriate partner, he got as far as a near-engagement. Käthchen Schönkopf and Friederike Brion were "beneath his station"—society, a successor to the parents, forbade them to him. The famous Charlotte Buff was engaged and in *Werther* (under her correct first name!) inspired a whole generation to feeling, love, and suffering. I do not know whether she also inspired them to loving intimacy with children, which was her strong suit and remained so in real life. In any case, starting a family was not what Goethe had in mind. He went to Weimar and experienced his great spiritual, but not physical, union with the second Charlotte, the wife of the unloved equerry von Stein, and the mother of several children. Goethe said of her that she had been his sister or his wife in a "former life"—not his mother, and only in a former life. At the same time, he is said to have occasionally shared a lover with his friend and sovereign Karl August.

Goethe's often-used resolution of an important relationship, flight without taking leave, led him from Weimar to Italy, the country "where his father had been" and the goal of his life's desire. Only then could Lady von Stein say, justifiably, "Goethe has become sensual." Very shortly after his return, in his midforties he met the very young Christiane Vulpius, and there was every indication that he was bound to her by an enduring physical love. He could, however, share with her little more than the sphere of sensuality, of home, food, life, and sleep. She was a young "great" mother, to whom his mother Aja was very well disposed as the "treasure of his bed," but whom he could hardly exhibit, whom he again was not allowed to possess fully and before all the world. He had five children with her, of whom only the unhappy August survived. After twenty years of living together, Goethe and Christiane married because of her courage in the face of the Napoleonic soldiers who wanted to occupy Goethe's house—as if with this she had finally proven her maternal protective attributes and only now had become worthy of the marital state. Thereafter Goethe was grateful to everyone who socially recognized the marriage. At the same time, he still needed official forgiveness for the fact of his marriage. After Christiane's and August's deaths, his daughter-in-law, Ulrike von Pogwisch, who from the beginning got along better with the old man than with her difficult husband, assumed the role of "housewife." Goethe died in her arms.

Before this, however, he came to love the beautiful and gifted Marianne von Willemer, though with full passion only after her patron and lover, a friendly and generous man, had married her. Goethe literally ran away from Marianne, too. The only marriage proposal he ever made, when he was a seventy-year-old man, was to a very young girl, Ulrike von Levetzow. He was refused, but Ulrike never married.

In this world of triangular relationships and forbidden, but nonetheless lived, unions, women more or less suffered at Goethe's hands, but all have been immortalized in his poetry. For Goethe deceived them all with what he inherited from his mother; as he states in a well-known poem, with his "love of poetic invention," his poetry. (In the meantime, the first volume of K. R. Eissler's splendid psychoanalytic Goethe-study [1963], which was previously unknown to me, has appeared in German. It is not the mother

who appears there as the beloved and forbidden woman in Goethe's life
but his sister, who is, naturally, likewise unattainable. In spite of this, I
would like to let my series of triangles stand, since the conspicuous
tendency toward the "damaged third party" and toward women who are
"forbidden" remains valid.)

It is not known whether Goethe was jealous during this long life full of damaged third parties. Perhaps—no, certainly— the refuge in creativity saved him.

The resolution appears different in less significant biographies. Misfortune
is less honorable, the participants less noble, and according to Freud, jealousy
is a necessary condition of this kind of love. It is almost as if these people
can only believe in their own commitment if they feel jealousy as a kind of
proof. Furthermore, part of this type of object choice is that a "decent"
woman never exerts the same attraction that a sexually disreputable woman
can. This quality can vary from an inclination to flirt to conspicuous promiscuity. We feel that the expression that Freud uses, "love of prostitutes," is
quite pejorative in terms of the life-styles and forms of love now considered
permissible. However, one can empathize with the phenomenon of a tendency
to choose directed not toward a final victory but toward constant risk at the
hands of a third party, with its concomitant jealousy as well as its mixture
of fascination with, and denigration of, the desired person. In this way, the
childhood situation that was not satisfactorily resolved is conjured up again
and again and, because it was indeed forbidden, is destroyed again and again.

A man has been married for ten years without having consummated the
marriage. The marriage is tender and good, but although both of them
want children, they are afraid to take the decisive step. Then the man falls
in love with a young girl who has already had several boyfriends. She
seduces him. He moves out of the marital home. His wife also finds a
boyfriend with whom she finally makes love. After some time, the
husband's relationship to the young woman falls apart because of jealousy
that was probably, for the most part, unfounded. Now he is able to have
intercourse with his wife, but the marriage is clouded by the husband's
mistrust, which in this instance is related not to men, but to money. (The
equation, money = fortune = potency, has been demonstrated many times
over by psychoanalysis.) The couple's desire for children can no longer be
realized. Now that it would finally be *physically* possible to become
parents themselves, and no longer to remain just delicate children, a
psychic barrier is erected. Seen in oedipal terms, self-generated siblings are
a monstrosity to gods and men.

The marriage ends in divorce because the husband and wife have new
relationships, in each instance with childless partners. The husband's
girlfriend must at first conceal her new love from her husband. She does

this very skillfully, and her boyfriend accepts it with a mixture of happy self-esteem and a bad conscience. The new couple eventually marry. The husband knows that his wife frequently had affairs on the side in her first marriage. He says that he had not known "such women" until then, and that his mother and first wife had been completely different. He develops borderline jealousy that torments his wife so much that she gets another divorce, although she still loves him a lot.

This man could not believe nor endure the fact that he was the only one who was to be the final victor. His unconscious arrested him on a child's level where this condition—physically, as well!—was impossible to produce and where his desire for sole possession of his mother could not be fulfilled and was severely condemned. Moreover, this completely contemporary case may perhaps make understandable to doubters how impotent sexual enlightenment often is, and how correctly and accurately Freud's incisive statement hits the mark, even if it is still provocative: "whoever is to become truly free, and thus happy in his love life, [must] have overcome his respect for women [and] have reconciled himself with the notion of incest with his mother and sister" (Freud 1910, 86). Naturally the word "notion" is important here (not implementation!) and, furthermore, the mental addition of the concepts "childhood" and "transference."

2. Jealousy as a Desire

Behind every jealousy, on the whole, there are always desires that are expressed, blocked, or punished by fears. A special variant has been worked out by Robert Seidenberg (1953). He follows Freud's observation that the man with whom the beloved is unfaithful in fantasy, that is, the one who causes the jealous torments, often bears traits of the jealous individual. Seidenberg is therefore fascinated by two situations, adapted for the theater, in which jealousy of a *Doppelgänger* plays a role. He is first concerned with the classical story of Amphitryon, which he cites in Giradoux's conversational version (and not in Kleist's Molière adaptation, which is condensed and tightened and endowed with a more profound mystical meaning). Jupiter can possess the virtuous Alcmene, who loves her husband Amphitryon more than anything, even more than the highest of the gods, only if he assumes her husband's form. Who is jealous of whom in this situation? Who still has "cause" to be jealous? Most likely Jupiter, but he also gets what he wants—he does not at all want *more*, Alcmene's lasting love.

   A similar entanglement occurred to the Hungarian Franz Molnár: a husband disguises himself as a guard and, in this form, seduces his own wife. As it is later revealed, however, she has seen through the deception from the beginning (as Alcmene did in the Giradoux comedy—a modern, frivolous addition). What is the position of fidelity and deception in this situation? After the deed has been done, the hero of Molnár's play says to a friend, "Pity the husband, but congratulate me." Both, however, are one and the same person.

What is important in this—and herein lies Seidenberg's psychoanalytical starting point—is the equation of the deceived person with the deceiver. In the psychopathology of neurotics and psychotics, this naturally never comes to a comedic resolution by itself, but often enough to a tragic one. The cases that Seidenberg cites all point in the same direction; they presume in a quite carefree manner a great deal of training in how to think in psychoanalytical terms, they are only described representationally and diagnostically, and we learn nothing of the therapy. As an illustration, I have chosen the simplest case and shall make some interpretative comments on it.

A twenty-two-year-old student comes to a psychiatrist because of severe depression accompanied by attacks of weeping, disquiet, and anxieties, which are also expressed in somatic symptioms. He loves a young girl whom he would like to marry, but is deeply tormented by the knowledge that she has already had previous sexual experiences, which is also true for him.

Up to this point, it would be easy to surmise hetero- as well as homosexual projections of infidelity. Relief, the "economical advantage," as Freud called it, would then be achieved by an unburdening construction, which would sound like this: "It is not I who would like to be unfaithful, it is of course she" (the man's heterosexual desire to be unfaithful). Or it could sound like this: "It is not I who love other men, it is of course she who does this" (resisted homosexuality on the man's part). In both cases, the jealous individual saves himself, through his suffering, from the condemnation of his desires by his own superego: "How could I desire such a thing—I am suffering so from it!"

Seidenberg, however, now reports that these explanations did not suffice but that therapy uncovered a deeper level, a further mechanism: already as a child, the young man had been fascinated by stories about "easy" girls. In his present situation, jealousy compelled him to elicit more and more, and ever more precise, information about sexual details. He felt himself deeply tormented: he could not marry the girl because of her "promiscuity," but also could not separate himself from her. Rather, he returned again and again in order "to cry in her lap."

Besides a hot-tempered father's rejection and exploitation, and intense rivalry with an older brother, more exact exploration of his family history primarily yielded the fact that his parents, although belonging to a strict religious community, ran away from home before their wedding. From this the boy had developed fantasies that his mother could perhaps have been pregnant before marriage and was therefore a girl of "easy" virtue as defined by the religious group.

Seidenberg writes briefly that the boy's daydreams about his mother's promiscuity were, at first, pleasurable. But when his notions of sexual "looseness" were transferred to the mother substitute, his girlfriend, "his conscience could no longer allow him to feel pleasure in his incestuous thoughts. Pleasure is replaced by melancholy and despair." That is just a bit hasty. Let us simply ask, naively, Why incest? The girl *is,* after all, not his mother! It is, however, just not that simple.

The author continues to follow Freud's essay on the "special type of object choice by the man" without explaining it more precisely. There it says that, after the boy can no longer maintain the fiction of his mother's asexuality ("others may perhaps do such a thing, but not my parents!") and after he has heard of prostitutes, he often says to himself, "with cynical correctness, that the difference between his mother and a whore is not so great after all, that they basically do the same thing" (Freud 1910, 73). We may add that this is especially the case if dubious details from the mother's biography become known, as happened with Seidenberg's student. A person who is oedipally bound while growing up can then revive the fantasies of the small child, which were suppressed in the latency period. He has the mother and later her successors (Freud calls them "mother surrogates") appear in daydreams and onanism fantasies as other men's love partners. This fantasy is at first pleasurable and pleasant, as is, therefore, the patient's fascination with sexual gossip in his childhood and youth.

In the choice of beloved or wife, Freud's type, as well as Seidenberg's cases, manifests the bond to the mother by maternal traits and similarities. Freud very fairly compares this phenomenon with the consequences of a difficult birth: "After protracted labor, the child's head must represent the discharge of the maternal birth canal" (Freud 1910, 71).

A series is therefore formed: *the* woman ("the beloved, the irreplacable, the only one," the mother) is like *all* women (like my girlfriend), all do the same thing. They are tender or sensual not only with me, but also with many other men. The *fascination* with this notion continues to exist (the beloved must report precise details), but it is accompanied by torments instead of by pleasure. Why? The superficial explanation, that the patient is now the one who is deceived, is obvious, but does not suffice. Many men would deal very differently with the same facts. It is more understandable to say that he is concurrently the person deceived in reality (in psychoses, often only in his delusion) and the deceiver in unconscious fantasy (here we have the proximity to Amphitryon). One may empathize with the fact that a painful and even insanity-producing tension arises from this. At the same time, the torments of jealousy respond to guilt feelings due to the fulfillment of forbidden incestuous desire by the beloved, who is unconsciously felt to be the tabooed mother's successor. Seidenberg points out that the fears that usually accompany jealousy are castration anxieties, that is, disguises of the fear of the central punishment that threatens oedipal desire according to the orthodox Freudian conception: "Fear of losing the home, anxiety for the family's reputation, fear of insanity and physical collapse."

One may or may not take literally the small boy's fear of losing his penis— the incestuous desire is still always extremely dangerous and forbidden, and in the figurative sense it is also a horrible mutilation for someone not to get free of his parents for his whole life. The inability to distinguish between the mother and the beloved lies at the root of Seidenberg's cases. Therapy must elicit this distinction, and consequently overweening jealousy will disappear.

3. Jealousy and Guilt Feeling

The relationship between jealousy and guilt feelings, only hinted at by Freud in his 1922 essay, was especially noted and further researched by his disciples and successors. In 1930 Ernest Jones, one of Freud's most loyal supporters through all schisms and later his reverent biographer, gave a brilliant lecture at the Sorbonne to an academic lay audience. The lecture had the concise title "Jealousy." Like Freud (1917), Jones cites the classical passage from Diderot's philosophical and satirical dialogue, "Rameau's Nephew": "If the small boy were left to himself, if he retained all his naiveté, and if the passion of a thirty-year-old were added to the slight rationality of the child, then he would strangle his father and sleep with his mother." According to Jones, remaining internally suspended in the oedipal grip engenders consciousness of guilt, which is suppressed with difficulty and is constantly inclined to uncomprehended outbreaks. It makes so-called love an extremely fragile and risky occasion. He emphasizes the feeling of moral inferiority that lurks in people who are inclined to jealousy. In order to avoid this and instead to prop up their low self-esteem, they need to be loved. These two trains of thought are the main elaborations that Jones contributed to the discussion of jealousy: the role of narcissistic needs, and the dubiety of what we call love. We are reminded that, at least since the time of Augustine, it is said, "He who is not zealous does not love." And neither we nor Jones have much to say against that proposition. To be sure, if the weight in this equation is shifted, the matter becomes more difficult. If it is said, for example, "Only he who is zealous loves," or even, "Only he who is *very* zealous really loves," as many jealous individuals would like to hear, then a question mark is most likely appropriate.

Jones emphasizes the reactive character not only of heterosexual love in the case of repressed homosexuality, but of genital love *per se*. He says that the unconscious disguises more hatred than one would generally suppose. "The characteristic resistance of this hatred [is] to be seen in the development of a surfeit of affection, so that the sum of affection becomes larger than it would have become without the hatred." Through a change in the supporting circumstances (marriage, a love relationship), usually caused by the appearance of a real or imagined rival, hatred will become all the more evident the more necessary it was for the "loving one" to love. Our newspapers are full of reports of such ruptures, whose backgrounds naturally remain unclear. As an illustration, therefore, I chose a drama by Calderón that is little known in Germany. It deals with the story of Herod and Mariene, about whom Hebbel also wrote a tragedy. Hebbel's drama, however, seems to me much less successful than the Spanish play, because of its ideological superstructure and because of its convulsive efforts to establish universal-historical correlations. Calderón's play is called *The World's Greatest Monster* ([1637] 1951).

The figures in the jealousy triangle are the Jewish tetrarch, Herod, who is the Roman emperor Octavian's viceroy; his wife Mariene; and the emperor himself. That Calderón's typical jealous contemporary apparently could, even though in awe, identify with these characters shows the powerful narcissistic pretension of even "normal" jealousy. Emperors and kings are indeed often the idealized parental image in dreams and fairy tales, so that the oedipal parallel is obvious in the competition between Herod, who is actually a king by birth but only delegated to rule, and the omnipotent Roman emperor. One puzzles over what the world's "most gruesome, horrible, and strongest" monster is, for an astrologer prophesied to Mariene that she will unjustly meet her end because of it. At the same time, her husband's dagger will kill what he loves most in the world. There is no doubt as to what that is: his idolized wife is thus fearful and very worried. To reassure her, therefore, he pulls his dagger from its sheath (!) and throws it into the sea, only to get it back in the most miraculous way. It becomes embedded in the shoulder of a shipwrecked officer who is swimming toward him and who tells Herod about the failure of his ambitious plans: his fleet, allied with Antony and Cleopatra in an attempt to overthrow the emperor, has been destroyed by a storm. From happiness to unhappiness: such schematic vicissitudes of fortune, which seem almost like events in puppet theater, are frequent in baroque drama. This makes Herod sad for only one reason. He says that nothing defeats him

> but that I must see,
> that I was not man enough
> to make Mariene the empress of the world,
> and in this, so you will claim,

> as will everyone, I am
> out of my senses; do not be afraid,
> for where love leaves us our senses,
> there is no love . . . (act 1)

Thus, as he himself is aware, it is an exaggerated and insane love from which he draws his entire self-esteem. And upon more exact consideration, it seems totally logical that the dagger, the symbol of his aggressive, incalculable/calculable masculinity, returns to him. For nothing in this masculinity has changed by virtue of the external defeat. As Calderón has his hero clearsightedly say during an amazing conversation with his wife, perhaps

> the greatest monster of the world [is]
> that it is indeed my love
> which threatens you so terribly;
> for since I love you,
> I strive for so many things,
> that I fear love will be
> your misfortune and my badge of glory.

Naturally, however, the "world's greatest monster" is not love, but that known to us as the one with green eyes—jealousy. Herod has barely realized—again, a baroque plot complication—that Octavian has fallen in love with a picture of Mariene, when he is convinced that he, the vanquished, will be replaced by the victorious emperor even as a lover and husband, after his own execution. In his desperation, he immediately hatches a plot in prison to have Mariene killed.

> Even if I should die, I will die with the knowledge
> that Mariene, my queen,
> will die together with me . . . ,
> for there is no lover nor husband
> . . . .
> who would not much rather see
> his lady dead, than alien and taken from him. (act 2)

We will not deal here with the third act's suspenseful events, which are designed with utmost cunning in the style of cloak-and-dagger dramas. At the end, the completely innocent Mariene, who stands the test in an entirely regal and strong manner and tries to resist her husband's claims to possession (very unlike Desdemona), is mistakenly stabbed to death in the dark with Herod's dagger. During the entire play, she is paid homage in the most magnificent verses. However, in a much cruder sense than Freud ever intended, she is an "object" and nothing more than that. In the great final scene, Herod says in addition to everything else,

It is not I who killed her.
But who then?
Her destiny—
because since she died of my jealousy,
she fell at the hand
of this world's greatest monster. (act 3)

We will return to Jones: what characterizes the love of jealous individuals "is, taken precisely, that it is not love, but a torturous desire *to be loved*" (1930). In order to fulfill this desire, like an addict one makes the most insane efforts because one cannot consider oneself worthy of love as a person alone. One concurrently needs reinforcement. Only the partner, the "beloved" other, gives one "love, esteem, and self-respect," which mitigate the unconscious guilt feeling. "The relentlessness of his hatred, which is engendered in him by betrayal," derives from this. Does Herod love Mariene? Or has his hatred perhaps only waited to kill her? In the oedipal context she is, of course, as a wife the successor of the unattainable mother. Is it possible that a severely disturbed individual unconsciously only waits to avenge himself as an adult in this kind of gruesome way on the mother-woman and sibling-children for the unbearable frustrations of his childhood, in which his uncertain self-esteem is rooted? The murder of the children of Bethlehem is something else that has been transmitted to us about Herod, and Hebbel relates the jealousy story to this. Calderón's Herod even says that it was not he, but "it," "destiny"— an early indication of the power of drives eliminated from consciousness. For Herod has no proof of his wife's infidelity. At the end, he does not even have the conscious intention of killing her; nonetheless he is irresistibly driven to the fatal solution. In this context, the phallic symbolism of the dagger and the tower (from which he throws himself into the sea) can only delight the Freudian.

In Jones's essay, his negative judgment of such immature individuals, indeed his near-indignation at them, emerges only too clearly. He even reprimands his audience because of the tolerance that was common in France for crimes of jealousy and concludes with the concise sentence, "Jealousy is a sign of weakness in love, and not of strength; it more likely originates in fear, and in unconscious guilt feeling, than in love."

4. Men and Women

In the context of the Oedipus complex, which is so important for sexual identity, it must be possible to answer the frequently posed question about the differences in jealousy for men and women. Male and female experiences of the first triangle are, of course, not mirror images of each other. Freud, like Jones in the essay discussed above, was at first concerned only with the Oedipus complex in men. Until the very end of his life, he considered his views about feminine nature "incomplete and fragmentary." In the new series of his lectures, he advised his audience to consult their own "life experiences" or to turn to the "poets," if they wanted to know more about this topic (Freud 1933, 145).

This is not the place to deal with the many changes that Freud's views on the Oedipus complex have undergone in his theory or in the theory of his successors. What seems important here is that throughout his life and thought Freud held to the notion of a fundamental psychic bisexuality. Thus the decision to take on a predominantly female or male role is required of every individual as a life accomplishment. This is also expected by the culture in which the individual lives, and it is expected that it be accomplished in a way the culture deems "normal" (cf. Mitchell 1974, 127). Given these assumptions, the development of the Oedipus complex in boys and girls is described here.

At first the pre-oedipal mother, the merging object and omnipotent giver of the world and of life (potentially the *taker* of life as well), is of central importance to both sexes. This also holds true as far as identifying with her is concerned. During the oedipal conflict, that is, during that phase in which the importance of their own genitalia becomes clear to all children, the last stage of the first period of sexual development (which occurs in two phases only in humans) is achieved. The boy remains oriented toward the mother while, in his budding sexuality, he would like "the woman" for himself. During this time, however, he begins to feel himself to be a "little man," as Freud repeatedly notes. The boy's preoccupation with his penis in deed and thought (while masturbating or fantasizing, somehow to do the same thing as his father) is threatened by the possibility of having it cut off, taken away, thereby making the little person incomplete, mutilating him. He concludes that this can actually happen because this significant "more," which, as the little boy already knows quite well, is the source of so much pleasure, is not present in some people. The effect of these frightening observations is intensified when adults threaten to make the child's fears come true. Freud believes that such threats are frequent, even commonplace. Added to this are the guilt feelings that must necessarily arise when the child in so vitally important a relationship to two people, his father and mother, concentrates on just *one*, thus wanting to reduce the triangle to a biangular relationship. In pointed terms, the boy finds himself confronted with the alternative of either having to give up his penis or his desire for his mother. Narcissistic self-interest triumphs, that is, the desire to remain unmutilated.

In order that the unrealistic, one-sided, and sexually possessive love for the mother, as well as the hostility toward the father, can be buried, nothing is left but to internalize the parents' demands. These form the basis of the superego, the conscience and, as it were, the receptive agent for the demands of culture and society. The boy no longer wants to assume the father's position ("to marry the mother"), but rather identifies with him. He wants to become like him at some future time. The penis is indeed preserved by this but for a time is paralyzed in the literal sense. The latency period begins, in which sexual interests largely recede until puberty. In the best of cases, the fears that originate from the guilt feeling are also disposed of with the surrender of the undesirable desires.

The girl too at first primarily experiences the relationship to the great, omnipotent, pre-oedipal mother. As she begins to explore her sexual identity, she notices that she is missing something when she compares herself to a brother, father, and male playmates. According to Freud, she necessarily experiences herself as castrated (and is not, like the boy, afraid of the not-yet-executed castration), especially since she perceives the pleasure-giving clitoris phallically. The girl must compensate for a lack instead of fearing mutilation. The result is penis envy, a difficult construct that was already questioned during Freud's lifetime (by Ernest Jones, Karen Horney, and Melanie Klein, among others). However, let us at first stay with the assumption that the identity feeling of one-half of humanity is actually based on "being different" because of a deficiency. The little girl would then unequivocally like to have the desired "more" in some way. She fantasizes about it and believes, above all, that the mother, with whom she is angry because the mother has equipped her so imperfectly, prefers all people with a penis, especially her brothers, to the daughter. Since the seeds of sexuality are germinating even in the girl and are growing toward "the man," she would like to have her father's penis and later, in its place, a child by her father.

After the early years of an almost exclusive bond to the mother, therefore, a change in the love object takes place—a different situation than in masculine development. But for all that, the identification image remains constant: mother—girl—"little woman." This is a line of uninterrupted continuity, and perhaps this calmer developmental lineage provides the explanation for what can so often be observed: that girls are "further along" than boys of the same age. Narcissism in the boy leads to his making the laws of his omnipotent, forbidding parents, who harshly refer him to reality, his own for the sake of his integrity. Narcissism blossoms in the girl in that she makes her entire body pleasant and attractive. In crude terms, she has no penis, "only" a clitoris, but even so she can be lovable and respectable to the extent that a boy can never be (because it is not necessary for him). There is no compulsion to make a deep internal incision in order to avoid the external incision. Disappointment sets in only gradually at the fact that the father can really not be possessed (and in marriage counseling, one hears much more often about early incestuous relationships between small daughters and their grandfathers, fathers, brothers, or uncles, than one hears of the reverse situation, i.e., sexual abuse of small boys by mothers or their representatives). Freud, therefore, infamously ascribed to women a weaker superego, less social sense, a

more unstable morality, and a lesser capacity for sublimation. Juliet Mitchell
has summarized this softer, as it were more lascivious, development as follows: "The situation adds up to the fact that the shock of her lack, her
'castration,' and the end of her pre-oedipal mother-love forces the little girl
to *take refuge* in the Oedipus complex. Exactly contrary to the experience of
the boy, it is a haven from the castration complex, a love nest in which the girl
can gain the love she requires by winsome flirtation and pretty ways. . . . There
is an obvious link between the security of Oedipal father-love and the happy
home and hearth of later years" (Mitchell 1974, 117–18). Thus, placed in a
cultural-sociological context, even penis envy can be better understood as the
expression of disadvantage in a male society.

Later I will deal with the changes that this developmental schema has
undergone. Here the first question is, What can one conclude from this in
terms of the different forms of jealousy in men versus women? More precisely,
toward what are anxieties, desires, and aggressions oriented?

5. The Eternal Second

Men primarily fear castration, women the loss of love. How can these ciphers
be applied to triadic relationships? The man can feel himself to be the eternal
second: at first with his mother, he is second to his father. If he does not
succeed in feeling himself to be worthwhile and self-reliant while at least
partially independent of the relationship to his parents (and in this he is very
dependent on his parents' understanding and loving assistance), then he will
urgently desire to be the first when he finally has his own relationship with
a female partner. This desire will appear in puberty, at the latest, and the
female partner should naturally be "genuinely feminine." If she is, however,
then she will desire a child. And since, according to Freud, this is of course
the replacement for the venerated penis, desire's goal and all the world's
crown, it can easily happen that the man feels himself used to deliver the
actual fulfillment of his wife's femininity. And in view of the terrible importance of the children, he is again second best. Jealousy of the children
comes up frequently in marriage counseling. It is all the more difficult for
men to acknowledge it, the "more modern" the family is and, therefore, the
more clearly he knows or believes he knows that it is vitally important for a
child to have its needs treated as centrally important in its early years. A
"maternal" stance is thereby likewise desired from the men. In many cases,
this stance, even when they are consciously convinced of its correctness,
unconsciously demands too much of them and actually violates them. Jealousy
is then a reaction that is easily accessible, a reaching back to something
familiar: again a mother, again the second, again aggression toward this
detestable but, at the same time, beloved first.

The resolution of this conflict depends on the fates of the individual Oedipus complex. To be sure, the power of the pre-oedipal mother intrudes here, as it does so often when one contemplates jealousy. If the man has internalized her norms, it will be easier for him to renounce his own satisfactions for a while in favor of his progeny. One may not, however, forget to what extent men are also justified in their sense of injury. Many women only too gladly seize the opportunity to withdraw from the challenges of an adult relationship between husband and wife. In oedipal terms, loyalty to the father, for whom they may finally raise the phallus-child, is more important to them than the partner, and pre-oedipally they comply with the omnipotent mother's mandate to be like her. What is the husband still good for, after he has fulfilled his duty to procreate? Anyone who finds this exaggerated should consider how often the wife's parents take on new importance after the grandchildren's birth—in my experience, much more often than the husband's parents. The husband's complaints ("interference, never alone") are parried by the wife when she says, for example, "What would I do without my parents—I really need them—who would watch the baby otherwise?" The husband cannot really object to this. (That it does not *have* to be this way, that small children can also be cared for other than with grandparents' assistance, is demonstrated not only by couples whose parents are not available. It is shown also by the certainly extreme and unhappy example of young families who refuse all contact with the grandparents because they do not want any influence to take place. One always finds a way to actualize what one considers extremely necessary.)

As a marriage counselor, I can add that not only complaints about the children's too great internal significance are part of the everyday experience of my professional life, but also complaints about wives' aversion to sex after the birth of the first, but especially the second, child. Husbands often suffer greatly from this because, upon close examination, not only time constraints and exhaustion due to new tasks are expressed in this aversion, but also the diminished significance of the relationship to the husband. That such neglect is possibly felt even more painfully than sexual frustration, however, makes clear as well that the husband unconsciously fears mutilation and fragmentation. It was evidently not he himself, as a whole person, who was wanted, accepted, and loved, but his procreative power; and after it has accomplished its task, he experiences it not only as superfluous and undesirable to the person to whom he gave it, but also as "cut off" from its original experience, that is, obtaining pleasure.

Jealousy of children or parents is often relatively unconscious. It is also not as "permissible" as sexual jealousy. One often has the impression that, when it finally looks as if there were grounds for quarrels with a "normal" rival, all wounds actually implode into "proper" jealousy, which is thereby made possible.

6. Castration Anxiety

Is there really more castration anxiety than fear of the loss of love behind men's jealousy? The question is hard to answer. Jealous dread seems to me to be expressed in the following sentence more frequently by men than by women: "How do I come to be in this position?!" And the question indeed relates to "what has been taken away": in the first instance, the woman, but also respect, money, home, children. In my experience, violent, burning, active rage is also more frequent in the jealousy of men than of women and is similar to the reaction to the sudden pain of a bleeding wound. To be sure, if what is at issue is a penis substitute, what is lost also grows back again much more quickly in men than in women.

This is obviously linked to social and cultural factors. It seems as if a patriarchal society holds everything in readiness to compensate as soon as possible for the wound inflicted upon King Phallus. The younger generation is certainly entitled to their hopes for change. One may still say that a deserted husband is more likely to be held in contempt in our society, whereas a deserted wife is more likely to be pitied. One may, however, also say that a man on his own is more easily tolerated at many social occasions (proper seating at table!) than a woman on her own. In any event, one finds it inappropriate, but in no way abnormal, if a man links up with a women twenty years younger than he. The reverse case still has the effect of being very conspicuous, if not scandalous, and also occurs much less frequently. The opinion that a man cannot live alone, but that a woman can manage very well on her own (the household!) remains widespread. In divorces, small children are usually felt to belong to the mother. The man's experience in this is that, on the one hand, one begrudges him his children but, on the other hand, one also does not expect him to take care of them and he is consequently freer to form new relationships. "Staying with the father" is more frequent in the case of half-grown or adult children. In such a situation, the woman, older and, because of this, more likely to be on the fringes of the partner game, is left doubly alone.

In summary, one may say that, from the perspective of the castration complex, men certainly have a greater and more aggressive anxiety. Women, however, in a case of jealousy conflict must suffer for a much longer time, and more intensely, from the fact of their castration. In the context of marriage counseling, it is difficult for me to view this psychoanalytical symbolism other than from the perspective of predominantly sociopsychological aspects. It remains a question of interpretation as to whether one wants to consider the above-described phenomena, which are accessible to all of us, as expressions of a phallo-centric world image or "only" as those of a male culture. Nonetheless, the treatment of extreme states, as always holds true for jealousy, casts glaring light back on normality. I shall here refer to a case of pathological jealousy that Gerda Barag (1949) cured in a one-year analysis.

Her patient was a thirty-three-year-old kibbutz Israeli, married for ten years, with a nine-year-old son. With diminishing sexual potency, the man was seized by violent, exaggerated jealousy for his wife Noemi, whom he had loved until then. He accused her of infidelity with two kibbutz colleagues with whose wives he himself had had sexual relations before their marriage (but during his own). The patient developed an almost psychotic condition. He felt persecuted, screamed for help during the night, could not work, and believed he could not live without his wife. His central dream was described as follows:

"I had a very important dream that I do not understand; it is a homosexual dream. I am going on a trip with Noemi. She is walking in front of me in the most extremely provocative manner. She is dressed very remarkably. She has wound a shawl around her head and is wearing a close-fitting coat whose hem is turned down. Several kibbutz colleagues come toward us, and I recognize Schmuel and Jochanaan. [Schmuel is a fantasized rival and Jochanaan has gone through analysis.] Jochanaan goes up to Noemi, turns around toward his colleagues, and says, 'Just look at her;' (with which words he wants to indicate her vanity) 'a few more steps and she would have been under these ruins and been killed by them.' When I go on a few steps, I see the ruins of a wall that has just collapsed, and I am very afraid. We go on, Noemi still in front of me . . . and come to a place where there are a lot of boys. Noemi gives one of them a playful slap on the head, and he wants to run up behind her, but another boy stops him and they begin to fight. In the meantime, Noemi disappears and I wake up."

The analyst jokingly says that Noemi seems like a wandering phallus. Thereupon, the patient produces a series of associations agreeing with this statement: he has always been anxious about his penis and has even been afraid that it would be destroyed in the vagina (the collapsing wall). Now he understands why the loss of Noemi seemed to him just as bad as death—the whole kibbutz would then have known that he was impotent.

The equation, penis = woman, which here becomes clear, reaches far back into childhood. The patient had great difficuties in making the transition from pre-oedipal love of the father, which was very strong in him, to oedipal love of the mother. He fantasized that his father's penis (he slept in his parents' room until he was thirteen) was in danger in his mother's body. He also felt envious of his brother, four and a half years younger, who originated in her body. As a salvation from his own aggression, he identified with his little brother = the mother's body content = penis. (The assumption that small children want to incorporate the mother's body content by devouring it, i.e., oral-aggressively, originates with Melanie Klein. Not only milk, but also the father's penis and unborn siblings are part of this bodily substance; see chap. 17, sec. 2). It is not far from here to homosexual love, and the patient in fact had a lengthy period in which he assumed the active role in relationships to other boys, that is, he stood between an identification with the father and one with the mother. His numerous sexual relationships with women remained extravaginal until his mother's death. It was with his wife that he was first able to have "proper" intercourse. He fell in love with her at first sight shortly after his mother's death, and she was so similar to his mother that he often misspoke and called her "Mama."

Yet the ties to his father, as well as his mother, were too strong and frightening, and when his wife, to whom he was basically bound incestuously and not personally and maritally, became aggressive because she was not being satisfied, jealousy emerged. The jealousy went somewhat according to this formula: *She* loves other men. It was not: *I* have loved many women, perhaps *in order to* leave her unsatisfied, for I love my father and mother and brother males more than my wife. Further: I am afraid for my penis, and my wife represents it, not herself. Rather love, rather be horribly jealous, than risk the penis.

Anyone unaccustomed to viewing things in this way may find such interpretations extreme. The unconscious forces in operation here may certainly be understood differently. Jungians, for example, would have spoken of submission to the great mother, the abdication of the patient's anima to his wife, or the patient's possession by the primordial image of the "extraordinarily potent" (see Neumann 1952). Adler's disciples would have spoken of male protest, inferiority feeling, and the striving for superiority (see Adler 1956). All, however, proceed from the assumption that here the unconscious is operating in an inhibiting, limiting, and mutilating way. This is also, of course, only too apparent after all the *conscious* solutions, which were not all mentioned—marriage, fatherhood, sexual training, giving away one's inheritance to sisters, life and work in the meaningful kibbutz society—had so clearly failed that the patient could barely go on living.

It remains to report that the analysis lasted only one year and that the patient, previously tormented by suicidal thoughts and death fantasies directed against the people closest to him, became fully potent after therapy, loved only his wife, and become capable of a self-assured relationship with his kibbutz colleagues. Furthermore, after his wife had lost the fervently desired second child in her fifth month, which coincided with his analysis—as we would see it today, probably because of the strong psychic pressure that her husband exerted on her—a healthy second child was born at the time of catamnesis. Obviously, the jealousy had also disappeared.

7. Fear of the Loss of Love

Being completely whole only by being loved, loving primarily in order to be loved in return— is it really this that characterizes women? A man, a woman— it often seems to me as if the opposite of what I have just said about this is also true. So many role changes have taken place before our eyes, even and especially under the influence of psychoanalytical thought (one must only consider its importance for the protest movements of the sixties), that many of Freud's constructs, findings, and speculations seem doubtful in a totally different way than when they originated. It is understandable that a convinced psychoanalyst, such as the one in Janet Malcolm's excellent journalistic study of this "impossible profession," says, "And what is happening here is something that never ceases to amaze me—namely, that the insights of psychoanalysis are never taken for granted from one generation to the next" (1981, 158). He says, "The Oedipal period—roughly three and a half to six years— . . . is the most formative, significant, molding experience of human life, is the source of all subsequent adult behaviors. If you take a person's adult life—his love, his work, his hobbies, his ambitions—they *all* point back to the Oedipus complex. That's a fantastic thing to say. And we have found this out. . . . But what we take for granted the lay public continues to challenge" (158–59). The interviewer answers, "This idea is hard to accept." And the analyst says, "Sure it is." Let us therefore continue to register our doubts, but not be intimidated by what is hard to accept.

What primarily causes us difficulties is that Freud's leading concepts are entwined in the patriarchal order. This order can, however, be perceived in all its force in the everyday experience of marriage counseling. (To be sure, the subterranean cracks also become apparent there, sooner than on the rough surface.) We do not live among the Hopi Indians, or among the happy Samoans who are free of jealousy, as Margaret Mead has described them. Her findings have, moreover, been called into question. Rather, we live in a society in which one can still not speak of equality in many areas.

It appears that real maternally oriented conditions have never existed anywhere in the world. What has been maintained or poeticized about this turns out to be resistance to or justification of patriarchal power (Wesel 1981). The omnipotent mother exists in very early childhood and later in adults' dreams and fantasy, but she never existed in historical reality. If the father- and male-oriented order has been the only one in operation among us for thousands of years, how are women not to feel themselves to be the "second sex," as Simone de Beauvoir termed it (1949)? Therefore it seems all too easy to understand emotionally that women very often describe their jealous state as the feeling of having lost their footing. Their position in the world was defined by secure belief in their husband's love. In other words, they desperately ask, Who am I now that he has turned away from me? They do not ask, as men do, How will I come to terms with the wound that she, whom I perceived as part of myself, inflicts in detaching herself from me?

The fear of the loss of love is closely connected to female guilt feelings, whose origin is difficult to pinpoint and disputed in the psychoanalytic literature. Janine Chasseguet-Smirgel (1974) is of the opinion that the experience of an evil, denying object (the mother's breast which is withdrawn), which was first sustained at the hands of the pre-oedipal mother, leads to the girl's search for a better goal for her love. According to Chasseguet-Smirgel, this cannot be thought of in any other way than that everything evil is projected onto the mother, and everything good onto the father, at least temporarily, but for a time that is very important for imprinting. With this, the girl again gives up the tolerance for ambivalence (the mother is good *and* bad), which was just learned from the mother's example, and idealizes the father and what he has to offer (phallic symbol). The object change, infidelity toward the omnipotent mother, could not be justified other than by the illusion of a totally good father. When, in spite of this, aggressive impulses against the father arise, they must be repressed and transformed into self-reproaches. These specifically feminine guilt feelings then arise again and again when the adult woman perceives in herself the anal-sadistic component of sexuality (which, in terms of developmental history, is older than the oedipal-genital component). This component of sexuality is radically opposed to idealization. One must not, of course, command or control a man who is *only* good or make him dependent on one's own needs. Such a man would do everything of his own free will (with this, we are again on familiar ground: the model of the great, good mother).

This complicated derivation confirms what personal observation demonstrates: women are more strongly inclined toward guilt feelings by culture, upbringing, and psychic development. Even in the case of triadic relationships that occasion jealousy, they are more likely to ask, and ask more urgently, what role they themselves had in love being withdrawn from them. Only in very severe cases do they want to get from therapy what Seidenberg claims (1967, 599), that is, confirmation of their suspicions and reinforcement of their mistrustful stance. Based on my own experience, a case from our counseling work is characteristic.

A woman with several children was completely thrown off course by her husband's superficial (as seen from the outside) interest in another woman, which never led to intimacies. She repeatedly wanted to escape the bottomless pit, into which she had fallen, in the bottonless peace of death. Primarily ''because of the children,'' she entered into lengthy counseling. Today she thinks that it saved her life.

Long-term therapy is never only salvation, but also enrichment. One may not, however, forget what strain the woman took upon herself with this psychic effort. After this, together with her very pleasant and winning husband, she entered into group therapy, where she was again advised not to take the matter so seriously. Only about fifteen years after the ''outbreak'' of her jealous loss anxiety had she become sure enough of herself that she dared to think, and could say, "Why did it never occur to anyone that my husband could change something too?"

This is certainly an extreme example of a woman raised for love, but the reverse situation, that is, such an effort on the part of a man, is difficult to imagine, just as it is unlikely that there would be a feminine mirror-image correspondence for the following case.

A man is suffering greatly from his wife's passionate affair which, however, is over. She says that she *still* has no great desire to sleep with him, but she is honestly convinced that she would never have been able to conduct a marriage with her lover. Her husband's reproaches are directed not only against her infidelity, but also against other tendencies toward greater freedom (having a profession, participating in sports). She should change this. He imagined things differently when he married her. He compensates for the lack of sexual intimacy with pornographic magazines containing the crudest depictions of genitals—body parts, not people. The wife is revolted by this. The husband feels himself terribly restricted. He cannot think or work because of his unalloyed sense of injury. His solution is escape into a new love for a young woman, whom he has liked for a long time and whom he had renounced because of his marriage. He said that he was wanted there and was understood as a whole person, rather than only as someone who brought in the money or as his children's father, who had to put aside his sexual needs if that was desired.

This man too wanted to be loved, but what is obvious is the difference between his aggressive claim to genital confirmation and the desire of the woman in the previous example to take upon herself the greatest exertion for the sake of being loved (which also represents an exorbitant demand placed on her partner).

I would like to conclude this section about men and women with two references to statistical studies. In a study conducted by a psychoanalyst-gynecologist from Geneva, the following question was asked: "If you were forced, which of the following situations would you choose?" (1) Your partner makes love to you and, while doing so, thinks of another person. (2) Your partner makes love to someone else and, while doing so thinks of you.

Seventy percent of the men chose situation 1 because they thought it less alarming; almost as many women chose situation 2 (Rusconi 1982). Thus here too we see the need women have to be loved, not to lose their partner's love even under the most extreme circumstances. In addition, we see women's traditional resignation vis-à-vis male infidelity. Boldly stated, men on the contrary are more concerned with phallic confirmation, and the loss of love, even if it happens in their own arms, is feared less. Unfortunately I was unable to get more detailed information about this study, which therefore, as regards this question, almost remains in the realm of parlor games.

A more serious survey (Buunk 1982) of fifty Dutch couples who had had extramarital relationships shows, to begin with, a greater inclination toward jealousy among the women: 22 percent are "often jealous," compared with 2 percent of the men, even if in an acute triadic relationship jealousy is as good as unavoidable. In such a situation, 82 percent of the women and 86 percent of the men were jealous. But dealing with jealousy varies. Women attempt to work through it with a cognitive reappraisal of the relationship more frequently than men. They also withdraw from their husbands in the critical situation with significantly greater frequency. "This finding possibly still reflects the traditional way in which a wife was expected to react to infidelity in her husband: not making too much trouble, not showing jealousy, looking for the faults *she* has that push her husband to another woman, and just waiting for him to give up his wrong behavior (16–17)" It is noteworthy that even in the case of this test group, which is well above average educationally, professionally, and financially and which may without a doubt be viewed as very progressive in terms of sexual and communicative practices, the author reaches the conclusion "that sexually open relationships bring more costs and less benefits for the woman compared to the men (17)." He stresses, however, that jealousy is unavoidable and that, in the case of neurotics (who see themselves as nervous, pessimistic, tense, and worried), there is the danger that they will withdraw into themselves, deny conflicted feelings associated with the affair, or try to solve them entirely on their own. Furthermore, because of this, the partners will really be driven apart.

I would like to add to this that, regardless of what the statistics show, the distinction between "masculine" and "feminine" may shift and sometimes even disappear. Today we can see more clearly than before how right Freud was when he (as did, by the way, Jung and Adler too) used these concepts as ciphers for behavioral attitudes, rather than to characterize the respective sexes.

8. Aggression toward Whom?

The lack of rigor distinguishing gender-specific behavior especially applies to the direction aggression takes. Who is attacked, hated, and in extreme cases killed: the rival, the partner, or the jealous individual him- or herself?

The earliest consideration known to me of the question of jealous aggression is Edmund Bergler's (1939). For him, the choice of target for the jealous individual's aggression is dependent on the type of love at issue. His thesis is that in love, as it were, a role distribution of different psychic facets takes place: at any given time, the ego and the ego-ideal are involved. If one who loves activates the loftier, ideal conception of oneself, one's love will be active, solicitous, giving, domineering, and protective. If one sees one's ego-ideal in the beloved ("my better self, my better half"), then one will sub-ordinate oneself to the beloved; the individual will primarily admire, claim, enjoy the beloved, thus want to be loved passively. Although wanting to love can be schematically designated as masculine, and wanting to be loved as feminine, both forms can be found throughout both sexes; in Jürg Willi's terms, what is at issue is a progressive and a regressive position (1975, 1978). For Bergler, all the torment of jealousy is explained by the fact that one's own ego is *always* involved. In the case of infidelity, the actively loving person becomes aggressive toward the rival. One is thus so narcissistic that the beloved (the representative "only" of the ego and not of the much more highly valued ego-ideal) is actually not as important to one as the rival, in whom one is more likely to see an equal. The unfaithful person is thereby unmistakably shown that she or he is the "object" and that the matter will be settled between two acting subjects of disproportionately greater impor-tance than the one who is unfaithful. Bergler is of the opinion that the ho-mosexual explanation has no place here. The opposite seems to me to be the case. Only the partner of the same sex is fundamentally worthy of notice and aggression. The person of the opposite sex is more likely to be held in contempt and disregarded, and this goes on over her or his head.

In the case of wanting to be loved, the situation is different. The ego-ideal of the jealous individual is here stricken by infidelity. The person expresses disillusionment by directing rage and hatred against the unfaithful partner. Since the partner has played the main role in the life of the loving person and thus is much more significant than the loving person him- or herself, the rival is more likely to remain outside the field of confrontation. This pertains especially to jealous alcoholics (Llopis 1962), who indeed demonstrate with their addiction the extent to which their ego needs external reinforcement, and who almost never attack the rival.

Let us consider the major literary cases from this perspective: Othello and Pozdnishev, both very "masculine" men, kill their wives under the influence of an unbearable compulsion. Something that is beautiful literally "beyond all measure" is lost to both—Othello suddenly, Pozdnishev in a slow, carefully prepared process of disgusted disillusionment. It is perhaps not apparent at first sight that both men primarily want to be loved. It is obvious that they suffer from the ego-ideal ("the human being should be this way, and I would also like to be this way"). A story about jealousy in Boccaccio's *Decamerone* ([1348] 1981) also demonstrates this mechanism.

In Paris, Bernabo swears to his wife's unique fidelity and virtue, while all his fellow merchants believe in that of their wives no more than they believe in their own. Bernabo bets Ambrogiulo that the latter would not be able to seduce Bernabo's wife. Ambrogiulo tries but is unsuccessful.

However, by a series of cunning tricks, he obtains circumstantial proof that he has succeeded. Under the pretext of temporarily storing valuables, he has himself carried into her room in a trunk, uncovers her during the night, and sees a mole surrounded by golden hairs under her left breast. "When Bernado heard this, it was as if a knife had penetrated his heart. His pain was that great. And the pallor that suddenly suffused his entire face, even if he had spoken not a single word, would have been a manifest sign that it was as Ambrogiulo had said." Bernabo therefore loses the bet and part of his fortune (!) and assigns a servant the task of killing his wife (199ff.).

It is not of interest here that the story nonetheless has a happy ending because the servant is merciful and because the wife is not only virtuous but also clever, energetic, and adaptable. What is of interest, however, is the unambiguous and unquestioned aggression toward the previously idealized and then disappointing wife. Nevertheless, from a psychololgical perspective, the husband in this marriage may be "feminine" and the wife "masculine," that is, on top of everything, disguised as a man, she rises in the world under the aegis of a sultan (as can be read in the *Decamerone,* day 2, tale 9).

Such a clear division of aggression based on wanting to be loved or wanting to love seems to me problematical, because the aggression of jealous individuals often takes not only one direction but several. Nonetheless, the basic masculine-feminine assumption (anxiety about phallic confirmation, anxiety about the collapse of one's feeling of self-worth due to the loss of love) also fits Bergler's thesis. In the "masculine" case (as well as among phallic women), the one who threatens my phallus must himself be killed or at least castrated. In the "feminine" case (as well as among "feminine" men), I will attack the one who leaves me, and, in the worst situation, he must die.

Lagache's statistics are interesting in this context (Lagache [1947] 1982, 612). Of his 50 cases, 78 percent were preoccupied with thoughts of murder and suicide. *The most at risk were the men's female partners:* 11 men wanted to kill their wives and themselves; 1 his wife, the rival, and himself; 6 only the partner; 3 the partner and the rival. Thus, in 21 of 50 cases, the woman's life was threatened, at least in fantasy. *Among the women, aggression was more strongly directed against their own persons:* 10 women contemplated suicide; 5 of them, the exclusive destruction of their own life; the others, the related murder of the partner (1), the female rival (2), or both (2). In spite of all this, 2 women contemplated the murder of the rival and the partner without wanting to kill themselves. Since Lagache's statistics include more men than women (28 vs. 22), it is all the more noteworthy that *not a single man thought exclusively of suicide.* In almost half (10 of 22) of the female cases, and in much more than half of those who contemplated force at all (10 of 17), suicide fantasies played a role. On the contrary, thoughts of murder played a role in 22 of the 28 men. Every man who considered force also considered murder (22 of 22), 12 of them, to be sure, in combination with suicidal intent. Greater aggressiveness toward the other is obvious from this, as well as *the men's greater aggressiveness in general:* of the 28 men, only 6 did not contemplate force; of the 22 women, 5 did not have such thoughts, still a somewhat lower percentage.

Heinz Henseler's study confirms that *women commit suicide more frequently* than men (1974). He divided his 50 randomly selected cases of suicide attempts (39 women, 21 men) according to psychodynamic motivation in terms of their origin in oedipal, anal, and oral correlations (4 cases could not be classified in these terms). He demonstrated that a narcissistic crisis precipitates the related suicide attempt. *The largest group was the oral one* (20). Interestingly, *no triangles* at all played a role in this group, but rather often very minimal (as viewed from the outside) disillusionments intendant upon finally discovered, fragile, overidealized biangular relationships: arriving late, criticism of a hair style, among others. *The smallest group was the anal one* (8), and it was concurrently the group in which *jealousy* played a large role *in all cases;* for the suicides, however, it was jealousy suffered in the power struggle between the couple, not active jealousy. All 7 women in this group and the single (homosexual) man wanted to kill themselves because their *own efforts to gain independence* (separation, divorce, a new relationship) seemed to *fail due to the partner's jealousy,* control, and claim to possession. In terms of relational dynamics, one can understand this as the strong final trump in the power struggle, but on the other hand perhaps also as delegated aggression: the hate component of love does not indeed lead to the murder of the withdrawing person by the controlling person, out of rage at the threatened disassociation from his area of influence. Rather, the suicide is possibly guided not only by the feeling of not being *able* to live any longer, but also by the unspoken command denying *permission* to live any longer.

The *oedipal group was almost as large as the oral group* (17, 7 men and 10 women). Here it is remarkable that *insecurity about one's sexual role* played *a greater role than triadic relationships:* 4 men and 6 women attempted to take their own lives out of *disillusionment with* the partner due to his or her *intention to get a divorce,* but what was primarily behind this was despair at having failed as a husband or wife. (The difference with the anal group, where what was at issue was *one's own* forbidden desires oriented toward the outside, is striking.)

What follows from all these statistics is that women in jealousy conflicts are much more endangered by murder as well as suicide than men. Max Marcuse's essay (1950) even arrives at the conclusion that "the final *object* of jealous aggression is *always* the *woman,*" and Marcuse explicitly refers to Bergler's psychodynamic thesis.

In my thirty catamneses, one cannot confirm either the theisis that the person who is aggressive toward the partner primarily wants to be loved or the thesis that it is especially important to the person who adheres to the rival to be the actively loving party himself. Even Marcuse's thesis that aggression is always directed toward women does not hold true for our counseling cases.

Obviously I do not know my clients as precisely and as intimately as a psychoanalyst knows his or hers. Furthermore, one can always depend on the fact that desires and fears are constantly changing, and therefore, at the moment of acute risk, the constellation of forces was such as Bergler describes it. The response to the question of aggression, for which I asked by clients, refers to the case *as a whole* and not to an especially dangerous moment (see chap. 19, sec. 3). The clients reproduce their own evaluation of things. Mine was sometimes different.

Given these qualifications, I can say that the fields of aggression are very unclearly delineated. Many clients declared that they were enraged at *both* other persons in the triangle and, moreover, also at themselves. In some clients, aggression was plainly only directed toward the partner. ("The other women have nothing at all to do with me!") In others, it was only directed toward the rival. ("A power-hungry person—he was ready to use any means at his disposal. Had I met him on a dark street, I do not know if I would have been responsible for my actions.")

The homosexual role seems to me much more productive, both diagnostically and therapeutically, than the question of wanting to love or be loved. The last quotation, especially, admits of a homosexual interpretation, for what can the jealous man not be responsible for in the dark? Naturally, he consciously means that he would hit the rival on the head. In German, however, this expression is comically ambivalent (*Rübe,* "rape weed," is slang for "nut," "noodle").

9. More Women or More Men?

In the psychiatric literature, there are significantly more reports about masculine than feminine cases: Jaspers (1910), 7 men, 1 woman; Gausbeck (1928), 4 men, 1 woman; Todd and Dewhurst (1955), 9 men, 1 woman; Shepherd (1961), 63 men, 16 women; Vaukhonen (1968), 27 men, 18 women.

Jones and Mack-Brunswick (1928), on the contrary, assume it to be obvious that "women are more frequently afflicted by this emotion than men" (Jones 1930, 154). Vaukhonen's careful psychodynamically oriented study confirms this but also concurrently—and this is where the main difference probably lies—the unequivocal preponderance of severe psychiatric pathological syndromes among men. Vaukhonen comes to the conclusion that men "become pathologically jealous" more frequently, more seriously, and (in terms of age) earlier than women (1968, 171). Women, on the contrary, are more inclined toward neurotic jealousy. He declares himself to be opposed to the assumption of biological factors as the exclusive explanation for these differences: pyschological and sociocultural determinants also play a role. The contrast between severe psychotic ruptures in men and the reverse more-frequent neurotic, so to speak more ordinary, forms of jealousy in women seems to me to fit the different way of dealing with suffering in both sexes that was observed by Richter (1974). There too it looks as if women are provided with better antennae for suffering and risks and, as it were, suffer more persistently but therefore not as dangerously. Men, on the other hand, expect to pull themselves together, to have strength, and have a more inflexible self-image, which is more susceptible to radical damage precisely because of these high expectations. To express it somewhat cynically, "Women complain, men become ill" (Wirsching and Stierlin 1982, 35).

△ 17 △

FROM THE TRIANGLE BACK TO
THE BIANGULAR RELATIONSHIP

1. No Oedipus: Ruth Mack-Brunswick

Freud was of the opinion that severe cases of jealousy could be explained psychoanalytically, but that they could not be cured (Freud 1922, 1917, 254 ff.). In later years, he no longer commented on this, but could not have looked unfavorably upon a young disciple's splendid work. In a period of only two and one-half months, she treated the jealousy paranoia of a woman who was only slightly older than she and who, by the way, as a "proletarian" was completely different from the usual middle-class patients who underwent psychoanalysis. At the time this analysis took place, Ruth Mack-Brunswick was twenty-five years old (twenty-seven at the time the case was reported in print), and the patient was thirty. When one calls to mind the educational requirements of contemporary psychoanalytical institutes, it seems almost miraculous that so young a physician could handle the tools of her trade, which in the short course of its history had become quite complicated, with such assurance and competence.

The patient who was referred to Mack-Brunswick was "small, poorly developed, intelligent, and not entirely without charm." The diagnosis had been jealousy paranoia, and she was sent to Mack-Brunswick because the family refused to have her institutionalized. Her prehistory was horrible: "a desolate jealousy landscape, suicide threats, a serious suicide attempt at the police station," threatened institutionalization. The symptoms were many and varied: total frigidity, vaginism, two to three weeks of bleeding after every act of intercourse, the tortuous notion that her husband had a sexual relationship with her stepmother, the feeling that strangers were laughing at her on the street, periodic fits of rage accompanied by a "ringing and buzzing" in her ears, the feeling that an electric current was passing through her head. The family history sounds desolate: There were five children, of whom the patient is the youngest. After being ill for several years, the mother died when the patient was not yet three. A mentally retarded sister, who was ten years older, became the patient's protector and closest referent. This sister lived as a prostitute before she reached puberty, and died of progressive paralysis in a mental hospital at the age of twenty-nine (the age at which the patient's psychosis began).

Unfortunately, I cannot go further into the details of this plainly suspenseful study, which is also an introduction to the techniques of psychoanalysis as it was then practiced. I can only stress the main points. At the root of the matter is a seduction of the patient, who was very young at the time (her mother became ill before she was one) by her sister, which led to a varied sex life and a true love relationship between the two sisters. Freud has often pointed to the serious nature and formative impact of such early loves (for example, 1896a, 142; 1905a, 61, 129). The feeling of having done something forbidden remained deeply imprinted on the patient's unconscious, for those aspects of this "terrible love" that came to light were, of course, received by society with harsh threats and punishment.

With a lot of hard work, the patient and her analyst discovered that the reflected love for her stepmother, and the yearning for her real, deceased mother, were at the bottom of things. An enormous hatred arose in the small child whenever her sister, who went with boys at an early age, left her: "I wanted to have her to myself!" As a parallel to this, the grown woman hated her stepmother, whom she felt wanted to steal her husband, and later, through transference, also her analyst when the latter manipulatively (!) provoked her jealousy by having the patient's husband come to the analyst's office for a conference. As a consequence, a few days later the patient "suffers a panic attack, the outside world suddenly ceased to exist, she was only aware of a horrible ringing and electrical buzzing in her head, and she was seized by the thought that I would like her husband better than her. She bit her hands and knew that she had no choice but to commit suicide" (Mack-Brunswick 1928, 480).

In dealing with this transference of jealous love, one can show in a nutshell what takes place in an analysis: just "remembering, repeating, working through." By means of the analyst's realistic and matter-of-fact refusal to respond to the patient's erotic overtures, which this time, however, unlike the young woman's earlier experiences, were not associated with punishment or condemnation, she could correct the experiences. It could no longer be said, If I love, things must go badly for me because that is forbidden. Rather, the love was permitted to exist, but just as would be the case with a good mother, it was lovingly frustrated and redirected toward its "proper" object, the husband.

After love has been experienced, it becomes possible to experience hate. In a hallucination she had at home the patient saw her deceased sister, who was laughing at her. "All her bitterness and repressed anger culminates in the thought, 'If only she were dead!' " (494). During analysis she recalled the above-mentioned scene with boys, in which she felt radically rejected not only by her sister but also by her stepmother, whose love she desperately sought as a substitute for her sister's love. Working through this central experience made it possible to bring the analysis to a conclusion.

In conclusion, it may be said that the patient—since her sister died so soon—could only experience the ineffectiveness of her death wish in analysis. Before that, her reemergent love for her sister (with her husband) forced her to remain caught in a literally maddening web of guilt feelings, hatred, and self-punishment. A developmental block arrested her in "the all-encompassing narcissism of the child, which . . . expects love and recognition everywhere" (496), because this expectation could, on the one hand, never be fulfilled and, on the other, was never sufficiently, phase-appropriately restrained.

"Narcissism" is a key term for the continuing development of research into the problem of jealousy. Mack-Brunswick was skeptical of the success of her treatment. Nonetheless, when viewed from the contemporary perspective, it seems to me that there is no doubt that a connection between cure and treatment does exist. During treatment, the many complaints disappeared; the patient's intercourse with her husband became not only possible, but even pleasurable; the relationships with her stepmother and her mother-in-law were normalized. Furthermore, all of this was still in effect and stable two and one-half years after the conclusion of the analysis. In view of these successes, I consider the well-worn skepticism of physicians, "post hoc or propter hoc" ("*after* treatment," simply because of the passage of time, "or *because of* treatment") to be exaggerated, as well as the supposition that it could be a matter of spontaneous remission, which even Shepherd asserts in connection with similar cases (Shepherd 1961, 702).

What is most conspicuous about Mack-Brunswick as a disciple of Freud is the *complete absence of the Oedipus complex,* in spite of the actual presence of a father. She explains this based on the fact that the patient, unconsciously but most profoundly disillusioned by the loss of her mother, was so spoiled and overgratified by her sister's surrogate love, that the reality of the masculine, and thus also disappointment at the clitoris, could find no place in her life. Only the confrontation with her husband's demands then made her "crazy." She projected her homosexual desires onto him and became "madly" jealous.

Freud himself stressed that Mack-Brunswick was the first one who was able to cure and describe a case of pre-oedipal fixation (1933, 140). She and other women such as Jeanne Lampl–de Groot or Helene Deutsch, as well as Melanie Klein and Karen Horney from whom Freud explicitly distanced himself with regard to this question (as he also did from Jones), apparently have, as Freud himself said, more direct access to the first maternal bonding than he. This is because, for them, maternal transference occurs more easily. Everything having to do with this appeared to Freud, even as an old man, "so difficult to grasp analytically, so ancient and shadowy, and barely capable of being revived" (1931, 519).

Nonetheless, even as a seventy-five-year-old, Freud was able to reformulate his ideas about female sexuality. This sexuality is closely related to the pre-oedipal mother. Her powerful image and its relationship to the development of individual narcissism have been heeded more and more since then. Indeed, it looks as if this uncertainty would call into question the central position of the Oedipus complex or at least cause its importance to be reassessed (see in this connection the publications of Kohut, Kernberg, Grunberger, and the popular studies of Alice Miller and Christopher Lasch, or Wangh's 1983 essay). For our purposes, it is sufficient for the time being to cite the definition of narcissism in the *Wörterbuch der Psychoanalyse* (Dictionary of psycho-analysis): "Based on the myth of Narcissus: the love that one has for one's own self-image."

In the early days of psychoanalysis, what was meant by this was primarily a disturbance, or even abnormal behavior. (In the beginning, the concepts "autoerotisicm" and "narcissism" were not clearly distinguished.) The con-temporary view distinguishes between healthy narcissism, that is, the feeling of self-worth that is in keeping with reality, and narcissistic disturbances that consist of a broad spectrum of retreat to one's own person. This can be a matter of a drastic overestimation of oneself accompanied by contempt, in-difference, and exploitation in dealing with other people. It can also be the opposite, drastic underestimation of the self (feelings of inferiority, depres-sions). In the extreme case, therefore, our triangle collapses into one angle. To express it differently, it collapses into a being centered on itself, which in the worst case (autism, catatonia) is totally immobile or, in a somewhat less severe case, revolves exclusively around itself or only communicates with something unreal, that is, one's own reflection. These genetically very early and often very severe disturbances were long considered to be incurable, because those suffering from them were viewed as incapable of developing a transference because of the basic malformation of the capacity to relate to an object. In the meantime, this has changed. Not only borderline and psy-chotic cases are treated, but sometimes, at least in view of published reports, it looks as if psychoanalysis no longer treats anything other than early disturbances.

Later I will deal with the connection between narcissism and the relation-ship to the mother, and its relationship to jealousy (see sec. 6 below), and thus return once more to Mack-Brunswick. In any case, long before the Oedipus complex was completely differentiated, it became clear that one could not continue with Oedipus alone. In 1922 Freud had already designated the wound to narcissism as one of the components of jealousy. Not only Mack-Brunswick, but everybody else who published something new on the topic, delved deeper and further back into the developmental history of their patients. The Oedipus complex did not thereby become insignificant but was understood more precisely in terms of its origin.

2. Incorporation

Even the layperson can perceive what sucks dry and is devouring in jealous love. Thus it is not surprising that, long before the narcissism discussion of the sixties expanded the theory of the relationship between self and object, therapeutic work on stress caused by drives paid attention to the earliest psychosexual developmental phase. In this phase the child experiences pleasure and the denial of pleasure primarily through the processes of nourishment, especially of sucking, that is, through the mouth (the oral phase). In this regard, it is important to keep in mind that one cannot eat something without destroying it. There is no more radical merging than that produced by eating, but also no more radical destruction. Thus, according to Karl Abraham, a large range of fundamental ambivalence (the oral-sadistic stage) appears here for the first time in human libido development (Laplanche and Pontalis 1974, 362), a range that has, of course, already frequently confronted us as the basic characteristic of jealousy. It is obvious that the relationship to the mother, thus a dyad, plays a decisive role in the oral stage.

In 1932 an Englishwoman, Joan Riviere, who worked closely with the German emigrant Melanie Klein, published a case history in which "jealousy as a mechanism of defense," that is, against desires to devour and rob, is described. What is interesting in this study is that jealousy was not the occasion for therapy, but rather "the achievement of orgasm" was, the elimination of the patient's frigidity. Jealousy only appeared incidentally, as a so-called symptom of passage, so that, precisely because of this, its origins could be clearly observed.

The patient, a young married woman with children, claimed never to have been jealous. Her husband was the most important person in her life. During analysis, when she engaged in fierce attacks against her husband and developed severe mistrust of the analyst while the external situation remained unchanged, the analyst, in keeping with already established tradition, at first thought of projections of infidelity. The patient flirted with success and pleasure. Thus it may also have been possible that she desired continuing infidelity for herself and put the blame on her husband to exonerate herself. These desires were responsive to analysis, but the jealousy symptom, which at this time was very severe and paranoid, did not disappear. What, therefore, was being projected? According to Riviere, it was more elementary, more aggressive, and therefore even more strongly resisted desires, "the ruling passion of her life," namely, to pillage and rob another person. A triangle was also necessary for this: the patient and *two* objects, of which only one unconditionally had to be a person. The other could also be a thing, but a thing that was valued and dear to the person who was to be robbed. If the second object was a person, then the person had to "belong" to the first. The patient tried again and again, as the central theme of her life, to fulfill this "dominating fantasy," which concurrently produced bad guilt feelings: for example, in flirting the issue was not that she liked the men but that she could take them away from other women; or she, who never had been interested in expensive clothing, had to have some just at the time her husband was in financial difficulties; or she haggled over prices while shopping or cheated outright.

Riviere, following Klein, traces the origin of this fantasy to the oral period, which goes back to well before the Oedipus complex: as a nursing infant, the patient, who Riviere assumes has an especially strong innate libido, wanted to suck her mother dry, devour her, and rob her of her entire body content, to which the father's penis, as well as possible unborn siblings, belongs (see Klein 1975). When the unconscious fantasy patterned after these archaic desires became too strong, or when it came close to being realized, fear of punishment became so great that the patient projected her desires, whereby she concurrently punished herself: that could happen only in jealousy, since she had in the meantime, of course, become a grown woman. In her jealous moods, she consistently complained that her husband and his other women stripped her of everything, ridiculed, tormented and dishonored her, robbed her of his love, her own self-esteem and her self-confidence, discarded her like a sacrifice that is helplessly exposed (Riviere 1932, 182). After the uncovering of this fantasy complex, jealousy disappeared, as did its reverse, the flirtations (i.e., the unconscious *active* living out of what is described above as endured).

I do not want to deal here with the fact that an analyst of a different orientation would, perhaps, have found other dreams in the patient that were satisfying and therefore could have helped in the cure. Nor do I want to deal with the fact that the husband, too, gave grounds for jealous suspicion (ibid., 177). Nor do I want to ask whether we can really believe, as Riviere claims, that in the case of such severe symptoms the mother was "especially loving and generous" (184), "was always present and always kind" (185). Nor do I want to discuss whether we consider it possible that a tiny child of less than a year could have an innate conception of the content of her mother's body, which also includes the father's penis (cf. Joffe 1969; Kernberg 1976, e.g., 118). What is important is that, in this severe form of jealousy, the "simple genital Oedipus complex" plays only a small role; that the problem was "genitalized" in order to make it appear less harmful. 'Triangle situations,' which one is after all accustomed to view as the expression of the highest object love, [can] *still* be rooted in narcissism (Riviere 1932, 188, emphasis added).

In order to understand this better, we must continue to keep in mind that adult neurotics revive what was not worked through in their earliest childhood. To give just one innocuous example, anyone who has once seen an adult experience a breakdown knows what a terrible impression childish behavior, such as uninhibited crying, foot stamping, and thrashing about, makes and how inappropriate it is in adults. A woman who literally wanted to eat, suck dry, and dismember her mother or a mother substitute would be frightening as well. It is then understandable that the reemergence of the oedipal situation where, in spite of everything, three conscious individuals are involved who perceive themselves as such and not as body parts (penis, breast, the so-called partial objects), is more acceptable than confession of the desire to incorporate and rob. As far as the reinterpretation of the Oedipus complex is concerned, let us remember the prerequisite of the "damaged third party," which surely is invested with a more profound meaning by Klein's theory.

3. Wanting to See and Having to Show Oneself

In jealousy, as in every addiction, the fact that delight and torment coincide becomes obvious again and again. An author rarely cited in later studies asserts briefly and schematically, "The jealous individual's masochistic delight is secondary, and corresponds to an erotization of punishment by the superego" (Bergler 1939). With this, Bergler points to a psychic way of working through things, which can be found especially in the most extreme form of masochism, masochistic perversions (Eisenbud 1967, Stoller 1975, Reik 1940). Something very damaging, that is, punishment for discovered guilt by the successor to one's real parents, the superego, is transformed into a source of delight—a victory of Eros over pain. To be sure, in perversions the delight is consciously experienced, while in jealousy it is only "unconsciously enjoyed." As Stoller writes, if in manifest perversions "trauma becomes triumph," whereby the trauma remains unconscious and must be uncovered by analysis, then in jealousy the reverse is true: the trauma or its repetition is conscious, or at least closer to consciousness, while the triumph is hidden deep in the unconscious.

Masochism, the self-tormenting satisfaction that is so difficult for jealous individuals to perceive, much less to admit, is primarily evident in what Bergler calls the "visual imperative" of jealous individuals: they "must" repeatedly look at, think about, and imagine what takes place between the partner and the rival. All explanations—oral, oedipal, as well as sociological and relational dynamic—struggle with this central riddle. In the relationship to the partner, the masochistic compulsion to look is often connected with sadistic behavior, which is its twin and an integral part of it: for the jealous individual to be able "to see," the partner must be repeatedly subjected to the third degree and thereby tormented (see M. Balint et al. 1972). This is frequently found in cases treated in terms of the marriage and leads inexorably to divorce or at least to further distancing, when the partner withdraws from the sadomasochistic game, but the jealous individual wants to continue with it because she or he cannot risk any progressive development. The disappearance of satisfaction is experienced as extremely threatening: for example, as reported by Ping-nie Pao, when the wife, reinforced by the beginning of her own analysis, refuses to submit to the eternal questioning, her husband often dreams that he is being killed, and develops a brief psychotic reaction (1969, 624).

From where does this voyeurism come? It is apparently strongly forbidden and appears to be permitted only under the umbrella of aggression toward the beloved. A Freudian like Bergler naturally thinks of oedipal fantasies in this context: "the repressed desire to observe parental intimacies [is] reactualized with subsequent guilt feelings" (1939, 387). The child, that is, the jealous individual, thereby plays the role of the raping father as well as that of the raped mother. As we may add today, however, the child perhaps also plays the role of the overpowerful mother and the overpowered father. In any case, the tormenting inescapability of the parental union, which the child cannot penetrate, is thereby experienced (cf. the dangerous unified father-mother imago in Kernberg 1976). In especially jealous individuals, the desire to look is simultaneously extremely seductive and extremely forbidden.

At this point, Bergler takes a bold leap: according to Freud, all voyeurism, as well as its reverse, exhibitionism, is most profoundly narcissistic. In this, he refers to Freud's theses about the antitheses active-passive (Freud 1914a, 222ff.), which may generally be found in love. In reference to voyeurism and exhibitionism, Freud is of the opinion that the child at first observes himself (Freud is again naturally unclear about what the girl-child, who got the short end of the stick, can observe), then turns to observing others, too. And when that is forbidden, the child prefers to have himself observed in order to regain, in this way, joy in his own body, being, and self. The underlying active component is never totally surrendered, "the older active drive orientation continues to exist next to the more recent passive component." Thus the links between voyeurism, exhibitionism, and the desire to display (in which one wants not only oneself, but also the beloved or the couple's sex act, to be observed by others) that crisscross the difficult paths to identification, are not only possible but are the rule. The exhibitionistic component can, in fact, often be observed in jealous individuals—once the dam has been broken, they must not only continuously look at it but also constantly talk about it and thus tirelessly show themselves in their entire unhappiness. The narcissistic, self-centered component is clearer in this than it is in staring at it. We are reminded of La Rochefoucauld's maxim, that "jealousy contains more self-love than love," and therefore understand the unattractiveness of people who are chronically preoccupied with jealousy: anyone seeking contact with them feels oneself constantly offended, because they are so much more important to themselves than all others.

4. Ego versus Ego-Ideal

Running headlong into the torment of looking and putting oneself on display is, as mentioned above, unconsciously pleasurable. That means the simple explanation that one is narcissistically wounded because the beloved does not love one, but someone else, does not suffice—for then jealousy would not be characterized, for example, by pathology, by not being able to let go. Rather the wounded person would overcome the injury and either return to him- or herself or turn to another object. She or he remains bound, however, to the unfaithful person and thereby to punishment by the superego. In order to explain the origin of this unconscious pleasure, Bergler predicates a genuine drama of, as it were, intrapsychic subcharacters. Bergler proceeds from the structure of the superego, of which Freud says that it has two faces: "Its relationship to the ego is not exhausted in the warning that you *should* be like that (like the father), but also contains the following prohibition: *You may not* be that way (like the father), that is, not do everything he does (1923b, 263; emphasis in original). Bergler (1939) intensifies Freud's description: he isolates the role of "you shall not" and calls it the "demon." As the "instrument of torture," this has the ego-ideal at its disposal, with whose help it provides the ego with guilt feelings. Moreover, it is opposed to every love. Considering the child's experiences with his or her real parents, this would mean that love remains the preserve of the parents and the child can look after him- or herself. Love per se, therefore, already awakens guilt feelings; and within such a cruel construct it is more than understandable that at least guilt feelings are then eroticized.

In its predicament, the ego grasps at a trick: since it would unequivocally like to love, it projects its ego-ideal onto the beloved, thereby mitigating the guilt feelings. In "love," which Bergler readily places within quotation marks, the split between ego and ego-ideal therefore disappears; they are one, and guilt feelings are silent for a time. If the object, however, becomes unfaithful, then the demon again has the upper hand: it "holds the mirror of the ego-ideal up to the ego," and the latter feels bad because it has chosen such an unworthy object in the first place. That, however, represents one's own ego-ideal, the better image of oneself, and the hopes that one has for oneself; even these now prove themselves bad, when the ego that is consciously experiencing itself does not, in any case, have a very high opinion of itself. No wonder depression appears "on the psychic surface." And the jealous individual declines in a devouring maelstrom of guilt feelings and the partial relief of transferring guilt to the Other, all of which is eroticized again and again.

I have chosen to use lightly ironic language, because the conception of the marionette-like dance of these different psychic instances seems to me to go somewhat too far. One has the impression that Faust would be happy to harbor only two souls in his breast, and not the ego, id, superego, demon, and instruments of torture to which he had been helplessly delivered up. At least this is the way it sounds in Bergler. Although within psychoanalysis, fortunately, there is criticism of determinism as well as of anthropomorphic language (Kohut 1977, 248 ff.; Schafer 1976), I should remind the possibly confused reader that psychoanalytic essays generally are written about severe disturbances and not about "normal" phenomena that occur every day. Nonetheless, they are indispensable for the understanding of normality but most especially for the understanding of regressions that take place in every life during times of crises (and are often overcome, or simply outlived, without the help of a psychotherapist).

Bergler's argumentation, which is as complicated as it is incontestably convoluted, seems to me, however, to explain something important: the as it were dual participation of the jealous individual. "The most profound reason why jealousy is so tormenting is based on the disappointment in one's own ego-ideal. Thus one's own person is always affected. The disappointment that the jealous individual experiences in his own ego-ideal is, however, at the same time also disappointment in his own narcissism" (1939, 389–90). Almost three centuries earlier, La Rochefoucauld expressed it this way: "The pains of shame and jealousy are so sharp because vanity cannot serve to endure them" (1967, maxim 46). Thirty years after Bergler's essay, Kohut no longer speaks as Bergler did of "infantile delusions of grandeur," which should protect the ego-ideal, but rather of the grandiose self-image and self-objects (Kohut 1971). From the perspective of fantasies of omnipotence, Kohut sees in a new light the relationship between the experience of the self and the mother-child dyad, and thus the demand to control people close to one as it is expressed in jealousy.

What we can hold onto from Bergler is that, at least in the main section of his work, the triangle changes, approaching a biangular or even mono-angular relationship: the third party becomes remarkably diffuse and in the end even the second party almost disappears.*

5. *The Kreutzer Sonata* as an Example

Some consideration of Tolstoy's *Kreutzer Sonata* (1973) should show how much one is able to explain with the classical instrumentation of psychoanalysis, which is only interested in the individual and his or her intrapsychic problems.

The exhibitionistic compulsion of the main character, Pozdnishev, is only too apparent. In the frame story, he intervenes provocatively for a long time in the conversations of total strangers, until he can finally say, "I am Pozdnishev, the hero of the episode to which you are alluding, the episode that consisted of the fact that he killed his wife (96)." *No one,* however, had alluded to this. One of the people also traveling in the train compartment, painfully moved by Pozdnishev's violent attacks on the institution of marriage, had only tentatively acknowledged that "Yes, without a doubt there are critical episodes in marital life." Thereupon, everybody turns away in embarrassment, and leaves. One withdraws into sleep. The first-person narrator, who remains, becomes the auditor of the murderer's story of suffering and hate.

Pozdnishev feels himself, his real "ego" before marriage, to be crudely sensual, "dissolute" but, in this, completely normal in a society in which "one detaches oneself from moral duties toward the woman with whom one has sexual intercourse (98)." At least, if one is not married to the woman. Pozdnishev's desire, his ego-ideal, is purity. "I wallowed in the filth of vice, and at the same time looked around for girls who, in their purity, would have been more worthy of me (104)." Finally he finds one, beautiful but poor, so that he can feel himself free of materialistic intentions. He believes that she "understood everything, everything I thought and felt, and that she thought of and felt nothing but sublime things (104)."—the ego and the ego-ideal merge in harmony and communality. In retrospect, however, the demon says, "Actually it was nothing else but that her blouse and curls suited her face very well." And

---

*I use the term "biangular relationship," which may sound odd to some readers, in order to made clear that the basic configuration of jealousy remains the triangle. In the case of adults, the regression to a symbiotic-dyadic form of separation anxiety and surveillance between only two people, which in general parlance is also called jealousy, seems to me to be like the special case of a triangle whose third angle is eliminated, thus causing the two sides to collapse together. The term "dyad" has many positive aspects; "biangular" sounds more threatening and abnormal. This is what I wanted to express.

for several pages following, Pozdnishev comments sarcastically on the infamous tactics of mothers, who see through everything. They dangle their daughters, "with these vulgar jersey blouses, these padded rear ends, these naked shoulders and arms, and almost naked breasts," as bait before men whose impurity they know but deny. In this way women, who are without rights, rule the world: "You all want us to serve only to satisfy your sensual desires—fine! Then we will make you slaves through sexual pleasure (111)." The cutting masochism of a disappointed lover cannot be expressed more pointedly than in this description of the woman who, nonetheless, represents his own ego-ideal. During the engagement, Pozdnishev considers not only his fiancée, but also himself, perfect. He wants to live monogamously and faithfully—the demon has been silenced and the instrument of torture taken away from him, since there is no tension between the ego and its ideal.

This harmony already disintegrates during the honeymoon. The first quarrel opens up an abyss. Reality, at first viewed with disbelief ("She isn't at all like that!"), prevails over idealization: "Two egoists, total strangers to each other, who seek to get as much gratification from each other as possible, (120–21)" confront one another. Pozdnishev is at the same time attracted and repelled by the quality in his wife that he despises in himself yet feels is unavoidable: her sensuality. In the psychoanalytical sense, jealousy is a logical consequence of this: "throughout my entire married life, I never ceased to suffer the torments of jealousy (130)"— jealousy that is truly not because of love, but because of several levels of causality.

The realistic level is uppermost: he is especially jealous when his wife's physicians forbid her to nurse. Jealousy plagues him even more than usual when she is not pregnant, that is, when he notices that "previously restrained feminine coquetry was expressed in her with special intensity, (130)" and she can be psychically freer than when she is tied to her maternal function. He caustically recognizes his wife's sensuality, and sees the parallelism between "short-term prostitutes" (whores in the literal sense) who are despised, and "long-term prostitutes" (wives) who are esteemed. He sees her "mature beauty" when the physicians forbid her to have any more children after her sixth child, and she emerges out of the sphere of suffering and concern for her children; it is, therefore, only realistic to expect her to develop an interest in other men, which is later confirmed.

The second level of the causes of jealousy is that of projected infidelity: he who previously led a dissolute life and who does not love his partner, for whom he made the decision to be monogamous—how should he not have desires to be unfaithful, which he needs to repress? In transferring these desires to her, he exonerates himself.

The third level would, according to Freud, be that of homosexual projection—suppressed interest in the rival, which Velikovsky (1937) has shown to be valid for *The Kreutzer Sonata*. In fact, the extent to which the rival, Truchatchevsky, is endowed with feminine attributes is very obvious. It is also obvious how "a peculiarly fateful force" drives Pozdnishev "not to repel him, not to distance him, but, on the contrary, to pull him closer (152)." The (narcissistic) evaluation of one's own esteem (one makes oneself ridiculous when one is jealous) is presented as one explanation, among others, for this. There is, however, probably a deep-seated compulsion in this. It is not only the homosexual compulsion, but also the deeply rooted compulsion of the "oral pessimist" who, according to Bergler, repeatedly wants to put his wife, as his mother's successor, in the wrong, in order at least to derive satisfaction from having his prediction come true: "I of course always knew that you do not love me."

The fact that both come close to suicide is evidence of how strong and threatening the all-consuming demand of this evil symbiosis is. They cannot let go of each other or cling to each other, at least not affectionately. The enormously rich texture of Tolstoy's story allows us to trace jealousy in all its psychosexual developmental stages, not only in the oral stage, but also in the anal (the exercise of power) and the phallic (confirmation of one's own sexuality). However, the longing to be as one certainly is at the root of it. This longing cannot be fulfilled, its fulfillment is not even desirable, yet it is repeatedly sought in outbreaks of sexual passion that the married couple experience until the end. Sexuality, however, cannot replace paradise, that is, true love. Pozdnishev says right at the beginning that a person who has become a "whoremaster" will never again be able to discover "a straightforward, pure, sisterly relationship to a woman" (102). The desperate desire for an asexual relationship between two people with concurrent total fulfillment of one's needs is basically what is behind this. It is the desire for a relationship like that between mother and child in earliest childhood. For a long time, Pozdnishev ponders the ultimate nonnecessity of sexuality—the world need not continue to exist, it should perish (through abstinence!)—that is his utopia.

Since all of this is unrealizable, however, he himself produces the situation that, in the society in which he lives, gives him the opportunity for jealousy and thus for hate and sanctioned aggression: his wife's having a love relationship or, at least, a closer relationship to another man. It is, moreover, never said how far this relationship went on a physical level. He is acquitted in court and feels his deed justified on the basis of what he has construed from his own fantasies. "I saw the animal which dwelled in both of them and . . . asked: 'May I?' And the answer was: 'Certainly (154).'" A series of textual references indicates that Pozdnishev's wife and the violinist indeed felt the presence of this animal but dealt with it in a way that was permitted within the framework of societal conventions, references which therefore indicate that adultery did not take place. Nonetheless, there is something between the two of them that Pozdnishev cannot penetrate and that he does not understand (just as, in terms of psychoanalysis, he has not understood the primal scene): music. One has only to reread the unbelievable description of the effect the first presto of the Kreutzer Sonata has: "as if I felt something, that I actually do not feel at all; as if I understood, what I actually do not understand at all; as if I could do, what I cannot do (164)." The violinist and the pianist wife seem strict, serious, and transfigured; it is like a premonition of a sensual yet pure relationship, and this relationship exists for the other two, but not for Pozdnishev. In reference to the music, it seems as if the watching that is allowed (let me remind you of Bergler's voyeuristic thesis) has a liberating effect. Both spouses are "extremely satisfied" with the evening, and Pozdnishev thinks that "new unknown feelings emerged in her as in me; they rose up, as it were, out of memory (166)."

The utopia, however, is not sustained: human nature, which according to Tolstoy is most profoundly corrupted, again changes everything for the worse; friendly watching again becomes masochistically enjoyed voyeurism, to which Pozdnishev addictively surrenders himself. Compulsively, inescapably, he imagines what the two are doing: "I looked at these images and could not tear myself away from them (171)." They become reality for him. Punishment by the superego is inextricably tied to this, since what he imagines is indeed tormenting but, in the language of psychoanalysis, is eroticized: "With a kind of enthusiasm, I lacerated my own heart (171)."

Not only Pozdnishev's pitiable condition during the narration in the train, but also the confusion of images of murder and being murdered show the extent to which the punishment is meant not only for his wife, but for him as well. This is also shown by the dreadful parting from his destroyed wife on her deathbed, which is described with pitiless precision. It is a parting in hatred and without forgiveness. However, one reads, "For the first time I saw the human being in her" (187), for the first time he sees her and his own reality without projective distortion. He has gained insight through guilt, suffering, and condemnation—like Oedipus. "I am a ruin, a cripple! I have only one advantage over others: I know! . . . To recognize what swine we are is difficult, terribly difficult (133)."

Tolstoy dismisses Pozdnishev without reconciliation, but having become aware—almost as if through psychoanalysis. The symptom—jealousy—has been overcome. Unhappiness, to be sure, remains. As is known, Freud also wanted nothing more, and nothing less, than to transform "hysterical misery into ordinary unhappiness" (1986a, 312). As he says to his patients, "you will be better able to resist the latter with recovered psychic life." Has Pozdnishev recovered? Apparently not. He holds himself erect only with an enormous reaction formation, with hatred and derogation of the entire world of drives. He can only say, "Had I known what I know now, then . . . I would not have married her for anything in the world. . . would not have married at all" (188). What he cannot, however, say is, Then I would have been able to love her; I would have been able to have faith in her and in myself; I would have been able to accept sensuality, to remain within Tolstoy's relational frame, as God's gift. The world, which opens itself to him in music in the way of a premonition, remains closed.

Pozdnishev has, moreover, heard of Freud's great teacher Charcot: "Charcot would certainly have said of my wife that she was hysterical, but of me . . . that I am abnormal, and would perhaps have prescribed a cure for both of us" (140). Tolstoy's solution in the face of this fundamental human forlornness is known: it is that of Christian renunciation of the world, which goes so far that Pozdnishev says, "The words in the gospel, that everyone who looks at a woman to lust for her has already committed adultery with her in his heart, do not refer only to other women, but primarily to one's own wife (119)." Tolstoy, who depicts an important part of himself in Pozdnishev, never became healthy in the psychoanalytical sense. He was, however, perhaps "saved," elevated to the conception of a history of the world and life in which everything finally ends well. Tolstoy's wife, to be sure, was left behind in this attempt to save his soul and the soul of his many adherents. I shall speak of this later.

Psychoanalysis has nothing to offer that compares with hopes of salvation. Although areligious, it confirms in its own way the Christian concept of the absolute necessity of love, and its redeeming function. Pozdnishev would not have been incurable for psychoanalysis, because its goal is growth in the capacity for love (naturally asexual love *too*), and not its strangulation. Of course Pozdnishev would have had to be able to embark upon the adventure of a relationship for the purpose of being healed. This relationship can be called "love" only in quotation marks, but nonetheless is a form of love— therapeutic love in which he could for a time experience reliability, concern, unselfishness, and the central experience of being taken seriously. Pozdnishev can apparently not allow himself to love: "I avoided women who could have tied me to them by too great devotion or by the birth of a child (98)." However, only one who was once loved can love oneself. Only by means of this experience, thus our utopia, can jealousy's intensity contribute to the possibility of a positive change in both participants.

6. Omnipotence and Impotence:
Mother and Child, You and I

Pozdnishev, and every ordinary person who murders on account of jealousy, is a dreadful example of La Rochefoucauld's maxim, "Jealousy is the worst of all passions. It has no pity for the person whom it claims to love." The more Pozdnishev's passionate condition intensifies, the more unambiguously his only concern is doing what he himself wants. There is no longer a question of love, or of compassion, or even of interest in his wife and the violinist, whose intimacies he previously imagined in such a passionately and tortuously delightful way. When he murders, his only concern is the satisfaction of his own needs. The "love that one has for one's own self-image," narcissism, is here felt to be so dangerous that Pozdnishev can in fact do nothing but, in the most radical sense, eliminate from the world what endangers him. From where does this power come?

It may still be, and continue to be, surprising that, even in these most severe wounds to human reciprocity, psychoanalysis reaches back to early, even earliest, childhood. The myth of the innocent child and of the mother-child relationship as the exemplar of natural, instinctive love, cannot be destroyed; I believe that it is precisely this indestructibility that shows the denial, the not wanting to see, of all of us. This is, to be sure, a fairly new acquisition in our culture. Before the belief in the inherent goodness of humanity arose in the eighteenth century, and peaked in Rousseau's hope that if one would only return to nature, everything would become good again and remain good, the Christian image of basically corrupt humanity determined the Western conception. And in view of the contemporary state of the world, it seems as if the Christian view was more clear-sighted than the view of the high-spirited representatives of the Enlightenment. Pozdnishev, or his creator Tolstoy, stands for an extreme form of Christian pessimism. Psychoanalysis, thoroughly representative of the Enlightenment in this, nevertheless considers people to be somewhat educable, as well as reeducable. To be sure, it has nothing more to say about evil and aggression, even between mother and child, than all theories that came before.

It is enlightening that every aggression contains a narcissistic element, because it contains an element of self-defense. However, what makes jealous aggression toward the partner so difficult to understand is that it does not turn against an enemy, but against a person who is loved beyond all measure. It is this *immoderation* in love, as well as in enmity and the demand for control, that horrifies us, and every ethical and philosophical system condemns it as inhuman. Psychoanalysis calls it immature, unadult, "nongenital." In the presumed power of an (adult) person over another adult (or in another way over a child) psychoanalysis sees the result of an unclear demarcation between one's self and what psychoanalysis calls, so drily and unsatisfyingly, the "object," the beloved person. The beloved's rights, independence, and freedom of mobility are not recognized, as if one could dispose of that person as of oneself. And disposition of this self is not limited by any perception of reality, any social conditioning, any consideration of others or seeing oneself in reference to others. Megalomania and feeling of omnipotence are the catchwords for this phenomenon.

As an explanation of this severe disturbance and, consequently, its cure, theory, especially that of the last two decades, reaches back to the early mother-child relationship. It understands even pathological jealousy, among many other phenomena, as the reactualization of an unsuccessful, not satisfactorily experienced or resolved part of this primal relationship. Here it is no longer a matter of the classical triangle, but of only two people.

The pertinent theory is oddly complicated, multilateral, and difficult. (One can find summaries that are easily readable, for the layperson as well, but nonetheless well-founded, in Henseler 1974, and Kutter 1977, 116 ff.) Here I will mention only the following: for various reasons, a harmonious primary state (primary narcissism, according to Freud) can be assumed for the unborn child, who already exists as an independent organism. This state is a paradise, a heaven (another world) in which all needs are dependably and happily taken care of without stress. After birth, the struggle with this world begins, whereby memory of the past and yearning for it continue to be unconsciously preserved. The child at first experiences itself, even as it is breathing the air of the earth, as not yet separated from the mother, and at the beginning many mothers also feel intensely that their child is still part of them—how could it be otherwise, since each individual cell, except for the one cell that necessarily comes from the man, is generated from the mother's body.

The way in which separation proceeds decisively determines the self-esteem of the human being in the process of becoming. This separation is obviously very much a matter of letting go of the mother *and* being able to hold fast to her, of her giving and denying to the baby. For in this earliest period of life, the baby gradually learns to distinguish between him- or herself and the world. The baby "forms" internal representations of him- or herself and of the human referent who at this time is essential for physical survival, usually the mother. Various technical terms used for these representations are "images," "imagoes," "representants." Since the mother is experienced as omnipotent, life-giving, and life-threatening, and since the child is at first everything to her, as she is to the child, the first conceptions of self as well as of the object are idealized and powerful. Gradually they are separated and understood in terms more in keeping with reality. However, the possibility of reverting to desires for omnipotence and merging still exists. This recourse (regression) will look different depending on the different stages of psychosexual development: it is always possible in crises as an attempt at salvation. Without the basic certainty in one's relationship to oneself that is gained in the earliest period of life (opinions vary as to precisely when, as they do about all other details), one can barely exist.

Let us schematically consider the case of Mack-Brunswick's patient (described at the beginning of the chapter). Her mother apparently frustrated her too much (the mother's "guilt" does not interest us here). Because of illness, she had deserted the patient after her first year of life. The child could therefore develop neither a good feeling about her own power, her own worth, nor a sufficiently good feeling about her mother, who had exercised her omnipotence only in the most terrible way, by deserting her. In this basic uncertainty, the sister's love and seduction do not appear as equal to the mother, of course, but nonetheless as a replacement for her as the caregiver. The adult patient still regresses to feelings of omnipotence, because she has been neither satisfied nor frustrated in keeping with reality. She wants to kill herself, thus being able in the world of her unconscious to take and give life like her mother, and her feeling of self-worth is unrealistically so threatened by the rivalry of another mother (the stepmother) that she has fits of rage meant to destroy the world. Mack-Brunswick writes, "She had remained a child in the truest sense of the word" (1928, 505).

Where does a jealous individual get the strength or the power to demand total control over the beloved, which can go as far as murder in extreme cases? The answer is, Out of the expectation that you and I should always and in fact (and not only in the brief moments of sexual, erotic, or spiritual merging) be one; that you should make no demands of your own, or only those of which the ego approves. If the "you" makes other demands, then fear of them becomes extraordinarily threatening, perhaps so unbearable that jealousy alone no longer suffices as a defense mechanism (see sec. 2 above) and that the elimination of the recalcitrant object seems to be the only certain way out. The threatening aspect can be better understood if we remember that mother and infant are experienced by the jealous individual in the phase of normal symbiosis as "the unity of two within a common boundary" (Mahler 1968). If as an adult one regresses to this condition in a crisis, one experiences oneself and the beloved, to use a metaphor, like two people in one skin, whereby the external person exclusively determines the contact to the outside world. This metaphor easily allows us to conceive how life-threatening, how laceratingly painful, the independent, as it were nonsynchronic, behavior of the incorporated person must be. It also allows us to perceive how difficult it must be for the latter to break out of the symbiosis, and to what an extent he or she is also endangered when the "outer skin," that is, the incorporating partner, breaks away or forces the incorporated person into movements that are not appropriate to him or her.

In such symbiotic relationships, therefore, both partners are often jealous in the worst way. Tolstoy, with whose *Kreutzer Sonata* we just dealt, and his wife are an example of the torment, but also the strength and unavoidability, of such a relationship.

At the time of their courtship in 1862 (Tolstoy was thirty-four years old, Sophia Andreyevna eighteen), the following took place:

> "Just read what I am writing down for you here."
>
> "Fine," I agreed.
>
> "But I will only write down the initial letters; you are to guess the words they stand for."
>
> "But how? That is just impossible! Well, fine, write."

Tolstoy takes a piece of chalk and writes on a blackboard.

> Leo Nikolayevich writes, "Y.y.a.y.d.f.h.r.m.o.a.t.m.o.m.a.a.m.i.f.h."
>
> I read out loud, "Your youth and your desire for happiness remind me only all too much of my age and my incapacity for happiness."
>
> My heart began to beat rapidly, my temples were pounding, my face was burning. I had lost all sense of time and space, of everything earthly. I believed that, at this moment, I could lose everything, understand everything, grasp everything that was ungraspable.

She reads yet another sentence.

> Leo Nikolayevich was not even surprised—as if it were only a matter of what was most natural. We were internally so close to each other, that nothing else seemed to exist around us." (S. Tolstoy 1982, 23–24)

Just a few weeks later they were married. Like Pozdnishev in *The Kreutzer Sonata*, Tolstoy had his bride read his premarital diaries, which contained a record of the excesses of his bachelorhood, for he wanted her to know everything about him. He did not take into consideration what this did to her. He was, of course, not concerned with being considerate, but with being one. Sophia was deeply horrified. What she read unleashed her jealousy. On her husband's estate, she continued for a time to meet her husband's former lover on a daily basis. The lover was a peasant whose sensual power, among other things, Tolstoy depicted in the novella that first appeared in 1911, *The Devil*.

Sophia Andreyevna soon became her husband's indispensable collaborator, in that she copied his works, often many times over, so that he could continue to work on them. In the middle of her life, she copied the above-mentioned early diaries word for word for the archives, while being constantly tormented by retrospective jealousy. She became pregnant sixteen times and had thirteen children, the last when she was forty-five years old. Both spouses kept diaries and read these to each other again and again. For the most trivial reasons both of them experienced outbreaks of jealousy. They frequently made attempts to leave each other in desperate, rash ways (i.e. leaving barefoot in the snow) and were then unresponsive for days afterward to all efforts of those around them to bring them to reason. They were obsessed only by the thought of escaping from this inescapable closeness.

Sophia Andreyevna often thought of suicide. Tolstoy wrote her a farewell letter when he was about seventy years old, for he wanted to kill himself because of her platonic relationship to a mutual friend. He did not try to execute his plan, but she found the letter in a book on which he was working. Neither one of them would have been likely to call themselves happily married, but a great love bound them. Their respective enemies or partisans were agreed on this. Tolstoy felt himself misunderstood in his sectarian Christianity, in his ideology of selflessness and fraternity with the people—and was repeatedly unfaithful to his renunciation of the world in his sensuality with his own wife. Sophia sees herself in her diaries as incomparably more often exploited than loved, not to mention understood. One passage among many states, she suffers from his icy coldness, but then ''we again somehow reconciled. . . . And all at once everything was needed: the warm cap . . . , the fruit, the figs, my body, my work as a scribe—all of this was more than indispensable'' (2 November 1897). Leo Nikolayevich was at this time sixty-nine years old; she was fifty-three.

Written at the end of the 1880s, *The Kreutzer Sonata* was first published in 1891, after Sophia Andreyevna personally obtained permission for its release from the czar, who had banned it. She did not like the novella. She felt it was directed against her and felt humiliated by it. Nonetheless, she knew that she ''had never been guilty [of infidelity to her husband] with as much as a single gesture or a single unfaithful glance.'' Immediately following this, she says that *thoughts, potential* love for someone else are, of course, something else again (12 February 1891). And spouses living symbiotically can of course read each other's minds. Thus it is less unbelievable than it seems that Sophia in fact conducted a ''friendship,'' ''love,'' or whatever one wants to call it, with the composer and pianist Taneyev in the late 1890s, about ten years *after The Kreutzer Sonata* was written. Music played an eminently important role in this relationship. Since that time, Sophia often played the piano and frequently attended concerts. Music continued to be the only sphere of her life in which she was free, and she did not allow her right to it to be disputed. Anyone who plays the piano cannot be a scribe for a famous husband.

We know how the marriage ended: Tolstoy ran away from his wife at the age of eighty-two. Thereupon, Sophia Andreyevna threw herself ''into the pond in despair. Sasha [her daughter] and Bulgakov [Tolstoy's secretary] dragged me out, unfortunately! Then for five days I did not touch a single bite.'' Leo Nikolayevich survived the flight for about ten days. He died at a train station, and his followers and the couple's three children who were with him allowed his wife to go to him only at the very last moment. "They forcibly held me back, bolted the doors, broke my heart" (9 September 1910). Until the end, Sophia was tormented by hatred for her husband's adherent and friend, Chertkov, who later become the publisher of Tolstoy's works.

Especially in Tolstoy's final year of life, the late diaries, which he wanted to entrust to his friend and not his wife, were the object of a struggle in which eavesdropping, mistrust, and the cultivation of allies within his family and household figured prominently. Sophia's thoughts, her intolerably controlling behavior, her exclusive preoccupation with her husband's relationship to her rival, were one to exchange Chertkov's name for a woman's, cannot be distinguished from violent jealousy due to love.

These two people increasingly came to live in totally different worlds—Tolstoy in his art and his political-religious ideology; his wife with the children, her concern for material security, the huge family's maintenance, and society. Both ever more intensely despised the other's sphere. Both were full of desperate reproaches that they were not understood by the other. The formula goes something like this: "The other unconditionally wants to be with me, but whenever possible without knowing about me"; "I should 'be available' or 'not be available' as the occasion demands." This last sentence does not come from the Tolstoys, but is a citation from Alice Balint's fine essay, "Love for the Mother and Mother-Love" (1939), in which she clearly describes the intermingling of childlike expectations from the early years, and their neurotic reactualization in disturbed adults. As the author describes it, even as exemplified by primitive peoples the mother is seen in the sphere of archaic love as someone who has a self-evident power of disposal over the child, just as later the neurotic "child" presumes for him- or herself power over the mother's life. This power is not experienced as guilty but, as it were, bestowed by nature. This is shown especially clearly in transference during the analytic working relationship. The other person's needs are not heeded. Balint cites a dream in which jealousy is also at issue.

> The patient has the following dream: when he enters his apartment, he sees a large tube in the middle of the room. He lies down on it just as on a bed. A bed (or divan) is just what it becomes, but it soon turns into an old woman who is making lascivious grunting noises. It disgusts him, and he climbs down from her, in spite of the fact that she tries to hold him back. The actual occasion for the dream was the observation of how his mother spoiled her grandchild and wants to have the child totally for herself. With strong disapproval, he recognizes the repressed eroticism in her actions and at the same time feels his own jealousy with embarrassment. Behind and besides jealousy there is, however, also pity for his small nephew, who has

the same fate in store for him as the patient. The nephew, too, will at some time want to get free of the grandmother, and she will hold on to him, just as she had held on to him, the son. (A. Balint [1939] 1965, 119ff.).

Getting free of the mother and thus achieving relatively healthy adulthood is only—or at best—possible in continuing development of *both* partners that is enduring and reciprocal (in Stierlin's terms, "related individuation"). Through breaks and destruction the person who is tied to the mother by invisible, but unbreakable, bonds is destroyed in his or her entire relationship to reality, and especially to social reality.

In the case of a genius like Tolstoy, one has the feeling that he must continuously create a fictitious (and, in the fiction, thoroughly real!) reality, because he does not sense or achieve actual reality. Alice Balint writes, "Tact, insight, respect, gratitude, tenderness (in the sense of inhibited sensuality) are signs and the result of the dominance of the sense of reality in the sphere of emotion." One cannot say that this happened very often in the case of the two Tolstoys. The following quotation from the seventy-seven-year-old Leo Nikolayevich is convincing proof of the insolubility of very early deprivation. At the age of two, Tolstoy had lost his mother.

> Throughout the entire day a feeling of stifling oppression. Toward evening, this state of sadness changed into tender emotion, into the desire to be comforted, caressed. Like a child, I would like to cuddle up to a loving, empathetic being. . . . To become a child again and to cuddle up to my mother, as I imagine her to be? Yes, you, mama, whom I never called by name, because I could not yet speak. . . . Yes, you, the highest ideal of pure love which I could ever imagine; of human, warm, maternal love. My tired soul longs for this. You, mama, you, comfort me, lighten my heart. (Quoted in S. Tolstoy 1982)

To cite Balint once again: "The love for the mother is originally a love without a sense of reality. The father, on the other hand, we love and hate—even considering oedipal feelings—realistically."

By now it should have become clear what a great advance the achievement of the oedipal triangle is in the child's development, and that one can most probably view the "genitalization" of two-sided into three-sided jealousy as the expression of a desire. A client with episodes of delusional jealousy once said to me that he could imagine himself no longer having to be jealous, if his girlfriend, due to illness, would become sexually incapacitated, useless, and thus have no sexual needs and, in spite of that, stay with him. Then he would see that the sexual satisfaction that she received and desired from him—actually for his own pleasure too!—was not her main priority. He could believe that other men were unimportant to her and that she loved him only for himself. Since this man too, however, like each of us, could not feel "like himself" without his sexuality, one can emotionally comprehend that, in spite of all its torments, jealousy continued to be the better, more adult, and more vital solution, when it is contrasted with the notion of an asexual, undemanding mother-wife who is completely oriented toward her partner. In his fantasy he naturally remained potent ("powerful!"). The men whom he imagined for his girlfriend were always older, superior, and more significant than he— wishful images of a father whom he did not have, because his own father had been the gentle one in the family, while his mother was strict, powerful, and domineering.

7. Retrospective on Oedipus

The Oedipus myth can be read also as the renunciation of the pre-oedipal mother, here in the literal sense: as the condemnation of her power to give and take life (by exposing the infant) and likewise claiming the husband and father for herself. In the oldest transmitted version of the myth, in the eleventh book of the *Odyssey,* there is clearly talk of the "monstrous deed" of the woman there called Epicaste, who "in her ignorance committed the sin of marrying her son" after he had killed his father (11. 270ff.; in German translations, Wolfgang Schadewaldt renders it as "the unreason of her mind"; Johann Heinrich Voss, as "with blinded soul"; Roland Hampe, as "unknowing," which reduces the meaning to pure not knowing, which is apparently not wanting to know). Even in Sophocles, traces of a *conscious* deed can still be found. Why was Jocasta not reminded of anything, given both Oedipus's youth and his maimed feet? (See in this context Christlieb's somewhat crude, psychoanalytically ignorant study [1979], which is nonetheless worthy of consideration.) Bachofen reads the Oedipus tragedy as the "condemnation of that impure, hetaera-like, telluric motherhood, to which Oedipus is indebted for all his suffering" ([1861] 1980, 274). Homer assumes that the gods would have *immediately,* that is, before the incestuous conception of children, perceived and punished the calamity, and Oedipus would have continued to rule over Thebes after the queen's suicide. Thus in Homer one reads that they left "Oedipus to suffer all the horrors that a mother's curses can inflict." For, as Bachofen continues, Oedipus is "one of those great figures, whose suffering and torment lead to more exquisite human civilization; who, even while still supported by the old order, and having proceeded from this order as its last great sacrifice, nonetheless at the same time stand as founders of the modern age" (273).

The anger of the gods cannot be palliated, the condition of the city cannot be restored to healthy order (the "plague" that oppressed Thebes was the occasion for King Oedipus's investigations) without the struggle with the mother, which in the tragedy directly causes her suicide (in antiquity, the classical form of suicide in cases of impossible, impermissible passionate love is hanging from a high beam). Just as essential are ignoring Jocasta's imploring objections to the process of inquiry and relentlessly jeopardizing oneself. According to this reading, Oedipus would not be punished primarily for his impulse-driven, unwitting seizure of power, but rather for detaching himself from the mother's lovingly binding power in the most painful way, and assuming total responsibility for himself and for the people entrusted to him.

Bachofen assumed that a real matriarchal epoch had existed. Oedipus then symbolizes the transition from a lawless culture of sensuality driven by power and revenge, in which there was no marriage and thus no clear patriarchal line because of women's availability to all and their lack of constraint, to the "new, gentle law proclaimed by Apollo." Marriage and the family only now become the guaranteed bases of society. "The woman, who in the earlier order is the source of every malediction, now becomes a blessing unto herself and the man. Love's self-denial takes the place . . . of the hetaera's lust" (ibid., 275). Ismene and Antigone, who accompany their blinded father into exile, are symbolic representatives of this new female role.

This sounds beautiful, convincing, and humane—and it is this, too. The image of women that evolves from this is of course the image of a patriarchal culture. Within this culture in Greece, literature, especially the drama, had an eminently political significance. Indeed, more recent studies refute Bachofen's assumption that there was a matriarchy existing at some time in the distant past (Wesel 1981). Instead they furnish evidence for cultural variations—for example, in Crete and in Egypt, which are less misogynous, as opposed to repressing women. Athens in the Periclean age was extraordinarily restrictive for women. They were hardly allowed to go outside and had no power at all. Thus one must understand many myths about violent and fearsome women, sorceresses and witches, Medea, Circe, Clytemnestra, the Sphinx, and the Amazons, or even Jocasta, in a new light, as figures of the projective defense of a male-dominated society that justifies itself through this depiction: women must be tamed and subordinated to a patriarchal culture, for if one gave them free rein, then they would be *like that!*

Oedipus and no end in sight! Anyway, we will not get any further with one-sided interpretations. One may notice the renunciation of maternal power or not; one may be indignant that Oedipus stands there as the "guilty child" (Miller 1981) or, like Freud, find the play "immoral" because it "abolishes moral responsibility, shows divine forces as arranging for the crime, and shows the impotence of the moral impulses of people who resist the crime" (1917, 343). The spectator or reader in any case will not come away without feeling fear and pity and experiencing catharsis through the plain encounter with truth and justice in their internal contradictions. As Freud writes in the same place, all objections are irrelevant to the effect of the drama, for Oedipus has to do with us.

Even in reference to jealousy? I believe yes. To be sure, there is never talk of the jealousy of the Oedipus character (although there is of his violent anger). His jealousy must be deduced. Was Oedipus jealous? Not in the drama by Sophocles, but probably in his autobiography as the stepchild of Polybus and Merope and certainly in the original form of the myth, in which each deed, from patricide to maternal incest, takes place knowingly. Jocasta, however, is certainly jealous in the sense of taking possession in a symbiotic, incorporating way: she fights with all her power as queen and authority figure, even denying the truth of divine oracles, to keep Oedipus for herself, in her sphere of influence. And when she is not successful in this, when he moves on to his own truth and consciousness and becomes responsive to the demands of the polis, which thereby becomes the third point in the jealousy triangle, nothing remains for her but to kill herself. In hanging herself from a high beam, she literally loses her balance. Another possible interpretation is that the great mother has become the binate wife. She who originally was the heiress to the throne subordinates her life to the power of men. Reigning in submission is a risky game in the world of men; anyone who attempts this exposes herself to the dangers of life-threatening jealousy.

Reflecting upon Oedipus as the leading myth of psychoanalysis has made clear to me what a fruitful choice Freud made when he selected Sophocles' tragedy. It is extremely likely that, given his thoroughly classical nineteenth-century education, he was familiar with the myth's prehistory and propagation, even if he does not mention it in his works. Oedipus interested him only as the fearless individual who seeks the truth. Freud, however, unconsciously paved the way for us to be able to make the Oedipus myth the basis for theories of the family even today. The Sophoclean *Oedipus Rex* is of course only one strand in a whole web of stories and traditions. An interpretation of the entire myth in terms of family dynamics could teach us much about conformity and freedom in families.

The entire story is full of ambivalences, full of moderation and immoderation, love and hate, wisdom and ignorance. To be sure, the ninety-year-old Sophocles, in *Oedipus at Colonus,* allows the now truly wise and mellowed old man to depart the world reconciled: without actually dying, he is summoned to the kingdom of the dead in a kind of assumption into heaven. No one may approach the place where he was carried off to the gods. In the meantime, as the model of patient long-suffering, he has almost become a saint.

According to another tradition, his grave becomes a place of veneration. On painted urns, young women and men, perhaps a bridal party, visit the grave (Kerényi 1951, 2:88). And here an interpretation presents itself, with which Freud would have been in agreement: loving young life can unfold itself where Oedipus lies buried. Anyone who has left the Oedipus complex behind becomes capable of forming a new, flexible triangle without rigidity and fatal entanglement: husband, wife, child—and everyone—can be there for themselves and with the others, without ambiguous roles and unions, in vital mutual development.

△ 18 △
GUILTY INDIVIDUAL OR MULTILATERAL ENTANGLEMENT

Freud and all psychotherapists oriented toward the individual—Jung, Adler, Perls, as well as the behavioral therapists—have always dealt with *one* person who was viewed as being ill or neurotic or as exhibiting symptoms—in short, as a patient. This was so, even though in the case of these individuals one was dealing exclusively with phenomena, in both the intrapsychic as well as the interpersonal realm, that originate in human communal living within families. The central therapeutic relationship was a dyadic one, that between physician and patient, in which the reality of other relationships was reflected and could be worked out. It is obvious that, in this situation, distortions and one-sided views could not fail to arise. It is just as superfluous to reproach Freud for this research orientation as it is necessary to expand the goals that psychotherapy sets for itself. It seems to me obvious that no progress will be possible without a fundamental understanding of the individual's intrapsychic processes—thus this book's extensive preoccupation with the jealousy of the jealous individual. This, however, must be placed within the context of a reciprocal relationship with those individuals who make up the surrounding world—their behavior, their history, and their being one way and not the other.

1. "System" and "Circularity"

Almost all books about marriage and family therapy take a stand or justify themselves in terms of traditional psychotherapy (cf. Richter 1963, 33ff.; Schatzmann 1973, 93ff.; Selvini Palazzoli et al. 1975, 133; Stierlin 1971, 104; Wirsching and Stierlin 1982, 50ff.; Bauriedl 1980, 28ff.; Willi 1975, 244ff.; Preuss 1973, 61ff.; Hoffman 1981, 3ff.). Everyone who has gone through individual psychoanalysis, or any other therapy leading to important internal changes, knows that it is not only the individual who changes, but also his or her environment. The issue here is the concept of the system, which has become so critical in current thinking: these effects are due to the fact that *everyone* is bound *to everyone else.* "Generally speaking, a system is a set of mutually inter-dependent units'' (Boszormenyi-Nagy and Spark 1973, 2). If one directs one's attention toward this interdependence and not toward the single link in a circular closed chain without beginning and end, then the usual linear causality at least becomes questionable. This linear causality was something obvious to Freud and has earned for psychoanalysis the reproach of being dominated by a more or less unavoidable determinism.

Circularity is the key word for what is repeatedly designated by family therapists not simply as an expansion of prior methods and theories, but as a change in the paradigm, as an introduction to a new fundamental concept of therapy. If we continue with the metaphor of the closed chain, it is clear that the convulsions of *one* link are propagated through the whole. With this metaphor, one can picture the chain's linkage and flexibility in different variations. To this, however, one must add the difference between inanimate parts of the chain in the metaphor, and those that are animate within the reality of a family system. Citing Gregory Bateson, Lynn Hoffman adduces the classic example of the difference between kicking a stone and kicking a dog. The energy that the kick transmits causes an accurately predictable effect in the stone. The dog does not react simply as a substance made of flesh and bone, but has its own source of energy and the outcome is unpredictable (Hoffman 1981, 7). Everyone can imagine what *could* happen. One does not know what *will* happen. If we also consider what effects kicking the dog can have, for example, on a watching stranger or on the owner's spouse, and so forth, and what repercussions result from this for the person doing the kicking, then we can certainly understand Freud wisely limiting himself to a concern with the individual. (Jürg Willi [1975, 244ff.] writes very impressively about analysts' difficulties with group therapies.) The circular way of looking at things often requires a very laborious rethinking.

2. A System with Concealed Jealousy

Let us take an example in which the issue is at first—in the traditional way of looking at things—the symptomology of the symptomatic individual. These symptoms can be explained in purely somatic terms, for example, by muscle tension in the neck, poor circulation in the brain, low blood pressure. Every general practitioner knows how difficult it often is to treat headaches. They ''always recur.'' This expression would already cause a Freudian to see an indication of a suppressed drive phenomenon. The displacement from below to above, from the sexual organs to the head, is a known defense mechanism; let us consider Oedipus, who, once he knows everything, puts out his eyes, and with Jocasta's pin at that. This is interpreted as a substitute for self-castration. Or consider the blinding of Gloster, the character who is King Lear's alter ego, by Lear's daughter, who with this act definitively wants to deprive him of power (''potency'').

Therefore, in a psychological interpretation of drives, the mother's headaches can be the expression of a conflict within the individual. She simply has a "conversion symptom," the headaches, instead of suffering from her sexuality, her failure to be satisfied by her husband, her bad conscience because of masturbation—or whatever one may want to imagine. Psychoanalytical derivations of headaches are correspondingly numerous (see Fenichel 1945, 2:89). Thus Frieda Fromm-Reichmann, for example, explains migraines as unconscious hostility toward the intelligence of others, "psychic castration," which is turned against oneself because of guilt feelings.

The more important the mother-child relationship became (among object theoreticians), the more plausible the following explanation would be: if the mother with headaches had herself had the much-cited "good enough mother" (Winnicott 1984), then, appropriately satisfied or frustrated (according to phase), she would have learned to deal better with the demands of life and what it has to offer, that is, with aggression and tolerance. Perhaps she would have been able to be a better mother herself and would not have needed a psychosomatic symptom to express her problems. The intellectual model is linear in both cases; in the first mind game, it is the suffering individual who is "guilty"; in the second, it is that individual's mother, and the cause lies in the past but is of course reflected in the present. It could also be worked through in the present, but only by concurrently attaining a better understanding of one's past history.

Let us now assume that, for the moment, the family living together consists of the married couple, a son, a preschool daughter, and an au pair. The wife's newly widowed mother lives nearby and often visits. And let us attempt to shed our customary linear way of thought: "The action of the one is the action of the other" (Stierlin 1971), and the mother's headaches are not simply *her* illness, regardless of its genesis. Rather she, the weakest and probably most attentive and responsible link ("the most loyal" in the sense of Boszormenyi-Nagy and Spark 1973), manifests that something is wrong with the whole system; therefore, that not only the mother, but all the others, have something to do with the illness, whether it is that they are suffering from it, profiting from it, distancing themselves from it, whatever. Let us assume for the moment that the father regards the au pair with lighthearted empathy. She is young, carefree, energetic, somewhat sloppy, and never has headaches. Does the mother create headaches for herself *because of this?* Family therapists assert that this is the false epistemological assessment. (Epistemology is the philosophy of knowledge under the aspect of the principles of how one gains knowledge. Mara Selvini Palazzoli [1975] points to the etymology of the word from the Greek *epistamai* "to attain an advantageous position in order to be able to observe something better.") Aside from the fact that the woman, like her mother before her, had perhaps always suffered from headaches, the following circle simply does not obtain—(husband's) flirtation, leading to (her) headaches, leading to even more flirtation precisely *because* of her headaches. Rather, her children go easy on their mother when she is lying in the dark, are nice to her, but romp with their father and the au pair during the times their mother is resting, really enjoying it. The grandmother, far from siding with her daughter—for she is "just" and all her life thought this to be one of her best qualities—reminds her that she herself never allowed her deceased husband to know she was suffering from headaches; that would have been an imposition. "Naturally he could tell; we were of course so very close." In any case, it remains an imposition on the husband to have a wife who is eternally in need of special consideration.

And—we would say, "naturally"—it is in fact an imposition. Plans for the evening, outings, and the choice of friends are all determined by these headaches. Perhaps an alliance is formed between the mother and her small son—she can talk with him "as with a friend." Is the father relieved or embittered, when he returns home in the evening from a sports activity or a business meeting to find his son in bed next to his wife and holding hands with her, while she has once again taken the strong sleeping pills that finally allow her to fall asleep? Let us assume that he still finds his wife desirable—in all probability, it is against the rules for him to say that he now wants to sleep with her once again and not just hold hands like a five-year-old. Enraged, he slams the bedroom door. His three-year-old daughter wakes up and cries; startled out of sleep, the au pair comes into the kitchen; perhaps because both look charming and sweet in their distress, the man shouts, "Women are nothing but trouble . . . !" and so forth and so on.

It would be natural to say that the only reason for this is that the wife has a headache; or that the man does not claim what is rightfully his; or the laziness of the wife who thinks that with two children an au pair is necessary; or the inherited disposition of the children, who are oversensitive; or yet again, the lax attitudes of the young—the au pair was not "modest" as would have been proper; or even that the wife tries to work through her jealousy in a way that is typical in a patriarchate: through silence and waiting for it to pass, perhaps even not wanting to acknowledge it.

All these hypotheses attribute the "guilt" to a part of the system: they assume that if this one part could behave differently, then everything would be fine. What they thereby overlook is the fact that the others, even if they consciously wish the symptom to disappear, unconsciously contribute to its preservation. Anyone having a scapegoat does not have to go into the wilderness oneself (Lev. 16:21–22; see also Richter 1963, 198). Change demanded of the system as a whole is often felt by the individuals as a "wilderness." The father would perhaps have to risk rejection on the part of his wife—he is so afraid of this that he would rather remain unsatisfied. The wife would have to take a more aggressive stand with the girl, and that would be even worse than headaches. The foreign au pair would have to look for contacts outside of the family that has become her temporary home—who knows to what prejudices and difficulties one would expose oneself in doing this! The grandmother would have to accept her loneliness, work through her grief, and create something new and valuable for herself alone in her twilight years.

Thus the varying desires, fears, and expectations intertwine. What is extremely important in this is that they *all* get something out of this situation, even the jealous individual suffering from headaches; and that no one "is risking his or her life," in Thea Bauriedl's ambiguous formulation: being alive is not possible without being at risk, but the fear of this risk is so great among the members of the family, it is as if they would literally risk their lives. Thus they would rather risk a kind of covert death.

3. But Is It Not Heredity after All?

One has always assumed that there is a connection between the patient's illness and his or her environment. "You are that way because you come from this family"—this observation could be found since biblical times and the time of the ancient Greeks, up to our own time, naturally with different symptoms and inferences. The more scientific the proof became, the more ominous and inevitable it had to appear. If a psychosis (jealousy paranoia, for example) or a person's "essence" (a fearful, mistrustful, petty character structure, for example) were anchored in the genes, then one could at most make it more tolerable, but not basically change or fully cure it.

Among the discoveries of nineteenth-century science, it seems to me, hardly any are as deeply engrained a part of every person's general knowledge as Darwin's and Mendel's genetic theories, which are also indispensable in the schools. In Germany, the fascist idealization of these scientific discoveries, even up to the present day, certainly continues to play a disastrous role in their promulgation and transmission—exculpatory for the environment and damning for the person for whom one can just not do anything "because of heredity."

Luckily, it appears to me as if science is fundamentally less convinced by the validity of the argument for heredity than the lay public is. In 1961, in a scrupulous study of sixty-six psychiatric cases of jealousy, it is made crystal clear that "it is not reasonable to assume that the tendency toward jealousy is genetically determined" (Langfeldt 1961, 64; the cases are from the forties). Another study (Vaukhonen 1968) no longer deals with the genetic factor at all but stresses the frequency of broken marriages and unpropitious social circumstances in the background of the vast majority of patients suffering from jealousy. It is frequently assumed that constitutional factors often play a role; these do not simply consist in inheriting jealousy, however, but, for example, in traumatic early-childhood events, illnesses causing irreversible changes, alcoholism, epilepsy, and physical defects.

It is pointless for a marriage counselor to deal with such problems. If it should really be a matter of heredity and predisposition—and I would not like to be suspected of simply dismissing the existence of such phenomena— then one can still learn to deal with this differently in therapy, especially in therapy with the entire family or even with the couple alone. An earlier example may show how one can often deduce environmental influences in cases where the authors would like to point to the illness of the individual and his or her heredity.

A twenty-year-old girl came to the hospital after attempting suicide by taking barbiturates. She had attempted suicide because she—incorrectly— assumed that her lover was unfaithful to her. Three years prior to this, she had been under psychoanalytic treatment for paranoia. She had believed that she was being pursued by four people (one of them her mother) who wanted to poison her. Her family history yielded the information that her father, an alcoholic, had been tormented by hallucinations in the last ten years because of his wife's alleged infidelity. He had occasionally become violent, and several times, for her own safety, his wife had to lock him in the garage or other rooms of the house. Although the delusion was fixed and constant, it became especially intense under the influence of alcohol. The man often accused his wife of meeting her lover, whereas she had really gone shopping with her two daughters. The parents finally were divorced. About nine months before the daughter was taken to the hospital, her mother died of breast cancer. During his wife's final illness, her husband had been extraordinarily attentive to her, and some weeks after her death he committed suicide by inhaling carbon monoxide (Todd and Dewhurst 1955, 370).

The authors adduce this case as an especially clear example of what in their opinion is the very frequent constitutionally determined and hereditary nature of jealousy in severe cases. One can perhaps speak of predisposition in the sense that in this family when crises situations arise, one becomes mentally ill, rather than suffering from gastrointestinal illnesses, high blood pressure, or headaches. However, the influence of everyone on everyone else is much more obvious even at a superficial glance. The parents probably exemplified a pathological and symbiotic relational style for their children, and the father's addictive illness also attests to this. Addiction, of course, always stands for dependency, for not being able to live alone. The mother certainly played along in that she remained married to this father for a very long time, and the divorce apparently did not do much to change this situation. According to recent research into the causes of cancer, it would be completely possible that her psychic stress played a role in her fatal illness. Since preventative checkups have for a long time been common practice and are highly recommended as a way of dealing with cancer in women, it is possible that ignoring the warning signs would even be an indication of a suicidal tendency. In any case, the parental bonding must still have been very close if, in spite of their divorce, the wife allowed her husband to care for her in her fatal illness. His suicide shortly after her death also speaks for itself.

The young girl, the "patient," therefore had lost both her parents, one after the other, at the time of her own suicide attempt, and in a way with which every "normal" person can come to terms only with great difficulty. (Family therapists speak of "index patients" in the case of a sick family, to indicate that the system is disturbed and that not just the patient is ill.) It is hardly imaginable that she had other than an extremely ambivalent relationship to her parents, and she therefore probably developed death wishes directed against her father and mother. Of course, the "fulfillment" of these wishes often leads to severe disturbances. The fact that, in her paranoia, four people wanted to poison her, one of them her mother, indicates what she suffered on account of her family, which consisted of four people besides herself. In such a situation, it seems to me completely understandable that the faintest misunderstood and incorrectly interpreted signs of her lover's estrangement could be so threatening; that the retreat into eternal sleep, to a paradise free of conflict, which is how death is fantasized by suicides (Henseler 1974), would appear as the best solution.

Seen in terms of family dynamics, the daughter—we hear nothing of her sister—was the weakest part of the torn, but still functional, system at the time of her suicide attempt. This may be interpreted differently. One could also say she was the strongest part, since a suicide attempt is not only an expression of weakness, but also of functioning energy and desire. In any case, her "illness" is not only hers, but the illness of the entire family.

4. From the Disturbed Child to the Parents' Marital Problems

The unburdening function of "heredity," that is, the rejected internal relationship to the disturbances of closer relatives, especially children, may have been of some significance for the development of family therapy. As it happens, the classic examples are almost always based on families with children as index patients. Even today, child-guidance clinics work much more frequently with *entire* families than do marriage counseling clinics. It is therefore no accident that the first German book about family therapy, Horst-Eberhard

Richter's *Parents, Child, and Neurosis* (1963), treats the role of the child in the family. In child guidance, moreover, the issue is very often the children's jealousy of each other and their parents. I prefer not to deal with this, not only because this theme would require its own book, but also because the focus is almost always turned away from the child, with whom the therapist is supposed to "do something" so that it "will be all right again," will again be "OK" or no longer worried, to the common entanglement, the circularity. The parents' marriage plays a decisive role in this. In the case described above, of the family with the mother suffering from headaches, there are still very few therapists who would try to eliminate the headaches through family therapy. On the other hand, headaches and their possible causes have of course played a role in many psychoanalyses and perhaps in even more marriage counseling sessions. To be sure, many child-guidance clinics could report on constellations similar to the one described. Only then it would not be the mother who would be the index patient, but a child for whose bedwetting, stuttering, aggressiveness, or exaggerated shyness help would be sought. Since as a symbol for the disturbed condition of the total family this symptom has a strong defensive aspect, the counselor often must make a laborious effort to shift the main weight onto the parents' marital problems.

As far as the adults' jealousy is concerned, not a single case is known to me from the literature, in which this jealousy was presented or understood as a symptom of the *total family.* (Should this be due to a gap in my own knowledge, the number of publications, which is so copious that one cannot keep up with all of them, should excuse me.) Even I have worked with families from this perspective in only two instances. In both, the mother's jealousy paranoia had been treated with drugs, and she had been referred to our clinic by her physicians. I would prefer not to report on these instances, because one case has not yet been concluded, and the other is too recent. It is also a fairly new development in marriage counseling for psychiatrists to decide to entrust patients to us for follow-up treatment. It seems that it is only gradually becoming known among psychiatrists that we can offer assistance that they themselves cannot provide—primarily time (!), but also experience in the understanding of what it is in interpersonal entanglements that can contribute to, if not cause, disturbances of various degrees, up to and including psychoses.

The "systems theoreticians" have altered, enlarged, and expanded the possibilities for this understanding. Of course many of them proceeded from research on schizophrenia, here too usually that of psychotic children and youth. Previous psychotherapies had all in all yielded little success in this area, especially because of the huge expenditure of time that psychoanalytic treatment of psychoses demands. In view of the high percentage, 0.8, of the population that is schizophrenic, and as much as about 5 percent with depressive psychoses (according to Kutter 1977), psychoanalysis could not deliver more than the proverbial drop in the bucket. The discovery of drugs for these illnesses led to a decisive turning point in psychiatry (in spite of all the uneasiness among lay therapists, which I also recognize in myself). The systems theoreticians stand shoulder to shoulder with the analysts in their view that this psychopharmacopoeia is only a stopgap, even if a very effective and often indispensable one, that treats the symptom but not the causes and therefore often leads to relapses and to so-called revolving door psychiatry. Otherwise, however, they do everything differently.

5. Rigidity as Basic Symptom

Each living system—a family, a couple, and the subsystem individual—has two opposing tendencies, which at best function dialectically: that toward homeostasis (toward persistence, repetition, remaining the same), and that toward change. Thus, in the case of health, development is possible on the basis of the stability of a form that is animated from within. It allows leaps and deviations, and even survives the elimination of parts—death, detachment, separation. A waterfall or a forest are good examples of this. Pathological systems, however, tend to overemphasize the homeostasis and no longer find a way out of a feedback control system that has become rigid. Freud's repetition compulsion belongs in this context.

For rigidity is actually the basic symptom with which all psychotherapy must deal. It is all too often the case, of course, that in marriages, and families who come for counseling, *too* much—and too little—happens. What happens is repeated again and again in a very similar way. Clients will not escape this deadlocked form of interpersonal relations on their own.

In order to help in this situation, the systems theoreticians did not proceed from emotions, drives, internal conflicts, fantasies, and interpretations, but from communication, the way in which one shares oneself, that is, from a conscious act. They were unconcerned about its integration within unconscious connections. Helm Stierlin cites one of the pioneers of systems therapy, Jay Haley: "The unit of treatment is no longer the single individual, . . . but rather the relational network, in which this individual is embedded (1975, 10). The issue here is not primarily understanding but solving problems or breaking up ingrained patterns that are the result of false solutions.

I cannot deal here with the general theoretical classification of group therapies, or with the many different therapeutic methods. Anyone who wishes to learn more about this will have to proceed from book to book and should guard against unconditionally accepting the obduracy and one-sidedness of the individual schools. I will limit myself primarily to the description and discussion of two therapeutic procedures, whose use is widespread in the German-speaking area: Watzlawick's communications-theoretical approach, and Jürg Willi's collusion concept. What is common to both is primarily that they take the couple seriously as a couple and not, for example, as two single beings whose neuroses one must as far as possible factor out in order to arrive at a good therapeutic result (this is the premise of Gertrude and Rubin Blanck 1968).

6. Jealousy as the Result of Misplaced Attempts at a Solution

All couples or families who enter into therapy or counseling naturally attempt solutions—only they do not always succeed in these attempts. Paul Watzlawick graphically describes the interaction of a married couple in reference to jealousy. The parties believe each is reacting in the most appropriate way to the other's undesirable behavior, but the marital system is thereby driven into an agonizing double bind.

The wife "may have the impression, that her husband is not open enough for her to know where she stands with him, what is going on in his head, what he is doing when he is away from home, etc. Quite naturally, she will therefore attempt to get the needed information in some way by asking him questions, watching his behavior, and checking on him in a variety of other ways. If he considers her behavior too intrusive, he is likely to withhold from her information which in and by itself would be quite harmless and irrelevant to disclose—'just to teach her that she need not know everything.' Far from making her back down, this not only does not bring about the desired change in her behavior, but provides further fuel for her worries and her distrust—'if he does not even talk to me about these little things, there *must* be something the matter.' The less information he gives her, the more persistently she will seek it, and the more she seeks it, the less he will give her. By the time they see a psychiatrist, it will be tempting to diagnose her behavior as pathological jealousy—provided that no attention is paid to their pattern of interaction and their attempted solutions, which *are* the problem" (Watzlawick, Weakland, and Fisch 1974, 35ff.).

Watzlawick writes that what comes to mind is the image of two people on opposite sides of a sailboat who are hanging out of either side in order to keep the boat steady. This is called "hiking out." The more one person hangs overboard, the more the other has to counterbalance. Watzlawick's opinion is that the boat per se would be stable on its own (and probably also make progress). "It is not difficult to see that in order to change this bizarre situation, at least one of them has to do something seemingly quite unreasonable, namely to steady *less* and not more since this will immediately force the other to also do less of the same (unless he wants to finish up in the water)" (36).

Once one has seen through this communicative feedback control system, the issue is how one will bring the two people, who are doing something so irrational and harmful because they consider it rational, to let go of this misplaced solution in favor of a better one. Unfortunately, Watzlawick does not report how he dealt with this case. He also fails to mention the possible solution, which would have consisted in one of the two individuals having had enough and simply letting him- or herself fall into the water, drown, or swim ashore. The other person could then also fall into the water; thereby the boat they shared, and in which they should have sat together, would become useless. Or the person who remains in the boat is adroit enough to regain control of the threatening rocking and, left alone, makes him- or herself comfortable in what remains of the marital communality. Or a storm comes, which forces both of them, because of real danger, to sit next to each other "up" on the gunwale and literally "pull together on one line": in keeping with the metaphor, to pull on the sheet with which they must hold the sail. In the case of a storm, this requires a lot of strength. Otherwise they would not reach the safety of shore. In the case of married couples with children, such a "storm" can also originate in the system itself: a child could become the symptomatic individual and force the parents to distance themselves from their own problem, the one that is here circumscribed by jealousy.

All these metaphorically acted out solutions occurred to me as changes in a marriage in which one partner is jealous. To be sure, however, I would prefer the two of them back in their boat.

Sight unseen, Watzlawick considers this boat to be stable. It could, however, be otherwise: leaky, old, outdated, too light, too carelessly put together: in short, unsuitable for transporting people or housing them. I will now disassociate myself from the already overdone metaphor: in the example that Watzlawick considers apt for a specific form of marital communication, he apparently has no doubt at all about the institution of marriage per se.

Exact observation and the playing out of a metaphor that has been introduced as a symbol is a psychoanalytical way of looking at things which many a systems therapist considers wrong. This does not mean that the choice of the metaphor is arbitrary—far from it. Therefore Watzlawick specifically (Schülein 1976), but also the general tendency of family therapy, has been accused of conformist conservatism (Pohlen and Plänkers 1982). Critics do not agree that the way something came to be—the history of an individual, a relationship, or an institution, especially marriage and the family—is of no interest to many systems theoreticians. They also disagree that the question of the transmissibility of hierarchical orders and power relationships and their ethical implications is of no interest to the theoreticians. The systems theoreticians are pragmatists who primarily want to help and solve problems, with the aid of their theoretical insights, experience, and authority.

As far as hiking out is concerned, Watzlawick's description of communication applies in many cases. To be sure, his example makes it seem that jealousy *always* originates in this way and that it is very simple to come to terms with it, if one only could find the proper screwdriver for the corresponding screw. To begin with, that does not seem exactly simple to me. In my experience it is rather difficult to get the husband to do "less of the same." As a woman, if I tried to motivate him to be more open and communicative, I would be in danger of coming to be viewed as the ally of his jealous wife. With some justification, he could say, "Whatever I do, she will never be satisfied. I would rather just let it be." Some partners in such a collusion have indeed had this experience. This introduces Willi's concept which, to be sure, refers less to communication than to *unconscious* interplay. If I try, on the contrary, to motivate the wife to allow the husband more freedom and, perhaps, purposefully do something on her own, then *she* would in all probability perceive me as her husband's ally and would be afraid that he would be *all the more likely* to draw away from her. She could then perhaps be jealous of me as an imagined sympathizer.

Even Watzlawick is hardly likely to use the method of direct intervention described here. He would not simply say to the wife, "Don't ask so many questions!" or to the husband, "Tell her a little more!" It is conceivable that he would recommend that the husband not speak with his wife at all anymore, since her plying him with questions is, of course, intolerable. It is also conceivable, that he would advise the wife to look through all her husband's dresser drawers, coat pockets, suitcases, and whatever else occurs to her, and prepare a precise report of what she finds. The hope would be that, through a surfeit of the now recommended ("prescribed") hiking out behavior, a "solution of the second order" becomes available: both have enough of more of the same and thus do less of the same, and see that one can live with this and even live better than before. In the best case, this would give rise to a positive cycle; the creativity to construct new forms of communication becomes possible.

I will later present some further examples that demonstrate how therapists successfully apply this principle.

7. Jealousy in Marital Collusions

In a certain sense, Jürg Willi's collusion concept overlaps Watzlawick's communications analysis. For Willi, too, the behavioral patterns of both parties intermesh. He also identifies schematic circular effects. In the case of hiking out in jealousy, such a circle would be: "I must be so controlling, because you are so reserved and uncommunicative." Thereupon the other person, reduced to using a formula, would answer, "I am so reserved and uncommunicative because you are so controlling." Incidentally, something similar appears already in Lagache's monumental study of jealousy in 1947. In his pivotal case, Anna, her friend Dmitri says, "I would marry Anna if she were not so jealous." On the other hand, Anna thinks, says, and demonstrates, "I am so jealous because Dmitri cannot come to a decision to marry me.'' (In accordance with his analytical orientation, Lagache treated only Anna, not Dmitri, much less both together.)

I find Willi's concept more useful than the therapeutic orientation that proceeds only from communication. The reason is that, in my opinion, it more honestly shows all that one must have understood and learned to be able, should the occasion arise, to give a prescription of the kind that I intend to describe later.

The application of Willi's collusion principles thus seems to be more complicated and difficult, while Watzlawick's *Guide to Being Unhappy* (1983) is probably more intelligible to a wider audience, and to many marriage counselors, than Willi's (nonetheless much-read) books about collusions in the neurotically perceived choice of a partner. In this choice, the husband and the wife put their unhappiness into one basket, so to speak, in order to make the best of it. To be sure, Willi's perspective also functions as liberating and enlightening. He never, however, gives rise to the seductive impression, as does Watzlawick, "Boy, is that simple!" To remind the reader briefly and superficially of the basic ideas: reciprocal supplementation, which of course is indispensable in every marriage, is not designed productively; rather, the roles assigned to each partner are those the other does not dare to live. Thus one partner, for example, *may* only look after and protect. The other *may* only be helpless, dependent, and childlike. The one partner *must* present and actualize him- or herself as a shining model. The other *may* only support and admire in this. If either one attempts to extricate him- or herself from this usually unconscious contract, to "progress" (to move forward) or to "regress" (to withdraw into less independent, "more relaxing," positions), where actually the opposite is expected of him or her, then a crisis develops.

Willi describes some typical collusions along the lines of psychosexual human development assumed by psychoanalysis. But even these already quite numerous configurations of collusive intermeshing often prove to be too schematic; that is, they only rarely and temporarily appear in pure form, in the face of the complex reality of marriages and similar relationships. Thus in his book Willi describes the "jealousy-infidelity collusion" (1975, 129ff.) as a subform of *anal* collusion, in which love is conceived of as one belonging completely to the other, and in which the issue is basically a marital power struggle in a ruler-subject collusion. One partner formulates it in this way: "I am so jealous only because you are so unfaithful." The other partner says, "I am so unfaithful only because you are so jealous." There was only one instance of such a collusion among the thirty cases of my catemneses. And even there it was only one component among many others in a thoroughly complicated marriage.

As he demonstrates in his second book, Willi's therapeutic intervention would consist of understanding the reciprocal fears and desires, that is, the progressive and regressive position in the unconscious circular game. It would possibly also consist of what he calls "therapeutic collusion" (1978, 112ff.). He *consciously* takes the stances that I described above as dangerous. To be sure, he does not do this before a good therapeutic relationship has been established, and only *if* it becomes necessary in the therapeutic process specifically because of the therapist's unease. Playing out the conflict between the therapist and *one* of the partners, which is similar to the conflict of the collusively enmeshed couple, can be exemplary. Since, thanks to the therapist's greater emotional distance and better knowledge of his or her own psyche, the therapist can deal more clearly with his or her own position in the countertransference, the hope is that the observing as well as the struggling partner will learn something from this struggle. And the therapist comes out of a possibly paralyzing bind—perhaps annoyance, lack of understanding, confinement, envy—with respect and profit in his or her stance vis-à-vis the clients.

In terms of my own experiences, it seems as if the jealousy-infidelity collusion, at least to the extent that it is partially conscious, is primarily limited to a specific social class. As Willi writes, it seems that it is only in this class that it is possible for the unfaithful partner "to present the description of his experiences with infidelity . . . to the partner with missionary zeal, apparently with the intention of moving him or her to a more liberated attitude, but effectively causing the intensification of the partner's anxious, conservative attitude" (1978, 126). In many marriages in which infidelity and jealousy occur, anything of the kind is completely unthinkable. Nonetheless, one must view the interplay of desires for freedom and fears of separation, on the one hand, and desires for closeness and the yearning for separation, on the other, as something that is at the basis of many, if not all, relational processes involving jealousy. At the same time, it seems to me that jealousy still contains the positive aspect of being interested in the continued existence of the relationship. There is, of course, infidelity that does not elicit any jealousy but rather is experienced with indifference or even satisfaction, and that perhaps opens up the possibility of achieving separation.

I would also say that the anal level—the ruler-subject collusion according to Willi—*always* plays a role, and indeed the more dangerously the more unconscious it is. Since the traces of all psychosexual developmental stages can be found in every person, however, jealousy can also be found in another, genetically earlier or later stage. As so often in connection with Willi's concept, the therapist's participation here seems to me to consist in that therapists, certainly in accordance with their own history and situation, see and feel *one* aspect especially clearly and work with this aspect (as the focus). For me, it is often unclear precisely which form of collusion is taking place. In this sense it seems useful to me to decide in favor of one hypothesis, which thereby becomes the focus, naturally keeping open the possibility of correcting oneself.

One could, for example, also emphasize the *narcissistic* aspect, instead of the schema "I must be so unfaithful, because you are so jealous" (cf. Willi 1978, 65ff.). More expansively than in this abbreviated form, it would look something like this: "You are preventing me from being myself. Therefore, I must be bad and ruthless and deceive you. I can only judge the fact that you are jealous by saying that it is your own concern. I cannot be myself with you, and therefore I must attempt it without you. If you feel this to be directed 'against you,' that's your bad luck." Since partners in a narcissistic union unconditionally need the other as the ideal self, they will simply attack the other again and again. They will not change their image of the partner and do not want to correct the other's expectations—and thereby contribute to the other's doing "more of the same," to use Watzlawick's terminology once again.

An *oral* collusion—love as caring for each other—could lose its equilibrium in terms of these formulations: "You simply have to allow me to have my friend—I need him, and we have always wanted to help each other. Just think how sad I would be if I had to give him up—you can't possibly expect that of me. How can you really behave in such a jealous way when you, after all, know that this relationship is so good for me! And on top of that, reject me when I want to be loving to you—for I do love you *too*—you really make it difficult for me!" The other will insist on the unconscious agreement, which Willi defines in the following manner: "The one thing that 'mother' was not 'allowed' to do was to deny her partner helpful devotion. The one thing that the 'ward' was not 'allowed' to do was not to express grateful recognition any more" (1978, 101). Jealous partners, therefore, will continue to demand reciprocal caregiving and will point to everything they have taken upon themselves and sacrificed in order to feather the marital nest, which the partner has flown. They do not dare to recognize their own desires to flee, and must therefore deny them.

In terms of individual history, the last part of the child's psychosexual development is the *phallic* phase. From the psychoanalytic perspective, this phase has such a molding influence that traces of it—repetitions, fixations, happiness, and unhappiness—can unmistakably be found in adulthood. In this phase, the issue is entirely one's own sexual identity—not identity as a whole, not the experience and demarcation of what is today designated as the "self," but the discovery of one's body and one's person as masculine or feminine. In behavioral patterns that can be traced to the phallic phase there are obvious, frequent traces of the earlier phase upon which these patterns naturally build. A jealous (hiking out) collusion on the phallic level could thus look like this: "We have of course found and confirmed ourselves as husband and wife, man and woman, and initially it was wonderful. But no one can tolerate the strange things that come over you in bed, or your denunciations in social gatherings. I just need someone with whom I am unreservedly recognized and desired as a man [or a woman], where my potency [or capacity to experience orgasm] is not constantly endangered or ridiculed. The best thing would be for you to look for someone else, too.'' The contribution of the jealous individual to phatic equilibrium can consist in his or her attempt to prove how ''good,'' that is, desirous, seductive, and yielding, he is as a man (or she as a woman) in spite of everything. In their interplay, this leads to the unfaithful partner again having the opportunity to say, ''That's just not the way it is! Now you do it on command, so to speak, and then it's worth nothing to me. And besides that, you've frustrated me for such a long time, that I no longer find you as attractive as before. How completely different my new partner is!''

These supposed examples of collusions, which are all based on counseling experiences, do not correspond precisely to Willi's categories (whose greatest danger, in any case, consists in that they can be taken too schematically in spite of the author's warnings). I adduced these only to demonstrate how many more collusive possibilities there are than those that Watzlawick describes all too simplistically. The examples cannot be ''arbitrarily'' multiplied, but they can be multiplied in various ways. I also consider it a certainty that both the jealous individual and his or her partner contribute to the jealousy, and especially to maintaining it for a long time, even though both consciously want to be rid of jealousy. I have attempted to clarify the intrapsychic reasons for this in the long sections that treat this theme. Perhaps the interpersonal reasons for it have now become somewhat more comprehensible.

8. Power: Understood as Linear or Circular?

The intermeshing of behavior that causes unhappiness is often all too apparent. In the case of delusional jealousy, it is so very obvious that one must ask oneself, for example, who is actually crazier—the wife, who imagines her husband's nonexistent sexual fascination for one specific woman; or the husband, who year after year allows his entire behavior to be controlled in every detail, and repeatedly tries to convince his wife in a loving way that he is faithful to her, apologizes if for once he has become enraged, and so forth.

Gesell's 1906 study contains two examples in which the role played by the environment can be clearly traced.

A twenty-three-year-old woman tyrannizes her husband. He does not dare to go out without her or to say one word against her. She dismissed all her female domestic servants and caused daily scenes because of her jealousy. This is a case of genuine insanity. Her body becomes rigid, and she is convulsed by cramps. Perhaps it will pass when she becomes a mother.

A forty-year-old woman is so jealous that she never allows her children to embrace anyone, not even their grandparents. Once, when her son was six years old and had received a piece of candy from his grandmother, she gave him such a slap in the face that he lost consciousness (464–65).

To my eyes, which are trained to fix on things that have psychoanalytic significance, both these cases would lead one to think of an oedipal problem. If such a family were to come to me, and if this assumption were to be confirmed on the basis of interactions, insights, and utterances, then I would attempt to understand the current situation better on the basis of what was observed: I would attempt to change the Here and Now of *all* the participants on the basis of the There and Then of only *some* of them. In this, I stand in a tradition that assumes that understanding and being understood cures, because paths to change are opened up once what is unconscious becomes conscious. All the collusive interactions that I described above could of course run their course consciously, but often will also do so unconsciously.

In this regard, I am by all means concerned with the exercise of power between individuals and occasionally also with power in powerlessness, but in any case with linear causality within circular causality. And my concern is with easing the *pathological* exercise of power, with an emancipatory process that I hope will make possible an increase in maturity, adult behavior, and perhaps even goodness on the part of the individual—in the best of cases, with the partner, but often by separation from the partner. All these words have become suspect because they have so often been misused within psychoanalysis, as well as by psychology, which has experienced a popularity explosion. In spite of that, I prefer not to dispense with them here. As far as power is concerned, the systems therapists counter my formulation with the terse utterance, "This conviction is false because power resides neither in the one nor the other. Power lies in the rules of the game which have been developed in the pragmatic interaction of all the participants" (Selvini Palazzoli et al. 1975, 15).

Thus the issue is to change these rules, and then the individual will become free. Then the "power relationships," which in this context must be placed within quotation marks, will change.

9. Examples of Systemic Interventions

A therapist must have the courage to intervene, for example, in the following way (and thus understand oneself as someone of whom this is not only expected, but who is also allowed, on the basis of one's own self-understanding, to do what would be unimaginable on the part of a psychoanalyst; Im, Wilner, and Breit 1983, 213): to demand that a wife break off a platonic relationship with her former lover because of her husband's jealousy. The case history reports that no fruitful discussion was possible before this took place. Or breaking the rules can look like this:

A real estate broker, recently divorced, entered into a relationship with a man fifteen years her junior and much less successful than she. He proved to be extremely jealous of virtually all her business contacts. At first she tried to reassure him that she had no interest in anyone else. When this failed, she attempted to use humor. Finding that her lover was offended by her attempts at levity, she decided to conceal information, in the hope of avoiding his jealous rages. On the occasions that he discovered her omissions, his jealous outbursts bordered on violence (ibid., 213ff.).

Here the couple's prior attempts at a solution led to an escalation of the undesired behavior, as in Watzlawick's pivotal example. The woman is given the directive to do "less of the same" by being "consistently and scrupulously honest," that is, flooding him with information (flooding is actually a concept used in behavioral therapy). She "recognizes the value of the strategy" but at the same time realizes that she is not committed enough to the relationship to be able to carry out the directive.

The difference from a therapy that considers itself bound by the psychoanalytic perspective is clear: the symptom is not of interest as the suffering of an individual, as the intrapsychic conflict between fears and desires or between tendencies to remain and run away. These tendencies are based on the fact that the couple has placed itself in opposition to societal norms because of the unusual difference in their ages and the woman's unusual greater professional success. Rather, the symptom is of interest as the problem of a system. Once the system has been "cracked," the therapist's task is completed. As one reads in another essay, the therapist perhaps perceives him- or herself "at best as a social engineer, who regroups structures, hierarchies, values, norms, roles and sequences" (Teismann 1979, 154). In the example just cited, one does not learn what became of the young man after the woman's refusal to carry out the therapist's directive. He came for counseling as the symptomatic individual, the index patient, but this therapist does not assume responsibility for the individual's growth. The reproach that one would level against psychoanalysis would certainly be that psychoanalysts exaggerate their own importance. The client will of course manage on his own or, if necessary, later seek out further therapy.

In psychoanalytic terms, the woman in the above example was requested to satisfy the young man's desires for total control, for total possession of the maternal figure—however in *reality,* not in fantasy, as would happen in psychoanalysis on the basis of the fundamental rule of psychoanalysis and on the basis of transference. There, too, what is actually supposed to be controlled and overcome, once the id has become the ego, is in fact promoted, released, and admitted. In this sense, psychoanalysis too has been interpreted as paradoxical intervention (see Watzlawick, Beavin, and Jackson 1967, 244ff.). The direct injunction to drive motivated behavior in reality, so-called acting out, and on top of this with the assistance of the object, would be totally unimaginable for a psychoanalyst.

The unambiguous moral evaluation of a marital crisis would be just as alien to a psychoanalyst.

When the husband returned to his wife after an affair with another woman, his wife could not let it rest. She was obsessed by thoughts of the other woman. This started a chain reaction. The more his wife rummaged through his past (telephone bills, clothing, his appointment calendar), the more irritated her husband became, because he was serious about returning to his wife. But his impatience and anger intensified his wife's feeling of being rejected and unloved.

"The therapist labelled the affair a crime against the marriage and suggested that much time would be needed to heal the wound and restore trust. The man was advised that a punishment would need to be imposed in order to help his wife to forgive him. The penalty prescribed was full disclosure by the husband about his former relationship. The wife would be allowed to ask any question she chose, and the husband would be obliged to reveal even the most intimate details about which she might inquire. The wife was to use a full evening and night for this purpose and she was not to censor any question that came to mind." This exercise became odious to the wife long before the allotted time had expired, and she stopped. According to the therapist's commentary, the directive served to validate the wife and to satisfy her need to punish her husband. In reality, she had already been punishing him by her moods, crying spells, and her attempts to find out everything she could. Thus something that previously took place covertly was made overt. "The couple was then better able to address the troublesome aspects of their marriage that had contributed to the husband's having the affair in the first place" (Im, Wilner, and Breit 1983, 214).

Here the therapist clearly sides with the marriage and, at least initially, against the husband's tendencies to independence, in which desire for freedom, independence, and development may be expressed, but which, for whatever reasons, he has already renounced through his return to his wife. In psychoanalytic language, her interest in the "primal scene," intercourse, was granted, even prescribed, for the wife, after she had herself repeatedly demonstrated this interest in an apparently neurotic way. However, it was also transferred to her parents' relationship, their ways of interacting, and their history and, succeeding them, to the relationship of another close couple. Here it is only this permission that appears to have dissolved the encrustation in the shortest time and that first made it possible to talk with and approach each other. Upon closer examination, it is in no way the case that the "systems theoreticians'' only turn the screws of the system, put it on a different track, and then pull back. By all means, talking, working up problems, and insight as the prerequisite for the desire to change appear in many syncretized techniques. In Germany, Helm Stierlin and his associates are the prime example of this. Even in their most recent publications, they find many intermediate forms possible, between ''cure through confrontation'' and ''cure through changing the system'' (Wirsching and Stierlin 1982).

Additional examples in Im, Wilner, and Breit show how far directives can go. Thus a woman who is jealous of her husband's relationship to his older sister, which is marked by his tenderness and gratitude, is simply directed to act as if she were no longer jealous. The therapist joins her in a ''strategic alliance'': she is the more flexible party in the marriage, and thus any change can only proceed from her. The woman manages the dissimulation, even though it is difficult for her. As the result of her behavior, her husband becomes friendlier to her, as one would expect on the basis of common sense. It is of no interest why the wife reacted so pettily to a completely plausible relationship—his older sister had raised the husband. There is also no discussion of whether she perhaps relates to others just as anxiously and possessively, or whether, because of intrapsychic reasons, she ''must'' deal with them in this way.

In a similar manner, a therapist makes a devil's pact with a newly married man.

His wife is a ''vivacious social butterfly,'' is bored in marriage, frequently stays away from home, and finally asks for a divorce. The young husband is directed to provide his wife with the excitement that she apparently misses in her marriage: he is to become less dependable, is no longer to let her know exactly and regularly where he is, is to make plans without his wife, and so forth. The man follows the directive and thereby discovers that he likes this new life, that he can find friends on his own, and that a female colleague at work even makes advances to him. With increasing self-confidence, he is able to give up his clinging, possessive behavior. His wife begins to worry about losing him and has no further reason to despise him for his fretful behavior (Im, Wilner, and Breit 1983, 216).

An even more intensive intervention consists in the suspected partner pretending to be jealous—the authors report on two such cases. The more insane the symptomology, the more effective such interventions are.

In the case of a jealousy paranoia that went so far as to express itself in physical assaults on the husband, he, a physician, had responded by avoiding social contact. His life became so constrained that he considered the idea of divorce, or having his wife committed to a mental hospital.

This man was instructed to act the part of a jealous husband, and since in the course of years he had studied his wife's behavior more than enough, he was preeminently successful in doing so, without his wife even noticing that his new attitude was only feigned. In contrast to his usual behavior, he called home often and at unexpected times; he asked his wife what she was doing just then; he criticized and suspected new clothing that she wore— whom did she want to impress with it?—and he expressed displeasure whenever she showed the slightest interest in the opposite sex.

"The result was dramatic. The wife, now feeling flattered by her husband's attentiveness and his newfound interest, lost her anger and jealousy. She became pleasant and loving toward her husband, and expressed remorse over her earlier behavior." At the eight-month follow-up, the husband reported that his "wife continued to be supporting and loving, but as a precaution, he was still practicing the role of the jealous husband from time to time" (ibid., 216).

Eight months are of course not a very long time. And what would happen if the wife were to notice that her husband had only feigned jealousy, and was not really jealous? The more extensive the delusion is, the easier it is to incorporate within it what is happening. Balint writes, "The building-up of a proper paranoid system is the work of a life-time" (M. Balint et al. 1972, 28). And this is preferable and more important to the patient than (almost) everything else. In a case with which I am thoroughly familiar, the wife, who had the most sensitive symbiotic antennae as far as her husband was concerned, in all probability would have seen through the game and interpreted it as her husband's organizing the whole thing only to be together with "this woman, whom he will never give up," with less bother.

To be sure, in the case described above something else occurred in terms of depth psychology: the devotion, which is so fervently hoped for and so clumsily requested behind the storm of accusations, is suddenly granted. In her husband's entire display of controlling behavior, the wife sees only its loving aspect, the aspect of being held and wanted, which she had to do without for such a long time, which of course was also determined in part by her own collusive behavior. With this, the struggle for the reinforcement of weak self-feeling through attention and appreciation on the part of her husband, a struggle that she had conducted in a way that was just as inappropriate as it was stubborn, suddenly becomes superfluous. Forces are activated that had lain dormant under the crust of an ingrained mutual and ongoing effort to do each other in. Moreover, on the basis of such a foundation, which continues to exist, even the forgiveness of the pretense would be imaginable after some time had passed. In my view, the therapist, but also the clients, were lucky that things turned out well. But of course every therapist needs luck; and the more diligent and experienced the therapist is, the more he or she will admit to what extent luck is necessary.

The therapist's unambiguous reinforcement and confirmation of the undesirable, delusional behavior of the symptomatic individual goes even further than the partner's conscious role playing. Since all others always *resist* the jealous person's craziness (and since, without a doubt, even in deepest paranoia, a part of him- or herself would still like to ally with these people, whom he or she of course claims to consider not normal), then one can imagine what a shock to the system it is when a person as important as the therapist suddenly shifts allegiance to the patient. To be sure, this is also done by the psychoanalytic therapist, who wants to promote the "restitution of the self" (Kohut) and who, for a time, assumes the role of the symbiotic mother for a borderline or psychotic patient, through empathy, emotional satisfaction of needs, and unlimited acceptance in therapy. But the analyst does this in a completely different way, not by giving advice and behavioral directives.

To the systems therapist, the exchange of roles—that is, the feigned jealous behavior of the partner who is considered to be unfaithful—was not successful in the case in question. "The effort failed, however, because of the clumsy manner in which the husband executed the directive, leading to the wife's discovery of her husband's deception."

She continued to persist in her delusional conviction that her husband was wildly attracted to blondes, especially to the blonde who had recently moved into the house across the street from them. In a joint session, the therapist says to the couple, "I am a Buddhist and therefore believe in karma and in the existence of past lives. I believe your husband's interest in blondes has its origin in his past lives, in which he rejected and hurt women with blonde hair. In order to undo his past deeds, he must show his love for blondes. That is the reason for his blonde complex. Now, you can help your husband get over this complex more quickly by strengthening his interest in blondes." Thus she was supposed to point out to him every blonde she saw on the street or on television. The therapist also had her point out blondes in magazine articles to her husband during the therapy session. After four weeks, the wife said to the therapist, "I am getting sick of this blonde business. I don't care anymore. If he wants to see them, let him see them. It's his problem anyway" (Im, Wilner, and Breit 1983, 218).

In subsequent sessions, the wife reported her insight that her jealousy was caused by her own feelings of insecurity. She had had an unhappy childhood and was used to suppressing her emotional needs because she was afraid that she would be loved less if she expressed them. Shortly after her wedding, she discovered that her husband was having an affair. For fear of losing him, she never talked to him about it.

The therapist stresses that the psychological insight followed of itself upon symptom removal, without the therapist's interpretative intervention, through, one could almost say, the "recasting" of the drama in which the wife assumed the role of helper instead of victim (ibid.).

I have experienced something similar, on the basis of follow-up counseling of psychotic patients who were treated with drugs. After its disappearance, the symptom of delusional or borderline jealousy, which led them to psychiatric treatment in the first place, is understood by them differently in terms of its relationship to reality. They then say, "I only imagined that." These experiences confirm my opinion that jealousy never stands only for itself, but always masks something else. Of course, the fact that all people are familiar with jealousy does not exclude the fact that one is always jealous *because* . . . : and what follows is always the respective individual background.

In many cases, therapy that neutralizes the system has the effect of exposing a conflict. Concepts like "scapegoat" or "lightning rod" (Hoffman 1981, 148) play a large role; in order that the worst and most shameful thing in the family (a secret, sexual failure, incest, or even irresoluble differences between the parents in a family whose highest good is decorum and harmony) does not come to light, a participant in the system becomes ill, psychotic, or delinquent and thereby draws all attention to him- or herself. This attention might otherwise be directed to the sore point. In this context, stress research is interesting. It finds "that events with presumably positive meanings, like 'marital reconciliation,' ranked as more stressful on the scale than some with negative connotations, like 'difficulties with sex' " (ibid., 162). Thus what counseling experience demonstrates is confirmed here, that the effort to define problems for oneself and to solve them, whether by reconciliation or separation, is unconsciously felt to be greater, and therefore is more feared, than the stress that is associated with the continuing endurance of difficulties manifested as a symptom.

One of Jackson's cases shows that the masked conflict can, in certain cases, also lie in resisted jealousy, which can be exposed by the therapist's paradoxical intervention.

A paranoid patient says that he suspects that a microphone may be hidden in the therapist's office. The psychiatrist does not interpret this suspicion, but also does not attempt to correct the patient's relationship to reality (as every other person would do if he or she were suspected in such a way!). Rather, he acts as if he is very "concerned," interrupts the session, and thoroughly searches every nook and cranny of the office with the patient. The patient becomes "increasingly unsure and embarrassed. But the therapist would not let the matter rest" (Watzlawick 1983, 243).

And here we certainly find an important stimulus of therapy. There is an immense difference between the tradition of the ideal (never totally fulfilled) of free association and giving "precedence to the patient," which is also one of the rules of marriage counseling, and picking up on what patients present but pushing them to the limit by forcing them to look through every nook and cranny, in spite of feelings of distress, and then pushing the confrontation between reality and fantasy as far as it will go.

According to Watzlawick's account of Jackson's therapy, however, a leap to another level apparently becomes possible because of this. In hindsight, the thorough search of the room seems only symbolic to the reader. An apparently real, but actually invented, actuality, stands for another even more real actuality that, however, unconsciously appears to the patient so urgent and dangerous in its reality that he does not want to confront it. Because

"the patient then plunged into a meaningful description of his marriage, and it turned out that in *this* area he had good reason to be suspicious."

By analogy with the old French saying that jealousy is worse than a toothache, one might say here that admitted jealousy is worse than paranoid mistrust of hidden microphones.

Back to the "blonde business": what repels me in the example is the nonserious manner in which a religion is treated. On the basis of the authority that the therapist represents for the couple and that is so great that even the husband's failed role playing does not shake it, it would have been possible to find another reason for the wife's having to help, a psychological reason: one linked to his ethnic origins or something similar. Even in this instance, what the wife is resisting would have been prescribed: her own interest in blonde women and, according to Freudian thought, repressed homosexuality is behind this. One can imagine in detail how many different types of blondes the patient observed, admired, hated, and compared herself with, in the four weeks before she had enough of it. The admission of what is repressed leads to this attrition, even in psychoanalysis.

10. Problems of the Therapist

In view of such an intervention, the question that poses itself—to the therapist and the marriage counselor, but also to the psychoanalyst who is open enough not to reject out of hand the systemic perspective and its goal of short-circuiting feedback control systems—is not that of the success of such methods, which can no longer be disputed. Indeed, even the successes of psychoanalysis often cannot be precisely proven. They often can only be subjectively experienced and are doubted. I can well imagine that Jung's statement about the successes of his own work applies to all psychotherapies: "One-third cured, one-third significantly improved, and one-third fundamentally unaffected!" (Jung 1981, 148). Willi notes "that the differences in orientation among various thera-

peutic schools are less significant . . . than the personality of the therapist"
(Willi 1978, 366). Thus the question that poses itself is that of the choice of
the form of therapy, and its compatibility with what therapists expect of
themselves and their clients. The question is actually how the therapist views
people.

In view of the current confusing and enticing multiplicity of methods, the
therapist must first of all ask, What do I want to be for the person who comes
to me for help? For only if I am in harmony with myself, will I be able to
help in the most effective way within the range of my possibilities. Anyone
who is all too doubtful of his or her method will become unsure, unclear,
and not believable. To be sure, *some* doubt seems to me to be not only
unavoidable but also a sign of openness, which I almost feel as the proper
decorum owed to colleagues whose approach is different.

For one who works within the psychoanalytic tradition, the first thing one
feels when confronted by directive-systemic interventions is, "I would not
like to be one of them; I do not want to approach my patients so technically,
so manipulatively, as if I knew everything already, so nonindividually, so
ahistorically. I would feel as if I were violating them. I do not like saying
anything but what I think. I do not like using tricks; I also do not like inducing
my patients to use tricks." (It should nevertheless be noted here that this
reaction is not only the "spontaneous" one, but at the same time the official
reaction of *the* psychoanalytic school, that is, the one that is prescribed as
well as sanctioned within one's own group.) The ideal behind this was expressed by Anna Freud in a letter to a fourteen-year-old boy: "If you want
to become a real psychoanalyst, you must possess a great love of both scientific
as well as personal truth, and you must consider this recognition of truth to
be more important than any unpleasantness associated with confronting unpleasant facts, whether they appertain to the external world or your inner
self" (cited in Mitscherlich-Nielsen 1982, 268). One might also add that this
truth will make you free (or at least freer).

Truth and freedom—who would not willingly agree that these merit great
exertions? This truth can only be the individual truth, that is, only a uniquely
personal truth, and never the general, objective truth. And what is perplexing
is that to deal with this truth, it just happens that one takes recourse to fantasies.
The person as a biologically determined being approaching his or her unique
truth by fantasizing—this appears to me to be the most important of Freud's
discoveries. With that, however, the unanswerable question poses itself over
and over again: "What is truth?" Consequently, the other question also follows: "What is freedom?"

In view of the history of psychoanalysis, and of how it has dealt with truth
and freedom, one must unfortunately come to the conclusion that, within its
own ranks, it neither protects against foolishness nor against political cor-
ruption or hierarchical coercive structures. It is often only too difficult to

locate the dialectical and emancipatory principle in psychoanalysis, which is especially stressed by Thea Bauriedl (1984) and which, moreover, would require one to recognize that one's own desires are at the root of the rejection in the series of reactions described above. To be sure, the criticism that has recently been publically levelled against their own institution by prominent psychoanalysts (see especially *Psyche* 7, 1984) is a convincing example of efforts on behalf of the tradition of truth and freedom. In the end one must ask, in which professional group in our society is it possible to observe something similar? Not in politics, not in medicine, not in the field of elementary or higher education—perhaps occasionally in the church. The similarity between "church" and psychoanalysis has been emphasized by many critics. At least in this regard, it is not the worst comparison that can be made.

Nonetheless, it seems to me that the danger of projective resistance cannot be overlooked in the psychoanalytic reaction ("I am against it; thus I am sure that I myself want nothing of the kind"). It is an absolute certainty that no psychotherapist, and thus no psychoanalyst, is protected by a charm against occasional fantasies and euphorias of omnipotence. Yet somehow what is behind these fantasies is the conception that one might be able to create better people with the basic attitude of depth psychology. And psychoanalysts naturally accuse the systems therapists of precisely these fantasies of omnipotence. "Here I sit, and create people in my image." (Goethe, "Prometheus"). We should not forget Freud's modest statement, "Why should it be assumed that the analysts are necessarily better? Analysis makes for unity, but not necessarily for *goodness*" (Freud's emphasis, letter to James Putnam, 7 June 1915, cited in Jones 1953–57, 2:182). Today one would perhaps find "unity" in the regained "true self." People who have gone through a long analysis directed toward this goal often strikingly confirm Freud's observation that moral progress is missing. In addition, neurotics are absolutely capable of convincing, nonneurotic, "mature" goodness.

Even in a case that has been concluded to the counselor's satisfaction, I think that marital and family counseling will not produce this harmony. Nor can goodness and moral improvement in any way be its goal, even if positive forces sometimes are thereby released, making possible actions that are traditionally considered to be "good": love of one's neighbor, commitment to others, serenity, giving up privileges. Nonetheless, moral criteria, that is, the counselor's value judgments, can never be excluded. They are there simply because the counselor is not a computer. Even the social engineer, which is how the cited systems therapists would prefer to see themselves, obviously finds certain things "good" and "bad," not to mention the fact that he or she experiences his or her own and others' modes of behavior as impressive, boring, foolish, intolerable, and so forth, and reacts to them accordingly. One of the axioms of communications theory is that "one cannot not communicate." That is a convincing assertion. In my view, the *kind* of communication is by all means linked to one's life history, and I have first had to relearn from Watzlawick et al. that there are differences of opinion about this among psychologists. Until then I thought that only individuals who knew nothing of the unconscious, or of childhood development, relational conflicts, and their possible effects, could hold such opinions. One kind of communication between client and therapist is the *form* therapy takes.

Without a doubt, freedom is not only made possible by making unconscious compulsions accessible to insight, but also by intervening in the pathological rigidification of a system by means of a directive. In a systemic case history, the wife of a jealous husband alternated between reacting to his drunken attacks with fear of violence and with rage at his distorted view of reality. This is what he was accustomed to. When such a man realizes that his wife—acting upon the therapist's directive—is not doing what has been repeatedly done and what is therefore expected in response to his latest fit of jealousy, that is, she is not fearful or enraged, but walks around the room and pulls her hair, then he will obviously be confused. If she responds to his inquiry—likewise, because the therapist advised her to so—that she is despondent because of her fear of losing her husband, then an interaction cycle has doubtless been broken. One of its basic components was that the husband was of the opinion that only he was afraid of losing his wife, while she could be sure of him and was not concerned about whether or not she would keep him (Teismann 1979). No marriage counselor would be likely to view the goal that is thereby attained, the relativization of one's own perspective by learning to empathize with the partner and taking into account his or her needs and concerns too, as something that the counselor could do without in the practice. But the traditionally oriented therapist would attempt to achieve this goal differently: by conversations, inquiries, reflection—never by following such a course of action.

Allow me to show my own colors: I have never yet given a systemic directive. In most of the described cases, I would count on achieving similar results with my own method. In the serious cases, such as delusional or borderline conditions, I would prefer to raise the question of whether the results are stable and whether there will be no new attacks or crises. Therefore, at least as far as jealousy is concerned, I am convinced that there are many ways to achieve the same goal, or even that all ways are uncertain and that one can at most approximate truth and freedom, but never completely attain them.

It is self-evident that one manipulates, even as an interlocutor with principles deriving from depth psychology. Even the use of interpretations has something directive in it; the "setting" of a marriage counseling session—for example, the decision (which largely lies with the counselor) as to whether to work with one or both partners, perhaps including the children, and the decision as to how often and how long they will work—already contains a value judgment, in favor of the system of marriage in the case of joint counseling, in favor of individual growth in the case of individual counseling. It is inherent in the process that, in the course of time, this value judgment can shift because of the therapist's unperceived alliances with one of the partners. What Fritz Simon, one of the members of the Heidelberg group that formed around Helm Stierlin, writes can (but doesn't have to) happen: "that precisely those individuals whose goal it is to make what is unconscious conscious, unconsciously do what the others do consciously" (1983, 311).

In the Federal Republic of Germany, there are many fewer competent teachers—and thus, in my view, many more amateurish attempts at therapy—in the area of systems therapy than there are in the area of depth psychology in its various branches. However, it seems to be part of the essence of therapies that are planned to be brief, that they do not demand less but rather more knowledge and know-how from the therapist than long and leisurely therapies, which have more possibilities of corrective adjustments by trial and error simply because the therapy lasts longer. This is true for focal psychotherapy (M. Balint et al. 1972) and for the strategic short-term therapies of the systems analysts. There is a quadratic solution for the problem of how one can get an egg to stand on end. Columbus solved this problem by denting the egg and then standing it on end. Anyone who wants to apply Columbus's solution to the problem either must be a Columbus, that is, a pioneer, explorer, or a charismatic personality, or must have seen it done before. One needs tremendous knowledge to be able to transfer such a solution to other problems. It is difficult to learn this from books, in which often successful examples alone are presented and in which any mention of the therapist's frustrations is rare. Even if I *wanted* to acquire such knowledge, that would be rather difficult in my situation and environment, at least in regard to the forms termed "classical" in the literature. It is simpler in the case of hybrid forms.

My personal argument for not using directive methodology, however, depends on the field that psychoanalysis designates with the terms "transference" and "countertransference." Systems therapists, of course, place themselves in the role of the omnipotent father who often insists on the execution of his directives without explanations. At most, they may occasionally make a joke or be a "good sport," for example, by making a bet with the client and staking their next conference fee (Teismann), but they never allow their actions to be called into question. Naturally, I also set certain preconditions without which I will conclude no "contract." A client who does not want to reflect and probe into feelings, who wants only to accuse and to be a passive recipient of help, who often does not keep appointments, and who wants to see only the client's viewpoint confirmed, is not acceptable to me. I do, however, attempt to relativize my authority. Nonetheless, I still retain more than enough of it—because of my position, my home-court advantage, and the client's distress—and I also do not delude myself into thinking that I can dispense with it completely. The clients, of course, look for the counselor's "experience" and also need it. For me, however, this experience consists in the knowledge that people in the worst crises will find an individual solution—often in crises in which I myself would have the feeling of not being able to endure! It also consists in motivating them to find this individual solution. In doing so, I would like to support them and not determine the way *for* them. This is precisely what the patriarchal father claims the right to do and, in so doing, often disappoints. Furthermore, his reign has not exactly improved our world.

In addition, I would like to structure my relationship to the client in such a way that I participate in his or her growth, that I see the changes (which the systems therapists of course also want to make possible) emerge—should I, together with my clients, be successful in initiating any at all. That is entirely a matter of taste; a matter of the pleasure principle, if one wishes to express it in those terms. It is simply more enjoyable for me. I would prefer to be cautious with any ethical classification or disqualification. After systemic prescriptions, therapists often initiate breaks in the therapy lasting several weeks, whereas I, as a rule, work at least once a week with my clients. I must put up with the reproach that I take myself too seriously, since I think that I could not endure the anxiety of not hearing for such a long time from people for whom I, through my own actions, clear the path to far-reaching, and possibly dangerous, changes in their lives. I can less readily accept the other reproach, that I am too serious and do not want to venture upon what is playful, imaginative, and creative in strategic interventions. A representative of this school (Teismann) calls this "serious playfulness"—and to direct in this way and to play along oneself is certainly pleasant for the therapist and, at best, useful for the client. However, in my counseling sessions, things are not always serious; we often laugh, and if a client can begin to laugh at him- or herself, I regard that as considerable progress and often as a sign of growth. However, I also do not want to run the slightest risk, just on the basis of the therapeutic structure, of secretly laughing at my clients—not because I would not sometimes feel the need to do so, or to get back at my clients in another way, but rather because I would not like it if someone were to deal with me in this way.

Moreover, I am conscious that, even after all the reflection I have devoted to my work, I still see myself, again and again, in the position of not being able to be consistent, but of "somehow" having to cope. To be sure, perhaps the following also applies: The more precisely I understand that, the less fanatical I am able to be, the more flexible I remain, and, I hope, the more helpful I am to my clients. Also, the older I become, the more clearly I experience a paradox inherent in therapy. This paradox, as it happens, has been imparted to us as a fundamental part of the human experience: the monstrous, unique seriousness of conflict and suffering, and the need to eliminate this pressure—and at the same time the inconsequentiality of those same phenomena in the face of life's fragility and brevity. I am not able to draw the conclusion from this that in the end it is consequently irrelevant whether I deal with my clients directively or nondirectively. What is remarkable, however, is that I am comfortable precisely within this paradox. The old saying applies somewhat—not completely!—to my work, and certainly to the work of all therapists: "I come, I know not whence—I go, I know not whither—I am amazed, that I am happy."

PART FOUR:
COUNTERMOVEMENTS

△ 19 △

THIRTY CASES FROM OUR COUNSELING PRACTICE

My work on this book was not only concurrent with ongoing counseling sessions in which jealousy played a role, but for the last two years I also surveyed and made use of thirty catamneses. Nine cases were brought to my attention by colleagues in the counseling center; one by the Ark, a suicide prevention clinic in Munich; I selected twenty from among my own cases, three of those from my private practice.

1. What Is a "Case of Jealousy?"

At first, my only criteria were for the case to have been concluded at least one year prior to work on the book and, naturally, for it to have involved jealousy. A peculiarity of the theme already manifested itself here: in no case did any of the clients forward jealousy as the symptom calling for attention. Rather, the predominant issue in twenty-seven of the thirty cases was that of triadic relationships: a partner had "strayed," as it is still so strikingly formulated. The extramarital love had remained "platonic" in three of the counseling cases. These are among the most difficult cases. In the twenty-four cases in which the extramarital partners were not only attracted to each other but also slept together, there were, in almost equal proportion, short-term relationships (one or two instances of sleeping together), longer ones (relationships lasting several months to approximately one and one-half years), as well as long-term relationships (lasting several years).

The three cases in which neither a fantasized nor a real extramarital partner was involved, but in which jealousy "only" manifested itself in surveillance, compulsions, and even rivalry with individuals who were part of the nuclear family (most often parents and children), were especially distressing and dramatic.

One already sees something that is perhaps unexpected: that there is generally no sense of proportion in jealousy, but also no correlation between its intensity, on the one hand, and the frequency or intensity of sexual contacts, on the other. Jealousy is not a predictable reaction in the "normal scheme of things," like the drop of blood that comes from the finger pricked by a needle. Rather, it is the variously determined symptom of an individual with his or her unique history within one or several life systems. In the cases that were worked up, the system is almost exclusively that of the family, which one can, of course, not conceive of other than as being itself integrated into various influencing matrices, such as the determining culture and religion, forms of government, professional associations, social circles, and much more.

The data manifest a striking gap: in not a single selected case had someone come for counseling who was the outsider in the triangle. At the same time, it certainly often happens that the "third party" is desperate, because the marriage or another love has been preferred to the third party, or because it was decided that the two were incompatible. This complex of problems does not surface in our examples. This may be due to the counselors' selection, but certainly also because one always views such suffering as being "not so bad," as something that one "can manage on one's own." On the other hand, it is viewed as more dangerous and more wounding for a person to have to come to terms with the fact that someone has invaded a marriage. This situation is also deemed to be worthy of greater exertions. Jealousy in marriage seems more justifiable in the literal sense of the word—protected and explicable by more rights.

This lacuna became clear to me only after I had worked through all the catamneses. At the same time, the third party had always been of special interest to me, and I paid very close attention to the fantasies that the wounded party in the marriage has about the third party. I likewise paid close attention to my own notions of what the rival, on his or her part, feels. It is, in fact, difficult to get to the reality of this person—except in reality! Without difficulty, I could point out a whole slew of such constellations among my male and female friends, from my own youth, and in triadic relationships in my personal social sphere. But those are not counseling cases.

I finally remembered a single case in which the issue was suffering because of rejection (which, moreover, most directly mirrors the oedipal problem, that of the single individual against an inseparable couple). However, this came to me too late for inclusion in this book. Furthermore I had already decided to present a case that, because of its unique structure, is not part of the follow-up data.

The lacuna seems to me to be indicative that there is a general consensus, to which even marriage counselors contribute: The individual who is wounded, and therefore jealous, in marriage or another long-term relationship deserves more protection and assistance than the intruder, or the individual in a rivalry who loses ground *before* the critical decision.

Once I had made this discovery, I could not suppress a feeling of indignation and dissatisfaction: when someone lets out a cry of distress because of an endangered marriage, we all gather together like colony of ants. However, if it is "only" a question of love, then we do not deny our assistance to those who are suffering—it would, of course, be given if it were requested—but we are simply not open to it without first giving it great thought. This is also the case if it is a matter of questioning our institutions, which in the final analysis is indispensable for all of us. In many instances these institutions may have become threadbare, but they are still protected by the state. Our own fears are naturally at the root of this.

But the admission of jealousy per se is already difficult enough. As I have already mentioned, this is demonstrated by the fact that the criterion, "the issue here is jealousy," does not come from the clients but from the counselors. The ineradicable painfulness and ambivalence of the entire complex is probably still, or yet again, mirrored in the reluctance to present jealousy directly as a symptom.

A client who had gone through lengthy and successful counseling was surprised when one of my colleagues who had worked with her called to ask whether she would be prepared to participate in a follow-up session about jealousy. She was of the opinion that her own case had nothing to do with jealousy, in the precise sense of the word. At the same time, she told me during catamnesis that, for a long time, she had thought of practically nothing but why her husband had a close relationship with a mutual friend, about which the friend had informed her earlier, and what the two of them might be doing together at any given moment. "During this time I barely noticed my children, although I conscientiously took care of their needs." And that was not jealousy? It turned out that the underlying fear of loss— she came from a refugee family—had imprinted itself upon her as the predominant concept.

My collection of examples does not contain any case of delusional or borderline jealousy. By this I understand jealousy of an imagined rival, or if a relationship actually exists, the evaluation is "false" within the terms of the system, and is thus isolated, "crazy." If such cases are treated at all and not simply endured, it is certainly not coincidental that they are more likely to turn up in psychiatric practices, or occasionally in psychoanalysis. As I have already mentioned, such cases are appearing more frequently in our counseling clinic, but none of us could produce a case that had been concluded a sufficiently long time ago. At the time of my book's final editing, I myself had counseled four such cases to their (preliminary?) conclusion, which in each case, however, lay only a few months in the past.

Moreover in these cases, as well as in the cases that were worked up in catamneses, "conclusion" only refers to an agreement, discussed with the clients, not to have any more regular counseling sessions. The client usually says something like, "We want to see how we will manage on our own"; or "Right now we're not getting anywhere." Thus "conclusion" does not mean "the end of a development that satisfies the counselor." If I were to treat only such cases here, that would produce a prettified picture of the "success rate" of counseling, all my colleagues would have had even more difficulty in locating cases. Or perhaps they would have had no difficulty at all, for one remembers very precisely the few successes, of which one allows oneself to be really "proud."

The evaluation of outcomes is very difficult. In spite of this, I have attempted a rough division into "good, average, bad"— and the thirty cases could be divided evenly among the three categories.

2. Some Statistics

The thirty cases are certainly representative for a counseling center in a large city—my three private cases do not basically alter the picture—primarily and precisely because of their great diversity. One constant consists solely in class membership: roughly stated, all clients come from the middle class, more from the upper than the lower middle class. Age is also relatively homogenous: by far the majority of clients began their counseling between the ages of thirty and forty; some were older, but very few were younger. One other thing they clearly had in common was the frequency of the jealous individual's direct contact with the rival. Among twenty-one jealous individuals the rival was from the circle of friends or acquaintances, or an effort to establish contact was made subsequently.

Otherwise, however, everything was very incongruous. The *length of counseling* varied between three weeks and seven years; the *number of sessions* between three and approximately two hundred. At the time of the catamneses, the *beginning* of counseling lay between two and seventeen years in the past, the *conclusion* of counseling between one and ten years. In only one case did we stick to the one-year time period between conclusion and follow-up, which I had set—all other cases had been concluded at least two years before. The *length of the marriage* was between three months and twenty-seven years. In sixteen cases, the marriage was preserved after counseling; in another four cases, a separation agreement was concluded; in eight cases, divorce was the outcome. One female client was—and remained—single. One marriage ended one and a half years after lengthy counseling (sixty-one sessions in almost three years) with the husband's suicide.

The *number of children* is conspicuous and above average; only six couples had only one child; sixteen had two children; two couples had three. That still sounds "normal," but this no longer does: two of the thirty couples had four children, and two couples had five children. I could not determine any link between the kind of jealousy and the greater number of children. In any case, one may conclude that it is in the nature of things for couples with several children to be more motivated to seek marriage counseling, because of the greater seriousness of their responsibility, than childless couples would be.

In nineteen cases, the *party who was suffering* due to the external relationship was the woman, in eleven cases the man. This outcome seems to confirm the frequently expressed assumption that women are more jealous than men. In any case, it shows that women deal with their suffering in a more vigilant manner and that they are more active when it is a matter of doing something about it. This is certainly connected to the longstanding notion that interiority, "the psychic," is in the woman's jurisdiction, while men continue to understand themselves as those whose responsibility for the family must be proven "outside." In ten cases, during the course of counseling it turned out that the partner now the object of acute jealousy had at other times been jealous him- or herself, sometimes to the extent of becoming violent.

The *women's stronger motivation* is also evident in that counseling predominantly involved the woman in twelve cases; in fourteen cases it predominantly involved both partners; in not a single case did it predominantly or only involve the man. Usually we attempt to see both partners together at least once. Some other counseling centers handle this differently. It is often rather difficult to motivate the partner who came first to bring the other along or, to express it differently, to admit the other partner to counseling. For there is usually a transference problem: the jealous individual also does not want "to share" the counselor. The client fears the confrontation with the other's concrete reality, against which the client would perhaps have to correct his or her view of things, or even change it completely. In any case, the counselor obviously will experience the client differently, in a more three-dimensional manner, so to speak, once the counselor has at least once seen the client in contact with the partner.

That in spite of this the more traditional method of individual counseling often proves to be more beneficial or, for different reasons, to be the only form of counseling that is practicable, is an entirely different issue. Keeping in mind the comparison between what is internal and what is external will stand the counselor in especially good stead in these cases, precisely because the clients' fantasies in jealousy play a role that must be taken very seriously; they are often just as important as observed reality.

3. The Questions

I did not present the clients with a questionnaire but had conversations with them, which usually lasted an hour. All were asked the same questions in terms of content (if not in the precise way they were formulated).

They were to describe briefly to me the occasion that led them to seek out the counseling center. This was especially useful to me in cases that were not my own and in each case led to a reintroduction to the problem.

Had the difficulty changed, or did it still exist in the same way?

How did the client see the effect of counseling on him- or herself (especially in dealing with the main problem), on the partner, and on other individuals, especially the children?

What was the worst thing for him or her at the time?

Against whom was aggression directed—against the partner, the rival, or the jealous individual per se?

During counseling, did the client have the experience of reaching a turning point, did something "click" that especially stuck in the mind ("Now I've seen the light!")?

What was the counselor's role?

During the clients' narratives, as well as during my own questioning, I paid special attention to the relationship to the rival.

4. A Guide through Incongruent Realities: Reflections on the Catamneses

When I began to work on the catamneses, I had no idea at all what would come out of it. Nonetheless, I had great expectations: that at least some of the clients might have become free and assured enough to be calmly able to concede to the partner important, erotically colored relationships. Here I even had sexual relationships in mind, in keeping with the clients' age, social class, and mutual ideas about marriage. Thus the utopia of the elimination of jealousy was also present in my mind.

At first, I was correspondingly disappointed when some clients (even a man!) still cried some during follow-up sessions, even though it was long after the event and long after the resolution of the crisis. And even though they said that counseling had helped them tremendously! My ideal expectations, if they were that at all, were not fulfilled in a single one of our cases, and thus reality forced me to banish all my counselor's delusions of grandeur completely from my mind. I have only gradually come to understand that the realm that jealousy does not govern can, indeed, be expanded and that love, to a certain degree, can also evolve from holding on to letting go. However, somewhere there is always an enclave with the warning, "This far, but no farther!" These enclaves change from case to case, and it is likely that, from time to time, they require a new demarcation even among very generous couples. To be more precise, they require a new definition of what the person who grants the partner certain freedoms expects from the partner in return in the way of loyalty.

Parenthetically it should be noted that also at issue are things that, as a counselor, one hardly dares utter because of their "old-fashioned" and normative bourgeois aftertaste: tact, politeness, and respect for the other, perhaps just good manners.

Primarily two things have become clear to me: first of all, that every counseling only means escorting someone a part of the way, that "conclusion" never means the conclusion of a development, in keeping with the formula, "From now on I will never be jealous again." If in spite of this some clients can say, "That will never again happen to me," what is meant is that they trust themselves never again to wind up in a similar morass of suffering and desolation, because they would notice earlier and more precisely how and where the partner could endanger their own indispensable, basic needs.

I especially noticed to what a slight extent, as a counselor, one can foresee the further course of development when, in some cases, I still had questions about older catamneses after one year had passed. When I called these clients, I could regularly ascertain that their situation and emotional state had changed even more, and often in a totally unexpected manner. In this context, it should be mentioned that in precisely half of the cases, the clients had turned to further therapy—often to long-term group therapy, in three cases to psychoanalysis, but also to weekend encounter sessions and such like. The counseling process, which was registered in the catamneses, had often taken place in a piecemeal fashion with sizeable interruptions. Basically all psychotherapy, including even the longest psychoanalysis, is just crisis intervention. Without feeling that one has become stuck in a dead end, one will not call upon a "specialist" for help. Once one is again out on a thoroughfare, the direction that will be taken is unforeseeable.

The second important experience I underwent with the catamneses was that previously I had been unable to see so clearly how variable the interpretation of reality is. In jealousy conflicts, and basically in marriage per se, the issue is to harmonize individual realities. In counseling, the reality of the counselor must also be taken into account. Thus in catamneses there is not only a threefold reality, but a threefold memory as well. There is no question of objectivity.

One could describe a jealousy conflict simply as a conflict between two realities, as a kind of star wars: my world against yours. A solution is reached when the realities (again) are predominantly congruent and when certain free zones for individual realities outside of the congruence have been negotiated, worked out, allowed, and permitted, even though they are possibly inaccessible to the partner—or however one may wish to express what happens when jealousy is exploited as an opportunity. I have experienced again and again that this opportunity often comes when the two realities, which are convulsively clung to as identical but which have actually changed long ago, are finally *experienced* as having changed.

I was able to see especially clearly to what an extent reality, in the sense of modern systems theoreticians (such as Bateson, Glasersfeld, and Foerster, as well as Watzlawick), is indeed "invented," when the partners came separately to a follow-up session after having, in the meantime, been divorced (see the fall 1984 lecture series sponsored by the Siemens Foundation in Munich).

In the case of one couple, whom I thought I knew very well, the conclusion of counseling lay eight years in the past. From what I remembered, the husband had been especially jealous. In follow-up he said that he had actually not understood things in the same way—the really jealous person was actually his wife. *Both* assumptions were confirmed for me in rereading my notes. The husband saw his wife's intention to get a divorce as the reason for the conclusion of the therapy, since at that time she already had a boyfriend, who had free access to the husband's home without his knowledge. For her part, in follow-up the wife said to me that, at that time, her husband was no longer interested in counseling, for he had taken up with Anna and thus needed neither counseling nor his wife. I had heard nothing of the two new partners in counseling, which was very intensive and in which I perforce had to be satisfied that the symbiotic relationship was breaking up, because I could not imagine any joint development.

I do not believe that these clients were lying. They simply had different realities, and because of the divorce, which took place two years after counseling, it was no longer necessary to harmonize the two realities. In my statistical scale, I classified the outcome of this therapy as "bad," even though the clients saw it differently. At the time of the follow-up, the husband still suffered from intestinal problems, which had almost necessitated an operation the year before. My main impression was that the couple was suffering from communication disorders that were an obstacle to a clear resolution of the conflict. The continued existence of the psychosomatic illness, which is generally thought always to accompany such disorders, confirmed for me that I had never penetrated to the root of the problem at that time.

What was responsible for this became clear to me only in follow-up. The wife said that the whole dilemma had probably consisted in the fact that her husband had "let out his aggression toward his mother on her." An entirely new piece of reality now was added to the picture, and it had not been dealt with anywhere during the entire course of therapy. We had talked a lot about the wife's youth and her relationship to her mother, but

never about the husband's mother. He had probably still been sparing her
in his love-hate relationship and did not want to sacrifice her.

I felt as if I were suddenly seeing the final, inmost form or solid core,
like the chrysalis in the cocoon, which is no longer hollow and which all
the layers that enwrap it echo.

With this description, I would like only to demonstrate how presented reality
can concurrently be real and unreal. I do not want, for example, to maintain
that the reality that has "emerged from its cocoon" is the true reality. In this
therapeutic process, the realities of the husband and the wife, as well as my
own realities, were not "false" or "ineffective." They were very powerful
and very real. They were only different, perhaps understood differently, and
it could be that the last "invention" will reveal the pattern that, if changed,
could finally make the husband healthier.

The notes I made on follow-up conferences and the excerpts that I prepared
from tape recordings fill a huge file. Thus an enormous quantity of source
material derived from my simple desire to learn how our clients were now
dealing with their jealousy. I feel justified in deriving a theory of jealousy in
counseling from this. However, I would like to attempt to describe some of
the countermovements that were jointly worked up by clients and counselors.
The reader is certain to expect this and has a right to, even if I am not totally
comfortable with it, since simplification always concurrently means doing
violence to reality, and since I must explain involuted processes as if they
could be dealt with as single entities.

In any case, I would like to state most emphatically that in this part of
the book I in no way want to provide directions on how to deal with jealousy.
Of course, one could infer this information from the results of the catamneses,
but I would consider this to be in the first place dishonest and in the second
place totally ineffective. The multiplicity of solutions is precisely what is
significant, not the few principles that can be read out of the totality of all
cases. Thus, any person has radically misunderstood me who shows his or
her partner this book and says, "Look, that's the way we have to do it!" or
even, "If you don't do things in the way described there, it's your own fault!"
*I neither can nor want to show the way it must be done or should be done,
but only the way it has been done.*

△ 20 △

SHOCK, RAGE, PAIN

I was not wounded—I myself was nothing but a wound.

A client

It may sound strange that I consider something that looks like a symptom to be among the reactions that lead to the overcoming of the crisis. One can say, however, that without a shock there is no crisis, and without a crisis, no solution. This is one of the few basic assumptions without which I cannot imagine jealousy counseling. One can hardly imagine a way of dealing with jealousy without becoming clearly aware that one is jealous. Perhaps that sounds strange, since jealousy is, after all, there; there is a reason for it, whether it is to be found in the partner's liaison, in a "delusion," or in internal insecurity.

But not without reason did language need such a long time to find a word for this feeling (see chap. 13). Something similar is recapitulated again and again in individual destinies. Too many desires and bonds, ideal conceptions, and fear of change confront jealousy. Clients frequently lament that they noticed nothing about anything for such a long time, that "everyone" already knew about it, except for themselves. Often they are angry at friends who covered for the unfaithful partner. Some who had promised reciprocal candor are indignant that this promise has not been kept. The more taboo one's own aggressiveness is, the more difficult it is to understand clearly what has happened.

The unconscious fear of breaking the internalized commandment against rage, not to mention a rampage, is very great, especially among women. A female client had inherited from her grandmother and mother the recommendation "always to keep a low profile." Women frequently are under the mother's commandment to be gentle, loving, understanding, and pretty, "for their husbands." I believe that the amount of fear of unavoidable ugliness that aggressive jealousy has as its concomitant should not be underestimated. A female client felt herself to be so totally unattractive during the crisis that she refused to appear naked in front of her husband during this time.

266

This problem surfaces in a client's memory as under a magnifying glass. Her mother used to caution her by saying, "Girl, you've got a young husband!" When she came to counseling, the client was twenty-seven years old, her husband thirty. During follow-up, ten years later, she said, "Even today, I often think about the fact that my mother did not take into consideration that, after all, I was young too. . ."

In this case, the mother's influence was very great; not that it was conscious, but it was strong in terms of unconscious identification. The client functioned not only as the mother of her two children, but also as her husband's mother, although she naturally was also his sexual partner. She felt she was happy in this relationship. She expected husband and wife to be "everything" to each other, like in the early dyadic mother-child relationship. Her husband was very attractive and at least appeared to be worldly and protective, although he was basically childish and easily insulted. Like an adolescent, after some years of happy total union, he no longer kept appointments or met obligations, and he entered into relationships with other women. After an affair ended, he continued to return to his wife, long after their divorce, to have a good cry and even to have her comfort his rejected girlfriends. The shock the wife suffered when she became conscious that their unity was dissolving was immense. "I was never jealous before his first affair. I quite simply thought, 'Something like that cannot happen to us.' After that it preoccupied me incessantly."

It is as if she had been suddenly catapulted out of the stage of a mother in a symbiotic relationship with a child dependent on her, with whom "that" really cannot happen, headlong into the relationship with a man of the same age who, if he wants and has the courage to do so, can satisfy his sexual needs with someone other than her. (A small child cannot run away and get milk somewhere else!)

The awakening was terrible; "I did not believe that I could ever again lead a normal life. I thought it would be all over—if the husband were to desert his family, and above all if he were to leave me. I saw myself as having been cast aside, like a piece of furniture with two children. For he was everything to me at that time, and I was just—I had to come to terms with that—not everything to him." The dependence of one's own life on another is demonstrated very clearly here. One could almost say that if the partner's divine breath is missing, the wife will again become a lifeless carved statue. Such symbiotic claims are, of course, experienced with shared or reversed roles: in this situation, the wife did not see herself as a mother, but as a totally dependent child.

Anyone who experiences such an invasion, such a shock, such a regression, which I here claim to be beneficial, will somehow start hitting out because of fear and horror. Naturally, that person will not be capable of a blow of adult aggression, that is, of clear confrontation, of disagreeing and agreeing about the basis of reciprocal claims. The role change that this woman could manage was from trusting to controlling mother, and her aggressiveness also ran its course along these lines: in an energetic and imaginative manner, which was typical of her, she began to monitor and spy on her husband incessantly, which naturally led to her discovering more affairs, if not even to her inducing them.

Many clients have perceived the endangerment of supporting love as a question of life and death. After all, one-third of the respondents attempted suicide. In one case the suicide attempt succeeded, one and a half years after the conclusion of counseling, after a prior attempt on the wife's life.

Two more examples of the horror that arises when one becomes conscious of the danger:

"I appeared to myself as having been catapulted into space, as being totally alone in the world. I do not want to say that I was dead, but it was night. If I had not had counseling at that time—I do not know if I would still be here today." In this case, the wife was entirely certain that her husband had not slept with her rival, but had only flirted intensely with her. And in follow-up, seventeen years after the start of counseling, the memory was still so painful that tears flowed.

Another female client said, "It hit me like an avalanche, and I couldn't explain *anything* to myself. I always thought that I had done everything right, and that something like that couldn't happen to us because our relationship is so unique. It was so bitter—at that time, the press carried the picture of a Vietnamese who is shot to death and loses his weapon. You could see the man's disbelief: 'Why am I being shot to death now?' That's the way I felt. This: 'Why me! Why me?—After all, I do everything!'"

With these examples, it probably is clear that counselors are likely to be happy if aggression is talked about after the shock. One can work with this. However, it occasionally requires much patience before it may be clearly revealed.

During group therapy, a client who had accepted with conspicuous calmness a completely surprising divorce brought about by her husband's reviving an old love dating back to his youth, remembered an experience that she had totally forgotten: When she was five years old, two teenage boys from the neighborhood had teased her. She had become enraged and had thrown a pair of scissors at them. Unluckily, it had become so embedded in the area of one of the boy's kidneys that a doctor had to remove it and stitch the wound. The little girl was not scolded but had to go along to the doctor's office and observe the treatment.

This client became aggressive only one time in group therapy: when the leader asked her why she was never actually aggressive.

During follow-up after the end of group therapy—she had stopped, "because others needed it more than I"—she explained that she still had difficulties becoming enraged. Only once did she go completely out of her mind: when her former husband had had a child with his new wife, and her own ten-year-old daughter was so hurt by this that she spoke of "throwing herself in front of a train." "If my husband had not been two hundred kilometers away, and If I had had a knife—I believe I would have stabbed him to death!" If, If . . . But at least the aggression had come somewhat closer to consciousness.

The same woman was so afraid of the aggression that lay dormant in her that she hid a highly ornate weapon, which she had inherited from her father and which was actually more an ornament, on top of a wardrobe— "but in such a way that I cannot simply get to it with a chair, but first I have to go down to the basement and get a ladder. I think that will be enough for me to return to my senses."

That may sound theatrical—but in the final analysis a staging is already a conscious, even if still fairly indirect, way of dealing with a theme. In direct language, this client can become momentarily "out of control"— fighting words for many women—only *for* someone else, specifically, for her daughter. When her daughter had started to get into the worst difficulties at school after the unexpected birth of her stepsister—the suicide threat was associated with school problems—the mother tearfully cursed the responsible teacher, on the telephone (!). Certainly her aggression was still not directed where it should have been, but to her surprise the client experienced that "for the first, for the very first, time in all these years, others showed me understanding and sympathy, really and truly shown by other people"—and they did not show her only their displeasure and condemnation. She had so terribly feared this in other situations that she had not even risked attempting aggression.

Women's suffering and injury overflows to the children much more frequently than men's—this appears permissible, while the emotional tradition predominantly commends to women themselves tolerating, enduring, and waiting. Men, on the contrary, react more directly. To be sure, they also state that the shocking experience consisted in their having been deprived of their foundation.

A man stated, and was very agitated while doing so, "I believed in a world that was intact. I believed I could count on my wife—and then the egoism that breaks through here—I believed that it was irrelevant if the children suffered from this!'' Indeed, the children also play a role, but he apparently understood this intact world as something that vigilantly, and possibly aggressively, differentiates itself from the outside world: ''Do you know, when one stands back to back—and then has to learn that one is *not* standing . . .''

Aside from the fact that it is difficult to imagine what takes place sexually and emotionally between a married couple when the two are ''standing back to back,'' not a single woman expressed herself in this, or a similar, way. Even when, as frequently happens, desertion by their husbands has been experienced by the wives as especially unfair after they have jointly erected a structure, the issue in the perceived injury is not the struggle per se. The man in this example carried on the struggle alone after the shock, during which he, like many men, had lost a lot of weight and became almost incapable of working. Indeed, as he discovered, he carried on in a better and stronger way then previously. He discovered he was more independent professionally and that he had become significantly tougher. ''I did away with humane concessions in my business.'' However, he stated unequivocally, and to my amazement, that he did not feel this to be something that was good. But it just had to be. Somewhat later in our conversation, he was able to formulate it more positively: ''I do not attempt to exploit anyone, but also do not allow myself to be exploited.''

In any case, men have a very different way of dealing with the rival after the shock than women do—they are more belligerent, derogatory, and openly competitive. I intend to deal with this. Here I would like to present only a characteristic example for the kind of shock involved.

''I seemed to myself to be as idiotic as the biggest blockhead on God's earth. I could not grasp it, because I was adamantly convinced that my wife would never do something like that! And in critical situations when allusions were made, I also came forward as being 100 percent convinced of this. Later I thought to myself: How he must have been secretly laughing at me! Others, of course, have the right to laugh, but I will not concede that to *him* of all people!''

△ 21 △
A NEW REALITY IN
THE RELATIONSHIP

After the shock nothing remains but to come to terms with the new reality. Occasionally dreams manifest the whole horror: thus a woman dreamed— and she was familiar with this dream "emotion" from some other important radical situations in her life—that she was sticking her head through the outer skin of the globe, completely alone, "and the earth was desolate and empty." The uncertainty as to whether the rebirth is to continue is clearly manifest here. The most obvious thing would be to pull one's head back—but that was not possible.

Moreover, several clients reported on the struggle for their own perception of reality. On the behavioral level, this appears as the partner simply denying his or her suspicion about another love. Often it is formulated with the words "You're crazy!" On the relational level (see Bauriedl 1980, 86ff., on this differentiation), it is formulated in the following way: "Whose reality is stronger, yours or mine?" Sometimes, it is formulated as "Do I have to go crazy for love of you, because you want to force your reality on me?" One of our clients attempted suicide for this reason. Her husband simply said, "You have delusions." As the woman stated, gradually "I lost touch with reality, I lost my footing so completely that I no longer wanted to live."

At this point, by means of a short plot summary, I would like to refer the reader to a novella by the Spanish writer Unamuno, in which the strands of this struggle of realities are clearly delineated, up to and including what is murderous about them. Miguel de Unamuno (1864–1936) was for many years the rector of the University of Salamanca. He was proud and individualistic, "like a Spaniard," but an unbending critic of traditional Spanish values, whose exaggeration he made responsible for the country's political downfall. The jealousy reaction, which the Spanish male still had to demand of himself in the nineteenth and twentieth centuries, is one of these values. The story about a man who wanted to deny jealousy shows how strongly it clings to the unconscious. The story is titled "A Whole Man" (Unamuno 1979, 492ff.).

271

The hero, Alejandro Gómez, comes from the Spanish New World, from Cuba, where he has accumulated an enormous fortune. He is depicted as being coarse, energetic, and plebeian. He marries the beautiful Julia because her father is in financial difficulties. For the first time in her life, after undependable immature boys, she sees in him "a real man," but is not clear as to whether he really loves her, or wants her only as one more piece of property. She cannot perceive the answer in his tenderness, for there is "no intimacy between them" (which naturally does not mean that they do not sleep together).

She comes upon the idea of making him jealous in order to test his love, although he has said that he would never be jealous. His favorite word is "I," and his self-assuredness is so great that he maintains it would be completely impossible for *his* wife to deceive him.

Julia gets involved with a pampered nobleman who convinces her that her husband does not love her because, for example, he has allowed her the freedom to meet him, the count, alone. When there is gossip about "his wearing horns," Alejandro hits the person who has insulted him over the head with a bottle, in a highly unaristocratic manner, but very calmly. He rejects a duel, for he is not noble and thinks nothing of the whole code of honor.

This coarse proof of his love is still not enough for his wife, especially because he himself has a relationship with a maid, does not conceal it, and even says that he needs the contrast in order better to appreciate his wife's beauty. "This is my little monkey, and you have your count as a little cat; are we supposed to be jealous because of this?"

Julia's reality is a love about which one speaks, and which one demonstrates. Alejandro calls that a result of her reading novels. *His* reality is his image of himself: a whole man, self-confident to the last, who is not jealous and does not talk of love.

Finally she hurls the confession at him (which is only *almost* true): "He is my lover! The little cat is my lover!" Alejandro simply denies this. She must be insane.

After she screams that he is a coward—which perhaps goes somewhat too far for him—he resorts to the following: he confronts her with the count and two doctors. Julia stands by her confession. The count, however—a member of a caste despised by Unamuno—denies the relationship. Thereupon, Alejandro wants to have Julia declared insane. The doctors are afraid that the husband will kill his wife in the traditional fashion if they say what they see and know: namely, that Julia's view of reality is correct and that one should perhaps have Alejandro declared insane. They therefore commit Julia to an insane asylum, "perhaps in order to have a chance of saving her." There she raves against her lover's cowardice and her husband's harshness—and reaches the conclusion: "I love him—blindly, mindlessly!"

In order not to become really insane, she declares herself to be cured: she has only hallucinated the relationship to the count. When they meet again, Alejandro consistently refuses to forgive her—why should he? It was only a matter of hallucinations . . . In this situation, Julia asks her husband whether he loves her. Very briefly, an abyss is opened in this "horrible, lonely, reserved soul, which this favorite of fortune had until now jealously [!] locked." Two tears fall, and he passionately confesses to her that he "belongs to her more than she belongs to him." And now it is bluntly stated, "She believed that she had to become insane." After this experience, nothing remains but death: "Now I would like to die, Alejandro." But the passionate soul again closes itself, and the icy armor of the "whole man" is again donned.

This experience immeasurably intensifies Julia's loyalty. The count is invited to their home, and the couple most ceremoniously displays its joint reality: that Julia only imagined the affair. Even in a tête-à-tête she maintains this assertion. She is amazingly beautiful on this day but speaks "in a supernatural voice, and the words coldly and slowly flowed from her lips; but one had the impression that a consuming fire was concealed behind them." The count, who is confused, humiliated, and ridiculous, leaves the house never to see it again, for fear of becoming insane himself. Julia has entered the haughty, icy world of her spouse—she laughs at the count and does not believe him capable of becoming insane.

One reads that, after this, she becomes the "victim of a severe psychic illness," during which she often hallucinates and passionately desires Alejandro. At the cost of her life, she thereby asserts her reality: she loves the cold "whole man" only to the extent that he repeatedly assures her of his love, and passionately proves it; to the extent that he "descends into a state of continuous cold madness" in the face of her approaching death; to the extent that he even wanted to bribe the Crucified One with what he has gained with the most difficulty and has defended most keenly: "Take my own self!" The last thing Julia asks before her death is "Who are you really?" And he answers, "I? Nothing more than your husband. The person you have made me." Julia's reality has conquered. She can die blissfully.

And like those who are dying, as one often hears, in this situation his whole life passes before Alejandro's, not Julia's, eyes, "like a cloud of ice," this life "that he kept hidden from everybody, but especially from himself"—a horrible childhood, insane rage at the paternal world's guardian angels who failed him, the helpless shaking of the child's fist at an image of Christ. He writes his will and kills himself, falling across her body.

It would be a fine task for systems therapists to think of how they would have advised Julia, had she come to counseling. Since unconditional jealousy here expresses itself in the denial of jealousy, one can in any case say, "Plus ça change, plus c'est la même chose" (the more things change, the more they remain the same), the basic symptom for which systems therapists believe they know the remedy. Psychoanalysis would uncover the link to childhood (there is no talk of Alejandro's mother, good enough or not, but there are a few revealing passages about Julia's parents), and Jürg Willi's disciples would rub their hands in glee at an unadulterated narcissistic collusion. None of them could help. There are simply souls that are stronger than any therapy, and some destinies are fulfilled precisely in their incurability.

But let us remain with those who, unlike the couple in the melodramatic Spanish drama of ideas, do not want to equate love and death, but rather feel themselves bound to the earth with ties of duty and the more delicate strings of love. They must reclassify their reality.

A female client states, "I had arrived at the outer limit of my possibilities, so that I had the choice of either drowning—life is no longer worth living—or pulling myself out by my own hair."

Another female client states, "In front of the door of the marriage counseling clinic, he claimed once again that the relationship was over. And then, after we were inside, he said, it still continues to exist, after all, and there will again be a time when sexual contact will take place. And then he beat me over the head with twenty years of marriage, one year after the other, all of which did not suit him—and I was completely out of the picture, I did not know *anything:* that he didn't want children; that he at least didn't want the second child; that I put something over on him then; and whatever else he was dissatisfied with. In twenty years, I had understood nothing, nothing, nothing. I was blank, *so* blank—and that all hit home, for there was naturally something to it!"

A man states, "I always resisted and resisted and resisted, in order to get her back on track, where I want to have her, and that was absolutely wrong."

Another man: "The problem consists of being obstinate about something and contructing something that is false. After the break, at first I was often alone; I furnished my apartment and looked for new goals. I concentrated very intensely on myself. During my entire marriage, it had just seemed intolerable to do anything at all alone. There were mistakes somewhere, and I would not like to repeat them."

What one woman said sounds like a summary of this type of experience: "I really had strange ideas—probably those that are current: When two people love and marry, this feeling will last for eternity. I did not at all take into account that a person develops and is also allowed to develop. That came out very strongly in counseling: one also has the right to develop in a marriage, and one must have the courage to look this development calmly in the eye.''

The only client for whom Christianity played a predominant role in her life and her marriage, which also came out very clearly in counseling, said, ''One then starts to think about what previously seemed so established. I had very, very great difficulties with my faith: Does the Lord really exist? Why does it have to happen now, after one has done everything? How can he only look on, when so many marriages break down, even good marriages like my own? Previously, I did not want to consider these things, but when my husband moved out on me, I saw more, so much that I often thought, Are there only bad things left anymore?—And the bad sometimes completely overwhelmed me.''

SEEING ONESELF ANEW

> The highest goal a human being can achieve is consciousness
> of his own sentiments and thoughts, self-awareness, which is
> the prelude to an intimate understanding of the temperament
> of others as well.
>
> Goethe, *Shakespeare and No End*

Looking in from the outside, one may dispassionately say that in this situation the only road to take is obviously the one that goes forward: to accept the new reality, and come to terms with it. However, in the case of the female client who was quoted as being caught by the throat in the outer layer of the globe this would mean, for instance, that next time she would be required to dream that she is at least standing with both feet on the desolate and empty earth, and perhaps even making a start on subjugating it. Directives such as this are found in some essays that appear in women's magazines, as well as in books containing psychological prescriptions, even if expressed in somewhat different terms. However, it is usually not that simple. Somewhat later, the same client had the following dream:

She sees the complete and already floating hulk of a large ship lying on the calm open sea in the morning sun. She knows it must be improved and equipped, and she wants to help with this. But she also knows that one cannot improve and equip a moving ship, not to mention one that is still without a rudder, like the ship in her dream. To do this, it must be lying at anchor. But the anchor—a very gruesome image—goes through her body, penetrating the genital region, and continuing along her spine. The anchor chain has been fastened to her throat. Remarkably, this does not cause her pain, and her head is above water. The ship looks pretty and gay, like a child's drawing. "I do not feel bad, but I would very much like to get into the ship. But how am I supposed to do that?"

This dream proved to be extremely multilayered—I only want to indicate a few things: the sexual connotation is obvious. The mainstay of this woman's life was her love for her husband. Aside from that, she loved and, one could almost say, admired her children, because she herself had not had a happy childhood. Letting go of her children signified for her a separation from the "only good childhood she had ever experienced." Her sense of responsibility was great and justifiable: children need a sure anchorage where they can complete the construction of the ship in which they will set sail on the journey of life. But now there was jealousy—her husband really liked a mutual female friend, and although the client was convinced of his basic loyalty, this was very painful for her; she felt that she had been abandoned. But she also realized that her husband was not cultivating this friendship "in opposition to her"; she even felt that she profited by it when he was pleased and carefree because he enjoyed being with the friend. She said, "It is actually anything but adultery"—she merely had to concede to her husband something that she herself could not have: more freedom.

Since she had a special relationship to ships and the sea, she frequently dreamt of these things, as she did once in connection with her jealousy.

Women are practicing sailing with children in small sailboats on a body of water that has no access to the sea and lies in shadow. Out on the sea, under bright sun and gleaming colors, in waves with snow-white foam, the men are sailing in larger boats. This is exciting and dangerous, but they are sure of themselves, in spite of high winds. With them are happy young girls with wet hair and wearing yellow slickers, and the girls are cheerful.

The entire crux of the jealousy conflict is manifested in these images, primarily in the first one: How is one supposed to be anchor and shipbuilder at the same time? How is one supposed to hold tight and concurrently let go in order to be able to build? The dream described last, which was the earlier dream, offers solutions closer to consciousness that occurred to the woman only much later: a multiple exchange of roles could have taken place—the girls could temporarily take care of the children; the women could let the wind and water blow around them on the open sea; the men could have fun themselves by teaching the children how to sail and not relinquishing this task to their wives. And finally, the women could also trust themselves to take the helm, not only in the small practice boats but also in seaworthy ships, and demand that either the young girls or even their own husbands be assistants.

At first, of course, this new role distribution was only a fantasy—but experience shows that fantasy prepares the way for reality.

For a long time, I had counseled the woman who had these dreams. She was successful. But the metaphor of the anchor that wants to be a ship (to

reduce it to a short formula) is apt for almost all individuals, men as well as
women, who begin to attempt a new way of dealing with their jealousy. To
be sure, the women in the cases that I studied were much more prepared than
the men to begin the change by changing themselves—except for the first
shock situation, in which probably every person thinks, "If the other person
would act differently, everything would be fine again."

The question asked the counselor almost always takes the following form:
"What should I do?" or "What should we do?" or "How can I influence
my partner differently?" Several clients expressed their disappointment that
the counselor did not provide this assistance. The name "counseling center"
is misleading here; sometimes I try to redefine it as an institution in which
one does not receive advice but consults with others, in pairs, groups of three,
or with one's entire family. However, this is also not very helpful. "Therapy"
would be a better, even if still diffuse, designation for our work. However,
there is agreement that we may not call ourselves therapists. To be sure, it
is not entirely clear who is allowed to designate him- or herself as such. I
hope that the reader will tolerate this lack of clarity, which is a result of
professional politics.

In any case, the question "What should I do?" has changed for all clients
who have made progress into another question: "Who am I?"

"I puzzled over everything, except for myself. I am dissatisfied with me.
Fifty percent of my husband's infidelity is my fault. My self-confidence
had already been destroyed before. But I did not confront my situation. I
no longer knew what really interested me, and I hid behind the children.
He worked so hard, and I convinced myself that I had to do my bit by
burying myself completely in household chores. At first I was enraged—I
grasped the concept of 50 percent of the guilt fairly quickly. I had the
feeling that the counselor was talking nonsense. I had to get back to my
small children—and then to work through something like that with me!
Perhaps she didn't express it that way at all, but that's the way I perceived
it. I was just so wiped out! But gradually she helped me, to the extent that
I realized that I was sitting in a prison of my own making. She helped me
punch holes in the wall, through which I climbed by myself."

A young man said, "I gave up my music. I had a band before—that was
the greatest! I believed I was doing it for my wife, but that wasn't at all
true. I only wanted to keep an eye on whether she was also doing what I
wanted her to do. If I had given up music because I had had enough of it,
that would have been something else. But that wasn't the way it was. I
shouldn't have had to sit at her side constantly and stare at her adoringly,
but should have said to her, 'Please *believe* me, now do something that *you*
want to do for a while.' We had married very young—and then right away

the two children came along. I should have said, 'Of course I'm here, but don't worry about it.' Our relationship would have had to be far enough along so that one could say to the other, 'I'm going someplace now, and I'm *not* going to call you.' And the other would have had to say, 'You can come home whenever you want'. But if she came home one and a half hours late, I acted as if it were the end of the world. It was only my damned fear of being alone. And the desire to keep things under my control. At the same time, I wasn't an innocent lamb even before. And in the final analysis, now, after the divorce, I'm not living like a monk. Perhaps the fear was due to that—that I knew the way it can be; everything one can do with women . . . At the same time, she doesn't have a boyfriend, even now—I know that for sure. She only wanted to get away from my treating her like a child. After the divorce I was so desperate—I used other women so that I wouldn't become an alcoholic.''

Here someone is sensing something that I plan to treat in a coming chapter and that demonstrates the systemic aspect of jealousy: the intermeshing of letting go and returning. Additionally, however, the jealous individual must have the courage to recognize unpleasant, possessive, and clinging aspects in him- or herself.

A woman: "At first I didn't want to admit it to myself, because I wasn't aware of anything of the sort in me. If someone had told me about that, I would have said, 'That's not me!' '' Then later: "I was completely aware that I was anything but lovable. But I was so terribly afraid that I just couldn't do anything but continuously spy on my husband." And still another step further: "Certainly, I was often unhappy and never admitted it to myself—the eternal difficulties with my husband's mother, his indecisiveness—he never said an unpleasant word to his mother; of course, he didn't say pleasant words either, but was always totally passive; and he never defended me. And at night I lay awake, and he always fell asleep very quickly, escaped from me into sleep. I just couldn't cope with that. And then he was so alive, always taking the initiative with other women, in a way I had never seen even before our marriage when he was in love with me . . ."

The decisive sentence, which helped this woman to go forward, is "Certainly, I was often unhappy and never admitted it to myself." Jealousy, which is more understandable, more "permissible," than groundless "being unhappy" in a marriage with several children and in secure financial circumstances, particularly in the farming environment in which the client lived, functioned like a signal. She felt herself to be so endangered that she had to seek help—and found something that she had not sought at all: a clearer picture of her history, her total situation and consequently, above all, a new way of dealing with herself—and only secondarily, a new way of dealing with her husband.

"It was a great strain, but afterwards it's a great feeling! Sometimes I drove home screaming and had the feeling that everything was only getting worse because of my thinking about myself. We talked again and again about how important what others think of me is to me—and I thought I was so independent! Even today, I just don't understand how I came to think that. Probably my efficiency in coping with externals was the reason I thought that. Of course I always functioned; I always pulled it off—managing the house, the children, and a profession on top of it. And I'm still on top of things today. . . . It's possible that I was simply too efficient for my husband, and he therefore looked for other women. But with all my efficiency, at that time, even during the worst quarrel, I thought that he was right and that I was just the poor wretch. You see—a gigantic mix-up. And in this situation it's good for one to come to terms with oneself, really to confront oneself, and not only say all the time, I'm suffering. Then things gradually improved. Today I know that I also need quite a bit of room myself—space, as it's called—precisely what I had rejected and therefore could in no way grant my husband."

Another client who, like the woman above in catamnesis, said that she now felt better than ever before, today understands that jealousy helped her "find herself for the first time—for I had never had time for that before." The conclusion she drew from this could be engraved in stone—a citation, not from catamnesis, but from process notes: "The old way just doesn't work anymore!"

Every counselor will probably work toward leading the client to this re- alization through listening, questioning, and explaining. Whether the client accepts this offer is his or her affair. To outsiders, it would perhaps sound terrible if they could listen to a team reporting on a case that was concluded because the counselor and the client agreed that there was no progress, and then hear the counselor say, "Actually I was very happy about this—the husband simply did not want to work." Instead of this, was the counselor not required to make change possible for the husband? Actually, yes. But there are limits to counseling possibilities and patience, especially in jealousy cases in sadomasochistic marriages, in which the partners unconsciously de- rive much more satisfaction from their eternally tense situation than from its improvement.

Six years ago I concluded counseling with a couple in which the wife was clearly inferior to her husband in terms of her education. She had been employed in a sewing factory and was now a housewife. He was a departmental head in a large insurance firm, after having completed a course of technical training during his marriage (a course that he financed himself and not through is wife's support, which is common). He had a girlfriend but gave her up during counseling and seemed to me to have made a serious commitment to marriage. These are the things he wanted from his wife: more decisiveness (for example, she was to learn how to drive); somewhat less negligence about her appearance; somewhat more care in speaking proper German. The couple had moved to Munich, and the wife spoke such a strong Alemannic dialect that I could sometimes not understand her. She resisted independence because she feared that then he would just leave—a pattern that is frequently seen in jealousy counseling and that can only be broken when the delight in one's own independent action becomes greater than the need to maintain the cozy familiarity of the pattern by accommodation and warmth. The wife, who, moreover, had more premarital sexual experiences than her husband and who was his "first woman," drew the following conclusion from her situation and from counseling: "You don't allow me to be courageous!" She repeatedly frustrated his attempts to get close to her by retreating: "You just don't like me any more—what's the point!" When her husband met his girlfriend again, the wife fell apart. When he gave the friend up, she said, "Now he's with me again because the other woman doesn't want him." The husband was finally at his wit's end because of my interventions: "My wife is always the only concern, not that she's concerned about me."

The time that the wife wished to recapture was when the relationship to her husband had been very close because of his sexual fascination; the wife had the upper hand entirely. Now she stated, "You would let me go at any time." And he said, "I can't keep you from going." The wife had frequently said, in a totally convincing manner, "I'll do what I want." None of the three of us basically believed that she would go. For example, she got a rise out of me, as well as out of her husband, when she maintained, "Men want to be lied to, then everything's fine." At the end of counseling (thirteen sessions to which, significantly, the couple always came together), I felt I had made a great effort but achieved nothing. I expressed my conviction that nothing in the marriage would change if the wife did not reflect upon herself, instead of always only gazing upon the wounds that her husband inflicted upon her. She said, "I'm not going to allow myself to be told in counseling that my marriage is broken." When I called her for follow-up, she first urgently requested to be allowed to come. She did not want to bring her husband along at all. As later became evident, she had made him somewhat jealous with her appointment "for marriage counseling." He did not find it appropriate for her to tell "about things that came from the depths of her soul." Then, in the one hour that was open, she could not stop talking. She had become much prettier, and her speech was less dialectical. She also knew how to drive a car. Basically, however, nothing had changed. Meanwhile, her husband had moved out once; at that time, she felt fine; she went to discos with a girlfriend and "had peace at home." He returned to her and asked, "Do you still like me?" Her comment on this was "I'll never say I don't like you, for then I would somehow only be hurting myself."

Once during the six years there was a debate as to whether she should take her own apartment with the children. When she saw that would have pleased her husband tremendously, since he once again had a new girlfriend, she decided once and for all, "Ok! I'm not going to give you that pleasure, even if it kills me! I'll never move out."

Sometimes things are very good between the two of them. Apparently, the husband acts in a fairly ambivalent manner—he demonstrates jealousy, promises things that he does not deliver, and so forth. The wife said—and it seemed to me that she summarized the entire relationship with this statement—"It's funny—whenever my husband is nice to me because he doesn't have anybody else just then, I start to get fresh again. Because when someone crawls for me—I don't like it. Then I'll only kick him. Funny, isn't it? Then he says, When I'm nice to you, you exploit it—and because of that he's not nice anymore."

Her conclusion was "My husband hasn't changed, but I have become somewhat different because more things are irrelevant to me." About counseling, which she felt had failed, she said, "You wanted to change me, because my husband wanted that to happen. And one should take a person the way he is, and not the way he's supposed to be. That's a saying, but I believe it's true." My voice on tape sounds a bit desperate as I answer, "But I didn't want to change you—I found and still find only that you make too little of what you actually *are!*"

In writing this down, I again begin to reflect on whether I was not actually too much in league with her husband, whom, moreover, *she* constantly wanted to change and in no way to accept as he was. But of course it was he himself who said that I would be too concerned with his wife's development . . . And sighing, I will now remove myself from this maze of double binds. Where there is nothing (no motivation), the counselor has lost any claim.

△ 23 △

THE REALITY OF THE PARTNER

I had become entangled in the client's saying, that "one should take a person the way he is, and not the way he's supposed to be." But this saying is questionable if one makes it an absolute, for a new postulate of nonchangeability can easily arise from its apparent resignation. It does not seem bad to me as a working basis for the start of counseling, for the preliminary investigation so to speak, in terms of what applies both to the jealous individual and that individual's partner.

The clouds out of which jealous individuals fall when they make their discovery not only have veiled deficits in the relationship and overshadowed or glorified the jealous individual's own gestalt, but also have often wreathed the partner's image in mist.

At the age of thirty, a man who worked in the fashion industry had married a woman who was ten years younger than he. The division of roles was clear: she was the attractive young thing who admired him and whom he introduced to the great world; he was the successful, good-looking man whom she could confidently bring home to her parents. The young woman's bond to her father could not be ignored, but became clear to all three of us only in counseling, for, as is so often true in such cases, the relationship between father and daughter was rather tense.

Fairly soon after the wedding, it became clear that she was not only pretty but also energetic and intelligent. She began to grow as a person and studied architecture. A year after the wedding she already had a boyfriend and, after that, almost always had somebody else besides her husband. Furthermore, he adored her, becoming ever more fond of her, and knew nothing about his rivals.

At that time there was a recession in the fashion industry. The husband's business went bankrupt, and he began to drink. Because of this, the power relationships in the marriage shifted completely. For a time, the husband's life was even in danger. He regressed, so to speak, to the state of a nursing child and became fat and unattractive. His wife stood by him, but, as she later thought, she would not have managed this without the boyfriend she had at the time.

The husband underwent a rather brief alcohol detoxification treatment and remained on the wagon after that. At the time of catamnesis, he had been dry for eight years. Approximately two years after his treatment, the couple came to counseling because of marital difficulties. The man had vague jealous suspicions, and his wife denied everything. We agreed to attempt to clarify the relationship, which had been jolted by renewed significant change: on the husband's part, no alcohol but continuing professional difficulties; for the attractive architect, professional successes and constant contact with colleagues, clients, and workers whom her husband viewed with jealousy. However, as he said, his wife "purred around him like a cat." She loved to knit by the fire and, more than anything else, demonstrate for her parents the undisturbed harmony of a marriage rescued from alcohol. The husband was nervous, hesitant, and sexually uncertain: "You were more exciting before" or "You seem like a fish to me; I just had you in my hand, and then you're sliding away already . . ." In spite of that, he unconditionally wanted to believe in her loyalty. Meanwhile, he had reached the age of forty, and she was thirty. The desire for children, which both believed, in the final analysis, had bound them to each other, became a topic of discussion.

In this situation, approximately nine months after the start of counseling, the wife confessed: she had a steady friend, a colleague, whom she both admired and considered to be an impossible husband. He was married anyway. This was "zero hour" for my client. He had to begin to perceive his wife differently and correct the image he had of her. Strange to say, he affected me as being more stable and masculine than formerly.

I do not want to pursue the further convolutions of this counseling. The wife continued to appeal strongly for her husband's acceptance, as well as her father's. The husband, on the other hand, refused this: "You want to maintain that relationship and at the same time have me stroke you!" She was so caught up in oedipal bonds that, shortly before the divorce, she said, "My husband would be the ideal husband for my mother." In her unconscious fear of a bond to someone who would finally dethrone her father, she found herself yet another admirer, whereupon all three men became jealous of each other, and the woman behaved like a cute, scatterbrained child. "How *could* I just have left the letter from Würzburg in the file folder in which the plans for our joint building project went to my architect boyfriend!" The boyfriend from Würzburg had a pronounced similarity to her husband . . .

This mess disintegrated, to the husband's great distress. He had the satisfaction only of knowing that his wife's parents had learned the extent to which their daughter had merely acted the part of the model wife for them. He said, "I threw her out!" She said, "I finally went!" I asked where, whereupon she answered in tears, "To myself."

The husband rejected my offer of further counseling. he could not endure exploring his wife's new image with me. In a letter to me, he wrote as if he had awakened to a new reality: "How can a person change so quickly? Throw everything overboard that bound us together, with a masklike, cool smile. I feel that this is a defamation of her own ego. Is she the slave of her career? For me, an inexplicable being with a 'second nature'; I no longer understand the world."

At the time of follow-up, two years after that, the marriage had been terminated. The man was living with a woman who was "completely different." His wife, of whom he said that he could still easily put up with her, had been a "good buddy" to him, but basically cold. He thought that the worst thing about her was that she was so inconsistent, and he had hoped for lifelong continuity from her. "The other man was in no way terribly interesting to her. She often spoke very negatively about him, about his looks, his sloppiness—and she took up with him anyway. On the other hand, she still wanted the family, domesticity; she wanted to present our relationship to the outside as an intact world." This man was happy at having distanced himself from "this double life, this ambiguity," when he had finally understood her.

The woman came alone to catamnesis and indicated that the main result of counseling was that she now understood better why she acted as she did, and that the conflicts had at first intensified during our work, but had consequently become clearer. Primarily, however, she had become capable of leaving (!) her parents, and would now move to another city. Since the separation from her husband, she had indulged in more foolishness than ever before—she continued to have two boyfriends at the same time—but she had the feeling of finally having arrived. She had decided in favor of the man from Würzburg. Her career no longer seemed so important to her. It had boosted her ego, but primarily had allowed her to achieve her innermost goal: to be able to speak on the same level to her father (who had an entirely different profession, but a very high standing in that profession).

Here the more realistic perception of both partners shows that life patterns and histories led in different directions. Each had—terrible to say, but something often observed—a function in the other's life that was finished, superseded, no longer useful. At a greater remove, gratitude sometimes arises for such distances traveled together because, after all, each person has progressed and perhaps, in spite of all suffering, could progress only with *this* partner. It seems to me that a special kind of indissolubility often later becomes manifest in the old bonds. Naturally, this is different from the indissolubility that derives from the law or the church.

Continuing to live with the newly perceived partner is even more difficult than separation.

"I myself would have behaved differently. In the situation in which my husband found himself, I would have asked myself if it was worth hurting everyone so much [the wife, the girlfriend, the children]. What hurt me tremendously was that he was so presumptuous, as if he would be showing me, Of course, I can afford to do this, my family will just wait for me. I always saw my husband as a friendly person—and now he was so ruthless! However, I also understood that I cannot expect everyone to be like me. It wasn't easy, this putting myself into my husband's shoes. The counselor gave me a pillow and said, 'Pretend that that's your husband.' And I squeezed and squeezed the pillow—out of pure love, I thought. But the counselor said, 'Now look at the pillow'—it was completely crushed—'You're just smothering your husband! That showed me that one dare not prettify one's own thoughts.

"During the time he lived with the young girl [for two years], I became so independent that I was really hesitant about whether I should get back together with him. But now I know that it's over. And I like him the way he is. Before, we were so—so heedless of each other. Now I know that he is not only friendly but can also be awful. But nonetheless it's *he*—the man whom I fell in love with then, and with whom I want to grow old."

In this context, it seems to me important to work through the problem of why one still likes the other if the other is as bad as described in the accusations that follow the first—and the lasting—horror. Many jealous clients surprisingly say that, on their own, they would never have come upon this question. In counseling, the issue is to take love at its word and not only to affirm it solemnly. This takes tremendous effort. The unfaithful partners often do not know terribly much about this labor of love. If the jealous individuals did not themselves get something out of this; if they did not thereby again draw closer to the partner; if they could not live better with the partner—then one could sometimes despair about the injustice of the distribution of burdens in marriages. It is often the case that the person who loves more bears more of the burden.

"During the time of my second pregnancy, things were so good between us—I loved my husband as I had never loved him in my entire life. And precisely during this time he deceived me. In counseling I tried to project myself into his feelings, into his need for this damned 'space,' and I also sensed in what a terrible fix he was. He wanted to lead a freer life with her, travel and such things, and he had not actually wanted this late child. But the child just came along. Then, on top of everything, he had made a difficult catch—a girlfriend who managed to make him feel responsible for her. But that's all over, for years already. I would have the nicest life if I could forget it. But I can't. Do I still love him? I don't know. I was so proud of him—terribly proud! I always felt a little taller at his side—a handsome man, a respectable man, a dependable man. *My* man! Now that's all over.

"But I believe that it isn't the worst thing that this halo is finally gone. Because of that, I'm now really a little taller. I believe that he doesn't at all view me as being as small as I sometimes see myself, but as quite powerful . . ."

Another woman said, "My husband was not quite as strong as I would have wished, and I propped him up, from all sides, and constantly gave him support, warmth, and courage. Purely out of a desire to help, I so overburdened him that it was as if he were covered by a cocoon, from which he had to free himself. But I naturally ask myself whether this could happen only by means of other women. But we couldn't talk until it was over. I praised him to the skies—and then he was so weak, so pitiful, so ready. And also so—so slippery, when otherwise he had always been so clear, clean, and respectable.

"Today I view him in a completely different light: we live very well together. Great sympathy exists between us, but I also see his faults, which previously I never wanted to acknowledge. Naturally, he sees mine too, and we can speak about this very calmly. But at that time—I simply couldn't anymore. For me, he had become somebody different from the man I had loved. His indifference: 'Today I still don't know what I'll do in the future! Right now I don't have a girlfriend, but maybe I'll do that again. You're old-fashioned. One has to be modern . . .' And this glass wall between us, that he no longer demonstrated, I like you . . ."

This client had a dream that, as she stated in follow-up, was felt by her to be a key experience, and which plainly seems to me to have been dreamt vicariously on behalf of many jealous individuals.

She sees her husband on a kind of altar like an Old Testament king, in a rigid robe, "strict and superior." He wants to kill one of the children. She cries and fights, but he is unapproachable, inhuman. Finally, she wraps a piece of meat in paper and throws it at his feet as a substitution for the child. She becomes ill and runs away.

While telling me the dream, she wept profusely. Endless grief and despair finally seemed to be dissolving.

During the next session, she told about a solution to the tension between her and her husband. She said, "The rigid robe is gone," and then added an amusing detail: while crying in the last session, she had forgotten that, during the same night, after the horrible dream she had about the sacrifice, she had yet another, "completely cheerful" dream: "She is riding with her husband on the moped down an incline into a spring landscape. Both are very pleased." When I asked who was sitting in front, she laughed and said, "I was!" Until then, she was very afraid of driving a car, but had driven alone to north Germany during one of her husband's business trips, and afterwards had proudly reported to me, "I can fly!"

She had preferred to keep silent about the first dream, but had told her husband about the second. His comment was "You see, things are going downhill with us!" Apparently a phase displacement in the resolution of the conflict was present here. At the time of catamnesis, three years later, the couple had built a new house and had made some changes in how they lived. The wife said, "Things are better with us now than before the crisis."

△ 24 △

WITHDRAWAL FROM SYMBIOSIS

If I consider the acute jealousy crisis, it seems to me that the rival is not at all present in the eye of the hurricane, in the storm center. He or she becomes lost in the maelstrom of despair, to be sure for only a short time but often repeatedly. What is afterwards so frequently described by jealous individuals as a cry of help is a regression to the desire to be the other's whole world, because the other appears to oneself as the most important and only thing in the whole world. Very few clients have felt that the worst thing was that "someone else was present"; the majority, men as well as women, mourned the loss of trust, the destruction of unity. They said that "a world" had collapsed around them, or were horrified that they were not the "only ones, the most important, but simply unimportant."

This complaint is usually brought forward in an asexual manner, but it has much to do with sexuality. As jealousy often appears as the black sister of love, so the radical jeopardizing of one's own world brought about by the partner's rejection is the negative image of the joyful fulfillment of the world and merging in successful sexuality, where duality blends into unity and where my happiness is also yours. The jealous individual's demand is actually "You were happy when I was happy—now you should also be unhappy because I am unhappy. For we are one and joined with every fiber of our being." Since the person who is bound in this way is precisely the one causing the unhappiness and rupturing the unity, intolerable tension arises.

That again has to do with the pre-oedipal mother. I believe that there are many people who accurately sense that detaching oneself from one's parents, especially from the mother's power, becomes possible only by risking total engagement with another person. This total engagement is expressed in successful sexuality. One can perhaps understand the desire of today's young people for early sexual contacts as the attempt to remove themselves from the loving, understanding, in the Freudian sense eroticized environment of the nuclear family with its conscientious parents who want to get everything right—everything from tactile contact to the Oedipus complex and permission to masturbate. Earlier, with stricter, more distanced parents who understood a "good upbringing" much differently than we, this was perhaps not as necessary.

Young people's attempts often lead to disappointments since, of course, they are only a response to behavioral directives, "the pressure to perform." However, when the real "first time" takes place, it is terribly important. It also contains the possibility, and thus the danger, of a total bonding, out of which one must gradually evolve into yet another kind of adulthood if one does not want to mutilate oneself.

The "great love," in which, for a time, one person is everything for the other and, moreover, would like to "embrace the entire world" too, is probably a good hypothesis for managing jealousy as well. And naturally the prognosis is better if marital sexuality is felt to be satisfactory, which is often the case even in the worst crisis, than if the clients must say, "Things never really clicked with us."

Thus the dissolution of symbiosis as bonebreaking psychic work.

"I opened myself to him as I had never opened myself to anyone else— and now that he has the other woman, it's as if someone else were entering me along with him. Isn't it understandable that I'm horribly frightened?"

However, this woman also saw through her need for dual unity.

"I am much more sociable than my husband, and I flirt much more than he. But I can truthfully say that I'm also careful. If I were to get seriously involved with someone else, I would be afraid of my own passion. If someone were to declare a goal to me: 'With you!'—that would be dangerous, even almost irresistible."

Herein lies the danger of the entire game being repeated, and this was clear to the client. And jealousy, *her* jealousy in this case, embodied the possibility of distancing herself while maintaining love, continuity, and the fidelity of an already long-standing marriage. In the end, it would have been very inappropriate for the client to throw away this marriage.

Another woman who had been unfaithful to her husband with a mutual friend, one day flung a confession at him without any external necessity to do so. It was just as if, in doing so, she wanted to restore with common knowledge at least part of their unity.

She stated, "I clung to my husband for good or ill—*so much,* very fervently, and very closely. If he now thinks that he no longer means anything to me, that's simply not true. The fact is that I'm thinking of

myself more. I see our relationship from a different perspective—
somewhat looser, no longer as dependent on each other. And since then I
don't have this terrible fear anymore." For her part she had also been
entirely jealous and indeed, at least during the marriage, without "cause."

In this case, moreover, the meaning that a confession can have, which in the
customary sense is "meaningless," became especially clear to me: Why get
the other person worked up with a story that is long out of date, that was not
even especially nice, and about which he has not the slightest idea and would
never learn anything? On the one hand, I believe that in such a case those
who are "straying" want to get back to the legal marital bed (in which, to
be sure, they are already sleeping again, cozily snuggled up, in joy and sorrow,
thus possibly also in a sadomasochistic structure). On the other hand, they
are thereby drawn back into the symbiosis—however, with the unconscious
intention of rupturing it from the inside.

This statement precisely demonstrates the pressure of symbiosis: "I was
simply no longer I. This of course helped us to endure for decades a very
difficult working life. We were simply a unity, like Siamese twins. And
that is deceptive, that is deceptive! For I put aside everything that was
important to me for this marriage. I disposed of myself. At the same time
I used up all my batteries. I believe that I really invested more than he did,
but he was also constantly dissatisfied. Only, when he said, I don't feel
well—then I was there carping and said, Can I help? Maybe the other
women were good for this. For when he also showed me how miserable he
was, by that time I had finally had enough of helping. Naturally he also
had felt like the Siamese twins. It went so far that once, at a good moment
during the crisis, he said, 'You know what I wish most for you? *Just once*
to have a good relationship with another man!' That was finally the end for
me."

A client summarized in the following way the outcome of withdrawal from
the feeling of swimming like twins in the same amniotic sac: "To reveal
everything like before—that doesn't work anymore!"

WORKING THROUGH THE PAST IN MARRIAGE COUNSELING

If the jealousy conflict can to such an extent be traced back to symbiotic desires, that is, the experience of the early mother, is it not essential to confront the past directly and to treat the infantile conflicts as in psychoanalysis, by remembering, repeating, working through? *In fact* nothing of the sort is supposed to take place in marriage counseling, at least not in the precise psychoanalytic sense. Since this subject matter cannot be avoided, however, but is only too clearly introduced by clients, it occasionally contributes to the conscientious counselor's role conflict. *In fact* the issue should be just the actual conflicts and not communication, ego reinforcement, or possibly sustaining, but not revealing, work based on depth psychology.

I have discovered the following answer for myself: How am I to help my clients break through their role restrictions, to liberate themselves from traditions and decide for themselves what is appropriate for them, if I allow myself to be restricted by hierarchical precepts that, sometimes, I can in no way follow if I am to take seriously my responsibility for the client's well-being?

Therefore, in counseling conducted by me there is indeed a working through of the past; aside from the fact that every person becomes three-dimensional to me once I know something about the relationship to his or her parents, clients themselves often push in this direction. To a great extent, exactly the same thing occurred in the catamneses that I took over from colleagues. Thus, in twenty-one cases, working through the relationship to the parents played a role; in ten cases it played an important role. In catamnesis six of the thirty clients designated a clarification, resolution, or change in the relationship to their parents as the pivotal counseling experience. (In the final analysis, catamnesis was conducted from the perspective of jealousy and the triadic relationship, and not as a general check on the success rate.) In one instance, the following answer was given to the question about aggression: It was primarily directed against my wife's father. In another instance, this answer was given: It was directed against my partner's child. This certainly allows one to infer the existence of unfulfilled desires oriented toward the parents.

Here I would like only to point to these facts, and not to deal with them more extensively, since I want to maintain the focus on my chosen topic of jealousy. Counseling does not allow for very deep regression, and even transference can not usually be worked through, but only experienced. I would like to risk a—certainly controvertible—thesis to explain how it is possible that something may be present here that, in the orthodox view, can in no way be present: the more the counselor, because of his or her experience and an orientation toward depth and systemic psychology, is involved in viewing clients' relationship to their parents, as well as clients' childhood, as something of importance in jealousy conflicts, the more the counselor's unconscious will lead him or her to ask the right questions; to transmit the correct nonverbal messages; and, in the omnipresent transference situation, to behave as if the counselor can open up to the clients access to their archaic layers. The counselor *can,* but not necessarily will, do this. In successful cases, I have seen that only a few sessions suffice to lead to important insights and the liberating steps "outside" made possible by these insights. I also dare to hope that this is not only a transitory outcome, but an outcome that will remain stable. Or to formulate it even more carefully: clients perceived it in this way, and I had the impression that they were not acting out something for me.

Here I would like to present only one example—others are hinted at in several case histories.

A client was not finished with her husband's past love affair. Her mother had died six weeks before the start of counseling. Sometimes her agitation at the other woman was a thing of the past. Then it was as if something "switched her on" again, and she constantly had to dwell on the affair. In follow-up, three years after the conclusion of counseling, she told me that for about half a year she had been having a recurrent dream.

"I go to my mother's grave. I absolutely have to ask her what's going on with my husband's girlfriend. She'll certainly know. I go and open the coffin. My mother is whole, not damaged or decayed. I want to embrace her and ask. Then she's nothing."

I advised the client to continue with counseling. A colleague in our practice had to take over since I had no time.

One year after follow-up, I called the client, since I still had two trivial additional questions. Spontaneously she said that the most important thing in her counseling experiences up to now had turned out to be working through her relationship to her mother with my colleague. "I managed it; and the dream didn't recur." In the last year, she got to know a younger man who adored her, and fantasized about constructing out of this "something to parry" her husband's love. But then she had abandoned it—"it just wasn't all that important anymore." She also no longer interrogates her husband about his old girlfriend. Since she no longer presses him so much to be "more romantic" with her—"if he doesn't want to, then he just shouldn't"—he is again much more romantic. To be sure, in spite of this he still doesn't talk to her enough. Therefore, the couple once more want to have a joint session with my colleague.

Here it seems as if the conflict were finally localized at the proper point: the couple's relationship and communication. In spite of, or precisely because of, occasional glances or even climbing over the marital fence (by *both* partners), I had always had the feeling that the couple belonged together.

△ 26 △

THE MEANING OF THE RIVAL: FANTASY AND REALITY

"I didn't know her, but I hated *all* women. I could have screamed, Who are you?"

"She was actually a good guy."

Clients

At last we come to the rival: What is the rival's role? I would first like to repeat that I consider the perception of the rival's existence to be a step toward consciousness and therefore a step forward. The more unreal the rival is, the more dangerous the jealousy. If the third angle in the triangle is localized, if it has assumed the contours of a concrete person, then a piece of corrective reality has been gained with which to combat desires for symbiosis and merging. The proximity of these desires to psychosis is unmistakable. At the same time, a prerequisite is for the rival to have a real relationship to the partner, and this prerequisite was met in all cases examined in catamnesis. The situation in psychoses can naturally be different. At the same time, this real relationship—"she has something going with him, he with her"—embodies, in generally accepted reality, a relationship to the jealous individual, however distorted it may be. How did our jealous clients now deal with this relationship?

Certainly the current expectation, even of readers, is that there will be aggressive tension between the partner and the rival. However, my question about aggression showed a predominance of hatred or rage directed against the third party in only fourteen cases, less than half. In thirteen other cases, the main target of aggression was the partner. If there was no rival at all, it is of course obvious that annoyance, disappointment, and struggle will be borne with or unburdened on the partner. In *all* cases, there are always substitutes; aggression is not always directed where it "belongs," but against individuals who happen to be available, or "more appropriate" because they may be weaker than the real target: children, parents, professional colleagues, subordinates, pets, fellow motorists. But that is not the issue here.

Many clients indicated that their aggression was predominantly directed against *one* of the two individuals making up the new couple; many others said that, at the same time, they were also furious at the other party. During the course of further counseling, they frequently also became enraged at themselves. I believe that one manifestation of health is shown precisely in this variously oriented aggression. A fixed orientation appears to me to be neurotic; this orientation often cropped up in counseling sessions and lasted for a long time, but then began to give way. Aggressiveness that is too intense is also generally neurotic. If Bergler's thesis (see chap. 16, sec. 8) is correct, that the person who loves passively and primarily wants *to be loved* usually turns against the partner, whereas the person who loves actively and primarily wants *to be the one who loves* usually turns against the rival, then one may deduce from the changeability of aggression the changeability of needs due to love as well—and, in the final analysis, mobility is vitality and health.

In any case, the jealous individual's preoccupation with the rival, the alter ego, leads away from the partner, although one naturally can hate two individuals, just as one can love two individuals, at the same time. Therefore, let us stay with the rival: especially as long as one does not know the rival, or knows nothing specific about the nature of his or her relationship to the partner, the rival lends him- or herself very well to fantasizing and projecting. (Neurotics, or even psychotics, obviously can project things that are removed from reality onto individuals with whom they have daily contact and whom they know well.) The rival has something that the jealous individual, at least for the moment, does not have or believes he or she doesn't have, the partner's love. Why? What did the jealous one do? How is the rival better? The more distant the relationship, the more abundant the fantasies can or must be.

A man had a short-term relationship with his secretary. His wife now sees the secretary once a day in the small village in which she lives, on a specific path. What should she do? Naturally, choose another path. That won't work, the boy has to be picked up from kindergarten. Look for another kindergarten? That won't work, the house has just been finished. Arrange for the husband to change his job and therefore not see the secretary again? That won't work, he's lucky he was just made an executive. Attempt the same thing for the secretary, perhaps by intrigues or by speaking to her husband? That won't work—professionally, the same thing is true for the secretary that was true for her husband. The only thing left, therefore is, "to act as if it doesn't grate on me, to look away. . . . I also don't see in the least why I should change my life, in any case externally—I'll stay where I am."

The client did not seek out conversation with her rival, even though that would easily have been possible. She had only to interrogate her husband in a confrontational manner, whereupon he confessed the affair and immediately broke off the relationship. Thus the client knew nothing specific. The suspicious, psychoanalytic interpretation would be, she had arranged everything in order to be able to fantasize about it for years on end. I do not dare to judge whether this causality hypothesis is valid.

Things went on in the following way: for years, the client suffered the worst torments. She said that "it was a struggle between two women," and it was not clear to me whether the rival had ever noted anything of this struggle. "Every day she was with my husband for eight hours! Therefore I took over as much as possible of the extra work that he does at home [he was a city planner], as well as some of the work from the government office. I managed to bring it down to four hours." What was the rival like? "Black hair, well built, young—she had often had something going with married men, totally unlike me." Parenthetically, she noted that it was perhaps her husband's revenge for a "flirtatious verbal exchange" she herself had had with a young local pharmacist, whom the couple occasionally met socially. Again there would be a possible psychoanalytic interpretation: her guilt feelings were such that she had to punish herself with the torments of jealousy. In any case, she said that she "constantly had to suspect" her husband after her discovery—"That was bad for both of us." She had the "antennae" typical of jealous individuals.

"I simply no longer felt comfortable in our vacation home on Garda Lake. Then I asked him—and, in fact, it happened there, in *our* home, which we had so lovingly furnished. Since then, I can hardly drive there anymore. I have what I call my persecution delusion there. I try to repress thoughts of what happened there—but that's the same thing, you understand? I'm constantly preoccupied with it. And at every opportunity I scream at my husband that it's no longer a place to celebrate."

It is a certainty that we are here in the realm of oedipal fantasies. With this, I do not intend to assert that jealousy is "actually" aimed at the father, curiosity at the mother, and the compulsion to conceptualize it at the primal scene. Therefore, the last thing I want to do is to devalue the acute crisis by saying that none of this is valid, for it is only the expression of the desire to be the father's wife, and punishment intendant upon a bad conscience for wanting to assume the mother's position. Nonetheless, what is present seems to be firmly anchored in early problems, which contemporary treatment makes so "madly" difficult.

In terms of the solvability of the relationship to the rival, a case such as this is one of the worst that can be found in our counseling center. Indeed, it seems to me that this is true because of avoidance of direct confrontation and the inability to refrain from brooding. This client responded to the question of what was worst in the following way: "I myself. My inability."

Many others take the matter more directly in hand. They call the rival, meet alone with him or her, or even in groups of three or four, thereby certainly achieving very unpleasant scenes—but they retrieve a piece of reality from fantasy (and the fantasy and energy that they have reduced to their rage become free for other things).

In follow-up a client said, "Right at the beginning, my counselor asked me if I would like to see my husband's girlfriend. I said no. Today I have to say that it would have been better. Then this mystical aura would have disappeared. Then I perhaps would have had to say that he's actually a loving, nice guy, and I can understand that this happened to my husband. But this way, I was always searching: *Who is this woman?* I could hardly look at any woman. I could have wrung all their necks." For many reasons, this woman concurrently felt fear and desire when relationships to women were at issue. She desired and feared homosexuality and its transformations, but at the same time she desired and feared sexuality per se. Desire was manifested in the "search"; fear and resistance in "hatred." In this case, working through it in transference, especially with a female counselor, would certainly have brought about relief but was rejected by the client.

"So that the mystical aura can disappear"—this sentence could stand as the motto for all confrontations with the rival. One could also say, So that the other does not continue to be a god or a spirit with mysterious power, but that we may see and experience the fact that we are both human beings. The issue here is also the question of one's own reality, with which I dealt above. One case representing many:

A young woman had long sensed, "Something's going on with the neighbor's daughter." Her husband had denied it for a year. Finally she called at the counseling center. She had the feeling she was going crazy. She was given an appointment in a few days. Meanwhile, however, perhaps reinforced by being able to fall back on being helped, she had already hatched a plot with her girlfriend: she went on a weekend physical fitness course and had her girlfriend appear at the door earlier than the wife would usually return. The husband called out that he was already in bed and therefore did not want to open the door. Thereupon, the wife opened the door with her key. She had to search through the whole apartment. Finally she discovered the girl in the dark with the sleeping children. Now she wanted to speak alone with her husband, but he insisted that the girl be present. The wife got her girlfriend, who lived in the same building: "If

there are to be two of them, then I want there to be two of us present.''
One can well imagine that the conversation that ensued was not pleasant.
But the danger of ''going crazy'' was banished.

The very young woman felt herself to be the victor, and apparently
expressed herself in a fairly provocative manner. The wife, ten years older,
had finally found her place again. She did not allow herself to be provoked
and insisted that the girl's parents be informed. After this scene, the
husband continued to remain for a time in their apartment, and when the
wife saw ''how bad that was,'' she insisted that he move out. He stayed
away for one and a half years, but maintained continuous contact with the
family. Apparently he was in a predicament, for he wanted to return once,
but his girlfriend attempted suicide so that he thought he could not yet
assume responsibility for returning. During their separation, the wife had
become so independent that she was hesitant about whether she should get
back together with him.

What did she think of the girlfriend? ''The thing's over—but I don't
have the magnanimity to admit that she's OK. Maybe I expect too much
from others, because I also demand a lot of myself. I was enraged at the
girl—the children were still so little!—why did she stake so much on
taking their father from them? I thought to myself, I'm grown up, I'll get
over it; but the children? She was just too young. She probably didn't
understand what she was setting in motion.''

In contrast to the two previous examples, in which only fantasies played a
role, here the less ambiguous relationship to reality and the more dominant
way of dealing with the rival is presumably clear.

It is natural to ask about the difference in the way men and women overcome
a crisis; to me the difference seems considerable, at least in reference to the
above examples. Women view the rival more as a person who wants to take
their husband away from them. They more evidently suffer, but on the whole
are more inclined to reflect, to compare, and to see the parallelism between
themselves and the ''other.'' Indeed, in clear contradistinction to the assumption of women's greater emotionalism, they are more likely to be receptive to objective judgments. For the men in the above examples, the rival
was primarily someone to whom they wanted to be superior and whom they
had to devalue. Thus, the phallic-aggressive element was very much in the
foreground. Four of the eleven men had the wives give them an exact description of what had taken place. In such interrogations, which of course do
not occur in all cases, sadomasochistic titillation certainly always plays a
role, that is, a certain kind of frenzied excitement that probably is unconsciously enjoyed. However, the conclusion that they drew from this was that
they either felt themselves to be ''better'' than the other or used their findings
to ''put him down.''

A furious husband demanded that his wife provide him with a written
description of her affair down to the last detail—not only because he wanted
to know everything, but because he intended to show the written account to
the boyfriend's wife and other neighbors, "so that the snobs can't look down
on me." He later dropped this plan but in follow-up related with satisfaction
that he had afterwards once again "gotten hold of" the rival and verbally
abused him. The rival's professional, financial, and human inferiority was
stressed in all cases in which a man's jealousy was the focus of counseling.
After reconciliation with the partner, the men's main concern was seeing their
own sexual superiority confirmed.

Some significant utterances:

"For me he's an inferior subject who's out after all women."

"An old, grey-haired man—he has nothing, is nothing, and he was even in
jail once. Probably a charmer—she's always fallen for them . . ."

"That type—after he fell into all of my traps during a question-and-answer
game I played with him, and I had more or less pinned him—then he was
finished in my eyes, and I felt superior again."

"It was an insult to me that he was such a football-player type—
completely below par. And on top of that he's also a coward. He said that
if I were to come into his apartment, he'd jump off the balcony. Naturally,
the apartment was only on the second floor . . ."

When a wife, who was herself jealous, confessed to an affair conducted
out of revenge, a man even defended himself with the following
observation: "What—with that guy? Now that's a real embarrassment for
me!" For the wife, this was naturally totally degrading. However, even
years after their divorce, this man slashed his wife's tires when he learned
of a new love interest.

An especially amusing example parenthetically shows a skillful way of dealing
with the frequent and often especially problematic office-party flirtation:

At his boss's invitation, a man went with his colleagues to the Oktoberfest,
as is customary in Bavaria. The boss was a great womanizer, and my
client's wife was especially pretty. My client grimly stated, "He said he
wouldn't put up with driving such an attractive dinner companion up to her
house door without being allowed to go further." According to the client,
the boss brought the couple home "in his huge car," got out with them,
embraced the wife, and gave her "a good kiss." "For a second I saw red.
Then it occurred to me how to save the situation: I also embraced him, and
then gave him a wet kiss. First he was flabbergasted, but then all three of

us had to laugh. Afterwards, I felt great. That is to say, my boss is a good bit shorter and thinner than I, and when I had him in my arms like that, I—well—I pressed a little harder. I hope it hurt him a little. But naturally he couldn't say anything—how would he have looked in front of my wife! Both of us have often laughed about it. Unfortunately, no one else saw it."

△ 27 △

SEVERED CONSTITUENTS

An important aspect in looking at the rival is the insult caused by the rival's being different. This problem was at issue in fifteen of the follow-up cases discussed. As I have already shown, reproaches directed against the partner often relate to all that one has done for him or her, to what one has renounced, and what one has sacrificed: "And now that's the payback!" Consequently, at first a division originates within the long-term relationship: one party removes him- or herself from it, something the other does not, may not, or does not want to do. These three verbs signify an intensification of consciousness. "I won't do it" is the simple affirmation of a fact. "I may not do it" verifies that one is (apparently) bound by the couple's existent, if also often unconscious, contract and usually contains the reproach to the partner that he or she is the authority figure. "I don't want to do it" sees the "individual constituents" more precisely. This formulation corresponds more clearly to an individual decision, the roots of which can be different. The roots of such a decision are primarily internalizations of prescriptions, norms, and traditions but also, deriving from this, fears that prevent one from breaking through them. These fears, which are per se the result of an internal conflict, are neutralized by being channeled into the sphere of conscious decisions.

Why then does the other do what is forbidden? Why does the other feel he or she may do it, or want to do it? Likewise because of role-determined prescriptives, cultural programming, or familial tradition. A division of roles familiar to every German is that of the husband who must "go out into the hostile world" and the proper housewife who "rules the roost." No further commentary is necessary. Either one of the two may be annoyed at the assigned role. If he or she wants to assume the other's role, it would seem scandalous to that person. One can refer primarily to Thea Bauriedl and Jürg Willi for information about the psychological concepts relevant to this theme.

Yet another division arises between the jealous partner and the rival. The following pattern appeared more infrequently than I had expected: "What the rival is offering, she [or he] could of course also have with me." It was most

apt to appear in jealous men and be linked to sexuality. The assessment of
the rival as a person who is either completely different from oneself, or who
chooses completely different things, was much more frequent, whether it was
expressed or not. The standard of one's own values is applied to the rival.
Without being questioned, these values are viewed by the jealous individual
as the couple's mutual values—and this standard is unsuitable, even if it is
not shattered.

"Those are pseudowomen, female Casanovas. The men do it one way, and
they do it another. If a person lives that way, it's something dirty to me.
I'm not that kind of person." As perhaps can be concluded from this
statement, the client's husband had no relationships with barmaids or
prostitutes. Rather, during the course of a marriage that had lasted twenty-
five years, he had two long, fairly serious relationships. In follow-up, to
be sure, the female client, almost parenthetically, also narrated a love story
about which her husband, and above all her mother, for God's sake, could
not be allowed to learn anything. In this love, during her husband's
absence on a business trip, she had discovered great, if brief, happiness,
most probably as compared with her marriage and most probably full of
sensuality.

Obviously the notion that "the rival is what I am not" often proves to be
true: for example, when there is a large discrepancy in age, much younger
partners may get together with people their own age; or—as is very frequent
in our society—when a "crazy" man during midlife crisis abandons the wife
with whom he has created a family and a structure, in favor of a younger,
more liberated, emancipated woman. The reality of being different also holds
true in cases of physical and mental deficiencies, handicaps, differences in
education, depressions, and so forth. But the reverse can also be true. Handicapped individuals can be fascinating; older men can be more seductive than
younger men; ugly women more attractive than beautiful women; depressives
can exert an attraction on some individuals, which makes them "need" the
partner. Furthermore, my entirely personal experience is that the occasional
happiness of depressives, if they do not totally succumb to their depression,
is the most beautiful and infectious happiness that exists.

Thus everything also works in reverse. "It depends on an individual's
pain—not on an individual's wound"—and the most frequent pain of the
jealous individual is precisely that "everything came to be this way only
because your new love has something that I do not have."

Here one is confronted with yet another great psychic task: the issue is to
observe, to understand, to "analyze" how one is *oneself* different. After this,
one can either say that there is really nothing to change or say, I want to try

to develop in myself the "other thing," which I do not have (i.e., to integrate the "severed constituents"; or even, if one wants to use the language of family therapists such as Helm Stierlin, to live oneself the delegated characteristics and modes of behavior instead of leaving them to others).

I once had the opportunity to observe "in real life" such a separation. It reads as a pure curiosity, but in reality was connected with much pain. An already middle-aged married couple repeatedly stressed to outsiders that their decision to remain childless, which was mutually reached, had never been regretted by them. Perhaps they demonstrated their marital happiness somewhat exaggeratedly, but I believe that they were really happy, that they led an active life involving many cultural activities. They were liked and lacked for nothing.

One day, out of the blue, to the disconcerted amazement of all their friends and to the horrible pain of the wife, the husband suddenly left her. Since then, he has been living just as happily as before with another woman who has three children. He deals with these children in a thoroughly benevolent and paternal manner.

After some years, his wife married a man who himself had five children.

It is hard to imagine that other reasons, of which I am not aware, did not also play a role in such a striking shift in the choice of partners. However, I have rarely seen such a radical surrender of an intensely stressed and monolithic mode of existence in favor of another not previously lived. Certainly it demonstrates an unconscious need for "completion." Naturally this need was not experienced as a decision, but rather as being in love, as a new love for a "totally different" partner.

In speaking here of completion, what is at its root is the demanding concept that jealousy can *also* be a warning sign of human restriction, if not mutilation, which can be compensated for, at least to a certain extent. In our counseling cases, the solutions I liked best were the ones in which the jealous individual, to express it in formulaic terms, did not (or not only) say, "You may not do that, because I am different from your new love." Rather, they were the ones in which the jealous individual could arrive at a decision to say, "I want to stand by the fact that I *also* would like to have what the other has—whether it's with or without you."

In any case, the following example demonstrates how justified the outcry sometimes is.

A man lost his wife to another, was suffering greatly because of this, and was very jealous. He fell in love with a young nurse while he was in the hospital because of a compound leg fracture, that is, while he was in a condition in which "he couldn't go on anymore." The nurse was twenty years younger than he, had a more modest background, was friendly, pretty, and unpretentious.

She became pregnant by him, which for many reasons was a catastrophe. He was the only divorced member of a large, conservative family, and now, on top of that, had an illegitimate child, with a woman "socially beneath him!" The young woman did not want an abortion and for a time lived alone with her child in straitened circumstances. Finally he married her, not least because of familial pressure. For, in spite of everything, his family was pushing him to do "what was proper." When they were already married, but still lived apart, the woman came to his apartment a few times and discovered him engaged in profound discussions with former girlfriends—by candlelight, with music and cigarettes. "He was never that romantic with me." Nothing more than discussion took place, but the young wife was insanely jealous. These women represented everything she was not: they had time, did not have small children, and could carry on educated conversations.

The young wife truly could change nothing in the situation, and it was not possible to change herself while she was in this oppressed state. It was—naturally!—beneficial for the man that he was the superior one in this marriage and not the exploited party again.

At the time of follow-up, the situation had changed: nine years after the beginning of counseling, the wife had had a second child who was already beyond the stage of total dependency. She enjoyed having her mornings free, since neither of the children were then in the house. Furthermore, she was able to allow her husband to participate in activities, when before she had fantasized that he would only meet "sluts" while doing so. Now he enjoyed table tennis, folk music, photography. She states that her jealousy was a sign of her fear of losing him. "Jealousy is a sign of one's own insecurity and the other's towering superiority." To be sure, at the core of her being she was sure that her husband needed her and the child, and today she is even more sure of this. She looked charming, still very young, and was of the opinion that her twenty-year-older husband "to some extent danced attendance on her, more than she did on him."

Overcoming jealousy is sometimes also simply the result of patience, of being there and enduring, without which no marriage can survive.

As far as the integration or conquest of severed constituents is concerned, the issue is naturally liberation, not only from parental prescriptives and compulsions to assume certain roles, but also from ego-ideals that simply have to be changed from time to time. The issue is, therefore, emancipation in its broadest sense, and this requires courage, for it "causes fear," as Gambaroff (1984) has so excellently demonstrated.

28

HOMOSEXUALITY?

> Do you know, my love, why our relationship has become so great and so perfect? Now I want to tell you why. You are an *infinitely productive* being, I am an *infinitely receptive* being; you are a great *man*; I am the first of all women who has ever lived.
>
> Friedrich von Gentz to Rahel Levin, 1803

Of all Freudian assertions relating to the theme of jealousy, the assertion of repressed homosexuality is doubtless the most provocative. Freud sees it only in serious cases, and if one applies this criterion, then *one* path is cleared through the thicket of reality, in which one otherwise cannot find one's way. Of course, one must agree to the basic assumption that we are all fundamentally bisexually oriented and that the "normal" solution for us is, however, the heterosexual solution. I believe that one cannot simply say, The greater the unconscious homosexuality, the more severe the jealousy, even to the extent of psychosis. Rather, one can more clearly say, The greater the fear of the internal traces of earlier bisexuality, the stronger, the more lasting, the more tormenting jealousy is. At the same time it is essential to consider also the other side of this kind of fear—yearning, desires, longing.

Do such things crop up in our counseling cases? In my discussion of Freud's essay (see chap. 15, sec. 2) I maintained the opinion that one must be prepared to confront all three components of jealousy discovered by Freud, not only in the worst circumstances (those that are homosexually projective and develop into jealousy paranoia) but also in simpler cases, to be sure differentiated by the intensity of their distribution. These three components are simple rivalry; heterosexual desires to be unfaithful; and those naturally unconscious, homosexual projections of infidelity that are predominant in psychoses. I believe that each instance of jealousy, as well as each instance of love, contains traces of homosexual desires and fears.

We have gradually learned to view the psychoanalytic goal of lasting maturity as a utopia that is not even desirable. We have also learned to give

306

more than occasional credence to the regressive return to forms of sexuality that Freud called "polymorphous-perverse," but to view them as forms of sexuality that exist on an equal footing with genital sexuality, in the case of the partners' mutual understanding. (On the one hand, applying the concept of "polymorphous-perverse" to the infant's embryonic sexuality is not without its comical side. However, it demonstrates the extent to which Freud stubbornly held to the difficulty and precision of his thought and work, at the cost of rejection by almost all individuals with "natural feelings.") This insight has even found juridical expression, in that homosexuality among consenting adults is no longer punishable by law.

Paying attention in counseling to the sexual and relational anxiety of jealous clients has helped me enormously. To be sure, at the same time I could understand the fear of *homo*sexuality, in the cases worked up in catamneses, only as one aspect of the fear of sexuality and not as an isolated, unique form of this fear. This may sound somewhat mystical to the reader; but a counselor asks questions differently; other images occur to the counselor; the counselor even makes different gestures, in accordance with the connections he or she already has in his or her brain and the way the counselor manages to deal with his or her own fear.

In counseling centers, one seldom hears anything of direct homosexual contacts. Obviously homosexuals who would come to us with jealousy or other relational conflicts would be accepted, heard, and counseled like other human beings, and no one would try to "talk them out of" their homosexuality, at least, not a conscientious counselor who had decided to take on the case after a preliminary interview. This is something we do in *all* cases. Also, no one is "talked out of" something. However, expressing conflict can naturally lead one to abandon a desire, a partial aspect, a sexual tendency. Of course, such a conflict is present in every case of jealousy.

Only one time did I have a woman in counseling who was involved in a passionate love relationship with another woman. Previously I had only known of such cases from the literature, from the women's movement, and from "real life." This woman was playing with the idea of establishing a new household with her girlfriend and her own two children.
Understandably, her husband, whom she had previously loved very much and who was trying to understand, was extremely upset. Thus the triangle was for once constructed differently than is usual.

Infuriated, the woman called an end to counseling because she perceived me as her husband's ally, for she thought I had no clue about anything having to do with lesbian love, and saw herself *only* as an interesting case for me. Obviously the case was interesting, but many cases are. It would be terrible if this were not true. Indeed, I could understand the man, and found him very sympathetic. But I have also rarely liked a female client as much as I liked her—my own homosexual components! Perhaps we were both afraid of the transference relationship.

Approximately seven years later when, with some anxiety, I called the man because of catamnesis—I had counted on the couple having separated—he said that they were back together again, and everything was really fine. To be sure, after consulting his wife, she "no longer wanted to be reminded of the whole thing anymore," and the man was very busy with his profession. He had time—most likely for a telephone conversation, he said—only after the end of the deadline that I had set myself for the catamnesis. Here the only hope that remains is that the magnanimous "permission" for homosexuality—for a long time the man had observed the lesbian relationship, even though with great distress, without setting an ultimatum—made it possible for the couple to make a new approach to each other.

Something similar to this concession, only in a less explicit and explosive form, is perhaps a part of the solution in many cases of jealousy, and leads to reassurance and overcoming. Perhaps, however, the reader will ask where homosexuality exists in the usual cases—for, in the final analysis, those people want to have the partner back.

When this aspect plays an important role, what is most striking is the jealous individual's exaggerated preoccupation with the rival. One has the impression that the rival is much more important to the jealous individual than to the partner—for, in the majority of cases, the partner has lived out his or her sexuality with the third party! The discovery of an extramarital relationship sometimes pops the champagne cork that until then had plugged any interest in persons of the same sex.

In a case of borderline jealousy that I could not include in the catamneses because, even though it was concluded, it had not been long enough ago, I asked the client to describe his rival's characteristics. I was certain—and the client was aware of this—that this rival did not exist in "normal" reality but only in the client's reality, in which, however, he assumed an eminently important place. He described his characteristics—older, superior, professionally successful. From there, the client came to speak of a boss he had highly esteemed (and somewhat hated); and of his omnipotent, beloved mother; and repeatedly of his desires for tenderness, a tenderness in which he was permitted to receive tenderness.

From there he proceeded to his dissatisfaction with his totally affectionate girlfriend, with whom he got along very well sexually, but with whom—an understandable reaction—he no longer felt the same passion as at the beginning of their relationship. The couple were no longer terribly young and had lived together for about three years. For both, this was their "great love." Both had extricated themselves from mediocre, but not bad, marriages.

This all was brought up over the course of many sessions. What also recurred was the husband's bad conscience at having taken away another man's wife. One day the client came into my consulting room and, instead of a greeting, said, "Defregger!" Naturally, I was bewildered. It turned out that a reproduction of a painting in the style of Defregger, which he had passed at least twenty times, had, for the first time, struck him. For reasons unknown to me, the painting is on a door in our counseling center and depicts—somewhat tritely—a young peasant couple who are in love. The boy has apparently surprised the girl and wants to kiss her, and they are depicted in this situation—the girl already leaning into the boy's arms, alarmed and yielding at the same time, the boy bold and aggressive.

For my own part, I now took advantage of the opportunity, in as bold a manner as the peasant boy and perhaps just as excited as he, to ask the man jokingly whether he perhaps would not like to be taken like the young girl. This stimulus was not at all met with the rejection that I feared, but we were able to discuss it and then let the whole thing drop—because I in no way wanted to discuss it to death!—and occasionally take it up again later.

In the course of counseling, anxiety and borderline phenomena became fewer. Instead, "human nature" could more explicitly be discussed, as it had developed in the relationship experienced as so shining, ethereal, and unique. Moreover, at the beginning the woman had been much more active than the man. Grief at the passing of the great love developed out of jealousy. The thought was allowed to surface that it was perhaps possible to conceive of the couple's separation even *without* rivals, for some of their life-style conceptions did not coincide as precisely as the two had thought. It is possible—and this is what I hope—that precisely this admission of the "normal" possibility of moving apart, which in the end every relationship contains within itself, prevented the real separation.

I believe that it is not necessary, and is even harmful, to formulate the theoretical context of such processes in counseling. Perhaps one does not even have to mention the word homosexuality, although the designation of fears, their "verbalization," remains one of counseling's primary tools.

What is much more important is to find a new way of dealing with unfamiliar, anxiety-producing emotions. This man was in no way homosexual, but he was afraid of this without being aware of his fear. (I consider it likely that the threat of heterosexuality, with which they must of course coexist, plays a similar role in homosexuals' especially frequent and torturous jealousy.) Because I was able to make it possible for him to contemplate his own "feminine" desires courageously—and because I believed myself capable of this—these desires lost the sinister aspect they had had for him. (While writing this section I came to look more closely at the picture hanging on a dark spot of the wall [by the way, this picture is by Waldmüller]. I discovered a third figure in the painting: in darkness, behind an open door, an old mother/witch/ woman is lurking, in the attitude of one who is pandering, or perhaps lustful. Unfortunately, in counseling I missed the opportunity of working through the role of this woman. And once again, I made up my mind to be even *more* scrupulous in the future . . .)

Like all aspects of jealousy that are felt as negative, this aspect also contains the possibility of being positively transformed. One might say it contains the possibility of a re-experience. In keeping with Freud's classification, anyone who feels anxiety and grief at the "love object believed to be lost" can attempt to make something out of that grief. The image of sinking in water always occurs to me in relation to this. Not only that the water, in every case, will carry one to the surface if one does not foolishly flail about, but also that if one has sunk all the way down to the bottom, one can push off and rise even more quickly to the surface.

Whoever has suffered "a narcissistic wound" will have no recourse but to think of him- or herself; to show off his or her own virtues; and perhaps to obtain from someone else the confirmation denied by the partner. Perhaps the person will also have to rediscover, for example, the melancholy joys of lonely communion with oneself.

The person who "projects his or her own infidelity" can—naturally— attempt something with real infidelity. Many now do this, since it has become so much easier today to actualize something of the sort than it was earlier, though with variable success. Spiteful loves, "counterpunches," often yield nothing. Jealous individuals, however, precisely because of their unhappy state, can find no outright sexual contacts with the opposite sex, but only contacts of a different nature. They "cry themselves out." They tell women or men, sometimes total strangers, the story of their love and disillusionment. In doing so, they also satisfy the exhibitionistic component of jealousy (see Bergler), which, in Unamuno's story, Alejandro so painfully and "manfully" wanted to surpress.

And finally, the fear of homosexuality also contains the possibility that internal and external reality can be expanded: contacts with one's own sex as an "antidote." Of course, it is especially women who are great friends, often to their husbands' annoyance. Many of our women clients found comfort and sustenance with other women. But also they simply began to do "happy" things with them, and the tenor of these undertakings was, Doing them, we have no use for men. Often it is a matter of very simple things: excursions, conversations about their children, physical fitness courses, sewing circles; more rarely, concerts, movies, exhibitions. Among younger people, it may be visits to a discotheque where, to be sure, heterosexuality invading the female alliance once again becomes threatening. Jealous men more rarely seek the opportunity to talk things out with other men, just as it is much less common to have a "best male friend" than it is to have a "best female friend." But men, of course, move predominantly in the world of men on a daily, professional basis, and in our cases *one* sphere of activity was especially attractive, sports, especially "hard-core" sports: mountain climbing; high-speed skiing; working out on the more demanding gymnastics equipment; table tennis at a highly competitive level, where there are separate divisions for men and women; a few instances of flying. These are all activities for which "the women" are too weak, where it is possible to have a satisfied company of men after great physical effort has been expended.

I continue to hear the objection that this is, of course, nothing sexual. This is true—and is also not true. Several times I have indicated that sexuality is Freud's main rubric. Perhaps some would like it better if one were to replace "sexuality" with "relationship" or "interest." When he used the term "sexuality," Freud *always* concurrently meant "interested relationship." But what interested him in the relationship was not its cultural aspect, nor its financial, sociological, and other aspects, but specifically the sexual aspect. He said, "J'appelle un chat un chat," or "I call a cat a cat." This is the French saying for "calling a spade a spade," calling things by their proper names. It is only *one* name, but that name is clear. There is no one who can convince me that men or women who shower together do not compare their bodies. I will make more progress if I see offshoots of sexuality in this, than if I were to speak of beauty, fitness, age, and so forth. "But, of course, among themselves, men talk an awful lot and in a very vulgar way about women!" Yes, of course—but why? On the one hand, out of desire, naturally; but perhaps also in order to prove to themselves how heterosexual they are? For one also knows that many homosexual contacts take place in barracks, internment camps for men, and prisons.

I would like to present one more observation on the following question: If, therefore, (sexual) interest in the rival plays such a great role in jealousy, what is the situation in the case of direct contacts between the jealous individual and the rival? Once again the great frequency of these direct contacts should first be mentioned: twenty-four of the thirty jealous individuals personally knew their rival (and one must keep in mind that there was no rival in three of the thirty cases!). In seven cases, the affected person showed indignation (behind which there was always one part injury and grief) that the rival was "as it happened" a male or female friend.

"I admired her, she always gave me such good advice. We know her well because she and her husband had the rented garden plot next to ours. To be sure, she had always been referred to as 'the queer bird' in our group. She talks a lot and wants to dominate everything. I just didn't notice anything! I trusted her. I woke up from my dream of friendship only after I knew everything and talked to her about what she was thinking of by destroying marriages—her own and mine. And she even became outraged at this! I left and slammed the door behind me. The dream is over! Only after this did I see how unfeminine and materialistic she is. I think that I could have more easily forgiven my husband a younger and prettier one . . .''

Does this not sound like a love affair that has been destroyed? During counseling, a man straightforwardly stated,

''We were so close to each other—he was part of the family, and we all loved him. When my wife started something with him, she took him away from the rest of us. We and the children and he—there were the six of us. He left behind a void. Now there are only five—if that. I still don't know what will become of our marriage. My wife's away so often, and the two boys especially mourn for him because he could play with them so fantastically—much better than I can. And of course you see—I've lost ten kilos. To give up both of them—my wife *and* my best friend—that's just too much!''

Such unambiguous examples affirm the psychoanalytic thesis that, in its archetypal form, jealousy involves *two* beloved individuals who ''betray'' the third: they turn to each other and not to the third person. Aside from this, thirteen individuals (approximately half) had at least *one* conversation with the rival in which the rivalry was directly addressed. Naturally, the reaction was often violent. There were fights, tears, confrontations. In the end, however, the judgment made from a remove, especially by women, is not at all so hate-filled as one would perhaps expect.

A client's husband had frequently said to her, ''If you could only see her—you'd like her too!'' In catamnesis, the wife said, ''He gushed and talked. I was completely crazy after this. I thought to myself, 'that must be a fantastic woman!' That was simply inside me, even when I was in counseling. Then she called once and wanted to meet me, but I said no to that: 'No—I won't do it.' Then she said, 'What do you still want from the man!' She said it so brutally, as if I were not his wife.''

For years there were indirect contacts between these two women. They even formed an alliance against their successor. Later the client went once to her rival's house: ''I wanted to get to know her after all. I made myself pretty. I wore a nice pullover and a new skirt, fixed my hair, and put on some makeup. Later I heard that, after this, she was jealous of *me*! I found her—nothing special, somewhat ordinary. But now I think to myself that she wasn't so bad. Maybe if I saw her more often, I would like her. And the way she carries herself, which my husband claimed was so provoking: afterwards I thought, 'I didn't even pay any attention to that!' "

Here, I would once again like to remind the reader of the twofold meaning of "to be jealous of" (see chap. 13).

The oedipal conflict sheds light on the adult triadic relationship. The positive resolution of the oedipal crisis cannot be understood only as renunciation of the parent of the opposite sex and identification with the parent of the same sex. Rather, it must also be understood as a new relational definition; we (father and son) like the same person (the mother): why should we fight over her and not both "enjoy" her, of course, in the form that, after all, is recognized in our culture and with which we can therefore most easily live? The hate-love, the ambivalence experienced in forgotten childhood naturally permits the later manifestations divided into hate and love—rejection and interest, devaluation and idealization, or even a mixture of both, which is probably most "healthy."

For an adult triadic relationship, this means that an existent or once-existent external love must not necessarily lead to distancing. On the contrary, there are friendships, probably fewer among men than among women, that originated from previous rivalries, where the former beloved was almost ditched. And when one considers that sometimes (not always) the closest, most tender and dependable friendships between men and women derive from earlier love relationships, should one not grant these to one's partner, especially if one gets something out of it oneself? The subtle, wise aphorism (Loriot's), which contains so much truth, would thus ad absurdum be most beautifully and most charmingly taken to the extreme: "Men and women are just not well matched!"

This possibility—one sees this in the way it is formulated—seems *to me* to be the best, most humane, and sympathetic resolution to the jealousy conflict. However, I would like to formulate this in personal terms in order to avoid turning it into a didactic goal. In some cases this solution has succeeded in my own life and in my personal environment. In other cases it has not succeeded at all. It frequently occurs among younger individuals, when jealousy involves a person who reacted to rivalry and not to trespassing (see chap. 3). Obviously, the prerequisite is openness at the two other angles of the triangle: if fear, a sense of injury, and possessiveness cannot be overcome at one of the three points, either through contemplation, new experiences, or "time," then what will remain is a close alliance between two, or separation of all three. Naturally, this also holds true if the love that initiated the jealousy was only a matter of a fleeting opportunity for at least one of the participants, who then afterwards has no interest at all in the person who was loved or with whom he or she flirted. In spite of this, such unimportant relationships can lead to great conflicts, for of course the severity of jealousy often has nothing to do with the intensity of the wounding relationship.

Among my thirty catamneses, I found this utopia of mine approximately actualized in one single case. During the entire course of counseling, I had the impression that this couple was very intimately bound, in spite of what were, in part, very great difficulties. It was counseling that demanded great intuition in walking the narrow line between what was said and left unsaid. The wife had seen very clearly that her husband's girlfriend, a colleague at work, could speak openly and happily with him, in a way she herself could not and had never succeeded in doing with anybody. In the face of this, she was unable to see her own good qualities—she was charming and unique in her shyness and intensity—and it is very difficult to facilitate something like this in counseling. In catamnesis, she said,

"My husband and I have a relationship that is filled with tension because both of us like tension. Therefore, it's not necessarily negative for us. And he always had a *completely* harmonious relationship with this girlfriend. That's what makes me jealous and also somewhat sad, because we've never succeeded in achieving that.

"Nothing was going on with her, but at the beginning I was afraid that something could develop from it. We see each other fairly often, in a group of four, because meanwhile she has married. The two of them look at each other adoringly. My husband is completely unconstrained in doing this, and he has never hidden anything from me. I don't have to 'get anything out of him.' That would have been too stupid, I would never have spied, that's—well it sounds a bit arrogant—but it's beneath my dignity. I think that everyone should have his or her own contacts. Of course, I meet people on my own, too—even if those people are hardly ever men.

"That one falls in love during marriage—I wouldn't have anything against that, not fundamentally. Actually I think it's normal. It could also happen to me, only I would handle it differently than my husband. But that he can do something with his female colleague that isn't possible with me—discover this simple harmonious social atmosphere—*that* annoys me!

"I also like his girlfriend, really, she has her good side. I'll also concede to him that she likes him—really, she likes him a lot, and he likes her a lot. Why shouldn't someone like him—I like him too! But at the beginning, we generally quarreled when we were together. At that time, he was spending much more time with her than with me. They're both teachers at the same school, and I was working full-time as a physician and was exhausted in the evening.

"It wasn't that long ago that I grasped that I am *very* untrusting, even toward those whom I know very well and like. That's probably a painful experience for the others, too. In this, my husband and I are very different—he trusts everybody, even his enemies. I no longer consider that good, but that he has the capacity to surround himself with such a nice atmosphere of openness was one of the reasons I fell in love with him back then. Moreover, he has a very warm relationship with all women, not only with me. I knew that from the beginning, and thought, We'll see what comes of that—it could also turn out badly. It's been only a short time since I've believed it is not turning out badly. Somehow . . . and I also have the feeling that I no longer have any grounds for jealousy.

"Also he says that sometimes things between us are, after all, the same way as they are between him and this girlfriend. When we're in agreement, he thinks. Perhaps I don't see that in the same way— sometimes one digests good things, and then they're gone . . ."

These spouses dealt with each other so tentatively and thoughtfully, but also with such a strange form of movement and contact, that I had the impression of submerged emotion—a life in which one comes to an understanding by means of oscillation, rather than with words—subdued, slowed down, and with a peculiar gracefulness. Thus here a (tentative) positive triadic relationship was possible because of respect for commonality *and* difference on both sides.

29

LETTING GO AND RETURNING

"Just let him (or her) alone—he (or she) is sure to come back!" Jealous individuals often receive this wise piece of advice—from mothers-in-law, from liberated individuals, from sons and daughters. From the counselor as well? That is probably rare, even though the counselor sees more accurately than others that basically it is only letting go that makes returning possible. This is the point at which I most strongly feel the pressure of systemic counseling. It is here I most often wish that I could entrust my clients to a paradoxical intervention. For I too see what everyone sees: that in most instances of jealousy the long-term partner's love, his or her desire to remain with the other, does not grow stronger, but decreases. However, letting go is achieved not only by the stimulus of a prescription, but also by working on the relationship, on love for oneself and thus for others, as it were. Once the feeling that "you are my life—what am I to do without you!" is dissolved, once constraints are loosened and have become less threatening, what appears is what was predicted by the know-it-alls, whom the jealous individual initially rejected so indignantly. In one case, things even took their course "telepathically."

Working with the wife, the counselor had reached the point where the wife understood how little freedom her husband had. Moreover, the client was truly pleased that it was a *man* sitting there listening to her. She stated, "Of course, you simply have different feelings than we do." Her husband had moved out for a few months, not to a girlfriend's place, but because of the girlfriend—he was "totally infatuated with her." Finally the client was at the point where she could say, "Someone has to be the loser. I felt it was over. That's it. And now I want to accept it as being over." She reported precisely that this was what she had thought at five in the afternoon, but that night her husband called her up from the southern Tirol, where he was on vacation with his girlfriend, to say that he was coming back. "And then I was immediately optimistic again."

Sometimes very simple words prove true in counseling, and the client can ponder them. In this case, the counselor had come upon the catchword "suspended motion," and the client worked on whether she actually wanted to participate in this suspended movement between wife and girlfriend. Things went on for a time, but finally the husband returned.

In this case the symbiosis had been very intimate, almost fatal. The wife had attempted suicide. Her husband had arrived and wanted to force her to spit out the pills. She refused, whereupon her husband screamed at her, "Then go ahead and do it!" and added a vulgar curse. Among other things, suicide attempts are always power struggles. Thus the husband must have felt that he was being squeezed, and even squeezed to a pulp, if he could hit out in such a way in such a situation. It is easy to grasp emotionally the horror and disappointment the wife experienced, especially since she described her marriage in simple words, "The way we were before—at that time there was simply nothing that one of us couldn't tell the other."

However, her distancing from him did not simply mean letting go, but doing something for herself. It is hardly imaginable that an internal change will not also pull external changes in its wake. Now she grants herself more than before—leisure time, new clothing, and the pleasurable sensation that she is being generous to herself. She has also assumed more responsibility, for example, by controlling the money they share. On the other hand, he does not go out in the evenings any less often than he did before—he still goes several times a week. But she can allow him this, whereas before she found it intolerable and scolded him—and he went in spite of that. She says that she gives him a great deal of credit for "helping" her; she is able to believe him when he says that no women are involved, "because he demonstrates this to her," that is, makes it comprehensible to her, talks about it, and sometimes even takes her along.

The upshot for her is, "If something like that happens to me again, then I won't react the same way. I've achieved this attitude in group therapy. I have experienced the fact that I can go on if I am without my husband, that I can do something *myself*. Before it was—snap! just as if the rug had been pulled out from under me. Now I am independent enough to take my life in my own hands and not throw it away anymore." Upon reflection, she added, "It brought about much that was good. That one has to experience something like that in order to become a different person! That no one is able to point out another way first, in order to wake one up!" And smiling, she said, "I've even gained something external from it—I've gotten much thinner!"

In a fundamentally more complicated marriage, where the extramarital relationship had already gone on for many years and specific rights had become ingrained—the husband's right to a joint vacation with his girlfriend and occasional weekends, but naturally having to show a clear preference for his wife and children—the wife said,

"The only times it doesn't work are when I'm not feeling well, when I resist it, or when I'm not mentally at peace with myself. However, when I'm detached and calmly confront the situation as a whole, then we don't have any problems. And basically I know that the calmer I am, the fewer opportunities his girlfriend has. Only—I just can't do this all the time, and I also don't like demanding that he separate from her; who knows what would come of that . . ."

This woman came to counseling not to achieve separation, but only to deal better with the fact of the extramarital relationship, without separation. It seemed to her that the girlfriend actually had a terrible life—alone, depressive, eternally waiting, without friends, with a none too satisfying profession. She herself continued to have a sexual relationship with her husband which was, in part, passionate. A short time ago, he said, "If the whole thing were to start over again—you can rest assured that I would bring her home with me immediately. If she were friends with both of us, with you and our circle of friends, she would get much more out of it than she does with just me." However, in this case the two women had never seen or spoken to each other, but only knew each other indirectly through mutual friends . . . Otherwise, in the culturally fairly open milieu that obtained here, my utopian solution, described earlier, would have come to mind.

With "letting go" I naturally do not mean allowing more than one can endure. However, perhaps I do mean testing whether one can, in fact, endure somewhat more than one did before. This has a twofold aspect: granting the partner's freedom, but to this point and no further because one can no longer endure it. I have rarely experienced this twofold aspect so impressively as in the following case.

A man had worked very hard throughout his life. He was the head of a large German subsidiary of a Japanese firm. To his wife's horror, when he was approximately forty years old—at the classical age for midlife crises— he had an affair. He complained about being restricted. She digested this and since then had set down specific regulations for him, which did not exactly come easy to her: weekends free, separate vacations, and so forth. This worked for some years, and he did not have other women. Then a— passing—love interest again came along. Now basic things were at issue:

the husband said that he did not exactly intend to do something similar again in the future, but he could not promise that he would not do so. The marriage had been very close and affectionate, and even continued to be so intermittently. Because of this, the wife claimed that she wanted him to tell her everything. But if he were to tell everything, she would be unable to endure it. In this state, they came to counseling.

The issue was that they both felt burdened by their pact of mutuality. The wife fought her way clear to agreeing to his taking a long and expensive trip on his own. He had never gone to Japan except on hasty and strenuous business trips and for a long time had wanted to get to know the country better at his leisure.

For the wife, this meant that she, for financial reasons as well, had to spend her annual vacation at home, alone. During this time, I saw her several times, and she looked as if she were suffering from a severe illness.

Three years later in follow-up, she said, "It was terrible—I was still so dependent on him. I thought maybe he wouldn't return. At the time, I couldn't even begin to grasp the implications of this."

What was helpful to her during this time were counseling, good friends, and especially an old teacher who judged—as I did—her husband to be someone "who would return." Her two teenage children, who knew what was going on but resisted taking sides, were *no* help, since she was certain in her own mind that it was not permissible to burden them, because they were preoccupied with becoming able to leave the nest. "At the time I had *three* people who were beating their wings."

But he returned, exhausted from his trip, and immediately went back to his business. Their relationship hardly changed. The wife was also uneasy about an exchange of letters with an American student he had met in Japan. In the manner typical of jealous individuals, she brooded on this. One day it became plain to her: "I don't want to be the hearth anymore, where everyone gets warm, but no one gives any thought to what he's being warmed by."

She had never given up the connections to her profession as a radio editor. Now she took on a part-time job, with great joy and intensity. She also went to a lawyer for advice. The result was clarity: "I know what I'll have to deal with. I can manage financially if I work. Now I'm not afraid anymore."

When her husband heard that she "was going full steam ahead," he became indignant. But since then the relationship has improved.

The woman concluded counseling. Half a year later, she wrote me, "We're now more considerate in how we deal with each other. Being together is no longer something so self-evident, and perhaps because of this has become more intense. I'm very happy about this, but I probably will never again rest in absolute security. Good days are richer than they were before. I also allow my husband to approach me more often, and he comes. Everything is more detached, more relaxed.''

In this case, I do not believe that one can simply say the husband was afraid of losing his hearth, the financial question caused him anxiety, he was indignant that his wife really wanted to abandon him, and so forth. Obviously, all these things played a part. A true, great solidarity existed between these two, and the husband had always emphasized that he loved his wife. Without at first even being aware of it, relieved amazement was probably added to his rage at the threatened loss—which certainly was what first made him consciously aware of the seriousness of the situation: The hearth can leave! And further, ''I will no longer be warmed by it.'' Changes on his part became possible only because of this. Without these changes, the marriage would have been lost.

For this is simply the way it is in the case of symbioses: they are an attempt at internal and systemic perpetual motion—and this will go well, until one party detaches him- or herself. In a successful resolution *both* parties must change their mobility, and in doing so they do not become different people. Who could seriously doubt that this woman would maintain those traits that make her a ''hearth'' for her whole life, even if those traits become less dominant? And who would not like to have a hearth that can even move?

△ 30 △

NEW LIFE, NEW LOVE

> One forgets too easily that one is oneself a part of those active
> forces [nature] and may attempt, in proportion to the degree
> of one's personal force, to alter a small part of the inevitable
> course of the world—the world in which that which is small
> is no less amazing and significant than that which is great.
>
> Sigmund Freud,
> "An Infantile Reminiscence of Leonardo da Vinci"

At this point there has been so much discussion about psychic processes, partial aspects, and exertions that many a reader has surely become impatient and is asking him- or herself, "What, after all, have your jealous individuals done, in very concrete terms? What has become of them, in the completely normal bourgeois sense?" And yet another question may be posed: "What's with the partners? For indeed, they have often behaved in a really bad, ruthless, and egoistic manner—can they continue to do this?"

I would like to answer the last question first: it is the question of moral evaluation. Both in my personal introduction and in the chapter on group therapy, I have already dealt with this. At this point, however, I would like to say once again and unambiguously that I cannot a priori consider a marriage that has been preserved as good, and a marriage that has been broken as morally bad. I am well aware that marriage—one way in which men and women live together—still functions and will continue to function. I am also aware that it offers many couples the possibility of personal development, personal happiness, and remaining faithful to oneself as well as the other, also in the sexual sense. This holds true in spite of all justifiable attacks on the murderous attributes of the nuclear family, with which a marriage counselor, more than many others, is so well acquainted.

However, I also see the extent of self-restriction, even cruelty, that the claim to life-long exclusivity can contain. Furthermore, it has certainly often been made clear to the reader the extent to which I view adultery, and jealousy in response to adultery, as an opportunity to learn to live more clearly, humanely, and fairly.

My own moral partisanship is obviously present, but it does not always come down in favor of the jealous individuals. I do indeed sometimes find the partner who is breaking out to be cold, vulgar, and egotistical—but I find the jealous individual to be this way just as often. But it is not my task to be a judge, and these criteria evaporate in a surprising way once one has spoken to both parties, become acquainted with their history and motives, and seen and understood the suffering on both sides.

As far as a change in partner during or at the end of counseling is concerned: the transitional character of the jealousy phenomenon within a system is most clearly manifest here. If the jealous individual changes, the other no longer *can* be the way he or she was before. In many cases, this unfortunately or fortunately means that the couple will separate. In thirteen of our thirty examples, the outcome was separation or divorce.

In the other cases, the union continued to exist, and that meant the *changes* affect not only one individual, but also the union. Often these were apparently simple things: the husband more frequently and with more conviction helped out at home; the wife took more interest in him and his profession; the couple did more things together; they gave up impractical schedules. The sexual relationship, or the value placed on it, almost always changed.

Here I am again entering the realm of prescriptions, which I find unpleasant, and therefore I shall immediately exit it again. For example, even if one can say that it is certainly good for many marriages if the husband can withdraw for a half hour after he has returned from the office, there are others for which such a rule would not be appropriate. Clients themselves usually come upon practical remedies. Occasionally something that had long been planned, had been attempted, but had never before worked is suddenly successful, "like a miracle."

In a similar summary fashion, I would like to answer the other question, what the jealous individuals did. In the case of separation, as in that of staying together, they did not continue to do what was done before, except for the three cases in which, in my estimation, *no* solution has yet been arrived at, although in one of these cases a separation has occurred. In these three cases, the husbands continue to have girlfriends. To a certain extent, the wives can live with this, but the same suspended condition still marks the relationship. Jealousy occasionally flares up and then becomes less intense again—and the step forward that must be risked in all triadic states that are felt to be painful by at least one of the participants was not necessary, not possible, or simply so painful that continual tension seemed to be the best possible solution.

The others—yes, what did they do? Wives got jobs; husbands thought more about their wives; houses were built, apartments changed; hobbies were rediscovered or revived; the relationship to the children was changed. One group of clients had better experiences with new partners. Almost all jealous individuals expanded their own "space," after they had seen that they had failed precisely because they were so little capable of conceding the partner his or her own space.

And is there no talk of love here? Actually, love is always the issue for me! Marriage counselors, however, usually tread carefully with this most beautiful polestar of their work. This word is as dangerous as it is powerful, and therefore one can propagate more confusion with this word than with any other.

And justice? One can, of course, demand this at most from lawyers and judges, and one can argue about it with one's partner—but things become very difficult if one demands justice from life. Love is often "unfair," because it is more than fairness, and also less than fairness. Why this woman or this man must endure so much, when she or he has taken so much trouble, and even, has loved so much—I am unable to answer this question, unless the answer is that the trouble one has taken is its own reward. But here we are again entering the realm of religion and philosophy: so I shall stop.

LAUGHING AND CRYING

Even a couple of enlightened older women came riding up, and immediately radiated the good and open, or the open good atmosphere which, at certain times, is only at the disposal of old women who have seen other times, and no longer fear or desire anything for themselves. Nothing was said that a person was not allowed to hear, and yet nothing was left unsaid which could be brought forward with any degree of benevolent cheerfulness.

Gottfried Keller, *Green Henry*

This is a remarkable story. When I was writing it down, it again occurred to me that I had once read that the American author Henry James loved telling stories, because this brought into play "the blessed faculty of wonder" (Trilling 1971, 134). At the same time, this is the single case in my book that I can cite for the jealousy of the third party.

Five years ago a woman came to me who, at that time, was as old as I am now and who, I have to say, did not appear to me to be especially youthful. Nonetheless, she opened our conversation with the following statement: "I believe I'm lovesick." Saying this, she laughed a bit. It was a charming, almost girlish laugh. She said, "A classical case." Automatically I thought that her husband had taken a younger girlfriend. She had heard that I was interested in jealousy, and when she went on to say that "It has to do with jealousy," I was fairly sure. But it was something entirely different.

She also believed that she had already almost succeeded. I was only supposed to listen. There was hardly anyone with whom she could talk about it, and "things assume a different shape when one tells about them." This would be good for her. She said, "It's a bit ridiculous."

Actually, I believe that there are no ridiculous emotions, and that is what I told her—there is only a judgment . . . Smiling and crying a little, she said, "Well, fine—then we'll see what you say afterwards."

Two years ago, she had met again someone who had been her boyfriend when they were young. She had left him thirty-five years ago. Later he had married a much younger woman. She said that the wedding pictures showed a charming and delicate girl. This marriage had already lasted almost twenty-five years. And now . . .

I thought that perhaps her own marriage was not especially happy. In that case, friends of one's youth are dangerous. But she said—and in the few hours I saw her, I was completely convinced—that she had married her great love, and even today she would marry her husband at the drop of a hat.

But then what was the problem in meeting this friend from her youth? The long interval was striking to me. They had not seen each other for twenty years.

"As he had said then, his wife is 'very sensitive' and wanted their mutual pasts buried at the beginning of the marriage. But naturally she didn't have a past. She was eighteen at the time and had grown up in a very protective environment. He is fifteen years older, and he *has* a past—me, for one thing. So I was supposed to be buried for him! It's a mystery to me how one can accede to such a request. If a married couple can't tell each other anything about the past, that just has to come between them!"

She became very agitated, and the corners of her mouth were twitching. I could only contribute, somewhat helplessly, Other marriages, other customs— but was he perhaps to a certain extent happy to be rid of her? Why had she parted from him?

"God, I loved him a lot. He was my first real love. After 1945, between piles of rubble and hunting for coal, we had two very happy semesters together. He had survived the war as a very young officer and was studying history because he said he wanted to figure out what had actually gone on then. I learned two things from him: love and politics. As far as love goes—you know what it was like then. We didn't sleep together, didn't even come close. You know what I mean—it's still always a bit hard for me to speak about this. But what we did—kissing, embracing under street lights, walking arm in arm through Marburg—that was 'permitted' and was not accompanied by the awful threats that my mother always forcefully expressed. Basically, it was glowingly sensual. I believe that I have this time to thank for my good sexual relationship with my husband."

Then had she after all once been married to him?

"No, that's exactly it!" she said and laughed a bit. "Actually, it was terrible." Both of them had changed universities. They continued to meet, but only occasionally. "I wrote a lot of letters and waited every day for his, but they came very infrequently; he was immersed in his studies and was already working in politics at the time. I believe that he also sometimes had relationships with girls who weren't as straitlaced, and was a little embarrassed by this. For two years I was unhappy. The only high points in my life were in the university libraries—and then I got to know my husband."

Very soon, everything with her husband was open, clear, and good. It was simply "the right start." She wrote her boyfriend, who remarkably still felt that he was "engaged" to her, a long letter. By return mail, a brief card arrived on which he wrote that they would then probably not see each other again. He did not want, and was unable, to fight. As a counselor, what did I think of such a reaction?

Most probably that the notions they both held of how to deal with another, how to love another, were very different. Which does not mean that one cannot love the other in spite of this . . .

The client broke out in unexpected tears.

Once she was again able to speak, she said, "Basically I continued to love him for my entire life, and he continued to love me. But in spite of that I truly think each day about how wonderful it is that I found my husband. It's nonsense for people to say that one can only love one person at a time."

Exactly—that is also my opinion. But did she ever think of separating from her husband?

"It may of course sound strange, and perhaps that's something you simply anticipate in your marriage counseling, but I have never, not even in my wildest dreams, considered that there was even the possibility of getting a divorce from my husband.

"Even during the famous twenty years, I hardly thought of my former boyfriend. I didn't complete my studies, and had four children. He didn't entirely go along with his wife's prohibition, and wrote me once in a while. That was always very touching—he also has two children—but I soon forgot it again. Only later did I find out that, for some years, he and his family lived only a half hour's drive away from us. He 'was not allowed' to visit me, and probably didn't even want to. Apparently, he thought of me more often than I thought of him—no surprise, with his wife's prohibition!

"And I would have been so interested in his wife. Of course, one never knows about something like this beforehand—but friendship among the four of us could have developed."

Meanwhile, the reader can imagine that the client could be certain of my sympathy at this point. She had taken a few steps in the direction of the "utopian solution" but had only met with resistance. The further course of the story confirmed me in my conviction that prohibitions are no solution to jealousy, but are even what first elicits fateful entanglements. "Fate" had broken free for the client.

"Once, when unexpectedly I saw his name on a list of speakers—he went into politics and mainly works for developmental aid—I had the organizers tell me the name of the hotel where he was staying, and I wrote him a note to say that I would like to meet him. I simply *could* not conceive that the old problem still existed. After such a long time!

"Perhaps I should also say that I have also suffered much in my own marriage, in addition to having experienced great happiness. For we were pretty old-fashioned, the two of us. I was busy with the children, sometimes did some journalistic work—and my husband was also very tied up in his profession at the university, but much more open to contacts, trips, even to a social life. When I had any time at all in the evening, I was often very tired. He liked to flirt and even had a few more serious relationships with other women. I took great delight in the children, but you know—one also simply needs some external recognition. And as a consequence of 1968 and afterwards, there was the tendency to consider all of that 'bourgeois.' People talked about bringing up children in an 'antiauthoritarian' manner, and I couldn't go along with that. My husband also couldn't, but it was mostly *I* who lived with the children. At that time, some of our friends thought, Well, she's a nice little housewife and has 'great' kids—but the husband lives differently. And of course even great kids disturb adults' plans.

"The other women—gradually I learned not to place any restrictions on him, because he did this himself in the things that mattered. And our own relationship was *never* mute or dead.

"Perhaps it's something one must accept if people are generally sensual. I have experienced it myself—only I didn't have the kind of opportunities for it as my husband had. One simply cannot somehow divide oneself into two parts: How is one to live tenderly with someone and at the same time not notice that other people are *also* attractive?"

But her friend's wife? It probably depends on how one deals with these insights . . .

"Yes—highly delighted, this was the way he answered my note, and we met. And now it gets strange again. He had gotten fat, and his black shock of hair, which I had always loved so, was snow white. A highly active political functionary; a gentleman with important tasks; totally bourgeois— and I, of course, was already what people, somewhat strangely, call an 'older woman.' And these two—well, it completely threw me, and him too. All the fascination, all the old bonds, everything was there again. We talked and talked and couldn't stop. I was supremely happy and had the feeling of having received, as an unexpected gift, something that greatly augmented my life.

"I told my husband about it immediately. He said, 'You look like a young girl again . . . , nothing else. I looked forward to further contacts and immediately wrote a letter to my friend, addressed to his home. And now—he wrote in return that his wife had seen the letter, had a very 'sensitive' reaction to it, and reminded him of his old promise about the past. This time he said quite clearly that he wanted to spare her, and I should write to him at his office in Bonn.

"I did this without hesitation. I'm used to putting myself into the thoughts of others. Since the children have become older, I've become involved in environmental protection and am on the city council. I'm involved in seeing to the needs of various elderly people. But at that point I never gave a moment's thought to his wife. I felt that he was himself responsible for his marriage and the demands it placed on him, and that our old love was our own affair. I had given this woman so many opportunities, and when she still continues . . . Do you find this wrong?"

Before I could answer, she continued,

"It's irrelevant to me if you think it was wrong. I did it, and I was almost proud of it. My God—a woman around forty, and I was in my middle fifties—I found this jealousy incomprehensible and ridiculous. Today it's a wonderful time for women of this age—and I didn't want anything more than an occasional letter, maybe a meeting twice a year, and an uncensored exchange of thoughts. For I'm not someone who destroys marriages. She couldn't, of course, know how good things are for me with my husband in spite of everything. But of course she could have seen it for herself from the beginning.

"Sometimes he wrote too, again more rarely than I did, like at first, but it was very nice. Then once we spent a whole day prowling around Munich. For he never has time. It was only one day."

How was it? Probably not exactly the way it would have been if she had done the same thing with a girlfriend?

"No—you've hit upon an important point there," she said and again laughed. "It was—well, it was a totally passionate day. I would never have thought that something like that would happen to me again."

Did you also have . . . I thought I was being tactless and did not complete the sentence.

"No, no—I don't know—we're so old already, and I . . . well, I don't want to talk about that. But there was one thing I came to understand: how unimportant direct sexual contact can be. To go to a hotel, for a few hours, without any luggage—I wouldn't have known how to do that. I would have been as embarrassed as a young girl thirty-five years ago. That's also laughable, isn't it?"

More than anything else, I was touched by it. But indeed, I also sensed the fateful distance that had separated the couple from the other woman as well as from my client's husband. I sensed its presence even on this day, during which the only thing that counted for both of them was that they had found each other again.

"Then he left again. We both knew that there was never any question of something like a relationship for us. He took trips to his developing countries, wrote me cards and sometimes letters, and I addressed my answers to Bonn. His wife works with him part-time. Moreover she's also active in an equal rights organization. Because of this, I had some hope that he could perhaps convince her that she could depend on him, and on me too. But he didn't say anything at all. You know, if we had still lived in the same city—but this way . . . I think, I was just not worth it to him."

And at this point she cried a bit. I asked whether it was possible that he really wanted to spare his wife. For apparently he was gone so much, on trips, at conferences, reading papers . . .

"Yes, naturally, naturally. But listen: one day he wrote me a letter saying he had to break off all contact with me. While straightening out his mail, his wife had found a letter from me, opened it, read it, and, inundated with tears, showed it to him. She thought he was too trusting. I don't know anymore what was in the letter, but in any case it ended something like this: I embrace you—or something like that. And the whole tone was like that between two people who are very close to each other and know a lot about each other. That's just the way it is between us.

"And now something happened to me that I would never have expected. Regardless of the fact that I find it unbelievable for someone to open other people's letters (but maybe she had no opportunity to talk to him, for he doesn't say anything), I 'completely flipped out,' as my children would say. It hit me so hard. I had such a bottomless feeling of loss that I no longer knew any way to help myself. A dream also recurred, which I had dreamt at the beginning of our rediscovery of each other.

"I am in a back porch. My old boyfriend is coming toward me across the path into the garden. I'm very happy. From outside, he breaks out the pane of the glass enclosure. Air flows in. In some way it's nice. But the splinters of glass come to rest around my body like a coat of chain mail. I can no longer move because it would hurt tremendously.

"There I sat in my armor made out of glass shards, petrified, immobile because of pain, and to make matters worse I couldn't begin to do anything because of the inappropriateness of my reaction. I was torn back and forth between two emotions. One was that it served me right, because I knowingly did something that had to hurt the other woman. The other feeling was that I had put myself out for my husband to such an extent because I understood that I could only be happy with him when I let him be freer than was first acceptable to me. Couldn't I *once,* just one time in my love for this second most important man in my life, simply be blessed with a little joy and self-affirmation, without always having to earn it? In my profession, in being alone, in letting go of the children—in everything I *exerted* myself. Of course, I also got a lot in return. But doesn't this kind of justice exist—just once only to have to gather pennies from heaven, so to speak?

I thought that "justice" exists, at most, *within* the system and not as something that infringes upon the system. However, I did not want to say anything so cold and theoretical. For a time, we were silent. Then she said,

"I can also see what is riculous about this story. Don't you think I'm really pretty whiny? But it was just amazing: my husband didn't think that at all. I talked to him about it and he listened—and that was already a lot to ask of him. Once he very quietly said, 'This idiot has no notion of what he's letting get away.' And that did me an immense amount of good.

"Meanwhile our normal life continued to be alive and tender, and that's just fine. I said nothing more than I absolutely had to. But he was especially loving to me during this time. One day, in the middle of the winter, he said he had a surprise for me. Both of us cancelled all appointments at very short notice, which is something we almost never do, and he drove with me to Chiem Lake in wonderful weather—there was sun and snow. In the middle of the lake is the "Women's Island," and it's a place that played a role during our engagement. There was no ferry service, but he convinced a man to put the small ferry into operation just for the two of us. And then we walked around the island. He had put his arm around my shoulders . . . and with that I had the feeling that I was allowed to think of my friend. My husband was—it was as if the differences between husband and father had been nullified—he was both things to me, and he had simply 'validated' me. I had a stepfather who would never have had any understanding for such things.

"My husband was not jealous, but he got scarlet fever. A childhood illness! Thank God it's not dangerous today anymore because it responds to penicillin. But when he was a child, a brother of his died of it.''

The client had calmed down. She said that she actually had a whole bunch of trouble, a share of all troubles.

"Once it was behind me, I was happier and more active than before. 'I'm happy to suffer pain that is already under control'—primarily I understood that, having taken the trouble to be generous as far as my husband was concerned, had been worth the effort.''

Had she then been jealous?

"I don't know—I was upset that this young woman had so much power over someone who, somehow, belongs to me and will always belong to me. Because of this she can do what she wants—I know this well. Sometimes I think of the anger and aggression toward his wife that lies below the surface but that this inhuman proscription will have engendered in him. But perhaps he is totally unaware of it.'' She laughed again. "Two royal children, who are not able to come to each other, at the age of fifty-five!''

And how does she view him today?

"It's the same as before—I believe that he's never wanted to make any effort on my behalf. But I believe that he also doesn't make any effort on his wife's behalf. In some way, not even on his own behalf. He has cut everything off, sawed it off, like a furious child who is hacking off flowers—only so that he'll be able to work again. Don't you also often find that that's a common occurrence: women love and men are busy? I believe that was what I didn't want. I've seen with my own husband that it's possible to unite love and work.''

And what does she think of her—well, is it her rival?

"Now you're going to laugh again . . . While doing my daily chores, cooking, ectetera, when one always has so much time to think of something else at the same time, I often thought of her—thought about her perhaps doing the same thing at the same time. Crazy, isn't it? I believe that she loves him a lot. It's absolutely certain that she has to give up much of him—he's just always so 'busy.' Moreover, he also loves her— I've seen that—in a way that is at the same time distracted and according to the letter of the law. And if I thought that she had to be able to do what I had earned for myself with such difficulty—to grant someone what one cannot have oneself, but which is somehow due to that person—then that was probably inappropriate."

This unusual story remained in my thoughts for a long time. Somewhat reluctantly, I thought, What does this woman really want? She is happy with her husband; she has children who have turned out well; she has friends and a profession; she has something she is involved in that makes her feel good— what more does she want? Can't she be content?

And gradually it became clear to me: she wants everything! And at the same time I sensed that she was right in wanting this. In paradoxical terms, only because she refused to be content, can she be content with her life. Love always wants everything. Only someone who knows this about him- or herself, yet had to understand that it is simply impossible to have "everything," can also renounce—not only out of reason, but also out of love.

And the other woman? She also wants everything. She probably does not know this, but rather thinks, Of course, I only want this one thing, for my husband to let his past be past and for him not to meet this woman. *Beyond that* he can have everything . . . (To be sure, it is also a certainty that he can have no other women.)

And now the basic problem of jealousy is again in evidence: two individuals who want everything—that does not work. "You should love your neighbor as yourself"—this does not work either. For it remains a paradoxical concept. However, precisely in its paradoxicalness it is the most productive directive of how to deal with other individuals, the "neighbor," that I know.

When I called this client five years after our conversations, she had just celebrated her sixtieth birthday and said that no, she had no desire to have another conversation. If I really thought it was important, I myself could construct what she would say. "Getting everything down" had been very helpful to her at the time, and later she had come upon a letter of Goethe's mother to Bettina Brentano that expresses, in all modesty, what she had felt at the time.

I looked up this letter, and it reads as follows: the young Bettina Brentano had lost a friend, Caroline von Günderrode, to suicide. Thereupon, Goethe's mother had advised her, "My son said one must work through whatever is oppressing one, and if he suffered something, then he made a poem out of it . . . . In this way, one should bury great and rare events in a beautiful coffin of remembrance, before which everyone can pass and celebrate their memory'' (Arnim 1835, 37).

What again pleased me about this strange woman was the courage with which she held to her feelings. The "poem" to his mother in which her famous son had disposed of suffering was none other than *The Sufferings of Young Werther*. Nevertheless, when she gave this advice to Bettina, Bettina was not the great romantic author who has once again become fashionable, but simply an unhappy young girl.

I showed the client what I had written down for her. She changed some things, laughed again a bit, and said, "Well—that's *one* truth. But it *is* one, and it can stand. And now you surely want to know how it went on? But I'm not going to tell you that . . ."

FINALE:

THE SOLUTION OF THE GODS

The last example suggests that laughter—humor—can be a solution to jealousy, to be sure not *before*, but only after, the experience of pain. Laughter presupposes a certain degree of freedom, which is too excessive a demand to place on many jealous individuals. However, in some catamneses, couples were able to poke some fun at each other, to bring each other down a notch, or to warn the other jokingly against feeling all too secure—it's never too late for sweet revenge.

Even if it is not the couple's mutual laughter, laughing plays an important role in the story with which I would like to conclude this book. It is described in the *Odyssey* and once again summarizes, in terms of the elevated humanity of the Olympian family of the gods, much of what I was concerned with in this book. Contrary to the many serious and tragic examples from literature that were presented, the story told to Odysseus during his stay among the Phaeacians is narrated as a festive entertainment. Even better, it is sung to him, a kind of satyr play. I must summarize it here, although I would prefer to reproduce it in its totality. However, I advise everyone to read it for him- or herself (*Odyssey* 8.266–366).

The love goddess, Aphrodite, deceives her spouse Hephaestus, the god of fire, with his brother Ares, the god of war. One reads of "the many gifts Ares made her," and the adultery takes place in the marital house and bed. The sun, however, brings it to light: Helios, the god of the sun, informs Hephaestus. "When he heard the galling truth," Hephaestus goes to his workshop "with his heart full of evil thoughts." He, the one who is lame but extremely skillful, forges invisible chains "that could neither be broken nor undone" and throws this netting of chains around his own bed. He then makes a pretense of leaving.

Ares "had not kept watch for nothing." He runs to Aphrodite, she who is always ready, parenthetically puts Hephaestus down a bit—he is with the Sintians in Lemnos to listen to their barbarous talk, and, as is well known, he really likes being there—and takes his beloved to bed. "Whereupon the netting which Hephaestus's ingenuity had contrived fell around them," and they are held immobile in their position. To later artists, this was a welcome occasion to depict divine intercourse.

Informed by Helios, Hephaestus naturally hurries home and now has clear cause for his "spasm of rage." "He raised his voice in a terrible shout" and summons all the other gods to his side.

"Come here and you other happy gods who live for ever, come here and see a comic and cruel thing," and he once again tells about what of course cannot be overlooked: that his brother is deceiving him with his wife, while he "was born a cripple. And whom have I to blame for that, if not my father and my mother," Zeus and Hera, who should "never have begotten me." Now, however, since it has indeed come to pass, he wants to leave them both lying there, bound, until Zeus, who is also Aphrodite's father, has given back to him all the gifts he "made him to win this brazen-faced hussy."

Thus the gods enter Hephaestus's house, while the goddesses are "constrained by feminine modesty" and stay at home. In the face of the tableau vivant that confronts them, something unexpected happens: the gods are seized by "a fit of uncontrollable laughter." They begin to talk and negotiate. First, the reader is confronted by the satisfied statement, "Bad deeds don't prosper; the tortoise catches up the hare." Then there is speculation: how would one feel if one were oneself in this position? Asked this by Apollo, Hermes says, "Though the chains that kept me prisoner were three times as many, though all you gods and all the goddesses were looking on, yet would I gladly sleep by golden Aphrodite's side." The gods laugh once again.

Only Poseidon, the god of the sea and "earthshaker," does not laugh with them but offers himself as surety for Ares. Hephaestus does not immediately agree to this, and uses the opportunity to put his rival down once again.

"Even a surety for a scoundrel is a poor thing to hold in hand." And if Ares were really to get away and not pay, then it would be highly inappropriate for him to arrest an innocent god instead of Ares. However, Poseidon promises—and in doing so corrects Hephaestus's more limited conception of surety—that he will himself pay the fine should Ares repudiate the debt. Now Hephaestus finds that it would be unfair ("unjust") to reject the proposal. He undoes the chains.

Immediately the two sinners leap up and flee to far distant places: Ares to Thrace, but "laughter-loving" Aphrodite to Cyprus, her sacred precinct where she, the goddess born of foam, touched earth for the first time. There she is anointed with the imperishable oil by the Graces. The gods are recognized by the odor of this oil. And "when they had decked her out in her lovely clothes she was a marvel to behold."

Once again a triangle, formed out of the family of the "frivolous, pleasure-seeking gods." These are the words that Wagner uses much later in reference to totally different gods who, to be sure, are unimaginable without the ancestry of the Greek gods (Alberich in *Siegfried,* act 2, scene 1). No one behaves nobly here or in a manner that is divine in the sense of a higher morality. And it is just as difficult to deal nobly with jealousy. However, everything that happens is indicative of jealousy in a patriarchal society.

In the first place, the adultery is only understood as a wound to the husband. He is the acting subject who defends himself. We learn nothing of how the two adulterers feel, except that they are intensely drawn to each other and that Ares won Aphrodite with gifts, that is, almost bought her. It is presumed of Aphrodite, the great goddess of love, that she is always ready and has incomparable love pleasures to dispense. In accordance with the principle that "birds of a feather flock together," Ares is much more suitable for her than her spouse, Hephaestus. But he needs her more urgently than the beautiful Ares, for individuals who are malformed (handicapped, impotent, old, or alcoholics) are especially anxiety-ridden and sensitive to the wound of infidelity. The earliest researchers into jealousy understood this. They require more urgently than others the partner's love and confirmation, as well as the esteem of their peers, for the revalorization of their own inadequacy. A firm and dependable bond to a beautiful person provides this.

Since Hephaestus is a god, he can provide himself with all forms of gratification. Other jealous individuals can literally only dream of these things for which they unconsciously long, and try to provide for themselves with psychic ruses. Initially the voyeuristic component is predominant. What Freud called the primal scene is held fast by the invisible chains, so that not only the wounded one may view it but, moreover, the spectators *must* view it. Hephaestus is not only not able to "get his fill of the sight," and here one can most certainly also presume gratification of oral greed, but at the same time he seizes the opportunity to blame his real parents, Zeus and Hera, for having begotten him as such a cripple.

The oedipal dilemma is especially clear in a crippled child of the father of the gods, who possesses the eternally young and eternally beautiful mistress of Olympus, all the more so, of course, because one may not conceive of age differences among the gods. Hephaestus also has a unique (pre-oedipal) relationship to Hera: in Homer he stands as the son of both parents, but there are also reports that Hera conceived him alone, perhaps out of her thigh. In any case, a gloomy destiny is linked to his birth. If he is the creation of Zeus and Hera, he was, so to speak, born illegitimately, during the three hundred years in which the divine siblings only met secretly, without the knowledge of their parents (Kerényi 1951, 1:124). And he is an abortion of nature: his feet are turned backwards, fit only for a rolling movement of his whole body. At his birth, Hera was so upset at his ugliness that she flung him from heaven to earth.

Therefore, Hephaestus is a dyadically injured person. He is the unloved child of a mother who was narcissistically wounded by his ugliness. If a person is not beautiful, the person can compensate for this lack in various ways. Hephaestus does this in three ways: he is *capable*—for nine years he trains to be a skilled blacksmith and therefore is later highly esteemed by all the gods. Thus he becomes the one "skilled with his hands," even though he cannot walk properly. Second, he is *clever and cunning,* as is parenthetically stressed again and again, in our story too: the lame one has taken in Ares, who is "the swiftest of the gods who reside on Olympus." And third, he causes those around him to *laugh*.

The immortals have no sympathy for him, although he vehemently appeals to it. However, his exhibitionistic need in the jealouy scene is powerful. For eleven thundering verses, he speaks about the injury done him. However, what he finally demands is not sympathy, but justice: he wants back what he paid for his bride—money, if he cannot have any love. From this perspective, one must think of him as very resigned, for he has not won Aphrodite with love, but purchased her—and, indeed, at the price set by the mother.

Yet another story mirrors the wound inflicted upon him by the first woman in his life, Hera, and at the same time his ability to provide himself at least with power, which reaps him gratitude, since the affection he desires for himself, "because it is you," is denied him.

When the gods moved to Olympus, Hephaestus forged the thrones for the lofty couple. Hera happily sat down on hers and found herself not only chained, but even lifted up into the air. Her son had thought up this trick, because he continued to be angry with her. He himself had not yet been admitted to the seat of the gods, and refused to come. To the request that he help his mother, who was suspended between heaven and earth, he defiantly responded that he had no mother.

Various attempts to pull him onto Olympus fail. The one who has come off badly here exploits his power with pleasure, and even defeats his brother Ares, who tries to force the liberation of his mother by a fight.

She is saved as a result of orality: Dionysius gives Hephaestus wine to drink, of whose effect the god of fire is unaware. Dionysius then loads him onto a mule and leads him, in a caricature of a triumphal march, onto Olympus. The gods again laugh at Hephaestus. But at the height of his drunkenness, his mind remains unclouded enough to bargain for a price to liberate his mother. He demands marriage with Aphrodite, the most beautiful of all, and nothing is left but for the gods to agree to this, if their mother and queen is not to remain hanging in the air, bound for eternity. According to other sources, the spouse he demands is Pallas Athena, whom Hephaestus also marries, or at least tried to marry. To marry this notoriously virginal goddess was naturally difficult (Kerényi 1951, 1:98).

In any case, Hephaestus is unlucky in love. We modern readers of Winnicott, Kohut, and Alice Miller are able to say why, if he has not learned the way with a "good enough mother." The equation wife equals mother, as it applies to the invisible bonds, is obvious. We are also able to imagine the shape taken by the jealous individual's own participation in adultery. It is hard to think of Hephaestus as a tender lover. He can be thought of as sensitive, demanding, and greedy. It might be imagined that even an Aphrodite could not come to love this in return.

Finally, his need for revenge is satisfied. Both parties who insulted him have been made to look ridiculous, before heaven and the world. Financial compensation has been promised him. Homer is then no longer interested in whether he receives it. Hephaestus undoes the chains.

What now becomes of the adulterers? Ares flees to Thrace; not very important—a common saying among many peoples is that "a man does what he has to do," and what he "has to do" is what, in the end, he is allowed to do. A more ritual absolution is required for Aphrodite. She must first be washed and made pure and beautiful again. On Cyprus she is treated similarly to how she was treated when she first touched earth. Concurrently, she experiences a second birth. She, who came naked out of the sea and probably lay naked with Ares under the chains, is "dressed, crowned with a garland, and adorned" (Kerényi 1951, 1:58). Only then is she again truly acceptable to the gods, who of course are also the protectors of law and morality. We do not learn what she does next. Aphrodite's love stories are countless and endless.

And Hephaestus is also immortal—his story is not that of a person with only one life and who therefore must again and again make a decision that is unique and irrevocable, totally unlike the "holy gods."

The beautiful Harmonia, whose spouse is Cadmos, was born of the union between Ares and Aphrodite. Harmonia and Cadmos are the first couple who can be traced as part of Oedipus's ancestry. Yet other children of Ares and Aphrodite are Phobus and Deimos, "fear" and "terror," but also Eros and Anteros, "love" and "mutual love."

What can the modern reader get out of these old stories? Enjoyment, like the gods; something to consider and wonder at, like the many who have read and heard these stories before; perhaps self-knowledge, because the person rediscovers him- or herself at one point of the divine triangle. However, the solution of the gods primarily shows us that *we* are not gods. We have less power and less freedom, and it is precisely that which is the requisite for humanness.

WORKS CITED

Adler, Alfred. 1956. "The Individual Psychology of Alfred Adler: A Systematic Presentation." In *Selections of His Writings,* edited by Heinz L. Ansbacher and Rowena R. Ansbacher. New York: Basic Books.

Andreas Capellanus. 1972. *Regii francorum de amore libre tres.* Edited by E. Trojel. Copenhagen: Gad, 1892. Reprint. Munich: Fink.

Ariès, Philippe, André Béjin, and Michel Foucault, eds. 1982. *Sexualités occidentales.* Paris. Translated by Anthony Forster, under the title *Western Sexuality: Practice and Precept in Past and Present Times.* Oxford: Blackwell, 1985.

Ariosto, Ludovico. 1962. *Orlando furioso.* Edited by Carlo Muscetta and Luca Lamberti. Turin: Einaudi.

Arnim, Bettina von. 1835. *Goethes Briefwechsel mit einem Kinde: Seinem Denkmal.* Edited by Herman Grimm. Berlin: W. Hertz.

Bachofen, Johann Jakob. [1861] 1980. *Das Mutterrecht.* 3d ed. Selections edited by Hans-Júrgen Heinrichs. Frankfurt: Suhrkamp. Translated by Ralph Manheim, under the title *Myth, Religion and Mother Rights: Selected Writings of J. J. Bachofen.* Princeton: Princeton University Press, 1967.

Badinter, Elisabeth. 1980. *L'amour en plus.* Paris: Flammarion. Translated by Roger DeGaris, under the title *Mother Love: Myth and Reality.* New York: Macmillan, 1981.

Balint, Alice. [1939] 1965. "Liebe zur Mutter und Mutterliebe." In *Die Urformen der Liebe und die Technik der Psychoanalyse.* Stuttgart: Klett (translated by Käte Hügel and Martha Spengler under the title *Primary Love and Psycho-analytic Technique* London: Hogarth Press, 1963). Originally published in *Internationale Zeitschrift für Psychoanalyse* 24 (1939).

Balint, Michael, et al. 1972. *Focal Psychotherapy.* London: Tavistock Publications.

Barag, Gerda. 1949. "A Case of Pathological Jealousy." *Psychoanalytic Quarterly* 18: 1–18.

Bateson, Jackson; Haley, Lynn; et al. 1969. *Schizophrenie und Familie: Beiträge zu einer neuen Theorie.* Frankfurt.

Bauriedl, Thea. 1980. *Beziehungsanalyse: Das dialektisch-emanzipatorische Prinzip der Psychoanalyse und seine Konsequenzen für die psychoanalytische Familientherapie.* Frankfurt: Suhrkamp.

————. 1984. "Geht das revolutionäre Potential der Psychoanalyse verloren? Zur politischen Bedeutung der Psychoanalyse und zum politischen Engagement der Psychoanalytiker." *Psyche*, 38: 489–515.

Beauvoir, Simone de. 1949. *Le deuzième sexe* (The second sex). Paris: Gallimard.

Bergler, Edmund. 1935. "Stendhal: Ein Beitrag zur Psychologie des narzißtischen Voyeurs." In *Talleyrand, Napoleon, Stendhal, Grabbe*, by Bergler. Vienna: Internationaler Psychoanalytischer Verlag.

————. 1939. "Beiträge zur Psychologie der Eifersucht." *Zeitschrift für Psychoanalyse und Imago* 24: 384–97.

Die Bibel: Einheitsübersetzung. 1980. Freiburg, Basel, Wien: Herder.

Blanck, Gertrude and Rubin. 1968. *Marriage and Personal Development.* New York: Columbia University Press.

————. 1974. *Ego-Psychology: Theory and Practice.* New York: Columbia University Press.

Boccaccio, Giovanni di. [1348] 1981. *Decamerone.* Frankfurt: Insel.

Boiardo, Matteo Maria. 1963. 2d ed. *Orlando innamorato.* Edited by Aldo Scaglione. Turin: Unione tipografico editrice torinese.

Boszormenyi-Nagy, Ivan, and Geraldine M. Spark. 1973. *Invisible Loyalties.* New York: Harper Row.

Bowen, Murray. 1960. "A Family Concept of Schizophrenia." In *Schizophrenia and the Family. See* Bateson et al. 1969.

Buunk, Bram. 1982. "Strategies of Jealousy: Styles of Coping with Extramarital Involvement of the Spouse." *Family Relations* 31: 13–18.

Calderón de la Barca, Pedro. [1637] 1951. *El mayor mostruo del mundo* (The world's greatest monster). In *Obras completas*, vol. 1, edited by Luis Astrana Mari. Madrid: M. Aquilar.

Chasseguet-Smirgel, Janine. ed. 1974. *Les chemins de l'Anti-Oedipe.* Toulouse: Privat.

Christlieb, Wolfgang. 1979. *Der entzauberte Ödipus: Ursprünge und Wandlungen eines Mythos.* Munich: Nymphenburger Verlagshandlung.

Davis, Kingsley. 1936. "Jealousy and Sexual Property." *Sexual Forces* 14: 195–405.

Dross, Annemarie. 1978. *Die erste Walpurgisnacht: Hexenverfolgung in Deutschland.* Frankfurt: Verlag Roter Stern.

Duden, Barbara. 1977. "Das schöne Eigentum." *Kursbuch* 47 (March): 125–40.

Eisenbud, Ruth-Jean. 1967. "Masochism Revisited." *Psychoanalytic Review* 54: 562–82.

Eissler, Kurt R. 1963. *Goethe: A Psychoanalytic Study, 1775–1786.* 2 volumes. Detroit: Wayne State University Press.

Elias, Norbert. 1976. *Über den Prozeß der Zivilisation: Soziogenetische und psychogenetische Untersuchungen.* 2 volumes. Frankfurt: Suhrkamp.

Fenichel, Otto. 1945. *The Psychoanalytic Theory of Neurosis.* New York: Norton.

Freud, Sigmund. 1946–52. *Gesammelte Werke, chronologisch geordnet.* 17 volumes. Edited by Anna Freud et al. London: Imago Publishing Co. The volume numbers in the following Freud works refer to this edition.

_____. 1896a. *Studien über Hysterie*. Vol. 1.

_____. 1896b. *Zur Ätiologie der Hysterie*. Vol. 1.

_____. 1905a. *Drei Abhandlungen zur Sexualtheorie*. Vol. 5.

_____. 1905b. *Der Witz und seine Beziehung zur Unbewußten*. Vol. 5.

_____. 1910. *Beiträge zur Psychologie des Liebeslebens*. Vol. 8.

_____. 1913. *Totem und Tabu*. Vol. 9.

_____. 1914a. *Erinnern, Wiederholen, Durcharbeiten*. Vol. 10.

_____. 1914b. *Zur Geschichte der psychoanalytischen Bewegung*. Vol. 10.

_____. 1917. *Vorlesungen zur Einführung in die Psychoanalyse*. Vol. 11. '

_____. 1919. *Ein Kind wird geschlagen*. Vol. 12.

_____. 1922. "Über einige neurotische Mechanismen bei Eifersucht, Paranoia und Homosexualität." Vol. 13.

_____. 1923a. "Psychoanalyse" und "Libidotheorie." Vol. 13.

_____. 1923b. *Das Ich und das Es*. Vol. 13.

_____. 1926. *Zur Frage der Laienanalyse*. Vol. 14.

_____. 1927. *Die Zukunft einer Illusion*. Vol. 14.

_____. 1931. *Über die weibliche Sexualität*. Vol. 14.

_____. 1933. *Neue Folge der Vorlesungen zur Einführung in die Psychoanalyse*. Vol. 15.

Friedmann, M. 1911. *Über die Psychologie der Eifersucht*. Grenzfragen des Nerven- und Seelenlebens 82. Wiesbaden: J. F. Bergmann.

Friedrich, Hugo. 1949. *Montaigne*. Bern: A. Francke.

_____. 1964. *Epochen der italienischen Lyrik*. Frankfurt: V. Klostermann.

Gambaroff, Marina. *See* Moeller-Gambaroff, Marina.

Gausbeck, Hermann. 1928. "Über Eifersuchtswahn." *Archiv für Psychiatrie und Nervenkrankheiten* 84: 414–89.

Germano, Giuseppe. 1960. "Rilievi clinici e psicopatogenetici sul delirio di gelosia nella popolazione degli ospedali psichiatrici di Firenze." *Rassegna die Studi Psichiatrici* 49: 1–44.

Gesell, Arnold L. 1906. "Jealousy." *American Journal of Psychology* 17 (October): 437–96.

Goethe, Johann Wolfgang von. 1948. *Gesammelte Werke*. Edited by Erich Trunz et al. 15 vols. Hamburg: Wegner. The volume numbers in the following Goethe works refer to this edition.

_____. *Wahlverwandtschaftschaften* (Elective affinities). Vol. 6.

_____. *Maximen und Reflexionen* (Maxims and reflections). Vol. 12.

Grimm, Jacob and Wilhelm. 1854–1971. *Deutsches Wörterbuch*. Leipzig: Hirzel.

Grunberger, Bela. 1979. *Narcissism: Psychoanalytic Essays*. Translated by Joyce S. Diamanti. New York: International Universities Press. Originally published as *Le narcissisme: Essais de psychanalyse* (Paris: Payot 1971).

Gründel, Johannes. 1977. "Die eindimensionale Wertung der menschlichen Sexualität." In *Menschliche Sexualität und kirchliche Sexualmoral*, edited by Franz Böckle. Schriften der Katholischen Akademie in Bayern 77. Düsseldorf: Patmos.

Grzywacz, Margot. 1937. *"Eifersucht" in den romanischen Sprachen*. Arbeiten zur romanischen Philologie 42. Bochum: H. Pöppinghaus.

Guardini, Romano. 1949. *Der Herr*. Würzburg: Werkbund.

Henseler, Heinz. 1974. *Narzisstische Krisen: Zur Psychodynamik des Selbstmords.* rororo studium 58. Reinbek, West Germany: Rowohlt.

Hoffman, Lynn. 1981. *Foundations of Family Therapy: A Conceptual Framework for Systems Change.* New York: Basic Books.

Hoffmann-Axthelm, Inge. 1973. *"Geisterfamilie": Studien zur Geselligkeit der Frühromantik.* Frankfurt: Akademische Verlagsgesellschaft.

Homer. *The Odyssey.* 1946. Translated by E. V. Rieu. Harmondsworth, England: Penguin Books.

———. *The Iliad.* 1960. Translated by Samuel Butler, edited by Harry Shefter. New York: Pocket Books.

Im, Won-gi, Stefanie R. Wilner, Miranda Breit. 1983. "Jealousy: Interventions in Couples Therapy." *Family Process* 22: 211–18.

Jaspers, Karl. [1910] 1963. "Eifersuchtswahn." In *Gesammelte Schriften zur Psychopathologie.* Berlin: Springer. Originally in *Zeitschrift für die gesamte Neurologie und Psychologie.*

Joffe, Walter G. 1969. "A Critical Review of the Status of the Envy Concept." *International Journal of Psychoanalysis* 50: 533–45.

Johnson, Uwe. 1982. *Skizze eines Verunglückten* (Sketch of an ill-fated individual). Frankfurt: Suhrkamp.

Jones, Ernest. 1930. "Die Eifersucht." *Die psychoanalytische Bewegung* 2: 154–67.

———. 1953–57. *The Life and Work of Sigmund Freud.* 3 volumes. New York: Basic Books.

Jung, Carl Gustav. 1981. *Erinnerungen, Träume, Gedanken: Aufgezeichnet von Aniele Jaffe.* 11th edition. Olten and Freiburg: Walter. Translated by Richard and Clara Winston under the title *Memories, Dreams, Reflections: Recorded and Edited by Aniela Jeffe.* New York: Pantheon, 1963.

Kerényi, Karl. [1951] 1981. *Die Mythologie der Griechen,* 5th edition. 2 volumes. Munich: Deutscher Taschenbuch Verlag.

Kernberg, Otto F. 1976. *Object-Relations Theory and Clinical Psychoanalysis.* New York: J. Aronson.

Kinsey, Alfred C. et al. 1953. *Sexual Behavior in the Human Female.* Philadelphia: Saunders.

———. 1948. *Sexual Behavior in the Human Male.* Philadelphia: Saunders.

Klein, Melanie. 1975. *Envy and Gratitude and Other Works: 1946–1963.* London: Hogarth Press.

Klessmann, Eckart. 1975. *Caroline: Das Leben der Caroline Michaelis-Böhmer-Schlegel-Schelling: 1763–1809.* Munich: List.

Koenigsberg, Richard R. 1967. "Culture and Unconscious Fantasy: Observations on Courtly Love." *Psychoanalytic Review* 54: 36–50.

Kohut, Heinz. 1971. *The Analysis of the Self: A Systematic Approach to the Psychoanalytic Treatment of Narcissistic Personality Disorders.* New York: International Universities Press.

———. 1977. *The Restoration of the Self.* New York: International Universities Press.

Körner, Heinz, ed. 1979. *Eifersucht: Ein Lesebuch für Erwachsene.* Fellbach, West Germany: Amp-Verlag.

Kremers, Dieter. 1973. *Der "rasende Roland" des Ludovico Ariosto*. Heidelberg: Kohlhammer.

Kutter, Peter. 1977. *Psychiatrie: Eine Einführung*. Munich: Kindler Taschenbuch.

La Fayette, Comtesse Marie Madeleine de. [1678] 1950. *La princesse de Clèves*. Paris. Geneve: E. Droz.

Lagache, Daniel. [1947] 1982. La jalousie amoureuse: Psychologie descriptive et psychanalyse. Paris: Presses Universitaires de France.

Langfeldt, Gabriel. 1961. "The Erotic Jealousy Syndrome." *Acta Psychiatrica et Neurologica Scandinavice*, supplement 151, vol. 36.

Laplanche, Jean, and Jean-Baptiste Pontalis. 1974. *The Language of Psychoanalysis*. Translated by Donald Nicholson-Smith. New York: Norton. Originally published as *Vocabulaire de la psychanalyse* (Paris: Presses universitaires de France 1967).

La Rochefoucauld. 1967. *Oeuvres complètes*. Paris: Bibliotheque de la Pleiade.

Larson, Donald R. 1977. *The Honor Plays of Lope de Vega*. Cambridge: Harvard University Press.

Lasch, Christopher. 1979. *The Culture of Narcissism: American Life in an Age of Diminishing Expectations*. New York: Norton.

Lehmann, Hans-Thies. 1982. "Filme lesen." *Merkur* 411 (September): 931–84. Review of *Die Frau des Fliegers*, directed by Eric Rohmer.

Llopis, Bartolomé. 1962. "Die Eifersuchtsideen der Trinker." *Fortschritte der Neurologie* 30: 543–64.

Luhmann, Niklas. 1982. *Liebe als Passion: Zur Codierung von Intimität*. Frankfurt: Suhrkamp. Translated by Jeremy Gaines and Doris L. Jones, under the title *Love as Passion: The Codification of Intimacy*. Cambridge: Harvard University Press, 1986.

McGinnis, Thomas C. 1981. *More Than Just a Friend*. Englewood Cliffs, N.J.: GLP International.

Mack-Brunswick, Ruth. 1928. "Die Analyse eines Eifersuchtswahnes." *Internationale Zeitschrift für Psychoanalyse* 14: 458–507.

Mahler, Margaret S. 1968. *On Human Symbiosis and the Vicissitudes of Individuation*. Volume 1, *Infantile Psychosis*. New York: International Universities Press.

Malcolm, Janet. 1981. *Psychoanalysis: The Impossible Profession*. New York: Knopf.

Marcuse, Max. 1950. "Zur Psychologie der Eifersucht und der Psychopathologie ihres Fehlens." *Psyche* 3: 759–77.

Miller, Alice. 1981. *Prisoners of Childhood*. Translated by Ruth Ward. New York: Basic Books. Originally published as *Das Drama des begabten Kindes und die Suche nach dem wahren Selbst* (Frankfurt: Suhrkamp, 1979).

———. 1984. *Thou Shalt Not Be Aware: Society's Betrayal of the Child*. Translated by Hildegarde and Hunter Hannum. New York: Farrar, Straus, Giroux. Originally published as *Du sollst nicht merken: Variationen über das Paradiesthema* (Frankfurt: Suhrkamp, 1981).

Mitchell, Juliet. 1974. *Psychoanalysis and Feminism*. New York: Pantheon Books.

Mitscherlich, Alexander. 1969. *Society without the Father: A Contribution to Social Psychology*. Translated by Eric Mosbacher. New York: Harcourt, Brace and World. Originally published as *Auf dem Weg zur vaterlosen Gesellschaft: Ideen zur Sozialpsychologie* (Munich: Piper, 1963).

Mitscherlich-Nielsen, Margarete. 1982. "Zur Identität der weiblichen und männlichen Psychoanalytiker." *Psyche* 3:267–76.

Moeller-Gambaroff, Marina. 1984. "Emanzipation macht Angst" and "Utopie der Treue." In *Utopie der Treue,* by Gambaroff. Reinbek, West Germany: Rowohlt. Originally in *Kursbuch* 47 (March 1977): 1–25, and (May 1978): 24–36.

Moltmann, Jürgen. 1979. "Theologie heute." In *Stichworte zur geistigen Situation der Zeit,* vol. 2, edited by Jürgen Habermas. Frankfurt: Suhrkamp.

Montaigne, Michel Eyquem de. 1962. *Oeuvres complètes*. Paris: Bibliotheque de la Pleiade.

Neumann, Erich. 1952. *Zur Psychologie des Weiblichen*. Munich: Kindler Taschenbuch.

Das Nibelungenlied (Song of the Nibelung). 1973. Edited by Ulrich Pretzel. Stuttgart: S. Hirzel.

Ovid. 1977. *Ars Amatoria* (Art of Love). Edited by A. S. Hollis. Oxford: Clarendon.

Pao, Ping-nie. 1969. "Pathological Jealousy." *Psychoanalytic Quarterly* 38: 616–38.

Pfandl, Ludwig. 1924. *Spanische Kultur und Sitte des spanischen 16. und 17. Jahrhunderts*. Munich: J. Kösel and F. Pustet.

Pohlen, Manfred, and Tomas Plänkers. 1982. "Familientherapie: Von der Psychoanalyse zur psychosozialen Aktion." *Psyche* 36, no. 5: 416–52. Response by Helm Stierlin. *Psyche* 37, no. 1 (1983): 73–75. Commentary by Wolfram Lüders. *Psyche* 37, no. 5 (1983): 462–69.

Portmann, Heinrich. 1952. *Der zerbrochene Ring: Aus dem Tagebuch eines Ehegerichts*. Kevelaer.

Preuss, Hans G. 1971. *Illusion und Wirklichkeit: An den Grenzen von Religion und Psychoanalyse*. Stuttgart: Klett-Verlag.

———. 1973. *Ehepaartherapie: Beitrag zu einer psychoanalytischen Paartherapie in der Gruppe*. Munich: Kindler.

Reik, Theodor. 1940. *Aus Leiden Freuden*. London: Imago. Translated by Margaret Beigel and Gertrud Kurth, under the title *Masochism in Modern Man*. Expanded edition. New York: Farrar and Rinehart, 1941.

Renaud, Bernard. 1963. *Je suis un dieu jaloux*. Paris.

Richter, Horst-Eberhard. 1963. *Eltern, Kind, und Neurose: Psychoanalyse der kindlichen Rolle*. Stuttgart: Klett.

———. 1974. *Lernziel Solidarität*. Reinbek, West Germany: Rowohlt.

Riviere, Joan. 1932. "Jealousy as a Mechanism of Defense." *International Journal of Psychoanalysis* 13. Reprinted in *Zeitschrift für Psychoanalyse* 22 (1936); 177–87, with an addendum by Riviere, 188–97.

Roth, Klaus. 1977. *Ehebruchschwänke in Liedform*. Munich: Fink.

Rusconi, Maria. 1982. "E tu, che specie di amante sei?" *Espresso,* July 25.

Schadewaldt, Wolfgang, trans. 1975. *Ilias,* by Homer. Frankfurt: Insel.

Schafer, Roy. 1976. *A New Language for Psychoanalysis.* New Haven: Yale University Press.

Schatzman, Morton, 1973. *Soul Murder: Persecution in the Family.* New York: Random House.

Schlegel, Caroline. [1871] 1970. *Briefe aus der Frühromantik.* 2 volumes. Edited by G. Waitz; newly edited by Erich Schmidt. Bern: Herbert Lang.

Schlegel, Friedrich. [1799] 1964. *Lucinde.* Frankfurt: Insel.

Schleiermacher, Friedrich. [1800] 1964. *Vertraute Briefe über Schlegels "Lucinde."* Frankfurt: Insel.

Schleiermacher, Friedrich. 1919. *Friedrich Schleiermachers Briefwechsel mit seiner Braut.* Edited by Heinrich Meisner. Gotha, East Germany: F. A. Perthes.

Schmideberg, Melitta. 1953. "Some Aspects of Jealousy and Feeling Hurt." *Psychoanalytic Review* 40: 1–16.

Schülein, Johann August. 1976. *Psychotechnik als Politik: Zur Kritik der pragmatischen Kommunikationtheorie von Watzlawick et al.* Frankfurt: Syndikat.

Searles, H. F. 1959. "The Effort to Drive the Other Person Crazy." *British Journal of Medical Psychology* 32:1–18. Reprinted in *Schizophrenia and the Family. See* Bateson et al. 1969.

Seidenberg, Robert. 1953. "Jealousy: The Wish:" *Psychoanalytic Review* 40: 345–53.

―――. 1967. "Fidelity and Jealousy." *Psychoanalytic Review* 54: 583–608.

Selvini Palazzoli, Mara, L. Boscolo, G. Cecchin, and G. Prata. 1975. *Paradosso e controparadosso.* Milan: Feltrinelli. Translated by Elisabeth V. Burt under the title *Paradox and Counterparadox.* New York: J. Aronson, 1978.

Shakespeare, William. 1968. *Othello.* In *The Works of Shakespeare,* vol. 10. Reprinted from the edition of 1767–68. New York: AMS Press.

Shepherd, Michael. 1961. "Morbid Jealousy: Some Clinical and Social Aspects of a Psychiatric Symptom." *Journal of Mental Science* 107: 687–753.

Simon, Fritz B. 1983. "Linearität und Puritanismus: Das Selbstverständinis des Therapeuten und die Verwirrung des Kausalitätsbegriffs." *Familiendynamik,* 309–11.

Spanische Erzähler. 1979. Edited by Albert Theile and Werner Peiser. Zurich: Manesse-Verlag.

Stekel, Wilhelm. 1931. *Die moderne Ehe.* Basel: Wendepunkt. Translated by Allen D. Gorman, under the title *Marriage at the Crossroads.* New York: W. Godwin. 1931.

Stendhal. [1822] 1926. *De l'amour.* Paris; H. et E. Champion.

―――. [1835] 1981. *Vie de Henri Brulard.* Translated by Alfred Schirmer, under the title *Leben des Henri Brulard.* Zurich: Diogenes.

Sterba, Richard. 1930. "Eifersüchtig auf . . . ?" *Psychoanalytische Bewegung* 2: 167–70.

Stierlin, Helm. 1971. *Das Tun des Einen ist das Tun des Anderen: Eine Dynamik menschlicher Beziehungen.* Frankfurt: Suhrkamp.

_____. 1975. *Von der Psychoanalyse zur Familientherapie: Theorie/Klinik.* Stuttgart: Klett-Cotta.

_____. 1978. *Delegation und Familie: Beiträge zum Heidelberger familiendynamischen Konzept.* Frankfurt: Suhrkamp.

Stoller, Robert J. 1975. *Perversion: The Erotic Form of Hatred.* New York: Pantheon Books.

_____. 1986. *Sexual Excitement: Dynamics of Erotic Life.* Washington, D.C.: American Psychiatric Press.

Teismann, Mark W. 1979. "Jealousy: Systematic, Problem-Solving Therapy with Couples." *Family Process* 18: 151–60.

Todd, John, and Kenneth Dewhurst. 1955. "The Othello Syndrome." *Journal of Nervous and Mental Diseases* 122: 367–74.

Tolstoy, Leo Nikolayevich. 1973. *Die Kreutzersonate.* Translated into German by Arthur Luther and Rudolf Kassner. Frankfurt: Insel.

Tolstoy, Sophia. 1982. *Tagebücher* (Diaries). Translated into German by Johanna Renate Döring-Smirnov and Rosemarie Tietze. Königstein: Athenäum.

Trilling, Lionel. 1971. *Sincerity and Authenticity.* Cambridge: Harvard University Press.

Unamuno, Miguel de. "Ein ganzer Mann" (A whole man). Translated into German by Otto Büeck. *See Spanische Erzähler* 1979.

Valle-Inclán, Ramón Maria del. [1920] 1974. *Divinas Palabras* (Divine words). Translated into German by Hildegard Baumgart. Frankfurt: Spectaculum.

Varnhagen, Rahel. 1967. *Briefwechsel mit August Varnhagen von Ense.* Edited by Friedhelm Kemp. Munich: Kösel.

Vaukhonen, Kauko. 1968. "On the Pathogenesis of Morbid Jealousy." *Acta Psychiatrica Scandinavica,* supp. 202.

Vega Carpio, Lope Félix de. 1979. *Eifersucht bis in den Tod* (Jealousy unto death). Translated into German by Eduard von Bülow. *See Spanische Erzähler* 1979.

Velikovsky, Immanuel. 1937. "Tolstoy's Kreutzer Sonata and Unconscious Homosexuality." *Psychoanalytic Review* 21: 18–35.

Veyne, Paul. 1982. "Homosexualität im alten Rom." In *Sexualités occidentales. See* Ariès, Beijin, and Foucault 1982.

Vilar, Esther. 1971. *Der dressierte Mann.* Gütersloh, West Germany: Bertelsmann-Sachbuchverlag. Translated by Eva Borneman, under the title *The Manipulated Man.* New York: Farrar, Straus, Giroux, 1972.

Wangh, Martin. 1950. "Othello: The Tragedy of Iago." *Psychoanalytic Quarterly* 19: 202–12.

_____. 1983. "Narzissmus in unserer Zeit." *Psyche* 37, no. 1, 16–40.

Watzlawick, Paul. 1983. *Anleitung zum Unglücklichsein* (Guide to Being Unhappy). Munich: Piper.

Watzlawick, Paul, Janet Beavin, and Don D. Jackson. 1967. *Pragmatics of Human Communication: A Study of Interactional Patterns, Pathologies, and Paradoxes.* New York: Norton.

Watzlawick, Paul, John H. Weakland, and Richard Fisch. 1974. *Change: Principles of Problem Formation and Problem Resolution.* New York: Norton.

Weber-Kellermann, Ingeborg. 1976. *Die Familie: Geschichte, Geschichten, und Bilder.* Frankfurt: Insel.

Wesel, Uwe. 1981. *Der Mythos vom Matriarchat: Über Bachofens Mutterrecht und die Stellung von Frauen in frühen Gesellschaften.* 2d edition. Frankfurt: Suhrkamp.

Wetzer und Weltes Kirchenlexikon. 1886–1901. 12 volumes. 2d edition. Freiburg: Herder.

Willi, Jürg. 1975. *Die Zweierbeziehung.* Reinbek, West Germany: Rowohlt. Translated by Walia Inayat-Khan and Mariasz Tchorek, under the title *Couples in Collusion.* New York: J. Aronson, 1982.

———. 1978. *Therapie der Zweierbeziehung.* Reinbek, West Germany: Rowohlt. Translated by Jan van Heurck, under the title *Dynamics of Couples Theory: The Uses of the Concept of Collusion and Its Application to the Therapeutic Triangle.* New York: J. Aronson, 1984.

Winnicott, D. W. 1984. *Deprivation and Delinquency.* Edited by Clare Winnicott, Ray Shepherd, and Madeleine Davis. London: Tavistock Publications.

Wirsching, Michael, and Helm Stierlin. 1982. *Krankheit und Familie: Konzepte, Forschungsergebnisse, Therapie.* Stuttgart: Klett-Cotta.

Wydler, Walter. 1957. *Treue und Untreue in der Ehe.* Zurich: Gotthelf-Verlag.

INDEX

Abraham, Karl, 203
Addiction, 28, 110, 182, 229
Adler, Alfred, 189, 193, 224
Adultery, 100, 103, 114, 120, 126, 138,
    277, 337; with one's own wife, 116, 176,
    213, 218
Adulthood, evolving into, 290, 306
Aggression, 193, 268, 295; toward the
    "beloved" object, 150, 160
Alcoholics, 194, 229
Ambivalence, 26, 106, 116, 150, 259
Amour-propre, 129
Andreas Capellanus, 107, 114–18, 129
Ariès, Philippe, 131, 137
Ariosto, Ludovico, 119–20
Arnim, Bettina von, 332
Augustine, Saint, 137, 179

Bachofen, Johann Jakob, 93, 221–22
Badinter, Elisabeth, 81
Balint, Alice, 219–20
Balint, Michael, 42, 45, 206, 244, 251
Barag, Gerda, 42, 45, 187–88
Barthes, Roland, vi
Bateson, Gregory, 225, 264
Bauriedl, Thea, 46, 224, 228, 249, 271, 302
Beauvoir, Simone de, 190
Beese, Henriette, 132
Bergler, Edmund, 169–70, 193–96, 205–9,
    212, 296, 310
Bernays, Martha, 99
Biangular relationship, 199–223, 338
Bisexuality, 110, 150, 158–59, 170, 183
Blanck, Gertrude, 233
Blanck, Rubin, 233
Bleuler, Eugen, 49
Boccaccio, Giovanni, 194–95

Boiardo, Matteo Maria, 119–20
Bonding, 114–41
Boszormenyi-Nagy, Ivan, 37, 46, 83, 225,
    226
Bowen, Murray, 83
Brant, Sebastian, 108
Brentano, Bettine, 332–33
Brion, Friederike, 173
Buff, Charlotte, 173
Buunk, Bram, 40, 193

Calderón de la Barca, Pedro, 124, 180–182
Castration anxiety, 179, 183, 187–89
Catamneses: author's, 1, 196–97, 257, 262;
    questionnaire, 261–62
Cercamon (Provençal troubadour), 109
Cervantes Saavedra, Miguel de, 112
Champagne, Marie de, Countess, 115, 116
Charcot, Jean Martin, 213
Chasseguet-Smirgel, Janine, 190
Child: disturbed, 230–32; and mother; 214–
    21
Children, 260–61; as coalition partners, 42
Christlieb, Wolfgang, 221
Church, 137; against jealousy, 137–41
Cinthio, Giovanni Battista Giraldo, 154
Circularity, 224–25, 239–40
Collusion (Willi), 235–39
Communications theory, 232–33, 249
Confession, 291
Conflicts, internal and external, 152
Conservatism, 234
Corneille, Pierre, 121
Counseling: center, 260, 278; conclusion of,
    259–60, 263–64; homosexuals in, 307,
    309; individual, 261; and psychiatry, 48,

Counseling *(continued)*
  259; and therapy, 278; and working
  through the past, 292–94
Countertransference, 237, 251, 308–9
Courtly love, 114–18
Crisis intervention, 263
Crying, 324–33
Cuckold, 109, 121

Davis, Kingsley, 38
Death wish, 57–58
Deutsch, Helene, 201
Dewhurst, Kenneth, 197, 229
Diderot, Denis, 179
Discretion, 2–3
Divorce, 86, 100, 134, 139, 260
Doppelgänger, 176
Dross, Annemarie, 138
Duden, Barbara, 68, 69
Dürer, Albrecht, 108
Dyads, 338

Ego, 207–9
Ego ideal, 83, 193, 207–9
Eisenbud, Ruth-Jean, 205
Eissler, Kurt R., 174
Elias, Norbert, 81
Emancipation, 16, 74, 218, 292
Emotions: history of, 79–81; power of, 90–
  91
Ethics, French, 128
Exhibitionism, 28, 206–7, 338
Exploitation, 270
Extramarital love, 115, 126

Family secret, 246
Family therapy, 224; in jealousy, 14
Fantasies, 277, 296, 305, 308
Fantasy and reality, 295–301
Fenichel, Otto, 226
Fichte, Johann Gottlieb, 68
Fidelity, 63, 64, 66, 136
Fisch, Richard, 233
Fliess, Wilhelm, 150
Focal therapy, 237
Fontane, Theodor, 121, 139
Frazer, James George, 92
Freedom, 114–41; compulsion to, 71–75;
  and love, 100–105
Freud, Anna, 248

Freud, Sigmund, 16, 26, 28, 39, 42, 44, 45,
  62, 80, 85, 86, 89, 92, 93, 99, 103, 117,
  120, 135, 147–54, 157–79, 183–85,
  190, 193, 199, 200, 202, 206, 207, 211,
  213, 215, 222, 223–25, 232, 247, 249,
  306, 307, 310, 311, 321, 337; his "cure,"
  153; his own jealousy, 149, 162
Friedmann, M., 45, 145–47
Friedrich, Hugo, 119, 128
Frisch, Max, 168
Fromm-Reichmann, Frieda, 226

Gagnon, Henriette, 169
Gambaroff, Marina, 66, 173, 305
Gausbeck, Hermann, 197
Gentz, Friedrich von, 306
Germano, Giuseppe, 145
Gesell, Arnold L., 145–46, 239–40
Giraudoux, Jean, 176
Gods: envy of the, 95, 97; Germanic, 107,
  122–23, 337; Greek, 90, 107, 337
Goethe, August von, 174
Goethe, Johann Wolfgang von, 17, 29, 34,
  51, 56, 62, 108, 132, 136, 173–75, 276
Goethe, Katharina Elisabeth ("Lady Aja"—
  Goethe's mother), 173, 332
Gorky, Maxim, 32
Grimm, Jacob and Wilhelm (the Brothers),
  107, 110
Grunberger, Bela, 202
Gründel, Johannes, 138
Grzywacz, Margot, 108–9, 111
Guardini, Romano, 101
Guilt, 170
Guilt feelings, 34, 39, 69, 103, 170, 179–
  82, 190–91
Guilty individual or multilateral
  entanglement, 224–53
Günderrode, Caroline von, 332

Haley, Jay, 232
Hampe, Roland, 221
Headaches, 226
Hebbel, Friedrich, 180, 182
Hegel, Georg Wilhelm Friedrich, 68
Henseler, Heinz, 196, 215, 230
Here and now, 81, 297
Heredity, 228–30
Hiking out (Watzlawick), 232–35
Hoffman, Lynn, 224, 225, 246

Homer, 94–99, 221–22, 335–39
Homosexuality, 42, 110, 147, 211, 247; fear
    of, 298, 306–15; between Iago and
    Othello, 161–67; Shakespeare's, 161, 194
Homosexual projections of infidelity, 161–63
Honor: quest for, 123–26; sense of, 114–41
Horney, Karen, 184, 201
Hosea, 89–90, 102
Hostile feelings, 158
Humor, 252, 335

Iago as psychoanalyst, 156
Im, Wong-Gi, 240–42, 245
Impotence and omnipotence, 214–21
Incest, 92, 93
Incongruent realities, guide through, 262–65
Incorporation, 203–5
Infidelity: projection of, 151, 159–63, 177;
    toward oneself, 135
Insanity, induced, 50, 155, 272–73
Intervention: paradoxical, 316; systemic,
    240–47

Jackson, Don D., 246–47
James, Henry, 324
Jaspers, Karl, 45, 47, 145, 147, 197
Jealous individual, 25–31; parental
    relationship of, 171, 172
Jealousy: Achilles', 97–98; acknowledging,
    266; ascending scale of (Lagache), 47–58;
    borderline, 44, 259; of children, 26, 54,
    57, 185, 257; concealed, 225–28; as a cry
    for help, 289; definitions of, 124
    (Calderón), 115 (Andreas Capellanus),
    128–29 (La Rochefoucauld), 136
    (Goethe); denial of, 45, 259, 271–73; as a
    desire, 176–79; diagnostic criteria for,
    46–49; education against, 146–47;
    elimination of, 66, 91, 262; etymology of,
    106–13; God's, 82–89, 102, 109; and
    guilt feeling, 179–82; Hera's, 94–96;
    history of the concept, 106–13;
    justification and normality of, 44–49; as it
    is lived, 25–67; and love, traditions of,
    114–41; in men and women, 26, 197–98;
    and murder, 84, 86; in the Nibelungenlied,
    121–22; as an opportunity, 263–64, 310,
    317, 321–22; of parents and children,
    257, 292; in the popular imagination,
    120–21; prerequisites for, 152, 160;
    preventive measures against, 56; as proof
    of love, 115; psychoanalytic concept of,
    12; psychoanalytic and psychological
    theories of, 145–253; in the quest for
    honor, 123–26; as the result of misplaced
    attempts at a solution, 233–35; as
    romantic, 134–36; of siblings, 231, 243;
    as a sign, 126–30, 279, 304; in Spain,
    123, 271; of the therapist, 9; uncovering
    of, 246–47; and voyeurism, 13; in
    women, 121–23
Jealousy psychosis (delusion, paranoia), 14,
    26, 35, 45, 48–49, 111, 119, 128, 145,
    151, 199, 230, 239, 243, 259, 271, 272,
    295
Jealousy sacrifice, 86–87
Jesus, 83, 100–105, 137, 151
Joffe, Walter G., 205
Johnson, Uwe, 57–60, 171–72
Jones, Ernest, 99, 179–82, 184, 197, 202,
    249
Jung, Carl, 156, 193, 224, 247
Justice, 323, 330, 338

Kant, Immanuel, 68
Karl August, duke of Saxony-Weimar, 174
Keller, Gottfried, 324
Kerényi, Karl, 92–94, 96, 99, 223, 338,
    339
Kernberg, Otto F., 202, 205, 206
Klein, Melanie, 184, 188, 201–4
Kleist, Heinrich von, 176
Klessmann, Eckart, 132
Koenigsberg, Richard R., 117
Kohut, Heinz, 202, 208, 339
Körner, Heinz, 66, 69
Kremers, Dieter, 118, 119
Kreutzer Sonata (Tolstoy), 209–13
Kurz, Hermann, 112
Kutter, Peter, 215, 203

La Boétie, Etienne de, 131
La Fayette, Marie Madeleine de (countess),
    127, 129
Lagache, Daniel, 26, 36, 40, 45, 47–49,
    59, 60, 145, 167, 195, 235
Lampl–de Groot, Jeanne, 201
Langfeldt, Gabriel, 228
Laplanche, Jean, 202, 203
La Rochefoucauld, 128–30, 207, 208, 214

Larson, Donald R., 125
Lasch, Christopher, 202
Laughing and crying, 324–33
Lehmann, Hans-Thies, 25
Lenin, Vladimir Ilyich, 3
Letting go and returning, 316–20
Levetzow, Ulrike von, 174
Levin, Rahel, 306
Linearity, 225, 239–40
Llopis, Bartolomé, 166, 194
Love, 81, 103, 114, 135, 259, 286, 323;
    ambivalence of, 150; being in, 32, 39,
    118, 304; codes of, 114–18, 126–27;
    extramarital, 115, 126; fear of loss of,
    189–93; and freedom, 100–105; as a
    frenzy, 118–20; and jealousy, traditions
    of, 114–41; in marriage, 114–18, 130–
    31; marriageability of, 134, 136; new,
    321–23; paradox of, 126–30; as reaction
    formation against hate, 117, 179–80;
    romantic, 131–34, 140–41; therapeutic,
    213
Loyalty conflict, 170
Luhmann, Niklas, 117, 128, 131, 133, 136
Luther, Martin, 82–84, 86, 103–5, 108,
    110, 137

McGinnis, Thomas C., 99
Mack-Brunswick, Ruth, 45, 197, 199–203,
    216
Mahler, Margaret S., 216
Malcolm, Janet, 190
Male and female roles, 182–83, 277, 310–
    11, 313
Marcabru (Provençal troubadour), 109
Marcuse, Max, 46, 49, 70, 149, 196
Marriage, 61, 64, 68, 71, 74–75, 86–87,
    94, 95, 104, 114, 129, 130; ceremony,
    137; development in, 275; force in, 11;
    indissolubility of, 285; love in, 114–18,
    130–31; in the Old Testament, 86;
    parents', problems of the, 230–32; as a
    sacrament, 137; and sexuality, 137; as a
    symbol of the covenant with God, 88, 102
Marriageability of love, 134–35
Marriage counseling: Christian, 103; working
    through the past in, 292–94
Marwitz, Alexander von der, 113
Masochism, 30, 205, 297
Maternal bond, 93, 219–20, 264–65, 267
Maternal love, 214

Maternal relationship, 293
Matriarchy, 190, 222
Maturity, 240
Men, 195–96, 269–70; and women,
    statistics on, 193, 197, 261, 299
Merging, desires for, 216
Midlife crisis, 318
Miller, Alice, 89, 202, 222, 339
Mitchell, Juliet, 183–85
Mitscherlich, Alexander, 172
Mitscherlich-Nielsen, Margarete, 248
Molière, 128, 176
Molnár, Franz, 176
Moltmann, Jürgen, 74
Montaigne, Michel Eyquem de, 130–31
Morality, 321
More or less of the same (Watzlawick), 233–
    35, 238
Mother: and child, 214–21; the great, 92;
    the pre-oedipal, 183–84, 202, 215, 221,
    289–90, 337
Murder, 29, 50, 56–59, 84, 86, 99, 139:
    due to justice, 59, 165

Narcissism, 109, 125, 129, 201, 202, 205,
    215. See also Wound to narcissism
Neumann, Erich, 189
Nietzsche, Friedrich, 128

Oedipus complex, 39, 72, 93, 117, 168–70,
    190, 223, 283–85, 289, 297, 313, 337;
    absence of, 199–203; in boys and girls,
    183–85; parental involvement in, 158,
    169; positive and negative, 169–70
Omnipotence: and impotence, 214–21;
    fantasies of, 99, 165, 215–16
Oral greed, 337, 338
Othello, 154–67
Ovid, 107

Pain, 266–270
Pao, Ping-Nie, 42, 45, 206
Paradigmatic change in psychotherapy, 15
Paradoxical: directive, 15, 233, 234–46,
    252, 316; intervention, 316
Parents and children, alliance between, 52,
    92
Partner: of the jealous individual, 32–37; the
    reality of the, 283–88
Paternal bond, 283–85

Patriarchal society, 61–67, 83, 86, 94, 118, 120–21, 136, 187, 190, 222, 337
Passion, 120, 127, 136
Paul, Saint, 102, 103, 104
Penis envy, 16, 184–85
Perls, Frederick, 81, 224
Perversion, 205
Pfandl, Ludwig, 123
Plänkers, Tomas, 234
Plutarch, 106
Pogwisch, Ulrike von, 174
Pohlen, Manfred, 234
Pontalis, Jean-Baptiste, 203
Portmann, Heinrich, 43
Power, 239–40, 338
Power struggle, 317
Preuss, Hans G., 83, 85, 224
Primal: scene, 13, 163, 166, 206, 212, 242, 297, 337; triangle, 170
Projection, 41, 151, 296
Projective resistance, 51, 249
Property, claim to, 68–70
Psychoanalysis: and Christianity, 85, 89, 103, 151, 213, 214, 249; and marriage counseling, 292; and morality, 249; and romantic love, 135; versus systems therapy, 15, 18, 249
Psychosexual developmental phases, 196, 236–37

Rage, 266–70
Ratzinger, Joseph, 74–75
Reality: and fantasy, 295–301; invented, 116, 263–64; one's own, 271, 298; of the partner, 283–88; of the relationship, new, 271–75
Regression, 216, 289, 293
Reik, Theodor, 205
Relationship: new reality of the, 271–75
Renaud, Bernard, 83, 84
Returning, 316–20
Revenge, 161
Richter, Horst-Eberhard, 46, 198, 224, 227, 230–31
Rigidity, 2, 10, 29, 232–33
Rival, 38–43, 258, 295–301; sense of fraternity of, 39–42
Riviere, Joan, 203–5
Roles, assigned or assumed by the jealous individual, 29, 268, 303, 339
Romantic love, 131–34

Roth, Klaus, 120
Rousseau, Jean-Jacques, 214
Rusconi, Maria, 192

Sachs, Hans, 108, 122
Sadomasochism, 53, 280–82, 298
Scapegoat, 227, 246
Schadewaldt, Wolfgang, 98, 221
Schafer, Roy, 208
Schatzman, Morton, 224
Schelling, Caroline Böhmer-Schlegel, 132–34
Schiller, Friedrich, 132
Schizophrenia, 231
Schlegel, Friedrich, 112, 131–35
Schleiermacher, Friedrich Ernst Daniel, 112–13, 132–33, 140–41
Schmideberg, Melitta, 44
Schönemann, Lilli, 173
Schönkopf, Käthchen, 173
Schülein, Johann August, 234
Searles, H. F., 155
Second, the eternal, 185–86
Seidenberg, Robert, 42, 45, 176–79, 191
Self, 134, 136; actualization, 74–75; criticism, 158
Selvini Palazzoli, Mara, 224, 226, 240
Severed constituents, 236, 248–49, 302–5
Sex roles, 277
Sexual enlightenment, 176
Sexual revolution, 61–67
Sexuality, 137, 311
Shakespeare, William, 28, 154–67
Shepherd, Michael, 47, 197, 201
Shock, 266–70
Simon, Fritz B., 251
Social class of clients, 260
Solutions: destructive, 50–60; misplaced attempts at, 233–35
Sophocles, 221
Space, personal, 277, 280, 286, 318, 323, 330
Statistics: author's, 260–61; on men and women, 192–93, 197, 261; on murder and suicide, 195–96
Stein, Charlotte von, 174
Stekel, Wilhelm, 64
Stendhal, 47–48, 56, 169–70
Sterba, Richard, 106, 110
Stierlin, Helm, 15, 37, 46, 69, 75, 198, 220, 224, 226, 232, 243, 251, 304

Stoller, Robert J., 205
Suicidal fantasies, 57
Suicide, 29, 51–52, 56–57, 113, 229–30, 268, 271, 273, 317
Suicide attempts, psychodynamic motivation of, 196
Superego, 83, 207
Surveillance, 36, 268
Symbiosis, 93, 211, 214–18, 229, 264, 267, 273, 290, 317, 319–20; as danger, 162–63; desires for, 36–37, 63; withdrawal from, 289–91
Symptom transference, 46
System, 224–25, 232, 258, 279, 281, 316, 327: and circularity, 224–25; with concealed jealousy, 225–28; cracking the, 241
Systems theory, 26

Teisman, Mark W., 241, 250–52
Therapist: problems of the, 247–53; in the triangle, 2, 8–9, 45, 235, 237, 258, 261, 263, 264, 280, 307
Therapy: versus counseling, 278; methodological variety in, 248; short-term, 250–51; success of, 15, 247
Third party, 258; the damaged, 173–76
Todd, John, 197, 229
Tolstoy, Leo Nikolayevich, 3, 32, 99, 209–14, 217–21
Tolstoy, Sophia, 217–21
Traditions of love and jealousy, 114–41
Transference, 15, 45, 202, 251, 261, 293
Triangle, 25, 35, 39, 45, 46, 83, 136, 168–98, 202, 204, 205, 220, 257, 284, 313, 337
Trilling, Lionel, 324
Trojan War, 97–99

Unamuno, Miguel de, 271–73, 310
Utopia, 212, 213, 314, 318, 327

Valle-Inclán, Ramón Maria del, 139
Vaukhonen, Kauko, 46, 145, 197, 228
Vega Carpio, Lope Félix de, 50–51, 124–25
Veit, Dorothea, 133
Velikovsky, Immanuel, 211
Veyne, Paul, 118
Vilar, Esther, 69
Visual imperative (Bergler), 205
Voss, Johann Heinrich, 98, 221
Voyeurism of the jealous individual, 13, 28, 54, 112, 206, 212, 337
Vulgate, 109
Vulpius, Christiane, 174

Wagner, Richard, 122–23, 337
Waldmüller, Ferdinand Georg, 310
Wangh, Martin, 156, 163, 202
Wanting: to love, 193–94; to be loved, 29, 193–94; to see, 205–7
Watzlawick, Paul, 40, 233–39, 241, 246, 247, 250, 264
Weakland, John H., 233
Weber-Kellermann, Ingeborg, 137
Wesel, Uwe, 190, 222
Willemer, Marianne von, 174
Willi, Jürg, 62, 194, 224, 225, 232, 235–39, 247–48, 274, 302
Winnicott, Donald W., 226, 339
Wirsching, Michael, 15, 198, 224, 243
Withdrawal from symbiosis, 289–91
Women, 266, 269; and jealousy, 121–23, 197–98; contempt for, 117, 138; in the world of men, 162–63, 182
Wound to narcissism, 27, 29, 40, 120, 157–58, 338
Wydler, Walter, 64

You and I, 214–21